AN INTRODUCTION TO
Research in
English Literary History

THE MACMILLAN COMPANY
NEW YORK • BOSTON • CHICAGO
DALLAS • ATLANTA • SAN FRANCISCO

MACMILLAN AND CO., LIMITED
LONDON • BOMBAY • CALCUTTA
MADRAS • MELBOURNE

THE MACMILLAN COMPANY
OF CANADA, LIMITED
TORONTO

AN INTRODUCTION TO
Research in
English Literary History

by *Chauncey Sanders*

ASSOCIATE PROFESSOR OF MILITARY HISTORY
THE AIR UNIVERSITY
MAXWELL AIR FORCE BASE
MONTGOMERY, ALABAMA

WITH A CHAPTER ON RESEARCH IN FOLKLORE
by *Stith Thompson*

THE MACMILLAN COMPANY : NEW YORK

The author is indebted to the following for permission to use copyrighted material:

American Library Association for a quotation from Isadore G. Mudge, *Guide to Reference Books*, 6th edition (1936)

The Clarendon Press for quotations from R. B. McKerrow, *An Introduction to Bibliography* (1927) and *Prolegomena for the Oxford Shakespeare* (1939) and from Bernard Mandeville, *Fable of the Bees*, ed. F. B. Kaye (1925)

Reprinted by permission of Dodd, Mead & Company from "Homer and Humbug" by Stephen Leacock, in *Behind the Beyond* (1913)

Ginn and Company for two quotations from André Morize, *Problems and Methods of Literary History* (1922)

The Johns Hopkins Press for a quotation from Francis R. Johnson, *A Critical Bibliography of the Works of Edmund Spenser*

Journal of the History of Ideas for quotations from Professor Arthur O. Lovejoy

C. B. McKerrow for quotations from *The Works of Thomas Nashe*, ed. R. B. McKerrow (1904–10)

The Modern Language Association of America for quotations too numerous to mention specifically

Oxford University Press and the British Academy for a quotation from W. W. Greg, *Principles of Emendation in Shakespeare* (1928)

Sidgwick and Jackson, Ltd. and the author's representatives for quotations from Harold Jenkins, *The Life and Work of Henry Chettle* (1934)

The University of Chicago Press for quotations from Arthur H. Nethercot, *The Road to Tryermaine* (1940)

The University of Toronto Quarterly for quotations from Malcolm Ross, "Elizabethan Society and Letters" (1943)

Preface

An Introduction to Research in English Literary History is intended
for use as a text in courses in bibliography and method and as a
guide for students in the writing of theses or dissertations or other
scholarly papers. Although the book is designed primarily for students of English, it will, I trust, be helpful in other branches of the
humanities as well. What is said of printing and bookmaking, for
example, will have application wherever research involves books
rather than test tubes or mathematical formulæ.

There has been no attempt at an exhaustive treatment of handwriting or papermaking or book illustration, or of any other of the
subjects discussed in Part I of this book. Certain information not
ordinarily presented in the usual graduate courses seems to me of
value, or at least of interest, to students of literary history; I have
included as much of that information as I could. I have tried to keep
the treatment throughout simple and practical. If I have at times
committed the sin of explaining things that should be, and doubtless
are, obvious to most graduate students, my only defense is that that
seemed a lesser evil than to risk leaving even one student confused
for lack of explanation.

I do not pretend to have canvassed the whole field of scholarship
in English and American literary history in selecting the examples
used in Part III to illustrate various details of method. I have relied
heavily upon the *Publications of the Modern Language Association
of America* and *American Literature* because they are easily accessible to graduate students and because the wide range of articles in
them makes those two journals particularly fruitful sources of illustrative material. When *AmLit* and *PMLA* have failed to provide
the number or variety of illustrations wanted, I have, of course,
turned to other periodicals or to books. Wherever possible, I have
included examples from both English and American literary history

[v]

and from various periods. In all but a few instances I have refrained from comment on the books and articles used as illustrations; it seems to me that the student should be encouraged to form his own opinion as to the validity of an argument or the effectiveness of a presentation of facts.

In arranging the *apparatus criticus* it has seemed best to put each explanatory note on the page containing the portion of the text to which the note relates, and to collect the purely bibliographical references at the back of the book. Reference numbers for the explanatory notes are in roman type; those for the bibliographical references are in italic. When a bibliographical reference is required within an explanatory note, it is enclosed in parentheses. In the section devoted to bibliographical references, each verso page has in the upper right corner a combination of roman and arabic numerals to serve as a guide in using the notes: "III, iv, 29" would mean that note 29 for Chapter IV, Part III, is the first note that begins on that page. Similarly, in the upper left corner of each recto page is a symbol indicating the last note that begins on that page.

The number of friends who have helped me in one way or another in the writing of this book is too great to permit mention of them all. I should, however, be most remiss did I fail to name Professors Wallace Douglas, of Northwestern University, and Ralph L. Collins, Laurens J. Mills, and John Robert Moore, all of Indiana University; and Misses Marguerite Kennedy, of the Air University, and Marguerita McDonald, of the Montana State College Library. The authorities of the Houghton Library of Harvard University, the Yale University Library, the Folger Shakespeare Library, the Henry E. Huntington Library and Art Gallery, and the Huntingdon College Library have been most helpful. My thanks are also due to numerous graduate students who have used this book—or had it used on them—in manuscript; and to Colonels Wilfred J. Paul and Garth C. Cobb and to Dr. Albert F. Simpson, all of the Air University, for their interest and encouragement. My indebtedness to Professor Stith Thompson is obvious; and that to my son and my wife is greatest of all.

                                          CHAUNCEY SANDERS

The Air University
Maxwell Air Force Base
Montgomery, Alabama

Contents

Part I THE MATERIALS
OF RESEARCH

THE material with which literary research is primarily concerned is, obviously, the expression of human thought; but such expression must, for practical purposes, be recorded in more or less permanent form. A speech may be literature, but it becomes grist for the student's mill only when it has been recorded.

Various means have been used in the past—paintings on the walls of caves, carvings on stone or wood, impressions on clay or waxed tablets, inscriptions on papyrus or palm leaves—for the setting down of facts or ideas; but with these the student of English literature is not likely to be much concerned. Nor do we need to anticipate the complexities that may arise in future research from the use of photography or sound-recording devices as methods of preserving human thoughts. We shall be working with paper (occasionally, perhaps, with vellum or parchment) upon which thoughts have been recorded by hand or by means of a printing press—that is, with manuscripts and books.

I

Some kinds of research—biography and editing, for example—are likely to involve considerable use of manuscripts; and those who work in the earlier periods—prior to the Restoration, say—will need to familiarize themselves with the form or forms of handwriting practised during the age in which they are interested. This is not the place for a treatise on palæography; [1] but a few words of advice may not be amiss. So far as handwriting is concerned, Old English and Middle English manuscripts will cause the student less trouble

[1] For works on palæography see Appendix A, Part VIII.

[1]

than documents dating from the period 1500–1600. The older manuscripts were written by professional scribes, generally in what is known as *book-hand*; since these men wrote with care, the writing is remarkably uniform. If one learns the shape of the book-hand letters—by no means a difficult task—he is not likely to have much trouble in making out the writing of a mediæval scribe.[2]

After 1500, as more and more people acquired the art of writing, there is naturally less uniformity. Books were produced in the printing house rather than the *scriptorium*; hence the neat but rather laborious book-hand fell into disuse, to be commonly replaced by a more cursive, and consequently more rapid, form of writing. Such a hand had long been in use in the law courts, and was, after 1500, taken over by business men and others as such individuals came to write in their own persons instead of entrusting their correspondence to professional scriveners. The ordinary hand, therefore, of the sixteenth century—the hand that Shakspere wrote—was this English, or *Secretary*, hand.[3] But early in the century a form of writing imported from Italy had begun to achieve popularity;[4] by the end of the seventeenth century it had completely supplanted the English hand. During the Elizabethan age most educated persons wrote both the English and the Italian hands, using the latter for passages in Latin or in contemporary foreign languages and for proper names.

The Italian hand is not difficult to read; would that as much could be said for the English! Unfortunately, with both, the ink is often so faded as to be almost illegible; and the writing is almost always small and cramped, because paper was something of a luxury and the writer wished to get as many words as possible in small space. But with the English hand several of the letters

[2] The contractions in which mediæval manuscripts abound will be troublesome; for help with these one may consult the dictionaries of contractions and abbreviations listed in Appendix A, Part VIII.

[3] The Elizabethan writing masters recognized at least three varieties of English hands—Text (derived from and similar to the mediæval book-hand), Secretary, and Court; Hilary Jenkinson ("Elizabethan Handwritings", *The Library*, 4th Series, III (1922–23), 1–34) distinguishes nine kinds of English hands: Text, Exchequer, Chancery, Legal, Bastard Secretary, Set Hands (General), Pipe Roll, Secretary, and Free Hands (General). The non-specialist, however, will get along with a knowledge of the Secretary hand.

[4] There were actually two imported forms: the Roman, a somewhat upright script, from which the modern roman printing type is derived; and the Italian, which was similarly the ancestor of modern italic type.

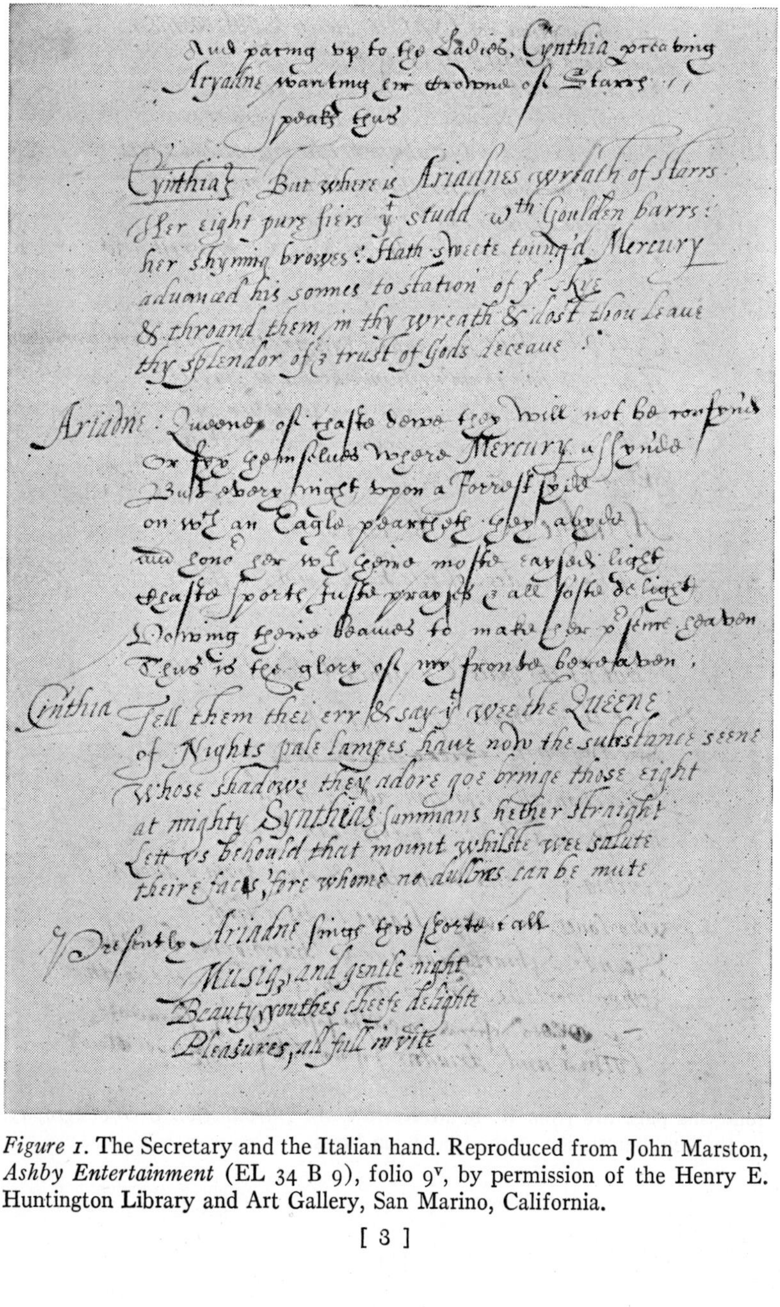

And parting vp to the Ladies, Cynthia wreathing
Ariadne wantinge her crowne of Starrs
speakes thus

Cynthia: But where is Ariadnes wreath of Starrs
Her eight pure fiers y studd wth Goulden barrs:
Her shyninge browes: Hath sweete tong'd Mercury
aduanced his sonnes to station of y skie
& throand them in thy wreath & dost thou leaue
thy splendor of y trust of Gods deceaue

Ariadne: Queenes of teares now for will not be confind
Or for them selues weare Mercury assind
But euery night vpon a Forrest wild
on wth an Eagle perch'd her glory abyde
and gone for with them no more earst light
great sports full wrapp'd all of the delight
Dorwing their beames to make her o sence garben
Teus is her glory of my from be borne born

Cynthia: Tell them thei err & say y wee the QUEENE
of Nights pale lampes haue now the substance seene
whose shadowes they adore goe bringe those eight
at mighty Synthias summans hither straight
Lett vs behold that mount whilste wee salute
theire faces fore whome no aultres can be mute

y Presently Ariadne sings these sportes i all
Musicy and gentle night
Beauty youthes cheefe delight
Pleasures all full invite

Figure 1. The Secretary and the Italian hand. Reproduced from John Marston, *Ashby Entertainment* (EL 34 B 9), folio 9^v, by permission of the Henry E. Huntington Library and Art Gallery, San Marino, California.

[3]

Figure 2. The Secretary hand: typical forms of the minuscules. This and the following page are from R. B. McKerrow, *An Introduction to Bibliography*, by the kind permission of the Clarendon Press.

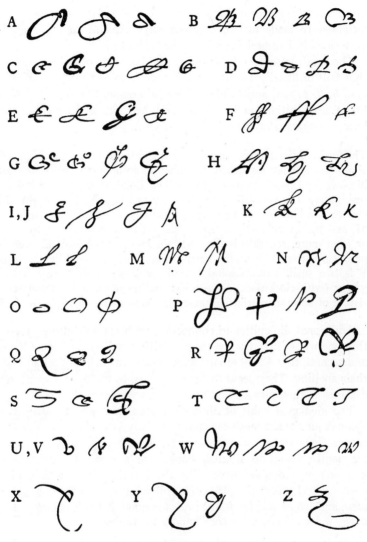

Figure 3. The Secretary hand: majuscules.

differ greatly in form from those we use today; moreover some letters were made in two or more ways. And of course individual variations in handwriting add to the difficulty.

The small letters—*miniscules*, in the language of palæographers—that will ordinarily be utterly different from the modern forms are *c, e, h, k, p, r, s,* and *t*. There were, of course, two forms of *s*—the long *ʃ*, used initially and medially, and the short final *s*. Of the capital letters—*majuscules*—Dr. McKerrow wrote:

The forms of these vary so much that it is difficult to say anything useful about them. They frequently resemble, more or less vaguely, the usual black letter [known to most of us as Old English] printed capitals, and fortunately it is generally possible to guess what they are meant to be. One or two hints may be given: occasionally a capital, especially B, H, M, and P, is very wide, so that it may at first sight appear to be two, or even more, separate letters; certain letters, especially L, are often practically the same as the small letter, only written slightly larger; F is two small f's; a capital I or J carelessly written may resemble g or y (with clockwise crossed tail); and an unrecognizable letter consisting of several interlacing curves is likely to be either C, E, or G.[1]

Additional difficulties in connection with capital letters are, first, that one writer may use two or more different forms of some letters; and second, that Elizabethans were erratic in their capitalizing as in their spelling. They seem to have felt free to use as few or as many capitals as they pleased and to use them wherever they pleased.

The mediæval habit of abbreviating carried over to some extent throughout the sixteenth century, especially in Latin texts. The Latin contractions are too numerous to be given here,[5] but the ones most frequently found in English books are a straight mark (like a macron) or a double curve (like the Spanish tilde) which, placed over a vowel, takes the place of a following *m* or *n* (mē or m̃e), for *men*, and frō or frõ, for *from*); qd. for quod (that is *quoth*); ẘ for *with;* ẘ for *which;* ẙ for *the;* [6] and ẙ for *that*.

---

[5] An account of these will be found in McKerrow, *Introduction to Bibliography*, pp. 320–24.

[6] "It should be superfluous to remind any possible reader of this book that in those abbreviations the *y* is the OE þ [*thorn*], and that it is only in quite modern times that any one has had the strange notion of pronouncing 'the' as 'ye'. In

The recommended procedure for acquiring a knowledge of Elizabethan handwriting is to secure a facsimile of a good clear hand, for which an accurate printed transcript is available,[7] and to study the facsimile along with the transcript until one is sure that he can read the manuscript letter for letter. Then one should imitate the handwriting, being especially careful to make the strokes in the right order and direction.[8] Having practised a hand until one is satisfied with his imitation of it—confident that an Elizabethan could have read it—one should study and imitate a variety of hands such as can most readily be found in *English Literary Autographs, 1550–1650.*[9] Such a discipline will enable the student to make his way among sixteenth-century manuscripts, if not with ease, at least with a reasonable degree of competence.

II

Instead of passing directly from handwriting to printing, we may well consider briefly the materials of which manuscripts and books are made. The words *vellum* and *parchment* seem not to have been distinguished in ancient times; but in modern usage vellum means calfskin prepared for writing purposes, whereas parchment is the skin of a sheep or goat. The very finest vellum is thought to have been made from the skin of an unborn calf, and hence is called *uterine* vellum. Instead of being tanned as for leather, hides intended for writing material were steeped in lime pits and then stretched on frames, where they were pared and scraped. Afterward they were rubbed and polished with pumice and chalk. In the whole process the hide was reduced to about half its original thickness.

Parchment—to adopt the old practice and use one term for both

---

reprints in which these abbreviations are not expanded a superior e or t should always be used, either above the y or following it as 'ẙ' 'yᵗ'. It is incorrect to print 'ye' or 'yt', which were at no period used as abbreviations in printed books." (McKerrow, *Introduction to Bibliography,* p. 322, n. 1.) Perhaps I should add that *ye* and *yt* would have been meant by the writer and understood by the reader to be the personal pronouns *ye* and *it*.

[7] A good and generally accessible facsimile is that of the letter addressed by Thomas Kyd to the Lord Keeper Puckering; it appears as the frontispiece of Kyd, *Works,* ed. F. S. Boas (Oxford: Clarendon Press, 1901).

[8] Dr. McKerrow gives (*Introduction to Bibliography,* pp. 344–50) information that will help the student to form the letters as the Elizabethans did.

kinds of material—has what might be called a right side and a wrong side; the *hair* side differs from the *flesh* side in being spotted with the follicles from which the hair has been removed. Mediæval scribes were careful to arrange the leaves of their manuscripts with hair side next to hair side, and flesh side to flesh side, so that the pages would present a uniform appearance; when the manuscript is opened, one sees either two hair side pages or two flesh side pages. Knowledge of this fact is frequently helpful in settling questions involving the make-up of manuscript volumes; if we find a manuscript in which hair side comes next to flesh side, we may properly suspect that the leaves have been disarranged, or that some portion of the manuscript is missing.

Parchment is still used for formal and decorative documents, such as diplomas; vellum is used occasionally for printing a very small edition of a work, or for a few copies of a larger edition, the other copies being printed on paper. For illuminated manuscripts vellum was desirable because the colors used did not show through; but for printing it is little better than good paper.

III

Traditionally—and probably—paper was invented in China; at least as early as the second century after Christ the Chinese were making paper from the inner bark of a kind of mulberry tree. In the eighth century the Arabs learned the secret of papermaking from some Chinese prisoners of war, and soon hit upon the device of using linen and cotton rags instead of "raw" vegetable fibers. The use of paper spread westward and was introduced into Europe by the Moors. By the twelfth century paper was being manufactured in Valencia and in Toledo. The Moslems also introduced paper into Sicily, and a paper mill existed in Italy, near Ancona, as early as 1278. Before long the art of papermaking was known to the French and the Germans, and in 1495 a paper mill was set up in England by John Tate. "In England, and indeed in any civilized part of Europe, paper was evidently procurable without difficulty from the beginning of the fourteenth century." [3] Nevertheless, paper was not very commonly used until after the invention of printing had stimulated quantity production.

*   *   *

Mr. Esdaile defines paper as "vegetable fiber disintegrated and reintegrated in water; this distinguishes it from vellum and parchment, which are animal skins, and from papyrus, which is vegetable leaf not disintegrated but simply dressed by drying, rolling, and polishing." [4] Cotton and flax, both of which are used, not "raw" but in the form of rags, furnish the best fiber for papermaking. Esparto, or alfa, a grass produced in Spain and North Africa; "chemical wood"—that is, wood chips reduced to fiber by boiling under pressure in a solution of caustic soda, or a mixture of caustic soda and either sulphate of soda or bisulphite of lime; and "mechanical wood"—pulp produced by grinding wood blocks into what is practically a fine sawdust—are other sources of fiber suitable for paper. Mechanical wood, because of the shortness of its fibers, quickly turns brown and becomes brittle, as anyone who has occasion to handle a newspaper only a few years old can testify; it has nothing but its cheapness to recommend it. Chemical wood, if properly manufactured, produces a good quality of paper; a good book paper made of chemical wood can be secured for less than a third of the price of an all-rag paper. Esparto may also produce a good book paper, but it is chiefly used for "antique" paper and art paper.

*   *   *

All paper, down to the end of the eighteenth century, was made by hand; and the very finest paper is made today much as it was in the beginning of the craft. The rags, after being sorted and cut into small pieces, were boiled for several hours in a solution which removed traces of fat and dye, and tended to separate the fibers.[9] Then the rags were beaten with mallets until they formed a smooth pulp, to which water was added to make the mixture something like cream in consistency. A screen—made of interwoven wires, the longitudinal ones being fine and close together, with the crosswires heavier and spaced about an inch apart, supported by a light frame under-

[9] According to one authority (Frank C. Butler, *The Story of Paper-Making* (Chicago: privately printed, 1901), pp. 50–51) a more primitive method was to moisten the rags and pile them "in some warm, damp place, often in a cellar, where they were left to decay for a period—twenty days or more. During this time, the perishable portion, sometimes spoken of as vegetable gluten, fermented or decayed to such an extent that it could be washed from the fibrine, or long, white elastic filaments."

Figure 4. Paper making in the seventeenth century. In this instance the rags are macerated by trip hammers activated by a water wheel. Reproduced from a woodcut of 1662, which appeared in Lancelot Hogben, *From Cave Painting to Comic Strip*; by permission of Max Parrish, Ltd., London, England.

neath, and having above it another frame of the same size and shape, called the *deckle*—was used in converting the pulp to paper. These frames, or molds, were rectangular, the width being approximately three-fourths the length; and they varied in size from about 12″ by 16″ to about 15″ by 20″. The mold was dipped into the vat of pulp and lifted out containing an amount of pulp sufficient to fill the mold to the top of the deckle; thus the height of the deckle determined the amount of pulp taken up, and consequently, the thickness of the resulting paper.[10] As the mold was lifted from the vat, the water in the mixture began to drain away through the screen; at the same time the workman gave a horizontal shake to the frame. In this motion lies the secret of the papermaker's craft. There must be both a forward-and-backward movement and a side-to-side movement to make the fibers cross and interlock in all directions; it is this interlocking that gives uniform strength to the paper.[11] When the water had all drained away, the pulp, by that time in more or less solid form, was turned out upon a sheet of felt stretched over a board called a *couch*. Over this layer of pulp was placed another sheet of felt, then another mold of pulp, more felt, more pulp, and so on until there was a pile, or *post*, consisting of perhaps a hundred sheets. Pressure was then applied to squeeze out as much as possible of the water that still remained in the paper, after which the sheets were hung over ropes or poles to dry.

At this stage the paper was still what is called *waterleaf*—it would absorb water, like blotting paper. To give it a non-absorbent surface

[10] The term *deckle* is also used to mean the rough and uneven edge of a sheet of hand-made paper; nowadays this effect is admired and is often produced artificially on machine-made paper. The presence of the deckle-edge intact on the leaves of an old book is proof that the book has not been trimmed down in binding; if the margins happen to be very small, the presence of the deckle might be important as proof that no marginal notes had been cut away in successive rebindings.

[11] If a circular piece of hand-made paper be dropped onto water, it will turn up at the edge all around, until it is the shape of a saucer; machine-made paper will turn up on two sides only, because the fibers are matted only in one direction. Thus machine-made paper will withstand folding one way but will easily tear if folded the other. This fact is of importance in the binding of books: machine-made paper should be so folded that the binder's stitches cross the fibers of the paper; if the thread parallels the fibers, the stitches will cut the paper. Hand-made paper can be folded and sewn in either direction. It has been stated (Reginald G. Williams, *A Manual of Book Selection* (London: Grafton, 1920), p. 101) that a strip of hand-made paper, if suspended, would have to be over four miles long to break of its own weight.

that would take ink without blurring, the paper had to be *sized*.
The sheets of paper were dipped in a solution of animal gelatin,
made from clippings of hides, horns, and hoofs. After being sized
the paper was air-dried, smoothed, and pressed.

*   *   *

If a piece of hand-made *laid* [12] paper is held up to the light, it
will be seen that the wires constituting the bottom of the mold have
left their mark on the finished product in the form of translucent
lines running across the sheet close together in one direction and
about an inch apart in the other. The surface of the paper may be
quite smooth and its thickness uniform; but the lines, called, respectively, *wire lines* and *chain lines*,[13] show up because the paper
is less dense where the pulp rested on the wires than it is between
the wires.

It will also be discovered, if an uncut sheet of old paper is held
up to the light, that there is a translucent design near the center
of one half of the sheet.[5] This is the *watermark*,[14] the maker's device,

[12] Paper made in a mold such as has just been described would be laid paper;
most machine-made paper and some hand-made is produced on a mold which has
the crosswires closely spaced like the longitudinal wires, and is called *wove* paper.
When held to the light, wove paper will have a slightly mottled appearance, or
perhaps show a faint network of diamond-shaped markings.

[13] The chain lines and wire lines are sometimes both referred to as *wire lines* or
wire marks; chain lines are sometimes called *chain marks*; and wire lines are sometimes called *laid lines*. *Wire lines* and *chain lines* seem the most appropriate terms
and are probably now in most common use.

[14] *Wire mark* would be a more accurately descriptive term than watermark. The
standard work on watermarks is a treatise by C. M. Briquet, *Les Filigranes* (Paris:
A. Picard et Fils, 1907), 4 vols. Many watermarks are reproduced in this work;
thus one may be able to determine the place of manufacture and the date of a
specific sheet of paper. The usefulness of watermarks as evidence is limited, however. In the first place, the watermark is likely, in any book smaller than an
octavo, to have been trimmed away, or multilated beyond recognition, by the
binder; and in quartos and octavos the position of the watermark in the backfold
(see below, p. 35) may make identification impossible without taking the book
apart, a procedure which would seldom be permitted. Only in folios and broadsides
can one be sure of having the watermark clearly visible. Furthermore, as Dr
McKerrow observed: "Arguments from similarity or dissimilarity of watermark
must, however, be used with extreme caution, for it seems quite clear that many
printers bought their paper in job-lots, and it is common to find a number of
different watermarks in a book about the printing of which there appears to have
been nothing abnormal. At the same time, if we had reason for thinking that a
certain part of a book had been inserted after the original printing, and we found

and was produced by weaving the design with wire in the bottom of the mold. Thus the design shows up, as the wire lines and chain lines do, because the paper is less dense at that point, the pulp above the device having been thinner than elsewhere. The commonest designs were hands or *gloves,* ewers or jugs, pillars, and crowns; others ranged from simple stars, crosses, or initials, to coats-of-arms.[15] Beginning in the latter part of the seventeenth century and continuing through the eighteenth, paper manufacturers commonly put a second mark, called a *counter mark* and generally consisting of the maker's initials, in the center of the other half of the sheet.

* * *

To this discussion of the old method of papermaking may be added some comment on modern machine manufacture, introduced at the end of the eighteenth century. The preparation of the fibers is accomplished by a series of machines—the *thrasher,* the *cutter,* the *devil* or *whipper,* the *duster,* the *digester,* the *washers* or *Hollanders,* the *drainers,* and the *beaters,* all of which names are more or less descriptive of the tasks performed. Inferior grades of paper are sized and tinted papers are colored in the beater; that is, the size and the dye are put into the pulp at this stage in manufacture.[16] The pulp as it comes from the beater is known as *half stuff.* This solution, about 97 per cent water, is pumped out in an even layer onto a moving belt, which performs the function of the mold. It is an endless band of closely woven screen wire, supported and kept in motion by a roller at each end. *Deckle-straps* of rubber keep the pulp in place, being adjusted to provide whatever width of paper is desired; the thickness of the paper is not, however, regulated by the height of the deckle but by a mechanical spreader and gate. As the moving wire mold carries along its burden of pulp, it shakes from side to side, thus matting or interlacing the fibers in one direction.

---

that the paper, both before and after this particular section, bore the same watermark whereas this section itself had a different one, we could certainly claim the fact as strongly supporting this view." (*Introduction to Bibliography,* p. 101, n. 1.)

[15] Certain designs came to be associated with specfic sizes of paper, and many of our names for paper sizes came from watermarks. A tankard or vase suggested *pot*; a post horn gave its name to *post*; and *foolscap* and *crown* are self-explanatory.

[16] This method of sizing is known as *engine-sizing*; the better grades of paper are still *tub-sized* or *vat-sized* by dipping the finished paper into the sizing solution.

By the time the pulp reaches the end of the moving belt—having passed from the *wet end* to the *dry end* of the machine—sufficient water has drained away to leave the pulp in a semi-solid state; at this point it passes under a *dandy roll,* which compresses the pulp, thus helping to interlock the fibers, and imparts the watermark if there is to be one. The dandy roll also determines whether the paper is to be laid or wove. Since most machine-made paper is wove, the dandy roll is, in most cases, simply a roller of screen wire; but by the addition of crosswires an effect can be achieved much like the chain lines and wire lines of hand-made laid paper. The matted pulp—having now reached the place where the moving screen passes down around a roller to return to its starting point for another load of pulp—is taken between two felt-covered rolls and is then carried by a moving felt web to *press-rolls,* which squeeze out more water and smooth the surface of the paper. After this the paper passes around a number of drying cylinders and then goes to the *calenders,* which impart a smooth and even finish. For most papers this is the end of the process. High-grade writing papers, however, before being cut into sheets, are run through a size tub. If the paper must have an especially glossy surface—as when it is to be used for printing very fine-screen half-tones—a mineral coating may be brushed on and the surface then polished by *supercalendering.*[17] When the proportion of mineral is too high—more than one-fourth, say—strength and durability are sacrificed to achieve the requisite glossy surface. Folding a piece of such paper breaks the coating and leaves little fiber to hold the paper together; tiny flecks of the chalky clay of which the coating is composed can often be seen along the fold. Much better paper, with a surface smooth enough for printing all but the finest half-tones, is produced by *loading* the pulp, instead of coating the paper; that is, the mineral is added to the half stuff while it is in the beater, and the paper is then calendered or super-calendered.

The continuous web of paper is cut into sheets of the required size by automatic machines. Sizes and shapes vary according to the kind of paper and the purpose for which it is to be used. The *New International Dictionary* lists 152 sizes by name. Mr. Esdaile men-

---

[17] In supercalendering the paper is passed between pairs of rollers, one of which is of cast-iron—heated by steam—and the other is of compressed cotton or paper.

tions eight sizes as being most commonly used now for book paper
in England; [6] these are: Large Foolscap (13½ by 17), Crown
(15 by 20), Large Post (16½ by 21), Demy (17½ by 22½),
Medium (18 by 23), Royal (20 by 25), Large Royal (20 by 27), and
Imperial (22 by 30). In modern printing, paper is used in sheets two,
four, or even eight times as large as these basic sizes. An American
paper manufacturer lists nineteen sizes of book paper, ranging from
22 by 32 to 44 by 64.

*   *   *

Since modern books are printed on such large sheets, the paper
used does not have the same significance for the student as is the
case in old books.[18] A modern book which is advertised as being a
crown octavo may be composed of sheets folded so as to make sixteen,
thirty-two, or even sixty-four leaves; but the leaves will be of the
size which results from folding a sheet of crown paper in octavo
fashion—5" by 7½".

IV

The question of ink is one that is not likely to be of concern to
many graduate students, or, indeed, to scholars generally; but two
comments should, perhaps, be made. First, it is to be noted that the
ink used by writers of manuscripts is a material very different from
printer's ink. Early writing ink was commonly made by mixing soot
with gum and water; this produced a lustrous black ink, but it was
not proof against exposure to water. Like modern "washable" inks,
it could be removed by sponging.[19] Since the beginning of the Christian era a more permanent ink has been produced by mixing tannin
(generally secured from oak-galls) with sulphate of iron and gum.
Such ink, though reasonably permanent, tends to turn brown with
age.

From the beginning, printers realized that writing ink, however
well it might serve the scribe, was not the proper medium to be used

[18] See below, pp. 35–37.

[19] Mediæval writers took advantage of this fact to conserve paper and vellum;
many a classic was doubtless erased to make room for the recording of a dull sermon
or theological treatise. Fortunately, modern science has enabled us (see below,
p. 89) to recover the original reading of *palimpsests* and to read, literally, between
and under the lines.

in their craft. In the earliest days printing ink was what it is now—
a mixture of lamp black and varnish, the latter usually made from
linseed oil and resin.

The other fact to be noted about ink is that chemical analysis
of the ink used in a manuscript—or the pigment in illuminations—
may be of aid in detecting a forgery.[20]

V

The invention of printing constitutes a subject much too involved
for full consideration here; it is, moreover, a subject entailing a
number of problems about which has raged, and still rages, a good
deal of controversy. At least three cities in as many countries have
been credited with being the birthplace of printing as we know it;
and it has not yet been possible to prove or wholly to disprove the
right of any one of them to the honor.

*   *   *

Perhaps as early as the sixth century the Chinese were practising
a form of printing by using wooden blocks upon which characters
had been made to stand out in relief by cutting away the background. The raised portion of the block was inked, and a sheet of
paper pressed down upon it, the inked design being thus transferred
—in reverse, of course, mirror-fashion—to the paper. In the eleventh
century the Chinese were making types of clay or porcelain; later
they made molds of wood, from which clay types could be made.
These clay types, when baked, were serviceable, though they must
always have been rather fragile. If the Chinese language had been
based upon an alphabet, it seems very likely that the art of printing
with movable types, here begun, would have been perfected as it
was later to be perfected in Europe. But the Chinese language is
made up of more than seven thousand characters, and the advantage
of movable type over the wood block was so slight—in view of the
difficulties attendant upon setting and distributing so many characters—that the new method seems to have been discarded almost
as soon as it was tried.

Block printing was practised in Europe in the manufacture of
textiles long before it was applied to paper; and it was at one time

[20] See below, p. 144.

quite generally held that the invention of printing grew out of block printing through the following stages: (1) block printing on cloth; (2) block printing for playing cards; (3) block print portraits, generally figures of saints, often to be pasted into spaces left for them in manuscripts; (4) *block books* in which the portrait has an accompanying text, printed on one side of the leaf only; (5) block books printed on both sides of the leaves; (6) books printed from movable type. This lineal descent of modern printing from mediæval wood-cut printing is not accepted by most of the modern authorities. In the first place, there is some question whether playing cards were printed or drawn separately by hand. No block book is known certainly to have been produced before 1460, at which time printing with movable type was already under way. Block printing was carried on through the second half of the fifteenth century as an alternative and cheaper method of printing for certain kinds of books, especially religious picture books such as the *Biblia Pauperum* and the *Ars Moriendi,* and one book without illustrations—the standard Latin grammar of the period, "Donatus on the Eight Parts of Speech", commonly known as *Donatus.* Many copies and many editions of these books were printed, most of them—perhaps all of them—during the period 1460–1525.

*   *   *

If it is not certain that modern printing grew out of block printing, neither is it certain that the European practice of those arts came, like the use of paper, from the Orient. Either kind of printing, or both, may have been introduced into Europe by travelers from the East; either or both of them may have had an independent origin in the West.

There are records in Avignon in 1444 and in Cambrai in 1446 which may refer to printing with movable metal types;[21] but the language of the records is not altogether clear, and there are no specimens of the work done in those places at that time by which we can judge what method was in use. Consequently, the claims of France to have been the birthplace of modern printing have not

[21] It seems more likely that the method used in Avignon and Cambrai was to punch letters in a sheet of metal and then make a mold, like a modern stereotype, from that. See below, pp. 33–34.

generally been allowed, and opinion has been divided between Holland and Germany.

The Dutch claim is based upon two things: the existence of some rudely printed books, commonly called *Costeriana,* which have been assigned to a date earlier than 1440; and a legend which relates that the inventor of printing was one Laurens Coster, or Koster. The story goes that Coster, a wealthy citizen of Haarlem, while walking through a wood one day, idly cut some letters in a piece of birch bark, and afterward stamped the letters with ink on a piece of paper for the amusement of his grandchildren. It then occurred to him that this process might be used for the production of books. According to some authorities the Laurens Coster referred to was born in 1436; if he made letters in bark for the amusement of his grandchildren, he must have done so closer to 1480 than 1440. By the time *that* Laurens Coster could have been a grandfather, printing was well known. Even if we accept the Haarlem legend at its face value, there is nothing in it to justify our giving Coster credit for having been the inventor of printing; there is nothing in the story to show that he bridged the gap between wooden block printing and the casting of individual metal types, which latter is the essence of modern printing.

The rest of the Dutch claim is not so easily dismissed. Some of the Costeriana may have been produced by *metallography,* or *cast printing;* [22] others may actually be of a later date than the first German printed books. It is certainly possible that someone was working with movable types in Holland as early as in Germany, perhaps earlier; in fact, one document distinctly suggests that such was the case. On the authority of Ulrich Zell, Cologne's first printer, the statement was made in 1499 that printing was invented at Mainz, but that there was a prototype (*Vurbyldung*) previously invented in Holland. Unfortunately it is impossible to tell precisely what this statement means. If printing was invented at Mainz, what was it that was invented in Holland? If, on the other hand, Zell knew that the essential process was invented in Holland, why does he say

---

[22] In this method letters are stamped in molding sand, or clay, or metal, to form a mold; molten metal is then poured into the mold to form a solid plate, from which the printing is done.

explicitly ". . . this art was invented at Mainz, as regards the manner in which it is now commonly used. . . ." [7]?

At the present time it is generally conceded [23] that the individual
who made modern printing possible by inventing a method of casting
individual types was Johann Gutenberg, a native of Mainz. In 1455,
Johann Fust, a goldsmith of Mainz, sued Gutenberg for the recovery
of sums of money advanced in 1450 and 1452. The money was to
have been used in perfecting the art of printing; and Gutenberg
pledged the apparatus that he was making as security for the loans.
We know, then, that Gutenberg was at work on printing by 1450;
some small pieces he may have produced even earlier than that. In
1454 some Indulgences [24] were printed, apparently by Gutenberg, in
a small type evidently designed for the occasion. The first substantial
printed book appeared at some time before August 24, 1456; [25] this
is the famous Mazarine Bible (so called because a copy of it was first
noticed in the Mazarine Library), or, as it is now more generally
known, the "42-line Bible".[26] There is also a 36-line Bible [27] of about
the same date. It seems impossible now to determine exactly what
share in these productions Gutenberg himself had. No book bearing
Gutenberg's name as printer is known to exist. The financial transactions of 1450 and 1452 may have created a partnership in which
Fust contributed something more than money, and this partnership
was apparently dissolved by 1456, perhaps before the Mazarine Bible

[23] Pierce Butler, in *The Origin of Printing in Europe* (Chicago: University of
Chicago Press, 1940[c]) argues that the invention of printing was not the contribution
of any one man but the culmination of the efforts of many, and seeks to give more
credit to Fust and Schoeffer than to Gutenberg. There is doubtless much merit in
the first point. It is as unlikely that the invention of printing was the contribution
of a single man as that Bell was solely responsible for the telephone or Marconi for
radio. As for the other point, it seems impossible now to determine how credit
should be divided between Gutenberg and his associates.
[24] These were printed forms with blanks left for the name of the recipient and
the date. They were issued by the King of Cyprus, with the authority of the Pope,
to all who made contributions toward the expenses of war against the Turks.
[25] This date appears in one copy as the day on which the *rubricating* (coloring
with red ink certain letters, generally initial, for purposes of decoration) of that
copy was completed.
[26] It is printed in double columns, forty-two lines to a column.
[27] This is sometimes known as the Pfister or Bamberg Bible, because it was
printed from type afterward used by Albrecht Pfister of Bamberg, who apparently
acquired it from Gutenberg or his associates.

was printed. In 1457 a Psalter (printed in large type so that half a dozen members of the choir could look on one copy) was printed, bearing along with the date the names of Fust and Peter Schoeffer (who later married Fust's daughter) as printers. Schoeffer seems to have made himself expert in the cutting of type. It may be then, that all these works—including two editions of Indulgences (30-line and 31-line), and the 42-line and 36-line Bibles—were the productions of a partnership in which Gutenberg furnished the basic invention, Fust supplied the money, and Schoeffer designed and cut the type. It is rather more likely that Fust and Schoeffer separated from Gutenberg before 1455, and that Gutenberg printed the 31-line Indulgence and the 36-line Bible, while Fust and Schoeffer produced the 30-line Indulgence and the 42-line Bible.

Between 1456 and 1465, at which date he became a member of the court of the Count of Nassau and Archbishop of Mainz, Gutenberg may have been printing independently of his old partners; several books of that decade have been tentatively assigned to his press. Gutenberg died in 1468. The partnership of Fust and Schoeffer continued until the death of Fust in 1466, at which time his son succeeded him. Schoeffer died about 1502, leaving three sons, all printers.

The Psalter of 1457 is the earliest example of color printing. Among other productions of Fust and Schoeffer are a Bible of 1462—the first Bible with a printed date—and an edition of Cicero's *De Officiis* of 1465.

A fact that may be significant as supporting the German claim to priority in printing is that the men who carried the art of printing to all corners of Europe were not Hollanders but Germans. In Germany itself, as might have been expected, the art of printing spread rapidly. Before the end of the fifteenth century there were presses in fifty German towns, and more than two hundred printers were at work. German printers went out from their native land to Italy, France, Spain, the Netherlands—even to Oxford.

It is unnecessary to give here in detail the names and dates of those pioneer printers, or to list their productions. It may be observed, however, that in Germany most of the early books dealt with theology or jurisprudence; in Italy the classics were naturally popular, though interest also extended to history, romances, and poetry; in France the classics and the romances were the favorites, though there were notably beautiful service-books produced at Paris and Rouen. All of the earliest books were printed in Gothic—that is, black letter—type. But in 1464 a Strasbourg printer—formerly known as the "R" printer, from a peculiar upper case letter used by him, and recently identified as one Adolf Rusch—used roman type; in 1465 Sweynheim and Pannartz, pioneer German printers in Italy, used a semi-roman type at Subiaco, and in 1467 were working in Rome with a purely roman font. The roman style was really perfected, however, by Nicholas Jenson, a French printer working at Venice, in 1470.

Italic type is the creation of Aldus Manutius, of Venice; it was first used in a few words of a book of 1500, but was really designed for a series of pocket classics, beginning with a Virgil of 1501. The type was based on a scholarly fifteenth-century Italian hand—not, as has sometimes been said, that of Petrarch—and was at first called *Chancery* or *Aldine* type. The first italic font had no upper case, roman capitals being used instead.

* * *

It was at one time argued that the first printing in England was done at Oxford; a book printed in that city by Theodoric Rood, of Cologne, bears the date 1468, but it has been generally agreed that the book is wrongly dated.[28] William Caxton is now conceded to have been the one who introduced printing into England. Caxton was an English merchant, who lived for several years in Bruges; after holding the office of "Governor of the English nation"—referring to the group of English merchants in the Low Countries—he took service with the Duchess of Burgundy. In his new position, Caxton had leisure for literary work; hence he occupied himself with translating Raoul le Fèvre's *Recueil des Histoires de Troie*. This was printed in 1474—the first printed book in the English language. By the autumn of 1476 Caxton had returned to England and set up a shop at Westminster. Here he brought out the first book printed in England—*The Dictes or Sayengis of the Philosophres*—in 1477.[29]

[28] See below, p. 196.
[29] The first bit of printing done in England, presumably also by Caxton, was apparently an Indulgence, now in the Public Record Office, dated 1476.

Caxton, who continued to print until his death in 1491, was translator and editor as well as printer; judging from his productions that have come down to us—and they may represent a comparatively small part of the total amount of work he did—he was a man of broad interests and considerable taste. Among the works printed by him are two editions (from different manuscripts) of Chaucer's *Canterbury Tales*, Malory's *Morte d'Arthur*, Gower's *Confessio Amantis*, *The Book of the Subtyl Historyes and Fables of Esope*, *The Golden Legend*, *Troilus and Creside*, and *Eneydos*—the last his own translation of Virgil's *Æneid*. When Caxton died in 1491, his press was taken over by Wynken de Worde, who devoted himself mainly to carrying out plans made by Caxton and to the production of reprints of Caxton's works.

As we have seen, Theodoric Rood began to print at Oxford about 1478; and a year later a press was set up at St. Albans. In 1480 John Lettou—later in partnership with William de Machlinia—began to print in London, producing at first nothing but law books. From 1490 to about 1530 Richard Pynson was at work in London; he was the first to use roman type in England.

Among sixteenth-century printers may be mentioned John Day, Richard Tottel, Thomas Berthelet, Richard Grafton, Henry Bynneman, Reynald Wolfe, Christopher Barker, and John Wolfe, some of whom did excellent work. The seventeenth century is recognized to have been the worst period for printing in England and throughout Europe. McKerrow finds no press in England worthy of mention during this period except the Oxford University Press,[8] and Esdaile mentions in addition only William Dugard.[9] By the end of the century a change had taken place in the business of book-producing. In the early days of the Stationers' Company the functions of editor and publisher might be assumed by either the printer or the bookseller. If an author took his manuscript to a printer, the printer acted also as publisher and turned the completed book over to one or more booksellers, who acted simply as retailers. But if the manuscript came to a bookseller, he became the publisher; and the printer had no share in the work beyond the printing of it, for which he was paid the prevailing rate.

In the seventeenth century publishing came to be a separate function, and the names to be mentioned from this time on are generally those of publishers rather than printers. In the Restoration and eighteenth century we find Jacob Tonson and his successors, Bernard Lintot, Edmund Curll, and Robert Dodsley. In the eighteenth century also a stimulus was given to better printing by the new types designed by William Caslon and by John Baskerville. Charles Whittingham's Chiswick Press and William Morris's Kelmscott Press raised the level of English printing in the nineteenth century, the result being that excellent work is being done today both in England and America, not only by various private presses and by the university presses, but also by a number of commercial printers.

*   *   *

In the early days, the essentials of a printing establishment were a press and a supply of type, with two men to operate the press and at least one compositor to set the type.[30] The illustrations that we have of early presses would suggest that one man did the inking of the type [31] and the other placed the paper, operated the press, and removed the paper. But it is the work of the compositor that we must consider first.

When a manuscript was received in the printing house, it was handed to a compositor (or sometimes divided between two—or even more—compositors), along with instructions concerning the page size desired and the kind and size of type to be used.[32] The compositor

[30] McKerrow prints (*Introduction to Bibliography,* pp. 39–47) five illustrations of sixteenth-century printing presses. In four of these two men are shown working the press and two are setting type; the fifth shows only three figures—two at the press and a third casting type.

[31] The inking of the type pages was done by means of two balls—like overgrown bass drum sticks with short handles. The balls were made of leather and stuffed with wool or feathers or some such material. Ink was spread on a stone and taken up from there to be dabbed on the type pages. To ink type by this method and secure an even distribution of the ink must have required a very special knack, but the results are uniformly and surprisingly good.

[32] Type sizes were formerly known by such strange names as Nonpareil, Minion, Brevier, Burgeois (pronounced, for some reason, or perhaps no reason at all, "bŭrjoice"), Long Primer, Pica (pronounced with a long *i*), English, and Great Primer. Nowadays, however, these names have largely fallen into disuse; the point system of measurement has replaced the old nomenclature. A point is $\frac{1}{72}$ of an inch, and various types are designated by the mumber of points they measure in height. Thus an eight-point type is $\frac{8}{72}$ of an inch high The effect of *leading* (increasing legibility by widening the space between lines by inserting thin strips of type metal—*leads*—or of wood—*reglets*) is often gained by using type which has the face of

took a composing stick [33] in his left hand; then standing before the
case [34] containing types of the size and style required, he picked up
the types one at a time with his right hand and placed them in the
composing stick.[35] As the first line of type placed in the stick was to

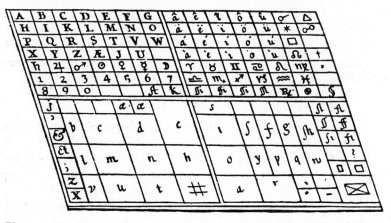

Figure 5. The "Lay of the Case": adapted from Joseph Moxon's *Mechanick
Exercises* (1683). Reproduced through the courtesy of the Yale University
Library.

be the top line of the page, the compositor, holding the stick upside
down, put the first type in the lower right-hand corner of the stick;
this would be the first letter in the upper left-hand corner of the
printed page. Each type had a *nick*—or notch—in the bottom side,

one size upon the body of a larger size, as, for example, a 10-point face on a
12-point body. Type of this kind is called *bastard type,* and a font of it is a *bastard
font.*

[33] Modern composing sticks are made of metal and are adjustable, so that they
can be set for whatever line-length is desired. The early printers, however, used
composing sticks made of wood, and must have had a different stick for each line-
length in use.

[34] Really a pair of cases, the upper—containing the capitals, the numerals, and
some other less frequently used characters; and the lower—containing the small
letters, punctuation marks, and spaces.

[35] It is often assumed, and there is some evidence to support the assumption, that
in the early days of printing the compositor had his copy read aloud to him. Dr.
McKerrow (*Introduction to Bibliography,* pp. 241–46) examined the evidence and
concluded that setting-up from dictation may sometimes have been resorted to but
could not have been the common practice.

so that the compositor could tell, by looking for the nick, that he had the type turned properly, i.e. upside down. If he found, as he approached the end of a line, that he had some room left but not enough for another word or another syllable, he might remove the

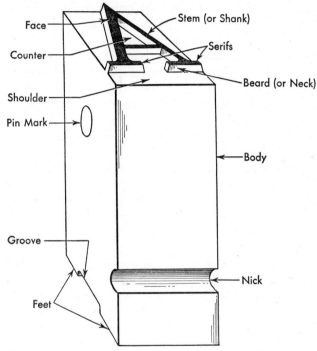

Figure 6. A type and its parts.

spaces [36] which he had placed between words and substitute thicker ones.[37] This process of arranging letters and spaces so that the right-hand margin of the page will be even is called *justifying*. Early

[36] The spaces are short types, which, having no *face* (the face being the part of the ordinary type that comes into contact with the paper), do not leave any impression on the paper.

[37] Between certain letters like *l* and *h*, as in the combination "small letter" or "final halt", the space can be increased without being made noticeable. Conversely, if the type-setter wishes to get one more letter in a line, he may reduce the space between letters such as *c, e,* and *o,* as in "public opinion" and "too early".

printers could and probably did [10] depend upon variations in spelling
to aid them in justifying. Thus the compositor could choose *chance*
or *chaunce*; *any* or *anie*; *mē, men,* or *menne*; *merciles* or *mercileffe*.

When the compositor has as much as half a dozen lines of type in
his composing stick, the weight of the stick will begin to be burden-
some and the danger of "pieing" the type already set by dropping
the stick, will become increasingly great. Nowadays he would transfer these lines to a *galley*—a shallow tray long enough to hold about
three pages of type. When galleys came into use is not precisely
known; but there is evidence that Elizabethan printers arranged
their type immediately into pages, perhaps placing the lines of type,
a few at a time, in a shallow box the size of a page, adding the catchword,[38] and tying the whole with string, to keep the type in position,
as soon as lines enough for a page had been composed.

If we assume that the proposed book is to be a quarto—the most
common format in Elizabethan times for the shorter, more popular
works, such as plays and "novels" like *Euphues, Rosalynde,* and
Pandosto—each sheet of paper will, before it is sewn and bound, be
folded twice. Thus each sheet of paper will constitute four leaves—
and eight pages—of the finished book. On one side of the sheet will
be printed pages 1, 4, 5, and 8; on the other side will be pages 2, 3, 6,
and 7. The type pages that will produce pages 1, 4, 5, and 8 are called
the *outer forme*; [39] the remaining four pages constitute the *inner
forme*. It will be seen that, if the inner forme is printed first,[40]
the press can be started to work as soon as page 7 has been composed.
But before any printing can be done, the printer must *impose* the
type pages, i.e., he must arrange them in the proper position with
relation to one another and then wedge them firmly in the *chase*—
a frame about the size of a sheet of paper—so that neither the inking
nor the pressure exerted by the press will disturb the alignment of
the individual types. In imposing the inner forme of a quarto book
the printer would put the top of page 2 opposite the top of page 3,
and the top of page 7 opposite the top of page 6; the left or inner
margin of page 3 would be next to the right or inner margin of

[38] See below, p. 44.

[39] So called because these pages are on the outside of the sheet after the first
folding.

[40] This seems to have been the usual practice; see McKerrow, *Introduction to
Bibliography*, pp. 18–19.

27

page 6, and the inner margin of page 7 next to the inner margin of page 2. When the type pages are properly arranged, the spaces between them, and between them and the chase, are filled with *furniture* [41]—pieces of wood below type height—and the forme is *locked up* by driving wedges, or *quoins,* between the furniture and the chase, so that the type pages are firmly fixed in place and the whole forme can safely be lifted and placed in the press. By the time all this has been accomplished, page 8 will doubtless have been set up; and the printer can proceed, in similar fashion, to the imposition of the outer forme. The top of page 8 is placed opposite the top of page 5, and the top of page 1 is opposite page 4; the left (inner) margin of page 1 is next to the right (inner) margin of page 8, and the inner margin of page 5 next to the inner margin of page 4. Thus when the sheet is *perfected,*[42] pages 1 and 2 will come on opposite sides of the same leaf, as will 3 and 4, 5 and 6, and 7 and 8. Now we come to the actual printing.

* * *

The process of printing involves two essential pieces of apparatus —a device for holding a sheet of paper in fixed juxtaposition to a page, or pages, of inked type; and a device for applying pressure to the paper, whereby the ink is transferred from the type to the paper. Since, in the early form of the printing press, the device for applying pressure depended upon the mechanical principle of the screw, and since, for convenience, the screw had to turn a little less than half of one revolution, giving a clearance above the paper of slightly more than half an inch, a third device was necessary—a means of sliding the paper under the pressure-applying device and out again.

A description of a press such as Gutenberg and his immediate successors used will serve to explain the technique of printing as it was

[41] The width of the margin is, of course, determined by the furniture. It will be noticed that in an attractively printed book the type page never appears exactly in the middle of the page of paper. The inner margin (the *gutter*) is always smaller than the others; then comes the top, or *head,* margin; then the outer, or *fore-edge*; and finally the bottom, or *tail.* A very attractive result is achieved when the height of the type page equals the width of the paper page.

[42] *Perfecting* is printing the other side of a sheet already printed on one side.

carried on down to the beginning of the nineteenth century. There
were refinements and improvements, to be sure; metal was substituted for wood in various parts, for example. But it was not until
steam power—later electricity—was substituted for man power, thus
permitting the use of larger sheets of paper and the printing of more
pages at one time, that there was any radical change in the design
of the press. We shall consider, then, such a press as might have
been found in an Elizabethan printing house.

A *spindle*—a cylindrical piece about eighteen inches long and
threaded for three or four inches of its length—was placed upright
in a frame in such a way that when it was turned by the pulling of
a lever it was raised or lowered according to the direction of the
lever's motion. Fastened to the lower end of the spindle was the
platen—a rectangular piece of hard wood; in one press its dimensions were 9″ by 14″ by 2½″.[11] Projecting from the framework in
which the spindle was fixed was the *plank,* so constructed that by
the turning of a crank it could be made to move in under the platen
and then, by a reverse movement of the crank, back out again. The
end of the plank nearest the platen had a frame 2′4″ long and 1′8″
wide, the bottom of which was a piece of marble or other smooth
stone. This frame with its stone—the *press stone*—was called the
coffin; it was in the coffin that the forme was placed.

Hinged to the end of the coffin away from the platen was a frame
covered with vellum, called the *tympan.* It had to be larger than a
sheet of paper, perhaps 18″ by 24″. The paper was laid upon this
tympan and folded down so that the paper came in contact with the
type. In order to keep the margins of the pages clean, it came to be
the practice—how early we do not know [12]—to make use of a
frisket; this was a second frame hinged to the tympan and covered
with a sheet of paper in which holes had been cut exactly the size
of, and in the position of, the type pages. Thus contact between paper
and type was made through the holes, and any ink that may have
been carelessly smeared upon the furniture surrounding the type was
taken up by the frisket and could not spoil the margins of the printed
pages.

In order to be sure that the pages on one side of the sheet would
be in *register* with those on the other side—that is, in the corresponding position—the sheet seems to have been folded before

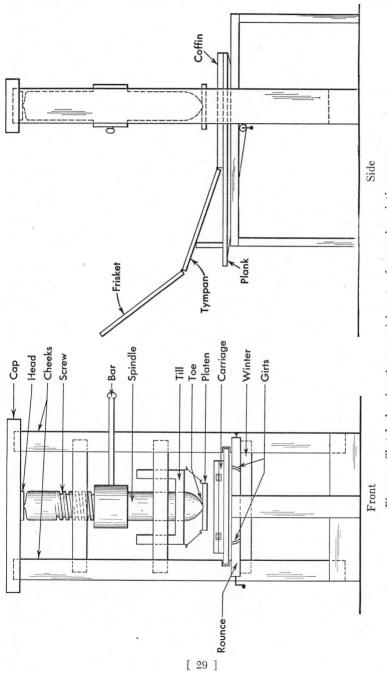

Side

Front

Figure 7. Sketch showing the essential parts of an early printing press.

Cap
Head
Cheeks
Screw

Bar

Spindle

Till
Toe
Platen
Carriage
Winter
Girts

Rounce

Coffin

Frisket

Tympan

Plank

being put on the tympan and then placed so that two pins, fixed in the middle of the long sides of the tympan, pierced the sheet through the fold, one on each side of the sheet.[43]

When the paper had been placed in the proper position, the frisket was folded over upon the tympan, and frisket and tympan together —with the paper between them—were folded over upon the forme. The printer, by turning a crank at his left hand, caused the plank— bearing forme, tympan, paper, and frisket—to move to a marked position under the platen. Then, reaching out with his left hand, he seized the *bar*—or lever—and pulled it toward him. As soon as the outer end of the bar—which curved away from the operator—came within reach, the printer added the strength of his right arm to that of the left; and the platen was brought down upon the tympan with sufficient pressure to transfer a clear impression of one-half of the forme to the paper. Then the bar was thrust back to its original position— thus raising the platen—and the plank was moved until the other half-forme came directly beneath the platen. Another pull of the bar completed the printing of the sheet on that side. The plank was thereupon moved back to its first position, the tympan and frisket were folded back, and the paper was lifted and hung up to dry.

If the printer had two presses—as several did—he could begin to *perfect* the sheet—print the other side—as soon as the ink on the first side was dry. If he had only one press, he would have to wait until all the copies required for the edition had been printed on one side; then he would remove the chase from the coffin, wash the forme with a solution that removed the remaining ink from the type, unlock the forme and remove the furniture, and then *distribute* the type—i.e.,

---

[43] When the forme was in the press ready for printing, the pressman (or, as the British call him, the machine minder) would *pull* a proof. This proof might reveal corrections to be made, but its chief purpose was to show whether the type page was giving an even impression—i.e., whether the letters all appeared equally black on the page. If one portion of the page pressed too lightly against the paper, so that the letters appeared gray, or too hard, so that there was tendency for the types to cut into the paper, the printer might be able to make adjustments in the type page by pounding down the types that were too high. But another device was frequently resorted to in this process of *making ready*. A piece of paper the size and shape of the area that was printing too lightly was pasted on the tympan at exactly the proper place to press the paper more forcibly—because of the greater thickness of the tympan at that point—against the portion of the type page that was too low and was, consequently, printing too lightly.

replace each type in its proper compartment, or *box,* in the type-case.[44]

Proofreading was done while the printing went on, usually by an employee of the printing house rather than the author; that this is true is indicated by the fact that the mistakes that are corrected are likely to be those that a printer would notice. Thus a letter of the wrong font will be changed, but some absurd blunder affecting the sense of a passage is likely to remain intact. Moreover, the sheets that had already been printed and consequently contained mistakes were not destroyed. You may find four variations—what might be called four issues—of one sheet: (1) both formes corrected, (2) both formes uncorrected, (3) the inner forme corrected and the outer forme uncorrected, and (4) the outer forme corrected and the inner forme uncorrected. If the press was stopped a second time for corrections—and that sometimes happened—the number of possible variations would be still greater.

The term *issue* just used may, perhaps, call for an explanation. When the type used in printing a book has been distributed, and then more copies of the book are printed from a new setting of type, the later copies represent a new *edition.* But when, as often happened, sheets printed from the original setting of type are put out with a new title page and perhaps some minor revision affecting only one or two sheets, these copies represent a new issue of the same edition. Since most modern books are printed from plates, a resetting of type occurs only when a book has been extensively revised. Hence most publishers do not today speak of editions but rather of *printings* or *impressions,* the two terms being synonymous and meaning, in the singular, the copies printed in one lot or at one time.

* * *

This is not the place for a discussion of modern printing, or of the different types of presses now in use. It has already been observed that the application of steam power and then of electricity to the

[44] If the printer anticipated a prompt demand for a second edition, he might keep the type pages intact by tying string around them. It could not have been very common, however, for a printer to have such a large stock of type that he could leave a whole book—unless a very short one—standing in type for any considerable length of time.

printing industry made it possible to use larger sheets of paper and print more pages at a single impression. Thus an octavo book nowadays is likely to be printed on quad paper, four times the size of an ordinary sheet, giving a signature of thirty-two leaves instead of eight. The printer may impose both inner and outer formes of two sheets, signatures A and B, let us say. If a quad sheet is run through the press and is turned properly in perfecting, the result will be two perfect copies of signature A and two of B. What would formerly have taken eight operations of the press is thus accomplished in two.

One or two other features of modern printing may briefly be touched on here. Most typesetting, except for very fine printing, is now done by machine. There are two kinds of machine: one, the *linotype,* casts a whole line of type in a solid slug of type metal; the other, *monotype,* casts individual types, so that a line is made up of separate types, as it would be if it were set by hand.

In the first kind of machine, which is universally used for newspapers and cheaper printing of various kinds, the compositor—in this case known as a linotype operator—sits at a keyboard much like a typewriter keyboard. Just as if he were a typist, he strikes the keys called for by the copy that has been given to him. As he strikes each key, a matrix or mold of the letter represented by that key slides from its magazine to join the other matrices that make up the required line. When the operator reaches the point at which another word or another syllable would make the line too long, he presses a lever; thereupon, the words constituting the line are automatically spread apart evenly so as to bring the line out to the right-hand margin—i.e., justify it—and then molten type metal is forced into the mold formed by the line of matrices. The metal is quickly cooled as the slug falls into a galley; it is then ready to be placed in the press. If the operator realizes that he has made a mistake somewhere in the line, he must, nevertheless, finish the line somehow; he cannot stop in the middle of a line and start over. Hence he fills out the line with some nonsense and begins the line anew, correcting the error as he proceeds. (The operator or proofreader is expected to remove the offending slug.) Generally the operator will fill out a faulty line simply by running a finger down the first two rows of keys; the result—"etaoinshrdluetaoin"—is familiar to the readers of all newspapers whose proofreaders are not infallible.

The monotype machine likewise has a keyboard, but here striking a key causes a certain perforation or combination of perforations to be made in a strip of paper that goes through the machine, like a typewriter ribbon but vertically instead of horizontally, from one spool to another. The perforated paper strip is then run through the casting machine; as in a mechanical piano player a certain perforation in the roll causes a certain note to be struck, so here the proper combination of perforations causes a matrix of the desired letter to fall into place. The matrix is filled with type metal, and thus a single type is formed. Monotype is commonly used for books and for better printing generally. It gives a rather more artistic result than is usually achieved with linotype; and it has the very great advantage that a wrong letter can be corrected by the substitution of the correct letter; whereas with linotype the whole line must be reset—with the ever-present likelihood that in the correcting of one mistake another mistake will be made elsewhere in the line.

The economy of mechanical typesetting is such as to compensate—in the opinion of the commercial printer, at least—for any lack of artistic quality such as may be achieved by hand composition; [45] for not only is the actual setting much speedier, but in addition the time formerly required in distributing the type is saved. With machine composition, once the type has been used for printing—or for making plates—it is thrown into the caldron to be melted up and the metal used over again. Another advantage of machine composition is that the compositor does not have to be on the watch to discard broken or defaced types, such as are to be found in any font of type that has been much used.

The mention of plates brings up another feature of modern printing. In the United States the actual type pages, whether set by hand or by machine, are not used for printing, except for small editions; [46] instead, a mold is made of the type page, either with plaster of Paris or, more commonly, a pulp—called *flong*—made of paper and paste. When the paper pulp is properly pressed or beaten down upon the type surface, a matrix is formed into which molten type metal can

[45] W. T. Crouch has an interesting comment on machine composition in his chapter, "Book-Making in the South", in *The Annual of Book-Making* (New York: The Colophon, 1938).

[46] In England the first impression of a book is commonly printed direct from type, plates being made for later impressions.

be poured to form a *stereotype* plate. Several matrices can be made from a type page before the type is broken up, each matrix can be used for half a dozen plates, and each set of plates can be used to print a great many copies of a book. Hence it is seldom necessary in these days for a book to be set up in type more than once, unless, of course, extensive revisions are to be made in it.

Another method of producing plates for printing is *electroplating*; in this process a wax mold is made of the type page, and the mold is then dusted with graphite, to make it an electrical conductor. By electrolysis a thin shell of copper is deposited upon the mold, which, when backed up with type metal, gives a more perfect reproduction of the type page and a more satisfactory printing surface than the stereotype plate. The electrotype plates are slower to make, however, and consequently more expensive.

One more kind of printing may be mentioned here in passing.[47] In *offset* printing the ink is transferred from type or plate to a rubber cylinder, then from the rubber cylinder to paper; this kind of printing is known to everyone through the rotogravure sections of Sunday newspapers, though it has other uses also.

VI

After the sheets have left the printer's hands, they are still to be made into books. The simplest practicable method of folding and fastening together sheets of paper to form a book is that in which each sheet is folded once across its smaller dimension and sewn, by means of stitches through the fold, to cords or tapes which hold it together with the other sheets comprising the book. This method of folding produces the *format* known as *folio*. Each sheet of paper forms two leaves (four pages) from eleven to sixteen inches high and from eight to eleven inches wide.[13] Since this method of construction causes all the folds to come together in the back, making the back edge of the book much thicker than the fore edge, and results in an unnecessary amount of sewing, it became the common practice to put two or more folio sheets together, one inside another, before sewing. If two sheets are placed together, making a *gathering* of four leaves (eight pages), the book is a *folio in fours*; if three sheets are

[47] See below, p. 52.

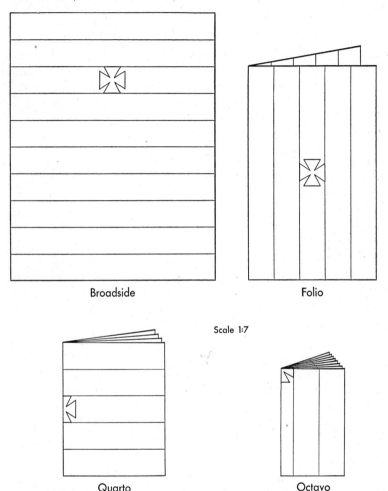

Figure 8. Sketches showing the direction of the chain lines and the position of the watermark in various formats.

used to a gathering, the result is a *folio in sixes*. One may find folios also in eights, tens, and twelves.

If a sheet is folded as for a folio, and then folded again across the other dimension, the result is a *quarto* sheet, with four leaves (eight pages) about seven inches by ten inches in size. Another fold, producing eight leaves from six to eight inches wide and from eight to eleven inches high, gives the *octavo* format. Still another fold produces *sextodecimo,* generally referred to as *sixteenmo*; and there are also such formats as *thirty-twomo* and *sixty-fourmo*. Other methods of folding will produce sheets or gatherings of twelve (*duodecimo*), twenty-four (*twenty-fourmo*), or even forty-eight (*forty-eightmo*) leaves. The common abbreviations for book formats are: Fol., 4to, 8vo, 12mo, 16mo, 24mo, 32mo, 48mo, and 64mo.

*   *   *

It has already been observed that the translucent lines crossing a sheet of laid paper and spaced about an inch apart are known as chain lines. Since we know that the chain lines always cross the sheet along its smaller dimension, we can make use of that knowledge in determining the format of a book. In folios the chain lines will cross the page longitudinally; in quartos, transversely; [48] in octavos, longitudinally again; in sextodecimos, transversely again; and so on, the direction changing with each additional fold. The direction of the chain lines in duodecimos and twenty-fourmos will depend upon the method of folding used.[49]

The position of the watermark—when one can be found—will serve to confirm the evidence of the chain lines. In folios there should be a watermark in the middle of one leaf of each sheet and none [50] in the other leaf. In quartos the watermark will be found on leaves 1 and 4 or 2 and 3 in the inner margin of the leaf, halfway between top and bottom. In octavos the watermark will appear—if it has not

[48] A book may be found of the right size for an octavo and with longitudinal chain lines but with four leaves to a sheet; such a book must have been printed on half-sheets of paper, and might be described as a quarto in half-sheets. Books are also sometimes found of quarto format but with vertical chain lines; these were apparently printed on half-sheets of double-size paper. See Allen T. Hazen, "Eighteenth-Century Quartos with Vertical Chain-Lines", *The Library,* 4th Series, XVI (1935–36), 337–42.

[49] Experiments with folding will show that a duodecimo gathering could be produced by folding a sheet once, as for folio, then folding it into thirds, and then folding once again. Or a sheet may be folded as for octavo, and a half-sheet, folded twice, inserted to make a twelve-leaf gathering. Or a sheet may be folded in thirds first and then folded twice again. And there are still other methods. (See McKerrow, *An Introduction to Bibliography,* pp. 169–73 and 325–28.) In any method, however, the final fold must involve all the leaves of the gathering so that they will all be held by the binder's stitches.

[50] Folios of the seventeenth and eighteenth centuries may have a counter-mark in the other leaf; see above, p. 13.

been cut away by the binder—at the top of the inner margin of leaves 1, 4, 5, and 8 or 2, 3, 6, and 7. Binders are likely to have removed all traces of a watermark from sextodecimos; but if any traces are present, they should be found normally on leaves 9, 12, 13, and 16 in the top, outer corner of the leaf.

* * *

In octavo and formats of smaller size some of the leaves are joined by folds at the outer margin, which must be cut through with a knife or trimmed off by the binder before the book can be read.[51] These folds are called *bolts*; [52] and pages are generally so imposed and sheets so folded that the bolts come in the second half of the sheet. Thus in an octavo, leaves 5 and 6 will be joined at the outer margin, as will leaves 7 and 8.

* * *

Two leaves that comprise one piece of paper—folded at the back and stitched through by the binder—are said to be *conjugate*. In an octavo sheet leaves 1 and 8 would be conjugate, as would 2 and 7, 3 and 6, and 4 and 5. *Cancels* [53] can often be discovered by the fact that the lines of print are not even with those of the corresponding conjugate leaf—as of course they should be if the imposing has been done properly—but are either higher or lower on the page.[54]

* * *

[51] A book in which the leaves have not been cut apart is described by bibliographers and booksellers as *unopened*. A book which is said to be *uncut* is one in which the margins are of the original width, indicating that the book has not been reduced in size by having been rebound. An uncut book is naturally more valuable than one which has been cut down; such a book is sometimes referred to as a *tall copy*. There is no premium on unopened books.

[52] Similar folds at the top edge of the leaves in quartos and all smaller sizes, and at the bottom of the leaves in some formats, are sometimes also called bolts.

[53] A cancel is a leaf in which some correction or expurgation or other revision has been made, so that the binder may cut out the original leaf and substitute the cancel. The leaf replaced by a cancel is called a *cancelland*.

[54] Cancels may also be discovered by the stub which the binder leaves when sewing the cancel into the book to make sure that his stitches will hold. Unless a book is very tightly bound, the stub of a cancel will be plainly visible. Another indication of a cancel is a signature on a leaf which would not ordinarily be signed. If, in a quarto in which only the first three leaves of a sheet are regularly signed, one finds a fourth leaf signed, he may suspect it to be a cancel. Any cancel would, of course, have to be signed in order that the binder will know where to insert it.

If one examines an old book or a modern book printed in England, he will discover a letter, or two or three letters, printed just below— and generally near the middle of—the last line on certain pages. This letter, or combination of letters,[55] is called a *signature*; it is intended to serve as a guide to the binder of the book. A signature will be found on the first page (the *recto* side of the first leaf) of each of the sheets—except the first—which when sewn together, constitute the complete book; the first sheet, since the first page of it is likely to be blank, or to contain the title or half title, and since it is easily recognized as the first sheet, is generally *unsigned,* i.e., bears no signature. In old books, the second, third, and sometimes other leaves of a sheet were also signed, the general—though by no means invariable—rule having been to sign one more than half the leaves in every sheet or gathering. In an ordinary quarto or octavo there is little reason for signing any leaf beyond the first; but suppose that the binder is dealing with a folio. He may not know at first whether it is an ordinary folio, or a folio in fours, in sixes, or in eights. He picks up the first sheet that comes to him and finds it signed B; another sheet, $B2$, is obviously intended to go inside B; seeing still another sheet, $B3$, he puts that inside $B2$. But is this a folio in sixes or in eights? Unless he stops to read the inside pages of $B3$, he cannot tell, in the absence of a signature, whether or not another sheet—$B4$—is meant to go inside $B3$. But if, on opening $B3$, he finds the second leaf signed (on page 3 of that sheet or page 7 of the gathering) $B4$, he knows that there is no other sheet to be inserted, that he is dealing with a folio in sixes. Thus the habit arose of signing quartos B, $B2$, $B3$, with the fourth leaf unsigned; octavos are likely to run B, $B2$, $B3$, $B4$, $B5$, followed by three unsigned leaves; and similarly with other formats.

I have used the B signature above as an illustration because it is usually—in first editions, at least—the first regular signature in a book. The reader may have observed that authors, even today, are likely to write the introduction to a book after the text of the book is finished. In the earlier days of printing it appears that the intro-

---

[55] In modern books a number is sometimes found on a line with the signature but generally near the inner margin; this number is a serial number assigned by the publisher to that particular work. If the work consists of more than one volume, the volume number is given also.

ductory matter—the so-called *preliminaries* [56]—was frequently brought to the printer after he had started work on the text of the book. Hence the practice arose of signing the first sheet or gathering of a work *B*, leaving signature *A* for the preliminaries when they should be ready for the compositor. As authors usually knew how to limit themselves in space (though not always in the warmth of their praises of the dedicatee and the reader), the printer was generally able to get all of the preliminaries in one sheet or gathering; sometimes he could even leave the first leaf blank. In the latter event, the title page would be *A2*; but it would normally be unsigned. The first signature, *A3*, would come on the third leaf (fifth page) of the sheet; and the following leaf, *A4*, the last of the sheet—if the book were a quarto—would be unsigned. If it proved to be impossible to get all of the preliminaries on one sheet, another sheet or half-sheet—signed *Aa*—might be used; or both sheets might be signed with asterisks, * and **, instead of letters.

One may wonder why binders found it necessary to use signatures when they could have guided themselves by page numbers instead, thus, in an octavo or quarto in eights, taking page 17 as the first page of the second sheet or gathering, page 33 as the beginning of the third, and so on. But a moment's reflection will show that for several reasons the signatures are more practical. In the first place, the pages of early books were seldom numbered. The manuscript practice was to number leaves rather than pages; hence when we find any numbering in early books—down to the end of the sixteenth century, say —it is likely to be *foliation* (numbering by leaves) rather than *pagination*. Of course the binder could have used leaf numbers as well as page numbers; but the fact is that printers were almost incredibly careless in their handling of such numbers, and the binder who tried to make use of the numbering, whether of pages or of leaves, would have found himself frequently at a loss. Moreover, the successive sheets of an octavo would not necessarily begin with pages 17, 33, 49, 65, and so on; even if the preliminaries are separately paged, as is the usual practice today, and the text begins on the first

---

[56] In Elizabethan times the preliminaries generally consisted of title page, dedicatory epistle, and an epistle to the readers; often commendatory verses—generally contributed by the author's friends—were added.

page of a sheet, there may be full-page illustrations which take up
one or more pages but are not included in the numbering.

If a second edition of a work was called for, the printer sometimes
found it possible to reduce the amount of space devoted to the preliminaries—perhaps by reducing the size of the type—and to begin
the text on *A4* instead of *B1*; then the page numbers at the beginning of the sheets would be 3, 11, 19, 27 (assuming that the book is a
quarto) instead of 1, 9, 17, and 25.

Since the early signatures were derived from the Latin alphabet,
in which *I* and *J,* and *U* and *V,* were not differentiated, printers used
either *I* or *J,* but not both, and *U* or *V,* but never both. *W* was
omitted, perhaps because it was felt to be literally a double-U or
double-V.[57] The signatures normally found, then, are: A, B, C, D, E,
F, G, H, I (or J), K, L, M, N, O, P, Q, R, S, T, U (or V), X, Y,
and Z. If the book contains more than twenty-three sheets or gatherings, the printer would start through the alphabet again, sometimes
using lower case letters instead of capitals, but generally doubling the
letter, either AA, BB, and so on, or Aa, Bb. There is seldom, if ever,
any significance to be attached to the style of type used in signatures,
as the compositor generally used type of the same font that he was
using in the line preceding the signature.[58]

American printers have, to the annoyance of British bibliographers,
devised a means of dispensing with signatures. Mr. Esdaile wrote—
with, I think, evident exasperation—

Will it be believed that all these complications, two volumes, separately
paged preliminaries, unpaged block pages, and no signatures, are introduced into a standard and finely produced recent book on printing,
written and printed by a modern American scholar-printer, in fact, no
other than Mr. Daniel Berkeley Updike's *Printing Types*? Koelhoff of
Cologne was more practical in 1472.[14]

But Mr. Updike and other American printers have been more concerned about the opinions of lay readers than about those of bibliographers. They apparently feel that if the signature—which adds
nothing to the content of the page but rather detracts from its appearance—can be eliminated without undue hardship on printers and

---

[57] Whenever a printer ran out of W's, as often happened toward the end of a long
signature, he got around the difficulty very nicely by using two V's, thus: VV.

[58] The kind of type used in certain signatures is sometimes mentioned in descriptions, however, as it may help to identify an edition.

binders, they will willingly bear the brunt of the disapproval of bibliographers, who will be constrained to refer prosaically to *p. 36* instead of using such esoteric terms as *Zzz3* or *P6ᵛ*. However, the bibliographers, being a conservative lot, will doubtless continue to ignore the page numbers and will write instead "[Zzz3]" and "[P6ᵛ]" [59] (the brackets indicating that the leaves are unsigned).

The method adopted by the American publishing trade to eliminate signatures is to print a spot of ink, generally square or rectangular, on the outer fold of each sheet or gathering. The spot on the first sheet is near the top of the fold, that on the second is just a little lower, that on the third still lower, and so on. Thus if a binder takes up a pile of sheets constituting, presumably, a complete copy of a book, there will be a line of spots extending diagonally across what will be the back of the book. If one gathering is missing, there will be a break in the line; if there are two copies of the same sheet, there will be two spots side by side; if any sheet is not in its proper place, the fact will immediately be evident. The binder can see at a glance, without stopping to look for, or at, signatures, whether the book is complete and whether the sections are in the correct order.[60]

The terms *sheet* and *gathering* are rather loosely used. Some bibliographers speak of a *sheet* (meaning the portion of a book comprising a single sheet of paper) when ordinary folios, quartos, or octavos are involved, and reserve the term *gathering* for two sheets folded together in folios in fours and quartos in eights, or three sheets folded together in folios in sixes, and so on. Others call the portion of a book bearing one signature a gathering, whether it is made up of a single sheet of paper, a half sheet, or several sheets.[61]

* * *

[59] *Verso* (left, as a book lies open) pages are distinguished from *recto* (right) pages by the use of a superior "v"; some bibliographers, however (Esdaile, *Student's Manual of Bibliography,* p. 259), use a superior "a" for recto and "b" for verso; they would write "B1ᵃ" instead of "B1" and "P6ᵇ" instead of "P6ᵛ".

[60] The method just described seems to have been used in my copy of Mr. Esdaile's book, from which I quoted above. Although the book was printed in England and contains a full complement of signatures, there are traces to be seen on several of the gatherings of ink spots that could hardly have served any purpose other than that of guiding the binder.

[61] Dr. McKerrow wrote: " 'Gatherings' are sometimes called 'quires', and the use of the word has good authority to commend it, but neither this nor 'gathering' seems appropriate when a single sheet is in question. 'Section' has also been suggested, but has the disadvantage that the word is commonly applied to divisions of a book's *literary* content. It would, I think, be better if some new word could be

When a statement concerning the printer or publisher of a book (or both printer and publisher) appears on the title page, it is called an *imprint*; when such information is given at the end of a book, the proper term is *colophon*. Most of the early books had colophons; but through the sixteenth century the tendency was for an imprint to take the place of the colophon, and after 1600 the colophon practically disappeared.[62] Imprints in sixteenth-century English books generally took such forms as these:

> Imprinted at London for Thomas
> *Cadman,dwelling at the great North doore*
> of S. Paules, at the ſigne of the Byble.
> 1585.[15]

> Imprinted at London,in Fleete-
> *ſtreate,beneath the Conduite,at*
> the ſigne of S. Iohn Euangeliſt,
> by H. Iackſon.
> 1584.[16]

> *At London*
> Imprinted for Wil-
> liam Ponſonby.
> 1584.[17]

> London.
> Printed by Ihon Wolfe for Edward White,
> and are to bee ſold at his ſhop, at the litle
> North doore of Paules, at the ſigne of
> the Gunne.
> 1587.[18]

> London.
> Printed by Iohn Wolfe,for EdwardWhite. 1588.[19]

introduced such as 'consute' (i.e. what is sewed together), which has no other associations." (*An Introduction to Bibliography,* p. 25, n. 2.)

[62] Colophons have, however, been revived in modern times. See, for example,
McKerrow, *An Introduction to Bibliography*: "Printed in England at the University
Press, Oxford / By John Johnson, Printer to the University" (p. [360]).

Printed at London by Roger Ward, for
Thomas Cadman. 1589.[20]

Imprinted by Iohn Wolfe, and are to bee fold at his
fhop at Poules Chayne. 1592.[21]

Imprinted at London for T.C. and E.A.[22]

Imprinted at London by Roger
Warde,dwelling at the figne of
the Talbot neere vnto Holburne Conduit.
1584.[23]

It will be seen from these examples that the imprint may or may
not give the name of the printer (unless he was also the publisher);
but it regularly gives the name of the publisher, that is, the bookseller. Thus the chief function of the imprint seems to have been to
inform a prospective buyer as to where he might find copies of the
book for sale.

Three of the books included above have colophons. *Arbasto* has
(on H3ᵛ) *"Imprinted at London by Iohn Windet /* and Thomas
Iudfon, for Hugh */ Iackefon. Anno. 1584."* (The "by H. Iackfon" of
the imprint is evidently an error; it should be "for" instead of "by",
as in the colophon.) *Gwydonius* has (on X2ᵛ) "AT LONDON /
Printed by T. East, for William Ponfonby. / 1584." In *The Myrrour
of Modestie* the colophon appears in the middle of a page (X7), with
decorations of type ornaments above and below it; the colophon
reads: "LONDON / Printed by Ro- / ger VVard dwelling at / the
figne of the Talbot, / neere vnto Holburne / Conduit. / 1584." The
last page of *The Spanish Masquerado* (E4) contains a decoration,
which may be the device of Ward or Cadman,[63] and may thus have
served the purpose of a colophon.

*   *   *

[63] I do not find it among the devices given by McKerrow in his *Printers' and
Publishers' Devices Used in England and Scotland 1485–1640* (London: printed for
the Bibliographical Society at the Cheswick Press, 1913); it bears some resemblance
to McKerrow's #179 and #378, but it is smaller and cruder than either of those.

We have found the word *register* used in printing to refer to the arranging of the type pages and the paper so that the impression on one side of the sheet corresponds exactly to that on the other side.[64] In bibliography a *register* is a list of signatures, sometimes found at the end of a book; by comparing the signatures given in the register with those on the sheets or gatherings as he brought them together for binding, the binder could tell when he had a complete book. If there was nothing unusual about the signatures,[65] a register was unnecessary, and hence is seldom found in English books. (Registers are more common in books printed on the Continent.)

*   *   *

From about 1520 down to the end of the eighteenth century it was the practice of printers to put below the end of the last line of each page, the first word—or the first syllable or two of very long words—of the following page. Such words are called *catchwords*. The practice may have been carried over from manuscript days, when catchwords, like signatures, served as a guide to binders; but Dr. McKerrow's suggestion—that the chief function of catchwords was to serve as a guide to the printer in imposing his pages [24]—seems a likely one.[66]

*   *   *

Large capital letters, whether woodcuts or metal castings, used at the beginning of a chapter or paragraph, are called *ornamental initials* or, abbreviatedly, *initials*.[67] Such letters are of great importance to bibliographers. Often they furnish the best—perhaps the

---

[64] The word *register* is also used to mean the exact correspondence of different impressions when two or more impressions are to be made on the same side of the sheet, as in color printing; see below, p. 53.

[65] For a case in which a register might have been helpful see Chauncey Sanders and William A. Jackson, "A Note on Robert Greene's *Planetomachia*", *The Library*, 4th Series, XVI (1935–36), [444]–47.

[66] The fact that John Johnson in his *Typographia* (II, 133, as quoted by McKerrow, *An Introduction to Bibliography*, p. 83) refers to catchwords as "direction-words" would support the belief that printers looked at the catchwords to see whether type pages were properly imposed.

[67] Strictly speaking, the term *capital letter* should mean a large letter used at the beginning of a chapter; but in common usage, even among printers, *capitals* or *caps* are upper case letters.

only—means of identifying the printer of a book;[68] and, what is more important, they may furnish information as to the date, or at least the order, of different books or editions.

An ornamental block with an opening in the center into which can be inserted an upper case letter from an ordinary font of type— whatever letter the text calls for—is called a *factotum* or *fac*.[69] Factotums were generally, if not always, cast; copies of the same design may be found in the work of several printers. For that reason they seldom offer much information to the student.

VII

Almost as long as there have been books, there has been decorating of books. Sometimes the decoration consists merely of such printed ornamental initials as have just been mentioned. Sometimes certain letters are colored, either by hand or by making a second impression with colored ink. Sometimes there are pictures—at first drawn or painted by hand, later produced by some form of printing—which are meant to elucidate or emphasize the text.

*   *   *

In the age of manuscripts the scribe frequently left spaces at strategic points, such as the beginning of a chapter, in which a *rubrisher*—to use the common English form instead of the Latin *rubricator*—painted letters in red or blue; such letters might thereafter be further adorned with silver or gold by an *illuminator*. The third step, applied in the finer manuscripts, was the addition of miniature paintings appropriate to the text of the work, such as the paintings of the Canterbury pilgrims in the Ellesmere manuscript of Chaucer's *Canterbury Tales,* now in the Huntington Library.

After the invention of printing, illumination gradually died out; when books became relatively cheap, there was no point in bestowing

[68] If it should ever be found that one printer borrowed a set of ornamental initials from another, many of these identifications would, of course, be invalid. It seems likely, however, that the possession of a fine set of initials would be an asset a printer would be reluctant to share with any one.

[69] Since a factotum is something which does all things and serves all purposes, a printer's factotum is well named; it enables the printer to make one ornament serve for all the letters of the alphabet.

expensive handwork upon them. Printed illustrations took the place of those done by hand. All printed illustrations fall into one or another of three classes: *relief, intaglio,* and *planograph.* In relief illustrations, as in letterpress printing, the background is cut away so that only the design takes ink and can be transferred to the paper. In intaglio work the design is cut into a block or plate. After being inked, the surface of the plate is wiped clean; when the plate is applied with strong pressure to paper, the ink remaining in the incised lines is transferred to the paper. In the planograph method the design is drawn upon a flat surface; we shall see later how such a design can be printed.

* * *

Line engraving on copper (an intaglio process) was known as early as was woodcut printing, technically known as *xylography*; but in the early days of printing, woodcut illustrations were more popular than engraved ones because they could be printed along with letterpress in one operation, whereas the printing of engraved illustrations requires such great pressure that it must be done as a separate operation. A distinction may be made between *woodcutting* and *wood engraving.* In woodcutting, which is the older process, the illustrator works with a block of wood planed with the grain—"on the plank"; with a knife he cuts away everything except the portions that are to appear black on the paper. In wood engraving the work is done on the end of a block of hard wood, usually boxwood, across the grain; with a *graver* instead of a knife the artist cuts into the wood the lines that are to be white in the illustration. Thus woodcutting is a black-line process, the design being the part that prints; and wood engraving is a white-line process, with the background taking the ink. Both are relief processes, however, since in both it is the high part of the block that takes the ink and transfers the impression.[70]

Woodcut illustrations fell into disfavor during the seventeenth and eighteenth centuries, but regained their popularity and remain popular today. In modern practice the printing is done not with the wooden block itself but with an electrotype plate.

* * *

[70] In recent times a good deal of work has been done using linoleum blocks instead of wood; the process is the same, and the result is similar but somewhat coarser.

The oldest of the intaglio processes is *line engraving,* at first on copper (*copperplate*), later on steel (*steel engraving*). In this method the artist cuts lines into the metal by means of a sharp tool called a *burin.* The ridge of metal (called the *burr*) thrown up by the burin is scraped away; then the plate is inked and wiped clean. When the plate is applied to paper with sufficient pressure, the paper is forced into the lines and the ink is transferred to the paper. If the paper is larger than the plate—as is usually the case—that portion of the sheet which was in contact with the plate will be smoothed and depressed by the pressure applied; the line between that portion and the margin of the sheet is called the *plate line.* The absence of a plate line is generally evidence that the engraving has been trimmed and is, consequently, less valuable, since lettering or even a part of the design may have been cut away.[71]

Line engraving was used as early as the fifteenth century, became popular in the sixteenth, and largely replaced woodcuts in the seventeenth. The softness of copper makes it impossible to make many impressions from a plate without damaging it; hence the first prints made from a plate are more valuable than later ones. About 1800, engravers began working on steel instead of copper; the harder metal made greater delicacy of line possible, even to the point of suggesting tone instead of line. (Earlier engravers had used cross-hatching for the purpose of suggesting tone, but without much success, as can be seen in the Droeshout portrait of Shakspere in the First Folio.) Toward the middle of the nineteenth century the practice of engraving on steel died out.

In the second intaglio process, *drypoint,* the design is drawn on copper with a steel point, like a pencil; the burr which is thrown up is not removed but is left to hold ink. The result is a softer line than that produced by line-engraving. As the burr soon wears down, drypoint is not suitable for illustrating a book of which many copies are to be printed.

The desire to achieve the effect of tone in engravings led to the invention in the seventeenth century of the process called *mezzotint.* In this method the engraver first roughens the entire plate by means

[71] In many book illustrations, especially in the first part of the nineteenth century, the printing was done on a large sheet, which was afterward cut up. Thus the whole sheet would have shown a plate line, but the individual illustrations do not.

of a curved tool called a *cradle* or *rocker*; thus the whole plate at this stage would print black. Then in the parts of the design that are to be almost as dark as the deepest black, the engraver lightly rubs down the burr so that it will hold less ink; the next lighter portions he rubs down still more; and so on, until he comes to the high lights, which are rubbed smooth and polished so that they will hold no ink at all. Mezzotint was very popular in the eighteenth century, rather died out in the nineteenth, but has to some extent been revived.

Several intaglio processes are forms of *etching,* in which the incising of the plate is done with acid. The etcher covers his plate with some waxy compound that is resistant to acid; then he generally smokes the surface by passing it above the flame of a candle or an oil lamp. This strengthens the resistance of the *ground* and also makes the surface opaque so that the etcher can see the lines as he draws them. With a sharp point (such as a steel phonograph needle) the etcher cuts through the soot-covered ground but avoids cutting into the metal. When the drawing is finished, the acid, or *mordant* (generally nitric acid diluted with water), is applied and allowed to *bite* into the plate wherever the ground has been removed. When the etcher thinks that the lines that are to be lightest have been bitten deeply enough, he removes the plate from the acid-bath and *stops out* those lines by applying fresh ground or varnish. He then replaces the plate in the acid, and continues to remove and replace until all the lines have been bitten to the required depth. Then the plate is ready for *proving*. The resulting impressions or proofs—whether one or many—constitute the *first state* of the etching. Generally the etcher is not satisfied with the result thus far achieved but proceeds to remove some lines and add others. When next a proof is pulled, it represents the *second state*. Every change that is made—the addition or removal of a single line—produces a new state; these are, however, merely *trial states*. When the etcher is satisfied, an edition is printed, which becomes the first *published state*.[72]

In *soft-ground etching,* tallow is added to the ground to make it softer and somewhat adhesive. Then a piece of paper is laid over the

---

[72] The *Encyclopædia Britannica* (14th ed., s.v. "Etching") shows four states of an etching of a bridge. The etcher was satisfied with the bridge in his first attempt; but certain shadows in the water were produced first with vertical, then with horizontal, again with vertical, and finally with horizontal strokes.

ground and the design is drawn upon the paper with a pencil. When the paper is lifted from the plate, part of the ground clings to the paper; where the pressure of the pencil was greatest, the most ground will be removed and the resultant etched lines will be broadest. Since the ground is nowhere removed so completely as it is by a point, the effect achieved is like that of a pencil drawing. A similar effect is attained in *crayon etching,* in which the lines are drawn in the ground with a *roulette*; thus each line is actually a row of fine dots. The regular spacing of the dots distinguishes roulette etching from soft-ground etching and from *aquatint*.

In aquatint the ground is made grainy by the addition of sand or powdered resin. Any portion of the design that is to be white is covered with stopping-out varnish. The first biting produces the parts that are to be printed most lightly; these are then stopped out, and the plate is bitten again and again until all the desired gradations of tone have been achieved. The sand or resin in the ground continues to resist the acid, so that there is an effect of white dots in the printed surface, as in soft-ground etching. Aquatint, though probably older than the eighteenth century, was most popular during that period; it died out in the latter part of the nineteenth century, but has since been revived.

* * *

In *lithography* the design is neither incised nor in relief; thus the process is a planographic one. It depends upon the principle that grease attracts grease and water repels it. The design to be printed is drawn with a greasy crayon or pencil upon a smooth stone; water is then poured on the stone and allowed to sink in, wetting the surface wherever there is no covering of grease. When the stone is inked, the water-soaked parts of the surface repel the ink—which is itself a form of grease—and the greasy lines attract it, thus leaving ink only on the lines that are to be printed. In practice, since a stone is not very portable, the drawing is usually done on paper and later transferred to the stone.[73] A great advantage of using paper is that one can make the drawing just as it is to appear, since it will be reversed in transferring it to the stone and reversed again in the

[73] A zinc or aluminum plate with an especially prepared surface is sometimes used instead of a stone.

printing; if one draws directly on the stone, he must make his drawing in reverse. Lithography was not very popular in England, largely because it was not very well done; since 1900 there has been considerable interest in the art and much good work has resulted. Colored lithographs—*chromolithographs* or *chromos*—were produced by using two or more stones, each inked with a different color; some of these were so inartistic that the word *chromo* has come to have a very bad connotation.

*   *   *

When the engraver or etcher is also the designer, the print is called an *original* engraving or etching. When two persons are involved, the designer's name, if given, generally appears in the lower left-hand corner, followed by the abbreviation *del* (for *delineavit*: "he drew it") or *pinx* (for *pinxit*: "he painted it"); the engraver's name then appears in the lower right-hand corner, followed by the abbreviation *sculp* (for *sculpsit*: "he carved it"). In describing such a print one should say "By the engraver, after the designer", as "Etching by Jackson after Turner".

*   *   *

The development of photography has led to methods of reproducing illustrations too numerous and too complex to be discussed here in any detail. It may be said briefly, however, that there are two kinds of photographic printing plates—*line blocks* and *half-tone blocks*. If the illustration is a line drawing, such as a pen-and-ink sketch, a photographic negative is made, in which, of course, the black lines of the original are white. Light is then passed through the negative so that it falls on a sheet of sensitized gelatine. The gelatine hardens when struck by light; hence the black lines of the original (the white of the negative) are hardened and remain when the unaffected gelatine is washed away. The gelatine mold—if one may call it that—is then transferred to a metal plate, generally zinc, and the plate is etched. The gelatine serves as a mordant-resisting ground; the white background of the original is etched away and only the black lines remain to take ink. The etched plate is mounted on wood to bring it to type height and is then ready to print. Such line blocks are called *zincographs* or *zincos* in England.

If gradations of tone are to be represented in the illustration, it is necessary to break up the dark areas into masses of tiny dots; the lighter grays will have smaller dots than the darker portions. To accomplish this, resort is made to a screen made up of two sheets of glass. Each of these sheets has opaque lines crossing it diagonally, from sixty to four hundred lines to the inch. The sheets are put together so that the lines cross, forming a latticework of black lines. The picture to be reproduced is fastened to a copy-board, and rays of light from powerful lamps are thrown upon it in such a way that they are reflected from the picture and pass through the aperture and lens of a camera, then through the screen, to fall at last upon a sensitized glass plate. Each tiny opening in the screen acts like the aperture in a pin-hole camera; thus the size of the image thrown upon the plate from each opening depends upon the amount of light passing through the hole. If the light is strong—as is that reflected from the white portions of the picture—the image will be large; the darker the area in the original picture, the smaller will be the corresponding image on the plate. By regulating the size and shape of the aperture in the camera, the distance between the screen and the plate, and the time of exposure, the photoengraver can manage to have the images on the plate corresponding to the white areas in the picture so large that they almost—but not quite—join; in the parts of the plate corresponding to the dark areas, the images are smaller and, consequently, farther apart.

Since the lens of the camera has reversed the image, it must be reversed again before being transferred to the half-tone block. This reversal may be achieved either by stripping from the glass plate the coating which contains the negative, or by turning the plate. Then a contact print is made from the negative upon a copper plate sensitized with gelatine and potassium bichromate. The color values will, of course, be reversed upon the copper; where the white images on the negative are largest (representing black areas in the original picture), relatively large dots of hardened gelatine will be produced by the action of the light; and in areas where the white images are smallest (corresponding to portions that are white in the original), small dots will be left on the plate after the unexposed gelatine is washed off. Resin is then added to form a better resist, and the plate is etched. The result is a copper plate with a surface irregularly dotted, with large dots—almost but not quite touching each other—where the original picture is black, and small dots farther apart where the picture is white. When the plate is inked and applied to paper, the large dots will produce the illusion of solid black, and the small dots, of white.

Coarse screen half-tones—sixty-line—are suitable only for such work as newspaper illustrations; in them the individual dots of the half-tone can easily be distinguished. Finer screen blocks require paper with a very smooth surface, originally obtained by coating, but now generally achieved by loading and calendering.

Other methods of producing plates for illustrations are *photogravure* (an intaglio process, like a photographic aquatint), *rotogravure* (a form of photogravure involving the use of a rotary press), *photolithography* (in which a design produced by photography is transferred to a stone), and *collotype* (in which the sensitized gelatine on a glass plate dries in fine wrinkles, producing a "grain"). Sunday newspapers have made everyone familiar with photogravure or rotogravure. It is an expensive process but is sometimes used for book illustrations. Collotype is particularly good for facsimiles of printed pages where it is desired to reproduce the color value of the original; where mere black and white will suffice, a line-block will serve the purpose.

The printing of an illustration may be either *direct* or *offset*; in offset printing the design is transferred from the plate to a sheet of rubber—generally a rubber-covered roller—and then from the rubber to paper. The elasticity of the rubber makes it possible to get a good impression on paper rougher than that required in printing directly from the plate; thus, for example, one may use a fine-screen half-tone without resorting to coated paper. In offset printing, of course, the plate and the print are alike, since the impression is reversed once when transferred from the plate to the rubber, and again in the transfer from rubber to paper.[74]

*   *   *

There are four ways of producing colored illustrations for books. The most primitive is to add color by hand to the printed impression;

[74] The fact that offset printing is used in the photogravure section of newspapers explains why, although the photogravure process is an intaglio process, there is no plate-line.

this was often done with woodcuts and later with aquatints. Or one might add the different colors to the plate or block and get a colored illustration from a single operation of the press; this method would obviously require great skill and care. Another method is to have two or more blocks or plates, one for each color to be used; each block or plate prints only the lines that are to appear in the color with which it is inked. The fourth method involves photography.

In the production of colored photographic illustrations, three half-tone plates are made, one to be printed in each of the three primary colors. Each plate is made, of course, from a photographic negative; and since the color values are reversed in the making of the plate, some way must be found to keep the light rays of the color with which the plate is to be printed from registering on the negative, so that they will be present on the plate. The device used is a color filter. The negative that is to be printed in red is made with a green filter that screens all the red values from the negative so that they will appear in the plate and hence in the impression made when the plate is printed with red ink. A second negative is made with a blue filter and a third with a red filter, and plates are made from these negatives. When impressions from the three plates—the first printed in red, the second in yellow, and the third in blue—are superimposed on paper, the three primary colors blend to produce natural color; but the inks must correspond exactly to the filters and the register must be perfect, or the result becomes a travesty of natural color. In *four-color printing* a plate printed in black is used along with the three color plates; it adds richness to the effect.[75]

VIII

When all the sheets that go to make up a work have been printed and arranged in the order in which they are to be read, they constitute what is, bibliographically, a book; but the services of a binder are necessary to put them in a form convenient for handling; only when bound (or *cased*) does the bibliographer's book become the layman's book.

*   *   *

[75] The effect of the four plates is well illustrated in the article on "Colour Photography" in the *Encyclopædia Britannica* (14th edition).

The binder, taking the sheets necessary to form a complete copy of the work, *collates* them, i.e., examines them to make sure that all the signatures are present and in the proper order. Then by means of stitches with strong linen thread, he sews the sheets or gatherings to stout cords or tapes (*bands*) placed at right angles to the back, or *spine*, of the book; the bands are then securely fastened to covers, or *boards*.[76] The outside of the book—covers and spine—is then covered with leather or fabric; and the raw edges of the covering material are hidden by pasting a lining paper (or a *doublure* of leather or cloth) to the inner side of the cover. Since this lining paper is twice the size of a leaf of the book, the free half becomes a flyleaf.[77] This much of the bookbinder's craft is called *forwarding*; that which remains— the adorning of the book with designs and lettering—is called *finishing*.

In English-speaking countries most books are now sold *cased* rather than bound; in such books the tapes are short, and a strip of something like cheesecloth is glued to the spine of the book, with a margin of about an inch extending beyond the spine on each side. The cover is made in one piece and is attached to the book by gluing the ends of the tapes and the margins of the cloth strip to the inside of the cover; in most instances the tapes and the cloth strip can readily be seen through the lining paper. On the continent of Europe it is still customary for books to be sold in paper covers; the purchaser then has them bound to his order.

What is called *library binding* is something of a compromise between true binding and casing. The sewing is done by machine, and the tapes—longer than those used in casing—are glued between split boards instead of being laced through a single, thicker board, as in true binding.

*   *   *

Probably the best of all leathers for bookbinding is what is known as *morocco* or *levant*; this is goatskin tanned with sumac. It has a

---

[76] In early bindings these covers were of wood; heavy cardboard is now generally used.

[77] It will be noted that the flyleaf is a binder's addition; hence it is not, bibliographically, a part of the book, and is not mentioned in a bibliographical description.

beautiful grain, and is hard and durable. *Straight grain morocco* is morocco stretched in one direction so that the grain forms parallel ridges. In *pin-head morocco* the leather is stretched in two directions, producing the effect suggested by the name. In *crushed morocco*—or, as it is more often called, *crushed levant*—the leather is crumpled, so that the surface takes on a pleasing wrinkled effect. *Niger morocco* is a thick, strong leather, generally dyed a light reddish-brown. *Cape goat* is good, but not as good as morocco.

Persian morocco and *French morocco* are inferior imitations, generally sheepskin. Sheepskin is not a durable leather for bindings, especially when it is split, as in *skiver*. *Roan* and *basil* are forms of sheepskin.

Pigskin is strong and durable but thick and stiff; hence it is suitable only for large books. It can be recognized by the presence of bristle-holes in groups of three. It has an attractive color and should not be dyed.

Many books are to be found bound in calfskin, an attractive smooth leather without a grain; it will take a pleasing polish (*polished calf*). Its chief fault is that it is likely to crack at the joints, or at least to become *fatigued,* as booksellers say. *Tree-calf* is a binding decorated with a tree-like design, produced by staining the leather with acid. *Russia calf* is scented by the birch oil used in tanning it; it is generally dyed a light chocolate brown, sometimes red. *Sprinkled calf* has a mottled effect, produced by sprinkling the leather with acid.

Books are often bound in vellum or parchment. When calfskin (for vellum) or sheepskin (for parchment) is to be used in bookbinding, it is not scraped thin as it is for use as writing material. Parchment is distinguished from vellum by the fact that it has a grain.

A *whole binding* is one in which all the outside of the book—covers and back, or spine—is covered with leather. In a *three-quarter binding,* the leather covers the spine and one-third of each cover. A *half binding* has the back and the outer corners of the boards covered with leather, the rest of the boards being covered with paper or cloth. In a *quarter binding* only the spine is leather-covered.

In the finishing of a binding, elaborate inlays of different colored leathers or enamel are often used; in early bindings *bosses* [78] and jewels are sometimes found. Generally, however, the ornamentation consists of a design impressed in the leather or fabric by means of a narrow wheel called a *fillet*, a wider wheel called a *roll*, or a *stamp*, or by a combination of these tools. The fillet is used to produce lines such as often decorate the borders or divide the surface into panels. The roll produces a continuous succession of figures, such as a row of flowers or of conventional symbols. The stamp—used with a press —produces a larger design; often the whole cover design is impressed by one stamp in one operation of the press. When the design is not colored, it is referred to as *blind tooling* or *blind stamping*. When gold is added,[79] the result is *gold tooling*. An *extra binding* is an unusually fine or luxurious one.

Some of the common terms used in describing bookbinding designs are:

ajouré—a cut-out pattern laid over a colored background

dentelles—borders of small, lacy figures

diaper—covered with small figures, often diamond-shaped

diced—ornamented with a pattern resembling dice or small squares; checkered

fleuron—a flower-shaped ornament

goffered (or gauffered)—having an embossed or indented design, as goffered edges

pointillé work—marked by small points or dots

repoussé—having a design in relief

semé (more often semis)—a powdering or sprinkling of small figures.

*   *   *

Styles in binding—in the early days, at least—are likely to bear the name of the person for whom the binding was done rather than that of the binder. One of the earliest is the so-called *Canevari*, named for Demetrio Canevari but now believed to have been de-

---

[78] Bosses—protuberances, generally of metal, placed in the four corners and often in the center of the outside of each cover—kept the surface of the binding from being marred by contact with desk or table.

[79] The heated tool is pressed into the binding through gold leaf dressed with a white-of-egg preparation.

signed for Pier Luigi Farnese. a sixteenth-century Italian book collector. This style is characterized by a rather plain tooled panel
enclosing an impressed *cartouche* (an oval or rectangle) with a large
cameo stamp in intaglio.

One of the most famous names in bookbinding is that of Jean
Grolier (1479–1565), who lived for many years in Italy. The *Grolier-
esque* binding has a pattern of interlacing bars, bands, or ribbons,
with delicate scrolls of slender gold line. The *Majoli* or *Maioli* style
is named for another Frenchman, Thomas Mahieu, secretary to
Catherine de Medici. Maioli bindings have a framework of ribbons
and shields, with interlacing scrollwork, partly inlaid, partly gold-
tooled.

The sixteenth century in France also gave rise to the *Lyonnese*
style, characterized by heavily tooled strapwork or by impressed
center and corner stamps, generally with arabesques on a background
of gold. Another French style of the same period is the *fanfare* binding, in which the back and sides are decorated all over with interlacing geometrical patterns, the intervening space at first blank, but
later filled in with sprays and wreaths of foliage. The name of
Nicholas Eve has been associated with this style, but actually Eve
practised a very restrained form of fanfare binding, using a central
design with corner fleurons and allowing plenty of leather to show.

A seventeenth-century modification of fanfare is the *Le Gascon*
style, in which *pointillé* work is used for the design, and the space
enclosed by the strapwork is decorated by inlays of colored leather.
In England there developed the style named for Samuel Mearne,
stationer to Charles II; *Mearne* bindings have designs made up from
various combinations of a few tools, such as a curve and tulip. The
Cottage style is a form of Restoration binding in which there is a
center panel with a gable at the top, or at both top and bottom.
Another development of the Restoration binding is the *Harleian,* in
which a center panel is surrounded by a broad border, both decorated.

One more style remains to be mentioned here—the *Jansenist*. This
developed in France in the latter part of the seventeenth century; it
is a simple style, in which a centerpiece—frequently heraldic or
symbolic—is repeated in each of the four corners, the rest of the
surface being left undecorated.

Of course the only way to learn about bindings is to study them

Maioli   Harleian

Figure 9. Examples of famous bindings. Reproduced through the kindness of William A. Jackson, Director of the Houghton Library, from books in the Harvard College Library.

at first hand; but even such cursory information as has just been given may help the student to visualize a binding from a description such as may be found in a bookseller's catalogue. Here are three, taken more or less at random:

2 vols., thick folio, magnificently bound in full crushed green levant, heavily gilt tooled, red leather labels, [80] raised bands gilt, inner dentelles, gilt edges, white moire end papers, . . .[25]

Full orange levant morocco, gold tooled back (uniformly faded), gold tooled inside borders, top edges gilt, other edges uncut.[26]

Contemporary [81] black morocco, thin line and ornamental borders, the

[80] Labels are pieces glued to the spine, bearing the title, the author's name, the volume number, etc.

[81] Meaning that the book was bound at about the same time as the date of publication of the work and has not since been rebound.

| Fanfare | Grolier | Mearne |
| LeGascon | Lyonnese | Canevari |

Figure 10. If some of these specimens appear not to correspond with the descriptions given in the text, it should be remembered that, though the shoemaker may stick to his last, he does not always use the same last.

side with a panel of conventional flowers on two stems surrounded with leaves, circles, etc., filled in with pointillé work, and with corner fleurons in gold, red end-papers covered with gold ornaments, metal corner pieces (one missing) gilt edges.[27]

Generally, however, descriptions are briefer than those quoted above:

"2 vols., thick tall 8vo, ¾ morocco (rubbed)"; "3 vols., thick folio, ¾ maroon morocco (one joint cracked)"; "thick 4to, blue buckram gilt stamped"; "12mo., polished calf, plates slightly foxed".[82]

*   *   *

Such, then, are the materials of research—the manuscripts and books, some witty, some wise, some poetic, some romantic, many, unfortunately, merely stupid and dull. Even the last, however, may have something to offer one who applies to them the tools of research.

[82] Foxed: spotted with stains caused by decay.

Part II THE TOOLS
OF RESEARCH

THE tools of research in literary history consist of bibliographies, a note-system, scientific instruments of several kinds, and a variety of forms of knowledge. The word *bibliography,* with its derivatives, has several meanings. Defined as "the science of books",[1] bibliography may be divided into four kinds:

(1) Historical, dealing with the history of book production—history of writing, printing, binding, illustrating, publishing, etc., . . .

(2) Bibliothecal, concerned with the collection, preservation, and organization of books in libraries (library science and history of libraries) . . .

(3) Enumerative, including lists of books of all sorts, which 'act the part of gentleman ushers toward other books by introducing them to the notice of strangers' . . .

(4) Practical, dealing with the methods of work of student and author —reading, research, compilation of notes and bibliography, the preparation of manuscript for the press, publication, etc.[2]

Still another meaning is attached to the word *bibliography* as used in research; thus all evidence derived from the physical make-up of a manuscript or book may be called bibliographical evidence. In speaking of bibliography as a tool of research, we are thinking mainly of enumerative bibliography.

I

This is not the place for an exhaustive list of bibliographies; every student interested in English literary history should have his own copy of Kennedy's *Concise Bibliography,*[3] or Spargo's *Bibliograph-*

ical Manual,[4] or Cross's *Bibliographical Guide.[5], 1* It may, however,
be worth while to consider here what kinds of bibliographies there are
for the student of English, and what aid one may legitimately expect
to derive from each kind.

The three guides mentioned above differ in details of organization
and arrangement, but all begin with a section devoted to books and
articles on bibliography; this section includes such works as Theodore Besterman's *The Beginnings of Systematic Bibliography,[6]* and
Bibliography, Practical, Enumerative, Historical, by Van Hoesen
and Walter.[7] Next comes a section listing works on research, including not only such standard treatises as Langlois and Seignobos, *Introduction aux Études Historiques[8]* and Gustave Lanson, *Méthodes de
l'Histoire Littéraire,[9]* but also books on the compiling of bibliographies (Martha Connor, *Practical Bibliography-Making)[10]* and the
writing of theses (André Morize, *Problems and Methods of Literary
History),[11]* on the use of public records (V. H. Galbraith, *An Introduction to the Use of Public Records),[12]* and on the use of libraries
(Margaret Hutchins, Alice S. Johnson, and Margaret S. Williams,
Guide to the Use of Libraries).[13]

The next section is made up of *universal bibliographies,* such as
those of Grässe (*Trésor de Livres Rares et Précieux, . . .*),[14]
Vapereau (*Dictionnaire Universal des Littératures),[15]* and Watt
(*Bibliotheca Britannica).[16]* As is to be expected, these universal
bibliographies, in which the compiler "lists every book he can lay his
hands on",[17] are not always to be relied upon. For the student of
English literature, Volumes III and IV of Watt, which constitute an
analytical subject index, will be most helpful; although the work is
more than a hundred years old, it is still indispensable for students
of the English literature of the eighteenth century and earlier periods.

Another section consists of *bibliographies of bibliographies,* the
classics in this group being Courtney (*Register of National Bibliography . . .*),[18] Petzholdt (*Bibliotheca Bibliographica),[19]* Stein
(*Manuel de Bibliographie Générale),[20]* and Josephson (*Bibliographies of Bibliographies Chronologically Arranged).[21]* Stein's work
may be regarded as a continuation of Petzholdt's; and Josephson's
serves as a continuation and correction of Stein's. The graduate stu-

[1] A briefer guide, consisting of 241 entries, is contained in Esdaile, *Student's
Manual of Bibliography,* pp. 274–347.

dent may be most likely to find what he wants in Clark S. Northup, *A Register of Bibliographies of the English Language and Literature,*[22] published in 1925.

Among the lists of reference books, the standard for American students is Miss Isadore G. Mudge's *Guide to Reference-Books,* of which the sixth edition appeared in 1936, with a supplement in 1939, and other supplements (by Constance M. Winchell) in 1941, 1944, and 1947.[23]

"General Catalogues and Lists of Books" will constitute another section. Here will be found first the trade-lists, such as the *London Catalogue,*[24] which in various editions covers the period from 1700 to 1855, and its continuation, the *English Catalogue,*[25] published annually; and the *United States Catalogue*[26] (to 1928), supplemented and continued by the annual *Cumulative Book Index.*[27] Second, there are the general library catalogues, such as those of the British Museum and the Bibliothèque Nationale. The old British Museum *Catalogue of the Printed Books*[28] (1881–1900) in 95 volumes, with a *Supplement*[29] (1905) of 15 volumes, is immensely valuable; but it is being superseded by a new *Catalogue of Printed Books,*[30] which, begun in 1932, has already reached Volume XXXVIII ("Buer-Bunn"). When completed, the new catalogue will comprise more than 150 volumes. The catalogue of the Bibliothèque Nationale in Paris,[31] begun in 1897, has proceeded slowly and is not yet complete; Volume CLVI ("Rose-Roug") appeared in 1939. For the United States there is a catalogue based on Library of Congress catalogue cards, which reproduces the information contained on each card.[32] Third are a few subject-catalogues, such as Robert A. Peddie, *Subject Index of Books Published before 1880.*[33]

In the next group are the check-lists and indexes to special collections in American libraries, such as the Wordsworth collection at Cornell[34] and that at Amherst,[35] American plays and poetry at Brown,[36] books on the history of science at the John Crerar Library at Chicago,[37] and American Revolutionary War pamphlets and other collections at the Newberry Library (Chicago).[38] Included in this group are also the *Check-List or Brief Catalogue of the Library of Henry E. Huntington* (1919), with its *Supplement* (1920);[39] *Incunabula in the Henry E. Huntington Library* (1937)[40] and *Census of Medieval and Renaissance Manuscripts in the United States and*

Canada, edited by Seymour de Ricci with the assistance of W. J. Wilson.[41] Another item in this group is Ernest C. Richardson, *An Index Directory to Special Collections in North American Libraries* (1927),[42] in which the arrangement is by places and by subjects.

Professor Spargo's Section VII has no counterpart in the *Concise Bibliography* or in the *Bibliographical Guide,* though many of the books listed there are mentioned by Professors Kennedy and Cross under other headings; this section is headed "Book-Building", and there are subheads: "Palæography", "Typography", and "The Parts of the Book". Most of the books in this section are mentioned elsewhere in the present work.

In another category are the encyclopædias, including the famous *Allgemeine Encyklopädie der Wissenschaften und Künste,*[43] commonly known, from the names of its editors, as "Ersch and Gruber", and, of course, the *Encyclopædia Britannica.*[2] There are also special encyclopædias devoted to religion,[44] names,[45] social sciences,[46] music,[47] education,[48] and the classics,[49] to mention only those most likely to be of interest to graduate students in English.

Another group of bibliographies is that made up of lists of learned societies—such as the Malone Society, the Selden Society, the Camden Society, the Early English Text Society, the Chaucer Society—or their publications.[50] Still another group consists of lists of dissertations.[51]

Another kind of bibliography is that which lists biographical material. In this category are such general works as that by Helen

[2] Isadore Gilbert Mudge, in her *Guide to Reference Books,* p. 44, wrote: "The 9th edition, under the able editorship of William Robertson Smith, was the high water mark of the Britannica, and its scholarly articles may still be used profitably for subjects where recent information is not essential. Many of its monumental articles have been carried over into later editions, sometimes abridged or revised. The 11th edition, though more popular than the great 9th edition, is more scholarly and more carefully made than the 14th; it (the 11th) is now, except for post-war topics or scientific subjects, where late information is essential, the most generally useful of the three editions [the 10th, 12th, and 13th were not really editions, but merely reprints with supplements], and its articles are more often useful than the more popularized articles in the 14th edition. The 14th edition, reset, with many new articles but not entirely remade, is a popularized and partially Americanized edition though still largely British in content and viewpoint. It contains many good new articles on timely subjects (sciences, post-war topics, etc.), but some of its older material carried over from the 9th and 11th editions has been inadequately revised or too much abridged; some of the new work is less accurate than the old, and its cross references are not always accurate."

Hefling and Eva Richards—*Index to Contemporary Biography and Criticism* [52]—and one by Phyllis M. Riches.[53] There are more specialized works for separate countries. Those for England will be of most use to students of English literature and English literary history; and it should hardly be necessary to remind users of this volume that the first work to consult for information about an Englishman no longer living—or, more exactly, one who died before 1940 [3]—is the *Dictionary of National Biography*, familiarly known as the *DNB*, just as *Who's Who* is the standard "first resort" for living Englishmen. For Cambridge men before 1751 a useful work is that by John Venn and J. A. Venn, *Alumni Cantabrigienses*; [54] and for Oxford men, Anthony à Wood, *Athenae Oxonienses*,[55] though more than a hundred years old and not always reliable, is still sometimes valuable. For the United States we have *Who's Who in America* [56] and the *Dictionary of American Biography*.[57] There are also, of course, a number of other biographical works for America, including a monthly publication by the H. W. Wilson Company; [58] mention should also be made of *American Authors, 1600–1900: a Biographical Dictionary of American Literature*; *Authors Today and Yesterday*; and *Twentieth Century Authors*, all three edited by Kunitz and Haycraft.[59] Obituaries in the *New York Times* are frequently very informative and can easily be located through the *Index*.

Dictionaries of anonymous and pseudonymous works constitute another class of bibliographies. In this field "Halkett and Laing" has long been standard; and there is now a second, fairly recent edition.[60]

A very important class of bibliographies is that made up of periodical indexes such as the *Readers' Guide to Periodical Literature*,[61] published since 1900, and the even more important—for graduate students in English—*Supplement*, begun in 1907 and known since 1913 as the *International Index to Periodicals*.[62]

The learned journals constitute another group of bibliographies. Strictly speaking, only those journals that provide bibliographies should be included; hence, Professor Cross lists only periodicals that contain reviews. These journals may be classified according to subject matter; Professor Spargo uses the following headings: "Bibli-

---

[3] The original publication in 66 volumes covered the period down to 1900, but a series of supplements, of which the latest was published in 1949, has brought the work down to 1940.

ography", "The language and literature of England and the United States, related languages and literatures, and linguistics in general", "Phonetics and speech re-education", "The drama and the theatre", "Comparative literature", "Folklore", and "Other pertinent materials".[63]

Then come bibliographies devoted to literature, classified according to country, to period, and to type of literature involved. Such general works as the *Cambridge History of English Literature* [64] and John G. O'Leary, *English Literary History and Bibliography* [65] are now supplanted—so far as the bibliographies are concerned—by the *Cambridge Bibliography of English Literature,* ed. F. W. Bateson, published in four volumes in 1940.[66] For the Old and Middle English periods there are Allen R. Benham, *English Literature from Widsith to the Death of Chaucer,*[67] and John E. Wells, *A Manual of the Writings in Middle English, 1050–1400*; [68] the latter originally appeared in 1916, but seven supplements to it have been published. For the period from 1475 to the present, one finds the *Stationers' Register,*[69] the *Term Catalogues,*[70] the Hazlitt materials,[71] and the *Short Title Catalogue* [72] (frequently abbreviated to *STC*), in addition to more specialized works.

Among bibliographies of poetry, the classics are Corser's *Collectanea Anglo-Poetica,*[73] Courthope's *A History of English Poetry,*[74] Saintsbury's *Historical Manual of English Prosody,*[75] and Warton's *The History of English Poetry from the Close of the Eleventh Century to the Commencement of the Eighteenth Century*; [76] there are more recent works in special fields.

For fiction the standard work is Dunlop's *History of Prose Fiction*; the edition by Henry Wilson is the one to be used.[77] For the English novel there is Ernest Albert Baker's *The History of the English Novel.*[78] There are also bibliographies for such special fields as mediæval romance, the novel of manners, the burlesque novel, and the like.

Bibliographies of the essay include Bryan and Crane's *The English Familiar Essay*; [79] there are also bibliographies of letters, diaries, and memoirs. For newspapers and periodicals, Crane and Kaye's *Census of British Newspapers and Periodicals 1620–1800* [80] and the *Times Tercentenary Handlist of English and Welsh Newspapers . . . (1620–1920)*[81] should be mentioned.

In the field of drama there are general works such as Creizenach's *Geschichte des Neueren Dramas* [82] and Allardyce Nicoll's *The Development of the Theatre: a Study of Theatrical Art from the Beginnings to the Present Day,*[83] and more limited works like Roy C. Flickinger's *The Greek Theatre and Its Drama,*[84] Kathleen M. Lea's *Italian Popular Comedy,*[85] and Karl Young's *The Drama of the Medieval Church.*[86] For England there are Sir Edmund Chambers's *The Mediæval Stage* [87] and *The Elizabethan Stage,*[88] Allardyce Nicoll's four works covering English drama from 1660 to 1850,[89] Greg's *A Bibliography of the English Printed Drama to the Restoration* [90] (of which only the first volume—to 1616—has appeared), and other books by contemporary scholars, as well as Collier's *History of English Dramatic Poetry,*[91] Fleay's *A Biographical Chronicle of the English Drama,*[92] Langbaine's *An Account of the English Dramatick Poets,*[93] and Ward's *History of English Dramatic Literature.*[94]

American literature has bibliographies which may be similarly classified. Among general works may be mentioned the *Cambridge History of American Literature,*[95] John G. Bartholomew's *A Literary and Historical Atlas of America,*[96] Charles Evans's *American Bibliography,*[97] and W. O. Waters's *American Imprints, 1648–1797.*[98] For the period from the beginning to 1783 there are *The Puritans,* by Perry Miller and Thomas H. Johnson,[99] and *A History of American Literature during the Colonial Times, 1607–1765* [100] and *The Literary History of the American Revolution, 1763–1783,*[101] both by Moses C. Tyler. The period from 1783 to the present is covered by such books as Patrick K. Foley's *American Authors, 1795–1895* [102] and Fred B. Millett's revision of Manly and Rickert's *Contemporary American Literature.*[103]

For American poetry there are such works as Gay W. Allen's *American Prosody* [104] and Oscar Wegelin's *Early American Poetry;* [105] for fiction, Lyle H. Wright's *American Fiction 1774–1850* [106] and Arthur H. Quinn's *American Fiction;* [107] for essays, Adeline M. Conway's *The Essay in American Literature;* [108] for diaries, Harriette Forbes's *New England Diaries 1602–1800;* [109] for periodicals, Clarence S. Brigham's *Bibliography of American Newspapers 1690–1820* [110] and Winifred Gregory's *American Newspapers 1821–1936;* [111] and for drama there are, among other works, Arthur H. Quinn's three volumes on the American drama from the beginning to the present day (or rather, 1931),[112] George C. D. Odell's *Annals of the New York Stage* [113] (fifteen volumes have carried the *Annals* to 1894), and Burns Mantle's *Best Plays*,[114] published each year since 1920.

Next may be mentioned bibliographies of individual authors; there are bibliographies for Chaucer,[115] Coleridge,[116] Dickens,[117] Donne,[118] Dryden,[119] Gray,[120] Hardy,[121] Housman,[122] Milton,[123] Pope,[124] Ruskin,[125] Scott,[126] Shakspere,[127] Shaw,[128] Spenser,[129] Swift,[130] and Wells,[131] among English writers; for Cooper,[132] Crane,[133] Edwards,[134] Emerson,[135] Hawthorne,[136] Howells,[137] Irving,[138] James,[139] Lowell,[140] "Mark Twain",[141] Cotton Mather,[142] Increase Mather,[143] "O. Henry",[144] Poe,[145] Robinson,[146] Thoreau,[147] Whitman,[148] and Whittier,[149] among Americans. Concordances exist for *Beowulf* [150] and the Bible; [151] for Browning,[152] Burns,[153] Chaucer,[154] Coleridge,[155] Collins,[156] Cowper,[157] Donne,[158] FitzGerald,[159] Goldsmith,[160] Gray,[161] Herrick,[162] Housman,[163] Keats,[164] Kyd,[165] Marlowe,[166] Milton,[167] Pope,[168] Shakspere,[169] Shelley,[170] Spenser,[171] Tennyson,[172] Wordsworth,[173] and Wyatt; [174] and for Emerson,[175] Hawthorne,[176] Lanier,[177] and Poe.[178]

In the field of literary criticism and æsthetics such general works may be mentioned as Gayley's *Introduction to the Methods and Materials of Literary Criticism*,[179] Gayley and Kurtz's *Methods and Materials of Literary Criticism*,[180] and Saintsbury's *A History of Criticism and Literary Taste in Europe*.[181] For England there are Gregory Smith's *Elizabethan Critical Essays*,[182] Spingarn's *Critical Essays of the Seventeenth Century*,[183] and a number of works on eighteenth-century criticism.[184] The works on American criticism include George E. DeMille's *Literary Criticism in America* [185] and more restricted works such as *Between Fixity and Flux: A Study of the Concept of Poetry in the Criticism of T. S. Eliot*.[186]

A consideration of bibliographies in linguistics and phonetics would begin with works like Leonard Bloomfield's *Language*,[187] Willem L. Graff's *Language and Languages*,[188] and Louis H. Gray's *The Foundations of Language*.[189] Following these might be mentioned works on the English language, such as Albert C. Baugh's *A History of the English Language* [190] and Edward D. Myers's *The Foundations of English*,[191] and then the dictionaries. First would

come the *New English Dictionary*,[192] familiarly known as *NED*,[4] *and*
other dictionaries of modern English such as *Webster's New International*; [193] then the dictionaries of Old [194] and Middle [195] English
and of English dialects.[196] For American English the most important
work is *A Dictionary of American English on Historical Principles*,[197] edited by Sir William Craigie and James R. Hulbert. This
dictionary, completed in 1944, is designed to be to the language of
America what the *NED* is to the language of England. Other books
on American English include George P. Krapp's *The English Language in America* [198] and Henry L. Mencken's *The American Language.*[199]

Other bibliographies that may be useful to graduate students are
those on rhetoric and oratory, on comparative literature, on literatures related to English (ancient Greek and Latin, mediæval, romance, Germanic, and Celtic), on folklore, and on history. In some
fields—such as the history of ideas—bibliographies of philosophy and
psychology, medicine and science, political science and economics,
education, and other subjects may prove very valuable.

It will, of course, be observed that many of the works listed above
are not bibliographies in form, or, perhaps I should say, are not
merely bibliographies. They are included here because they provide,
either in an appendix or in footnotes, bibliographical information
that may be more important for the graduate student than the text.

No student has need to know the merits and demerits of all of the
six hundred works mentioned by Professor Cross, or the eleven hundred named by Professor Spargo, or the seventeen hundred in Professor Kennedy's book. It is enough to know the relatively small
number of bibliographical tools that serve whatever field one is interested in, and then to know where to turn to find others as the
need for them arises. But to know bibliographies one must use them;
Courtney, Stein, Petzholdt, Watt—even *STC* and *NED*—are merely
names, sometimes names rather hard to remember, until one has had

[4] The *NED* is often referred to as the *Oxford Dictionary* and sometimes as
Murray's Dictionary (in honor of Sir James Murray, the first editor); it should
not be news to graduate students in English that this is the greatest dictionary in
the world, and that its greatness lies in the fact that it gives what amounts to a
complete history of every word listed, with the spelling, pronunciation, and meaning indicated whenever any change occurred during the word's existence as a part
of the English language.

the experience of seeking in the works for which these names stand some much-desired piece of information, and finding it—or perhaps not finding it. If the information is not to be found where one expected it, there is always some other authority to be consulted, some other way of achieving the desired result. But the student should first determine, if it is possible to do so, the reason for his failure to find what he expected. Sometimes it is a simple—and inexcusable—bit of carelessness, such as looking at the wrong place in the alphabet.

There are, of course, tricks to alphabetizing, as there are to all trades. One would look in vain in the Geographical Gazetteer of the *New International Dictionary* (First Edition) for *Cashmeer*, even though he also tried *Cashmere* and *Cashmir*; for the word appears, where doubtless it properly belongs, among the K's, as *Kashmir*. There is, to be sure, a warning note at the head of the C's: "For many names like Carlowitz, Cattegat, etc., see Karlowitz, Kattegat, etc., the preferable forms." There is no warning, however, that would lead one to look for the French town of *Ax* under the D's, where it appears as "Dax or Ax", with no cross-reference in the A's. Under "Van, Van der" there is a note: "For Dutch and Flemish names beginning with these elements, see the specific names". Hence one finds, as is to be expected, *Philip van Dyck* under D. But *Anthony* and *Ernest van Dyck* are listed under V. *De Mille, De Morgan, De Soto, De Quincey, De Vere,* and *De Wet* are all under D, as is also *Thomas D'Urfey*; but *Henri Duke d'Harcourt* is to be found under H, *Jean de Meung* under J, and *Alfred de Musset* under M. The *de Medicis* appear between *Medhurst* and *Meding,* all of them, that is, except *Marie,* who comes between *Marie Antoinette* and *Marie Louise. Röntgen* is found between *Ronsard* and *Rooke*; but where umlaut marks are not used—as is often the case—the fact that the vowel is umlauted is indicated by an *e* following the vowel (*Graesse* for *Grässe*), and the name may be alphabetized accordingly. Where an entry consists of more than one word, alphabetizing is sometimes by word rather than letter; thus *New York* would come before *Newton. McAdams* sometimes comes before, sometimes after, *MacAndrews*; and I have seen an index in which the Mc's and Mac's were all gathered together at the end of the M's, after *Myers.*

In the old *British Museum Catalogue* periodical publications were

grouped together under the heading "Academies" and listed alphabetically according to the place of publication. In the new *Catalogue*
the "Academies" classification has been abandoned; but periodicals
are still listed according to the place of publication, and the original
place of publication is the one used. Thus one finds the *Publications
of the Modern Language Association* under "Baltimore", though for
many years the periodical has been published elsewhere. And the
Journal of English and Germanic Philology, which has long been
associated with the University of Illinois, is listed under "Bloomington, Indiana" because it was published at Indiana University
from 1897 to 1902. All of these practices may be perfectly proper
and logical, but they emphasize the fact that one needs to have all
his wits about him in using any index; otherwise he is likely to
reach the quite erroneous conclusion that a particular bit of information is not to be found in a work that should—and actually does—
contain it.

One may also go wrong by looking for something that is not within
the scope of the work consulted. One would look in vain in the older
editions of Professor Cross's *Bibliographical Guide* for the *Publications of the Modern Language Association*; it does not appear in
Section VII, "Periodical Publications Containing Reviews", because
it did not publish reviews. But since 1922, when *PMLA* began publishing an annual bibliography, Professor Cross has included *PMLA*
on the ground, presumably, that a critical bibliography is equivalent
to a series of reviews, brief though the comments may be.

One must consult the list given at the beginning of each issue
of the *Readers' Guide* and the *International Index to Periodicals* to
determine just what periodicals are included in each of those works.
Likewise, in addition to the limitation set by the inclusion of the
dates 1475–1640 in its title, the *Short Title Catalogue* announces
other limitations to its scope in a note printed at the beginning [5]
of the volume:

. . . a catalogue of the books of which its compilers have been able
to locate copies, not a bibliography of books known or believed to
have been produced. The extension given to the word 'English' is that
adopted in the British Museum special catalogue of 1884, i.e. it includes
all books in whatever language printed in England, Wales, Scotland, and

[5] P. xi.

Ireland, and all books in English wherever printed, also Latin service-books, wherever printed, if for use in England and Scotland. It does not include works by English authors printed out of England in Latin or in any language other than English.

Time will be saved and errors will be avoided if the student will take pains to determine, whenever he has occasion to use a reference book with which he is not already familiar, just what help he may legitimately expect to gain from it—what information, that is, it may properly be expected to contain.

Still in the realm of enumerative bibliography, we may give more extended attention to the learned journals, some of which are tools in the special sense that they may be counted upon to give help in specific fields. Thus the bibliographer may expect to find something of interest to him in every issue of *The Library,* and the mediævalist may with like expectation take up any number of *Speculum.*

From 1884 to 1888 the Library Association [London] published *The Library Chronicle* (Vols. I–V). In 1889 this journal was super-seded by *The Library.* Vols. I–X (1889–99) of the latter were fol-lowed by a New Series, I–X (1899–1909), then by a Third Series, I–X (1909–19), and finally by a Fourth Series still in progress. The Bibliographical Society [London] published its *Transactions* from 1892 to 1919 in fifteen volumes. In 1920 the Second Series of the *Transactions* was combined with the Fourth Series of *The Library.* References to articles since 1920 are generally to *The Library,* though *Transactions of the Bibliographical Society* also appears on the title page. The journal, like most learned journals, is a quarterly. Since the first number of each volume appears in June of one year and the last in March of the next, a double year-date should be given: "*The Library,* 4th series, X (1929–30), 121–62". An index to the Third Series of *The Library* was published in Vol. X of that series. There is an index, published separately, to Vols. I to X of the Fourth Series. There is also an index to Vols. I to X of the *Transactions,* and an index to Vols. XI to XV was published in Vol. XV.

Speculum, a quarterly journal of mediæval studies, has been pub-lished at Cambridge, Massachusetts, since 1926. Each issue of *Speculum* contains a bibliography of the periodical literature in the mediæval field that appeared during the preceding quarter.

A journal devoted to Renaissance studies is *Humanisme et Re-*

naissance, which began publication at Paris in 1934. *Humanisme et Renaissance* is the continuation of *Revue de Seizième Siècle,* nineteen volumes of which appeared between 1913 and 1933, and which was itself the continuation of *Revue des Études Rabelaisiennes;* of the latter, Vols. I to X appeared between 1903 and 1912.

Another journal of special interest to students of Renaissance literature is *Studies in Philology,* which publishes in each April issue a Renaissance bibliography. *Studies in Philology* (commonly abbreviated *SP*) has been published at the University of North Carolina since 1906. There is an index for Vols. I to XXV. *now I to L.*

For students of the Restoration and the eighteenth century the *Philological Quarterly* (*PQ*) publishes in its April issue a bibliography covering the period 1660–1800. This journal has been published at the State University of Iowa since 1922.

E[nglish] *L*[iterary] *H*[istory], published at Baltimore since 1934, provided in each March issue a critical bibliography of the Romantic movement; this bibliography has recently been taken over by *PQ.*

Modern Philology (*MP*) has been published at the University of Chicago since 1903; as each volume begins in one year and carries over into the next, a double year-date should be given; but in citing a particular article it is perfectly proper to give only the year in which that article appeared. Beginning with 1933 *Modern Philology* has published annually a Victorian bibliography.

The *Publications of the Modern Language Association of America* (*PMLA*) began publication in 1884; there is an index for Vols. I to L. Since 1922—at first in the March issue but since 1931 in the *Supplement—PMLA* has provided a bibliography of works on modern languages and literatures, chiefly those by American scholars.

American Literature (*AmLit*), published at Durham, North Carolina, since 1929, has a current bibliography, in each number, of studies in American literature.

For students of folklore, journals of special interest are the *Journal of American Folk Lore* and *Folk Lore.* The former has been published since 1888, first in Boston, then in New York, and finally in Lancaster, Pennsylvania; there is an index to Vols. I to XL. *Folk Lore* has been published in London since 1890.

Other journals that every graduate student in English should know include:

Anglia, Zeitschrift für englische Philologie, which has been published at Halle since 1877. Vols. I to L have been indexed. *Anglia Beiblatt: Mitteilungen über englische Sprache und Literatur,* consisting of monthly supplements, has been published since 1890.

Archiv für das Studium der neueren Sprachen und Literaturen,[6] often known, after its founder, as Herrig's *Archiv,* has been published at Brunswick since 1846; there are indexes to Vols. I to L, LI to C, CI to CXX, CXXI to CXXX, and CXXXI to CXL.

Englische Studien has been published at Leipzig since 1877; there are indexes for Vols. I to XXV and XXVI to L. *Englische Studien* is sometimes abbreviated *ESt* or *Eng Stud*; but it is probably better not to abbreviate, since there is a journal *English Studies* published in Amsterdam.

Essays and Studies by Members of the English Association has been published at Oxford since 1910.

Huntington Library Bulletin began publication at Cambridge, Massachusetts, in 1931; eleven volumes had appeared by 1937, at which time it was succeeded by the *Huntington Library Quarterly,* published at San Marino, California.

Isis: International Review Devoted to the History of Science and Civilization began publication in Brussels in 1913; World War I caused a suspension from 1914 to 1919, and World War II brought an end to the Belgian *Isis.* No. 84 of Vol. XXXI and Nos. 85 and 86 of Vol. XXXII were ready for publication in 1940, but the war prevented their appearance at that time. A list of the contents of these issues is given in the new *Isis*—No. 87, Pt. I of Vol. XXXIII (1941), [41]–54—now published at Cambridge, Massachusetts.

The Journal of English and Germanic Philology (JEGP) began at Bloomington, Indiana, in 1897, as the *Journal of Germanic Philology.* Vols. I to IV were published between 1897 and 1902. Vol. V was published at Evanston, Illinois, during the years 1903 to 1905. Since 1906 it has been published at Urbana, Illinois, as the *Journal of English and Germanic Philology.*

[6] In recent volumes—since 1930, I believe—the last two words of the title have been dropped.

Litteris began publication at Lund, Sweden, in 1924; it suspended publication with the third issue of Vol. VII.

Modern Language Notes (*MLN*) has been published at Johns Hopkins University since 1886; it appears monthly from November to June. There is an index to Vols. I to L.

Modern Language Quarterly (*MLQ*) began publication at the University of Washington in March, 1940.

Modern Language Review (*MLR*) is published at Cambridge, England. It began in 1905; Vols. I to X are indexed in Vol. X, XI to XX in XX, and XXI to XXX in XXX.

Notes and Queries (*N&Q*) has been published weekly in London since 1849. From November 1849 to December 1923 there were twelve series consisting of twelve half-year volumes each, with an index for every series. Beginning in January 1924, the series number was dropped. An index to Vols. CXLV to CLVI (July 1923 to June 1929) was followed by one to Vols. CLVII to CLXVIII. There was also, from 1896 to 1901, an American *Notes and Queries*.

Osiris: Studies on the History and Philosophy of Science and on the History of Learning and Culture was started at Bruges in 1936. Seven volumes had appeared by 1939; the publication of Vols. VIII and IX was prevented by the war. The contents of these two volumes are listed in *Isis*, XXXIII (1941), [41]–54.

The Review of English Studies (*RES*) has been published at London since 1925.

The *Literary Supplement* of the [London] *Times* (*LTLS* or *TLS*) is a weekly publication, begun in 1902. There is an annual index. In the "Correspondence" columns are many items of interest to scholars.

These, then, are the journals within the pages of which the student of English—or American—literary history may expect to find much of the material with which he must work.

*   *   *

Let us turn now to another field of bibliography that serves the research student as a tool—what may be called descriptive bibliography. Bibliographical descriptions enable one to locate a copy of a desired edition (or issue) of a book, or to determine whether a given

copy belongs to the same edition as that represented by the copy
described. If one can bring the two copies together, the easiest way
to determine whether or not they belong to the same edition is to
apply the straight-edge test. Lay a ruler diagonally across a page of
one copy so that the edge of the ruler rests upon a definite point
(such as a period or the dot over an *i*) near the upper left-hand
corner of the page and upon a similar point near the lower right-
hand corner. Then place another ruler so that its edge rests upon the
corresponding two points on the same page of the other copy. The
two copies should then be carefully examined, line by line, to determine where each line is intersected by the rulers. If the two pages
are of the same setting of type—and hence of the same edition—
every line in one copy will be intersected at exactly the same point
as the corresponding line in the other copy; but if the two copies
are of different settings, there will be considerable variation. Even if
a compositor had been attempting to duplicate exactly the spacing of
words and letters in the copy he was following—and it seems unlikely that such a feat was ever attempted [7]—the irregularity of early
fonts of type would have made such exactness impossible. Strictly
speaking, the straight-edge test proves only that the two pages compared are of the same edition; the two copies might be of different
issues. By testing one page of the inner forme and one of the outer
forme of each sheet one can be reasonably sure whether the two
copies are of the same setting of type throughout.[8]

[7] Page-for-page reprints are seldom line-for-line.

[8] There are instances in which it would be necessary to test every page. Two editions of Robert Greene's *The Spanish Masquerado* (1589) are recognized in the
Short Title Catalogue; but there is some question as to whether they should be
regarded as editions or issues. Sigs. B to D are of different settings of type throughout. Two pages (E2 and E3^v) of the inner forme of the last sheet are of the same
setting except for the last line of E2 and the first line of E3^v; a third page,
E1^v, is of the same setting without change, but E4 is of a different setting throughout. The three pages of the outer forme (E4^v is blank) have been reset. A similar
situation exists in sheet A. Of the inner forme A1^v is blank; A2 has the first four
lines and the last two lines reset; and A3^v and A4 are completely reset. A1 and A2^v
have not been reset; A3 has been changed only by the addition or removal of lines
around an ornamental initial; A4^v is blank. Apparently the decision to issue a second
edition was made while the outer forme of sheet A—which would naturally be the
last to reach the press—was being printed; thus it was used for both editions (or
issues), rules on A3 being added or removed. Distribution of the type used in the
inner forme of sheets A and E was halted, and the type reset where necessary. The
type of the outer forme of sheet E had already been distributed; hence it had to be

Frequently—as when one copy is in the Huntington Library and the other is in the Bodleian—the straight-edge test cannot be applied.[9] Then the student must rely upon a bibliographical description. Perhaps two examples, with some comment, will make clear what difficulties are involved in such a description and what can be learned from one.[10]

THE SHEPHEARDES CALENDER   [First Edition] 1579.

Title: THE / *Shepheardes Calender* / Conteyning tvvelue Æglogues proportionable / to the twelue monethes. [this line in Black Letter] / *Entitled* / TO THE NOBLE AND VERTV / *ous Gentleman most worthy of all titles* / both of learning and cheualrie M. / Philip Sidney. / (∵) / [design, 20 by 20 mm., of type ornaments] / AT LONDON. / *Printed by Hugh Singleton, dwelling in* / Creede Lane neere vnto Ludgate at the / ſigne of the gylden Tunne, and [this line in Black Letter; the *n* in *gylden* is either broken at the top or turned, so that it resembles a *u*] / are there to be folde. / 1579.

Colophon: [N4ᵛ]: [band of type ornaments] / [ornament: a lady's head between cornucopias, 50 by 51 mm.] / *Imprinted at London by Hugh* / Singleton, dwelling in Creede lane [this line in Black Letter] / *at the signe of the gylden* / Tunn neere vnto / Ludgate (see Note 1 below)

Format and Collation: Quarto: ¶⁴, A-N⁴; 56 leaves.
   All leaves of each sheet signed, except ¶1, C3, C4, D4, H4, I3, K3, M3, M4, N3, and N4.

Foliation: Commencing with A1, leaves numbered *Fol. 1* to *fol. 52* in the upper right-hand corner of each recto page. *Errors in foliation:* 37 for 38; 39 for 40; 94 for 49.

Contents: [¶1ᵛ], Poem "To His Booke" signed "Immeritó"; ¶2–¶3ᵛ,

---

reset throughout. When nine-tenths of the type—or more—has been reset, one might well consider that he is dealing with different editions; if we are to be strictly logical, however, we should call these *issues* rather than *editions*.

   [9] Perhaps it should be noted that the straight-edge test can be applied to photostats; one photostat—representing a single opening, that is, two pages—would suffice to test both inner and outer formes of one sheet.

   [10] The first of these descriptions is taken from Francis R. Johnson, *A Critical Bibliography of the Works of Edmund Spenser,* pp. 2–3; the second from Nashe, *Works,* ed. McKerrow, I, [1]–2. I have made some alterations. For example, I have indicated the kind of type used on the title page of the Spenser work; whereas Mr. Johnson felt, rightly, that his reproduction of the title page made it possible for him to use roman type throughout his transcription.

Dedicatory epistle "¶To the most excellent and learned both Orator and Poete, Mayster Gabriell Haruey, his verie special and singular good frend E. K. commendeth the good lyking of this his labour, and the patronage of the new Poete." signed E. K. and followed by a postscript dated "from my lodging at London thys 10. of Aprill. 1579"; ¶4–¶4ᵛ, "The generall argument of the whole booke." [text in roman]; A1–[N4], the twelve eclogues, one for each month, each preceded by an illustrative woodcut and an "ARGUMENT" and followed by a "GLOSSE"; [N4ᵛ], Colophon, as described above.

The woodcuts occur on A1, A3, B4, [C3ᵛ], [D4], [F2ᵛ], G2, H3, [I3], K4, L4, and [M4]. Each has a design suitable to the subject of the eclogue to which it is prefixed and has the appropriate sign of the zodiac in the heavens. The argument of each eclogue is set in italic type, the poem itself in Black Letter, and the gloss in small roman.

Running-titles: ¶2ᵛ–¶3ᵛ, "*Epistle.*"; A1–[N4], different running-title for each eclogue, consisting of the name of the month in italic type.

Notes: 1. The Huth-J. L. Clawson copy has the earlier, uncorrected state of the outer form of the final, N, sheet. On N1, *fol. 49* has been misnumbered *fol. 94,* while on [N4ᵛ], between the ornamental band and the colophon, there is the same woodcut ornament of a lady's head between cornucopias which had been used as a tail-piece on G1ᵛ and I2ᵛ. The revised state of this form, found in all other known copies, has the misprint in foliation corrected and Hugh Singleton's device (McKerrow No. 198) substituted for the ornament on the colophon page. . . .

*   *   *

Thomas Nashe's *The Anatomie of Absurditie* (1589) might be described as follows:

THE ANATOMIE OF ABSURDITIE   [First Edition] 1589

Title: The Anatomie of / *Abſurditie:* / Contayning a breefe confutation of the ſlender / imputed prayſes to feminine perfection, with a ſhort / deſcription of the ſeuerall practiſes of youth, and / ſundry follies of our licentious / times. / No leſſe pleaſant to be read, then profitable to be remembred, / eſpecially of thoſe, who liue more licentiouſly, or addic- / ted to a more nyce ſtoycall auſteritie. / Compiled by T. Nashe. / *Ita diligendi ſunt homines, vt eorum non / diligamus errores.* / [design of type ornaments, 12 by 16 mm.] / *AT LONDON,* / Printed by I. Charlewood for Tho- / mas Hacket, and are to be ſolde at his shop / in Lumberd ſtreet, vnder the ſigne of / the Popes heade. / *Anno. Dom. 1589.*

Colophon: none.

Format and Collation: Quarto: ¶⁴, A-E⁴; 24 leaves. ¶1, probably blank, wanting.

First three leaves of each sheet and A4 are signed, other fourth leaves unsigned.

Foliation or Pagination: none.

Contents: ¶2, Title; ¶2ᵛ, blank; ¶3-[¶4ᵛ], Dedicatory epistle, "To the right worshipfull Charles / Blunt Knight, adorned with all perfections of honour / or Arte, *T. Nashe* wisheth what euer content / felicitie or Fortune may enferre.", in roman and italic; A1-[E4], the Text, in Black Letter, roman, and italic; [E4ᵛ], blank.

Running-titles: [3ᵛ]-[4ᵛ], "The Epistle.", in roman; [A1ᵛ]-[E4], "The Anatomie / of Absurditie.", in roman.[11]

* * *

The chief difficulty in arriving at a satisfactory bibliographical description lies in the transcribing of the title page. Except by providing a facsimile, one cannot very well indicate the size of the type or the spacing of the lines on the page. For illustration, consider a transcription of the title page reproduced on the next page:

[Within a rule, within a border of type ornaments, within a rule] *A* / Moſt pleaſant Co- / medie of *Mucedorus* the kings / ſonne of *Valentia* and *Amadine* / the Kings daughter of *Arragon,* / with the merie conceites / of *Mouſe.* / Newly ſet foorth, as it hath bin / *ſundrie times plaide in the ho- / norable Cittie of London.* / Very delectable and full / of mirth. / [rule, 50 mm. long] / [ornament, 13 by 19 mm.] / [rule, 50 mm. long] / LONDON / Printed for *William Iones,* dwel- / ling at Holborne conduit, at / the ſigne of the Gunne. / 1598.

In this example the words *A* in the first line, *Mucedorus* in the second, and *Mouſe* in the seventh appear in the transcription to be printed with type of the same font, though actually three sizes of type are involved; one certainly cannot show such difference when he is using a typewriter, and attempts to do so with type—except in facsimile—are not very satisfactory. Neither can one very well show how much more space there is between the seventh and eighth lines

---

[11] In giving running titles—or running heads, as they are often known—one may use the slanting or vertical stroke to separate the verso and recto readings. In the example cited, the verso pages from A1ᵛ to E3ᵛ would all have "The Anatomie" and the recto pages from A2 to E4 would have "of Absurditie." Errors or variations in the running titles should be noted.

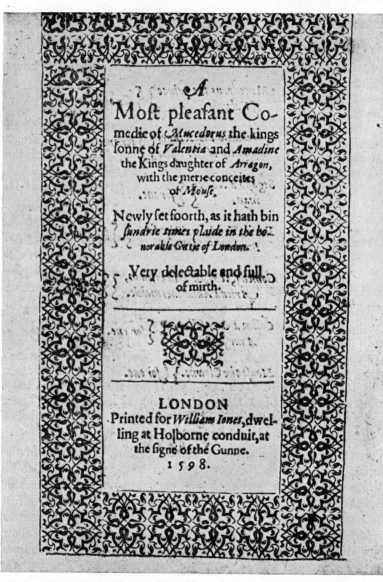

A
Moſt pleaſant Co-
medie of *Mucedorus* the kings
ſonne of *Valentia* and *Amadine*
the Kings daughter of *Arragon,*
with the merie conceites
of *Mouſe.*

Newly ſet foorth, as it hath bin
ſundrie times plaide in the ho-
norable Cittie of London.

Very delectable and full
of mirth.

LONDON
Printed for *William Iones,* dwelling at Holborne conduit, at
the ſigne of the Gunne.
1 5 9 8.

Figure 11. The Title Page of *Mucedorus* (1598). Reproduced through the
kindness of the Folger Shakespeare Library, Washington, D. C.

than between the eighth and ninth. In some descriptions an attempt is made to show roughly how the lines are spaced by varying the number of symbols used to indicate line endings; thus // represents a wider space between the lines it separates than is shown by /, and /// marks a still wider space.[12]

Other things not shown in the above transcription are the facts that the *ſt* of "Moſt" (line 2), the *ct* of "delectable" (line 11) and the *fi* of "ſigne" (line 16) are *ligatures* [13] and that the *A* in the first line and the *M* of *"Mucedorus"* in the third line are *swash letters*.[14]

The method used in the above transcription to describe the ornamental border is the more common and, I think, better one. Some bibliographers, however, would work from the outside of the page inward, thus: "[A rule enclosing a border of type ornaments enclosing a rule]". If there is an ornament other than one made up of type ornaments, it should be identified, if identification be possible; [15] if not, it should be described. The title page of Nashe's *The Terrors of the Night* (1594) might be transcribed thus: [16]

---

[12] In describing very early books one must use a vertical stroke to indicate the end of a line, instead of a slanting stroke (*virgule*), since the latter was used by the first printers as a mark of punctuation.

[13] A *ligature*, in printing, is a type in which two or more letters are united in a single character on one type-body. It is to be distinguished from a *logotype*, in which two or more letters appear on a single type body but are not united. (An upper case italic *W* is sometimes combined with a lower case *o* to avoid the unattractive separation resulting from the use of two types.) Modern fonts vary in the number of ligatures they contain; "ff," "ffi," "ffl," "fi," "fl," are usual, "æ," "ct," "œ," and "st" are sometimes found. Early printers used in addition "ſh," "ſi," "ſl," "ſſ," "ſſi," "ſſl," and several others.

[14] A swash letter is an italic capital with a flourish—generally produced by extending and curving one of the *serifs* (fine cross strokes at the end of a basic stroke of a letter) at the top or bottom of the letter or both. Such letters were used along with letters of the regular form, presumably according to the whim of the compositor. The older printers apparently had no swash forms for *F, L, O, S, W,* and *X.* Some modern fonts contain swash letters, some do not. According to the University of Chicago Press *Manual of Style* (8th edition), Scotch Roman (p. 250) has no swash letters, Garamont (p. 244) has ten, and Caslon Old Style (p. 230) has swash forms for all the letters of the alphabet except, *I, U. X,* and *Z.* The swash form of *I*—as it appeared in the old fonts, with a leftward curve below the line— is the ancestor of our modern *J,* and the swash form of *V*—curved instead of pointed at the bottom—is the ancestor of modern *U.*

[15] R. B. McKerrow, *Printers' and Publishers' Devices . . . 1485–1640,* contains reproductions of more than four hundred such ornaments; others may be found in R. B. McKerrow and F. S. Ferguson, *Title-page Borders Used in England and Scotland 1485–1640* (London: The Bibliographical Society, 1932).

[16] This transcription may be compared with the original by consulting the reproduction in Nashe, *Works,* ed. McKerrow, I, [339].

[Head ornament (17 by 70 mm.) with urn as central feature and volutes and leaves on each side of it] / THE / Terrors of the night / Or, / A Difcourſe of Apparitions. / *Post Tenebras Dies.* / THO: NASHE / [Danter's device (McKerrow No. 281)] / LONDON / Printed by *Iohn Danter* for *William Iones,* and are to be ſold / at the ſigne of the Gunne nere Holburne Conduit. / 1594.

In this example, the head ornament, which does not appear in McKerrow's *Printers' and Publishers' Devices . . . 1485–1640,* is described as definitely as seemed possible; the measurement is in millimeters, the vertical dimension being given first. If the book described is a rare one, and the same ornament occurs in some easily accessible work (such as McKerrow's edition of Nashe or Johnson's bibliography of Spenser), a note to that effect would be helpful to the reader who finds the description inadequate.

*   *   *

Sometimes, to what has already been given as characteristic of a full bibliographical description, there are added "justificatory words" —the first words of a certain page, often page 11—or the catchwords on certain pages. Frequently the wording of the entry of the book in the Stationers' Register is quoted from Arber's transcript or from Eyre's,[17] together with the proper reference. It may also be helpful to specify the copy of the work that was used in making the description; [18] then if some question of variant copies arises, students will know where to look for the particular copy represented by the description.

If there are ornaments elsewhere than on the title page, they should be identified or described; ornamental initials should also be noted, especially if they serve to identify the printer of the work.

*   *   *

In giving the collation, one must indicate any irregularities. Thus A–Z⁸—if the book is described as an octavo—represents a book made

[17] Arber's five volumes cover the period from 1554 to 1640; Eyre's three volumes carry on from 1640 to 1708.

[18] For some books a long line of previous owners is known to bibliographers; thus one copy of the Fourth Edition of *The Shepheardes Calender* is the Utterson—Carmichael—Hoe—Huntington—Hagen copy and another is the Bridgwater—Huntington—Clawson copy, while a copy of *Amoretti and Epithalamion* is the Holland—Utterson—Halliwell-Phillipps—Corser—Brooke copy.

up of twenty-three sheets, each sheet folded so that it constitutes eight leaves; [19] if the book were a folio in eights, it would have twenty-three gatherings of four sheets (eight leaves) each. But the sheets, or gatherings, do not always have the same number of leaves; we may have a collation: "A⁴, B–M⁸, N⁶, O–Y⁸, Z⁴". If the number of leaves alternates regularly, as sometimes happens, the fact may be indicated most concisely by the collation "A–Z⁸/⁴", which would mean that signatures A, C, E, and so on contain eight leaves each, while B, D, F, and every second successive signature have only four each. In referring to specific pages, the symbol for the page is put in brackets if the page is unsigned; thus all verso pages would be bracketed,[20] and—usually—the recto of the fourth leaves of a quarto and the sixth, seventh, and eighth of an octavo. When a book contains so many signatures that a second and perhaps a third alphabet must be used, one may use the symbol "₃K₂" instead of "KKK₂"; [21] it is customary to use Arabic numerals in citing pages even though the original may have been signed in Roman: "A₃" instead of "Aiij".[22]

In solving the many problems that may arise in connection with bibliographical descriptions, the student will find helpful, discussions by McKerrow,[200] Esdaile,[201] and Greg; [202] as a model for form, I know nothing better than the Spenser bibliography to which reference has already been made.[23]

* * *

Though the average graduate student is not likely to have occasion to describe a manuscript, it may be worth while for him to know

[19] In dealing with matters bibliographical one must be careful to preserve the distinction between *leaf* and *page* (one side of a leaf); as Esdaile points out (*Student's Manual of Bibliography*, p. 261) some bibliographers go so far as to speak of "title leaf" instead of "title page" when it is the leaf they mean. They would say "Title leaf wanting", for example.

[20] It is not really necessary to use brackets with verso pages, since it can be taken for granted that they are not signed. Brackets are sometimes omitted in referring to the fourth leaf of a quarto and to other unsigned leaves (Esdaile, *Student's Manual of Bibliography*, p. 259); but it would seem better, in view of irregularities in the use of signatures, to use brackets in all references to unsigned recto pages.

[21] It might be better, however, to save the numerical symbol for books like Robert Greene's *Planetomachia* which have two sheets bearing the same signature; then "₂B₃" would refer to the second "B" signature.

[22] In early printing, when lower case letters were used for Roman numerals, a *j* was used instead of an *i* for the final letter: "*ij*" and "*iij*" instead of "*ii*" and "*iii*"; "*iv*" was often represented by "*iiij*".   [23] See above, p. 77, n. 10.

something about such descriptions. Excellent examples are to be found in Volume I of Manly and Rickert's edition of *The Text of the Canterbury Tales.*[203] A full quotation would require too much space here; but each description includes the following items:

Contents: If the manuscript contains selections other than the *Canterbury Tales,* the titles are given, unless they are very numerous.

Form: Information concerning the material, the size and style of page, and the like.

Watermarks: If the material is paper, the watermarks are identified by numbers in Briquet's *Les Filigranes*; where there was doubt as to the identification, the number in Briquet that most resembles the watermark in question is cited.

Collation: The make-up of the MS is indicated (number of leaves in a gathering), any irregularities being noted, together with the presence of signatures and catchwords.

Date: Estimated as accurately as possible, mainly on palæographical evidence.

Writing: "We have tried to describe the hands in intelligible terms, . . ."[204]

Ink: Description of the color of the ink of the text and of corrections.

Supervision and Correction: Comment on the nature and extent of the work of supervisors and correctors.

Illumination: The main decorative features of each MS are noted; these are generally a "decorative initial joined by: 1) a conventional framework border extending around the whole page or three sides of it; or, 2) by hair-line sprays of varying lengths."[205] If the border extends around all four sides of the page, it is a *vinet*; otherwise it is a *demi-vinet*. A *champ* is a small gold initial—vinets and demi-vinets having a colored initial on a gold ground—"on a square of colored ground decorated at the outside corners with feathery sprays".[206] There are also initials with pen flourishes, generally in color. Four of the MSS have historiated initials (initials with figures), three have miniature paintings of the Pilgrims (Ellesmere has a full set of the twenty-three who told tales), and one has symbolic representations of vices and virtues.

Binding: The material, the style, and—where possible—the date of the binding are noted.

Figure 12. The beginning of the "Monk's Tale", showing the book hand and two types of illumination. Reproduced from the celebrated Ellesmere Chaucer (EL 26 C 9) by permission of the Henry E. Huntington Library and Art Gallery, San Marino, California.

Present Condition: A statement as to the present condition of the MS is made, chiefly to explain why some readings are illegible.

Order of Tales: The letter system of the Chaucer Society is used (A for the Prologue, the Knight's Tale, the Miller's Tale, the Reeve's Tale, and the Cook's Tale; B^1 for the Man of Law's Tale; B^2 for the Shipman's, the Prioress's, Sir Thopas and Melibeus, the Monk's, and the Nun's Priest's; and so on).

Affiliations and Textual Character: "Under this heading is given a brief statement of the genealogical position of each MS with a view to showing whether the MS is steady or variable in its relationships, and, if variable, whether the variation is due to itself or its ancestors." [207]

Dialect and Spelling: The dialect is indicated together with spellings that represent a variation from the norm for that dialect.

Special Features: This heading covers a variety of information: the presence of glosses, marginalia, etc.

Provenance: Two of the MSS have been traced to nineteenth-century owners only, thirty-nine have been identified—with more or less certainty—with fifteenth-century owners; the remaining forty-three have been traced to sixteenth-, seventeenth-, or eighteenth-century ownership.

II

So much for bibliography as a tool of research; let us consider now another tool—a note-system. We shall speak here only of the physical characteristics of a proper note-system; the method of using it may be more appropriately considered in another place.[24]

Professor Manly once remarked that the loose-leaf system was in use by scholars long before it was adopted by business men. The older scholars commonly made use of cards 3″ by 5″—the size of "bibliography cards", such as are found in the card catalogues of libraries. But most students will find the 4″ by 6″ size much more convenient. The larger size will accommodate in most instances—if both sides are used [25]—as much information as one is likely to wish to incor-

[24] See below, pp. 290–97.
[25] Professor Morize wrote (*Problems and Methods,* p. 293): "Never write on more than one side of the paper, . . ." But it seems to me better, if a note is very long—as may sometimes happen—to use both sides of the sheet than to clip two sheets together. Putting the word "over" at the bottom of the first side would prevent one's overlooking anything on the reverse side.

porate in a single note; whereas, with the smaller size, one is continually having to clip two sheets together, and the amount of space taken up in a file by a number of paper clips is not a negligible item. There is a certain amount of space wasted when the 4″ by 6″ size is used for purely bibliographical notes, but the convenience of having all of one's notes the same size justifies the waste.[26]

For one who expects to take a large number of notes, the use of cards, either 4 by 6 or 3 by 5, will prove expensive, both in initial cost and in the expense of providing sufficient filing space. Yet the paper slips, which may be secured, like the cards, in packages of fifty or one hundred, are not heavy enough to be satisfactory for anything but temporary notes. The ideal solution is to buy a ream of heavy ledger paper and have it cut into pieces 4″ by 6″. A size can be secured which will cut up with little or no waste; and hundreds, or even thousands of slips may thus be obtained at comparatively low cost. The right kind of paper will make slips heavy enough and stiff enough to handle as conveniently as cards, and as durable as can be desired, but thin enough to occupy little more than half the space in filing.

The student who looks forward to keeping a large body of notes accessible over a period of years will doubtless want a wooden or, better still, a steel filing case; but most graduate students will prefer the cardboard boxes of appropriate size that are procurable at any stationer's shop. Such boxes have the double advantage of cheapness and portability. To keep at hand a small sheaf of notes, 4″ by 6″ expanding envelopes of brown fiber, also relatively cheap and easily obtained, will be found useful.

When one has accumulated enough notes to begin filing them in a box or a drawer of a filing case, he will want division cards to keep the notes on one topic separate from those on another. Such division cards may be procured with ready-cut tabs for labeling, but for purposes of research it may be better to get cards about 4½″ by 6″ and cut out tabs to suit one's own needs. Different colors, as many as are likely to be needed, are readily available.

Sometimes a supplementary file, large enough to accommodate correspondence and reprints of scholarly articles, will be found desirable; the ordinary letter file—which opens up like a book and has

---

[26] Moreover, one should form the habit of turning purely bibliographical notes into critico-bibliographical notes (see below, p. 290) as soon as possible.

alphabetized division leaves—is inexpensive and will hold a consider-able amount of material.

III

Graduate students are not likely to be called upon to make use of scientific instruments—except, perhaps, a magnifying glass; but some notion of the contribution which science has made to literary research should be a part of every student's background. The *photostat*—a photographic device by means of which an image is thrown directly upon sensitized paper instead of plate or film—is familiar to most students. In a photostat the writing of a manuscript or the printing of a book appears in white upon a black background; [27] but once one has become accustomed to the appearance of the page, there is no difficulty involved in working with white-on-black material. The great value of photostats is that they enable any library—or any indi-vidual, for that matter—to possess an identical copy of the text of a rare book, not merely a transcript, subject to scribal errors, or a reprint, subject to editorial and typographical errors. The disadvan-tage is that certain marks—rust stains, for example—which, in the original, show up clearly for what they are, in a photostat will appear to be of the same color as the ink; thus a comma may look like a semicolon or an interrogation point.[28]

*   *   *

A somewhat less familiar means of reproducing books or manu-scripts involves the use of a small camera fitted with a long roll of film, like a motion picture film. A separate exposure is made for each opening of a book; thus the contents of two adjacent pages are repro-duced on each tiny frame of the film. Here again the reproduction is white on black. These microfilms are considerably less expensive than photostats, but they must be studied by means of a reading device which at once illuminates and enlarges the image.

*   *   *

[27] The process can be repeated to produce the more familiar black on white. The Huntington Library regularly sends black-on-white photostats at no extra cost; but to get black-on-white one generally has to pay double price and then gets both white-on-black and black-on-white copies.

[28] It is possible, of course, by means mentioned below, to screen out such marks so that nothing shows on the photostat except what is written or printed on the page.

Various kinds of lighting devices, either with or without color filters, are used in the examining and photographing of books, and, more particularly, manuscripts. Writing which is too faint to be read may be made legible and may even be photographed if light of the proper intensity be thrown upon the manuscript from just the right direction.[29] Filters make it possible to read faded handwriting, to photograph through stains, to contrast details through a microscope, and to compare the colors of inks and pencil marks. In comparing colors, Lovibond Tintometer Glasses are used.

* * *

Microscopes are used in examining handwriting, especially for the purpose of detecting forgeries, in transcribing manuscripts, in determining whether pencil marks lie above or below ink marks,[30] and in discovering the composition of paper. The microscope is also used, along with chemical analysis, in the investigation of inks and of pigments used in illuminations. Measuring instruments, of which there are at least fifteen different kinds,[31] are used in the study of handwriting.

* * *

Photography has many uses in literary research. We have already considered its value in the making of additional copies of the text of a rare work; photography may also preserve for posterity the text of a manuscript in which the writing is fading beyond the point of legibility, or the text of a manuscript or book which, for some reason or other, is disintegrating. Photography with infra-red light will bring out writing or printing on paper which is badly charred, and photography with Röntgen rays (X-rays) is sometimes also employed.

Perhaps the most interesting use of photography in literary research is that which makes use of the principle of fluorescence. Many papers fluoresce under ultra-violet light. If a piece of such paper has had writing on it, even though the writing be faded so as to be unread-

[29] An excellent account of the use of various scientific devices is to be found in Captain R. B. Haselden, *Scientific Aids for the Study of Manuscripts* (Oxford: The Bibliographical Society [London], 1935).

[30] See below, p. 144, n. 4.

[31] These are discussed by Albert S. Osborn in his *Questioned Documents,* 2nd ed. (Albany, N. Y.: Boyd Printing Co., 1929).

able, or has been erased (as in a palimpsest), the writing masks the fluorescence in such a way that whatever had been written can be plainly read and can be photographed. Writing done with invisible ink can be read in the same way. Sometimes it is the ink rather than the paper that fluoresces; sometimes both ink and paper fluoresce, but in such a way that the contrast between the two kinds or degrees of fluorescence makes it possible to read the writing. In some instances neither ink nor paper is fluorescent, but Captain Haselden has discovered a way of treating the manuscript with a chemical solution which makes the paper fluoresce,[208] so that any writing or printing that may have been on it can be read.

With all the skills and all the scientific aids now available, it is not too much to say that, although a literary fraud might go for a long time unsuspected, once it comes under suspicion and the forces of literary scholarship and science are marshaled against it, its fraudulent nature will inevitably be demonstrated.

IV

Whether or not he has occasion to make use of such scientific instruments as have been mentioned, the graduate student in English is likely to have need of certain equipment in addition to his knowledge of the English language and its literature. Just what equipment will be most useful will depend largely upon the period in which the student interests himself and upon the type of research he chooses to pursue. The most obvious item of such equipment is a knowledge of foreign languages. A thorough command of Latin and an almost equal knowledge of Greek used to be taken for granted as necessary for every scholar; nowadays a good many students get along with little Latin and no Greek. Nevertheless, if one is intending to work in one of the earlier periods—before 1600—he will find a knowledge of Latin highly desirable, if not absolutely essential; and in the later periods Latin is also a very useful tool. A knowledge of Greek is not essential in any of the periods, although it may be highly useful in all of them. Any one who plans to work in the Renaissance will find Italian almost—if not quite—a necessity. For the student of the seventeenth and eighteenth centuries French is perhaps the most useful foreign language; and one who is interested in the latter part of the eighteenth century or the nineteenth will find German valuable.

It goes without saying that one who is planning to work in comparative literature will need to have more than ordinary command of whatever foreign language his work involves. One who is interested in philosophical studies would doubtless want to be able to read Greek philosophy in the original language, and the student of ballads or romances would need a thorough knowledge of the older forms of English. Biographical studies of the older writers would require an adequate knowledge of Latin, since almost all records were for centuries kept in that language.

*   *   *

Foreign languages are not the only auxiliaries helpful to the student of literary history; almost any branch of human learning may at times prove valuable. A famous crux in *Beowulf* was cleared up with the aid of archæology. Early students of the poem had been baffled by the lines:

> Eoforlic scionon
> ofer hleorbergan gehroden golde,
> fah ond fyrheard, ferhwearde heold
> guþmodgum men.[32]

The words seemed clear enough, but how could boar-likenesses guard the lives of men? Then a bronze plate [33] was dug up, on which appear in relief two fully armed Viking warriors; atop each helmet, serving as a ridge or reinforcement, is the image of a boar. Thus the boar-likeness quite literally guarded the warrior's life by preventing his helmet from being caved in by a blow.[34]

A knowledge of architecture would be useful to the student of literature—not the architect's knowledge, which enables him to design buildings and to calculate strain and stress, but such familiarity with the architecture of a period as will enable one to re-create in

[32] Ll. 303–6; the lines may be translated: "Boar-likenesses shone over the cheek-guards decorated with gold; shining and fire-hardened, life-guard they held over the war-minded men."

[33] Pictured in *Beowulf*, ed. Franz Klaeber, 3rd ed. (Boston: D. C. Heath, 1936ᶜ), p. [v], fig. 2.

[34] An article (Eleanor Grace Clark, "The Right Side of the Franks Casket", *PMLA*, XLV (1930), 339–53) on the Franks Casket represents the converse of this kind of research; there literature contributes to the interpretation of an archæological relic.

imagination the houses in which the people of that period lived, the castles in which they assembled for protection, and the churches in which they worshiped their God. Only through such sympathetic understanding of the culture of a people can the literature of that people be fully understood.

It will readily be seen that a knowledge of political history is always valuable and often essential. An admirer of Browning once assured me that any one with an intimate acquaintance with the political history of thirteenth-century Italy could easily understand *Sordello,* regarded by most of those who have attempted to read it as quite unintelligible. A knowledge of economics and economic history is perhaps equally valuable; for an understanding of nineteenth-century literature it is essential. Social history is likewise important, especially in studies of the history of ideas.

An understanding of music, particularly the history of music, would be helpful in studying ballads and the songs in plays. The science of psychology enters into such works as Professor Lowes's *The Road to Xanadu.*[209] It has already been pointed out [35] that the ability to read the old forms of handwriting is required in working with manuscripts older than 1650; and biographical studies are likely to demand a knowledge of the idiosyncrasies of public records, a knowledge to be gained only by experience with the records themselves.[36]

*   *   *

The student, then, who is entering upon a career—whether it be for a year or for life—of research in literary history will do well to take stock of himself, to analyze and to rate conservatively his qualifications. If his language equipment is weak, and he has no desire to strengthen it, he should not undertake to work, except in a very limited way, in the older periods; he should certainly avoid any

---

[35] See above, p. 2.

[36] Even subjects so diverse as mathematics and wrestling may be made to contribute to literary research. An article on Spenser (Vincent Foster Hopper, "Spenser's House of Temperance", *PMLA*, LV (1940), 958–67) makes use of mathematics in arriving at an interpretation of part of *The Færie Queene*; and one on *Beowulf* (Calvin S. Brown, "Beowulf's Arm-Lock", *PMLA*, LV (1940), 621–27) interprets a passage in the poem (ll. 736–823) in the light of the author's knowledge of wrestling.

studies involving the influence of a foreign literature. If he has no interest in economics, he can hardly expect to become an authority on nineteenth-century English literature, though there are projects in that field which he may safely attempt—studies, for example, in technique. Finally, unless one is prepared to spend a period of apprenticeship in the Public Record Office in London, he would be wise not to attempt any extensive research in the life of one of the older English writers.

Part III THE METHODS
OF RESEARCH

CHAPTER ONE

৩৲ ৡৡ

PROBLEMS IN EDITING

PERHAPS not many graduate students will undertake theses that directly involve matters of editing; but every graduate student should understand the problems and the technique of editing in order that he may evaluate the editorial work of others—be able to discriminate between good and bad editions—and interpret rightly the notes and comments to be found in the critical editions with which he will have to work.

I

Editing, in the nineteenth century, was a relatively simple matter; the Reverend Dr. Alexander B. Grosart, one of the most prolific editors of the period, expressed the ideals of his art and science—for editing is both art and science—in these words:

Here I wish mainly to state, by way of General Preface, that with Greene, as in all my editing, my law and endeavour combined, is to reproduce the Author's own text in integrity, *id est,* without an attempt at (so-called) 'improvements,' or even modernisation of the spelling, punctuation, etc. The most of the original and early editions, having been printed in what is known as Black Letter or Old English—most trying of all types to read continuously—I do not profess to furnish facsimiles; but I shall be disappointed if it be not found that within the inevitable limitations of human fallibility, the *ipsissima verba* of the text are faithfully rendered—that text being in every case the earliest available. . . . Such few corrections of misprints and mispunctuations as it has been deemed expedient to make are recorded in the Notes and Illustrations, save trifles such as a reversed letter, as n for u; misplaced letters, as hwose for howse (= house); misplaced words, as 'yet if he doubting he' for 'yet doubting if he', . . . and the like. . . .

Throughout there are well-nigh endless allusions to classical-mythological names and incidents, not a few of them being oddly disguised by their orthography. Those merely trite are left unannotated; but in every case where an ordinary Reader may be supposed to wish information or elucidation, an attempt is made in relative *Notes and Illustrations* to render adequate help; while in the closing volume, under the Glossarial Index, etc., every noticeable word, name, and the like, may be looked for. . . .[1]

The editorial principles here set forth are not, so far as they go, very different from those we hold today; unfortunately, Grosart's practice, because of defects both in his temperament and in his method, was not as good as his preaching. In the first place, Grosart did not always make use of the "earliest available" edition;[1] the inadequacy of library catalogues was doubtless largely to blame, but a lack of assiduity in searching is also involved. Having found what he took to be the earliest edition, Grosart next hired a copyist to make a transcript of the work in question. It was this transcript that served as the printer's copy, and there is no indication that Grosart, or any one else, bothered to collate the transcript with the original; at least, the collating, if it was done at all, was done very badly. Thus the editor was at the mercy of his copyist; if the latter happened to be an accurate and painstaking workman, Grosart's text may approach—though because of the human fallibility referred to above, it seldom achieves—a faithful rendering of the *ipsissima verba*. More often, the transcript was grossly inaccurate:[2] words were omitted;[3]

---

[1] It will be seen later (pp. 100–13) that the earliest edition is not necessarily the one to be reprinted; but Grosart did not always use the earliest edition when he should have done so.

[2] One scholar who has worked much with Grosart texts assured me, almost seriously, that he could always tell when lunch-time or tea-time had been imminent in

"aníwere" became "and weare" (twice on the same page); [4] lines were omitted; [5] the Latin *"actum"* became *"etiam"*, [6] *"muto"* became *"motu"*,[7] *"eorum"* became *"coram"*,[8] and so on and on. But enough of bad nineteenth-century editing; what constitutes good modern editing?

We must first of all distinguish different kinds of editions. A children's edition has its requirements, which are different from those of an edition intended for use by high school students as a class text, and from those of an edition designed for the ordinary adult reader. We are here concerned with editions intended for scholars, for serious students of an author or a period. The requirements for such an edition—commonly referred to as a critical edition—are:

First, it should provide a correct text, representing as exactly as possible the author's final intention, with all errors [9] eliminated. Second, it should explain any allusions or other readings that are likely to prove difficult for the sort of person who may be expected to use the work.[10] Third, it should furnish a commentary that will serve to fit the work into its setting so that the reader may be able to appreciate its literary and historical significance. Fourth, it should, as Professor Morize wrote, "be easy to handle and convenient, arranged and printed in such a way as to afford instruction and pleasure, with notes that elucidate and do not submerge the text." [2]

The editor of a work of the seventeenth or an earlier century generally has to depend upon printed editions for his text; but if a manuscript is available, then a fifth requirement must be added: the critical edition should by means of textual notes, enable the reader

---

the copyist's life. As the transcriber grew more and more tired and hungry, the errors in the text became more and more abundant.

[3] For example, the word *then*: "and [then] to reueale" (Greene, *Works,* ed. Grosart, V, 63, l. 24); sometimes the omission, as of a negative, for instance, serves to change or destroy the meaning of the sentence: "haue been troubled" should read "haue not been troubled" (*ibid.*, XII, 126, ll. 21–22).

[4] *Ibid.,* V, 76, ll. 7 and 21.

[5] *Ibid.,* p. 78, ll. 6–7: ". . . and to tell him that / [íhe ío meanely accounted either of his períon or parentage, that] / after íhee had opened his letter . . ."

[6] *Ibid.,* p. 29, l. 23.   [7] *Ibid.,* l. 1.   [8] *Ibid.,* p. 35, l. 22.

[9] It should be noted that errors may be due to the carelessness of the author or of a copyist or compositor, or to the carelessness, ignorance, or prejudice of an editor.

[10] A good general rule is to explain words and constructions that are not made clear in a dictionary such as the *New International.*

to trace the development of the work from the earliest form available
—perhaps a rough draft—through successive versions to its definitive
form.[11] If there is no manuscript of the work it will suffice to give the
readings of the significant editions.[12]

II

The first step, then, in preparing an edition is to provide a correct
text; and to do that one must choose, from all the versions available,
a basic—or copy—text. By consulting such works as the *Short Title
Catalogue,* catalogues of important libraries, and other bibliographical tools, one should be able to discover all the versions known to be
still in existence.[13] But in the search for a basic text one is not concerned with all the versions that exist; since the editor's purpose is—
or should be—to use as his basic text that version which best represents his author's final intention, he need consider only those editions
in which the author is known to have intervened or may have
done so.

The available texts may consist of one or more of seven kinds: (1)
holographs;[14] (2) manuscripts not in the author's hand but containing evidence of authorial correction; (3) manuscripts derived from
an authentic text no longer extant; (4) editions supervised by the

[11] If the difference between versions is very great, it may be impossible to show
the development of the text by means of textual notes. In such cases the versions
may be printed separately, as in William Langland, *The Vision of William Concerning Piers Plowman,* ed. W[alter] W[illiam] Skeat (London: N. Trübner and Company, 1867–77), 5 vols.; or in parallel columns, as in the Chaucer Society's *A Six-
Text Print of the Canterbury Tales in Parallel Columns* (London: N. Trübner and
Company, 1869–71); or with such an arrangement as Professor Wilhelm Viëtor used
in his edition of *Hamlet* (Marburg: K. G. Elwertsches Verlagsbuchhandlung, 1891,
rev. ed. 1913): the lines of the First Quarto on the upper part of the verso pages,
the corresponding lines of the Second Quarto on the upper part of the recto pages,
and the First Folio version on the lower part of both pages.

[12] The significant editions are, of course, those in which the author may have
intervened.

[13] It is a good idea to consult persons who are familiar with the period to which
the text belongs; copies of previously unknown editions—and manuscripts—turn up
from time to time and may be announced in a letter to the editor of the *Times
Literary Supplement* or in a brief note in one of the learned journals. To make an
exhaustive search of such sources of information might prove fruitless; and the
prospective editor may save himself time by a tactful appeal to known authorities
in the field.

[14] A holograph is a manuscript written wholly in the handwriting of the author,
i.e., an autograph; since the term *autograph* is often used to mean a signature, it is
perhaps desirable to use *holograph* in referring to a manuscript.

author, the text of which—theoretically, at least—the author guarantees; (5) authorized editions, published with the author's approval—or, at least, without protest—but not corrected by the author and hence perhaps faulty in text; (6) editions published after the author's death, but containing his corrections or revisions and hence representing his final intention; and (7) unauthorized editions, printed before or after the death of the author, which may or may not represent his intention.

In choosing between a holograph and a printed text, one might think that the preference should always be given to the manuscript. What more, one might ask, could be desired than the author's words written out in his own hand? But there are circumstances which may make the printed text the proper choice. (1) The printed text, having been set up from the manuscript in question, may contain corrections or revisions made by the author in the course of reading the proof; (2) the printed text may be based upon a later manuscript no longer extant—or not known to be extant; (3) the printed text may represent an earlier printed text which was itself a later version than that contained in the manuscript; (4) the manuscript may be a careless copy of a printed text.[15]

A holograph—or any demonstrably authoritative manuscript[16]—would be preferred to the printed text (1) if the printed text is based on a version earlier than that represented by the manuscript; (2) if the printed text is unauthorized and differs materially from the manuscript; (3) if the printed text, though published under the author's supervision, is a careless and corrupt rendering of the manuscript, i.e., if it contains readings that are incomprehensible or inconsistent with the author's apparent intention, whereas the manuscript is both clear and consistent; or (4) if the printed text has been toned down from fear of censorship or changed in some way so that it does not represent the author's real intention.

[15] It is not likely, of course, that an author would make an autograph copy of any long work; but he might very well make such a copy, to serve as a gift or for some such purpose, of a short poem or essay. If such a manuscript contained important revisions, it would be taken as representing the author's latest intention, unless there were indications that the revision was intended for a certain reader or group of readers, rather than for the general public.

[16] A manuscript not in the author's handwriting may have all the authority of a holograph if it can be shown that the manuscript was written at the author's dictation, if it bears revisions or corrections in the author's hand, or if in some other way the circumstances indicate that it represents the author's intention.

In most cases, especially if the work be of a date before 1700, the prospective editor is not faced with the necessity of choosing between a printed text and a manuscript; there is no manuscript. Frequently, too frequently, there is no choice at all; the work exists in only one text, and an editor is constrained to use that text, no matter how bad it may be, how puzzling its cruxes. Of eighteen works by Thomas Lodge listed in the *Short Title Catalogue,* fourteen are represented by only one edition each; for twenty-nine of the thirty-eight works of Thomas Dekker the same thing is true.

If the work in question is represented by more than one printed text, shall one choose the first—or *princeps*—edition, or the last edition printed in the author's lifetime, or some other edition? Remembering that a critical edition should represent the author's final intention, one might assume that the last edition in which the author intervened—whether published before or after his death[17]—is the one to choose as a basic text. But two things are to be kept in mind: first, that the author must be shown to have intervened; and second, that his intervention must have been complete, or at least extensive.[18]

It is often impossible to decide upon a basic text until a comparison, called *collation,*[19] has been made of all the versions, whether edi-

[17] It is possible, of course, that there may be published long after an author's death, an edition which incorporates changes desired by the author—as indicated by a corrected copy or some other form of memoranda—and consequently represents his final intention.

[18] In the sixteenth century it was rather unusual for an author to make corrections in the second and successive editions of a work. This situation is to be accounted for partly by the fact that authorship as a profession was conventionally held in low esteem; hence, to be much concerned about the correctness of the text of a published work was something of a violation of Elizabethan decorum. A more important circumstance, however, is the fact that in the early days of the publishing industry an author invariably, I think, sold outright his interest in a literary work. Thus any profits that resulted from a popularity which led to the issuing of more than one edition were shared by the publisher and the printer; the author had no financial interest once a manuscript got into print, or, rather into the printing house. We find that Nashe seems to have intervened (see below, pp. 108–9) in some, at least, of the later editions of his works; but his practice was unusual. More often a publisher's allegation that an edition was "Newlie revised and corrected" had no basis in fact, or else the corrections were such as were made by the printer or his employees.

[19] It should be noted that this is a different use of the word *collation* from that mentioned in Part II, pp. 77–83, where a collation is a list of the signatures comprising a book. The word is also used to mean an examination of the signatures to make sure that all are present, as in Part I, p. 54.

tions or manuscripts, that have any authority—all those, that is, in which the author may have intervened. Such collating may most conveniently be done, if the text is not too long, by writing each line (of a poem) or each sentence (of a prose work) on a separate note slip The slips should be numbered in sequence, and the version represented should be indicated by some significant abbreviation—the initial of the owner of the manuscript, or the last two digits of the date of the edition.[20] When slips have been completed for one version, they should be compared, slip by slip, with another version. If the reading is identical, letter for letter and comma for comma, that fact may be indicated by using ditto marks or writing "Same", and then giving the symbol for the edition. Any variations that occur should be indicated as in the following illustration, representing the first quatrain of FitzGerald's version of the *Rubáiyát* of Omar Khayyám;

I, 1	1
Awake! for Morning in the Bowl of Night	59
Wake! For the Sun behind yon Eastern height	68
Same	72
Wake! For the Sun, who scatter'd into flight	79

I, 2	2
Has flung the Stone that puts the Stars to Flight:	59
Has chased the Session of the Stars from Night;	68
Same	72
The Stars before him from the Field of Night,	79

[20] Dr. McKerrow, in his edition of Nashe, used capital letters to distinguish different editions of the same year; thus the two editions of *A Countercuffe Giuen to Martin Iunior,* both of 1589, are referred to simply as A and B. When there are both editions of different years and more than one edition of one year, as is true of *Pierce Penilesse,* they are represented as 92^A, 92^B, 92^C, 93, and 95.

I, 3	3
And Lo! the Hunter of the East has caught	59
And, to the field of Heav'n ascending, strikes	68
Same	7²
Drives Night along with them from Heav'n, and strikes	79

I, 4	4
The Sultan's Turret in a Noose of Light.	59
The Sultan's Turret with a Shaft of Light.	68
Same.	7²
Same.	79

the collation includes the four significant editions. The figure in the upper right corner of each note is the serial number of the note; the figures in the upper left represent stanza and line; and those at the end of each line show the edition.

For longer pieces—novels and the like—it is best to secure, if possible, a printed copy of the work to be collated. Taking a concrete example, let it be supposed that one is to edit Robert Greene's *Groatsworth of Wit*. A copy of the work should be procured; I used Volume XII of Grosart's edition of Greene's works.[21] Editions of the *Groatsworth* dated 1592, 1596, 1617, 1621, 1629, and 1637 are known to exist. All of the seventeenth-century editions can be disregarded as having no independent authority, there being no evidence of authorial intervention in any of them. Since Greene died in 1592, before even the

[21] The edition by G. B. Harrison (London: John Lane, the Bodley Head, Ltd., and New York: Dutton, 1923) might have been used instead. Or a photostatic copy could be used as a working copy. Photostats can also be used satisfactorily—except for the possibility of mistaking a rust spot for an ink mark—for purposes of collation.

first edition was published, the edition of 1596 could have authority only if it could be demonstrated that the first two editions were printed from different manuscripts, both in Greene's handwriting or showing evidence of having been approved by the author.[22] Since no such evidence is known to exist, the edition of 1592 is the obvious one to choose for a basic text. It may seem that there is no reason to consider the 1596 edition at all; but for two reasons it will be wise to collate that text. First, it is always possible that the compositor may have had access to the original manuscript and may have consulted it whenever he was in doubt about the printed text that he was using as his copy, being thus enabled to correct mistakes in the first edition. Second, a sixteenth-century printer's guess as to the way to correct an obvious error—even though it was only a guess—might often be more reliable than that of a twentieth-century editor.[23]

In explaining the process of collation I am taking up the 1596 edition first only because I happened to collate it first; it makes no difference, of course, in what order different versions are collated. The copy used is the Huth copy in the Huntington Library; that is the copy from which Grosart printed his text and—according to the *Short Title Catalogue*—the only copy extant. In the working copy, on the page preceding the title page, should be written with colored pencil [24]—red, let us say—"96 Huntington 61157 (*STC* 12246")— representing, of course, the edition, the library call number of the

---

[22] Actually, the copy for the *Groatsworth* seems to have been submitted to the printer in the handwriting of Henry Chettle (see Chettle, *Kind-Heart's Dream*, ed. G. B. Harrison (London: John Lane, the Bodley Head, Ltd., 1923), p. 6); and there is uncertainty as to just what share Greene had in the work.

[23] Dr. McKerrow wrote (*Prolegomena for the Oxford Shakespeare* (Oxford: Clarendon Press, 1939), p. 38, n. 1): "The point may perhaps be made clearer by an imaginary example. Supposing that in an edition of a farce or a pantomime written about 1920 there occurred the phrase 'Yes, we have now bananas', a press corrector of the present day in charge of a reprint would at once recognize the meaningless popular phrase intended, and correct 'now' to 'no'. An editor of a hundred years hence, reprinting the play as a monument of Georgian literature, would (unless we suppose that editors of the twenty-first century will have a far better knowledge of the popular locutions of our own day than we have of those of Shakespeare's time) be far more likely to retain the text as it stood and to add a note on the popularization of the banana in England in the early years of the century."

[24] A pencil with a thin lead should be used, and one should keep a pencil sharpener at hand; a sharp point is necessary if the recording of variants is to be clear and sharply defined, especially when, as in the Grosart editions, the paper of the working copy has a somewhat rough texture.

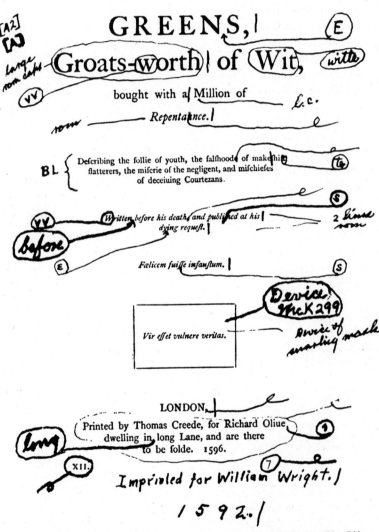

Figure 13. The Title Page of *Greenes Groatsworth of Wit* (from *The Life and Complete Works of Robert Greene*, ed. the Rev. Dr. Alexander B. Grosart (n.p.: privately printed, 1881–83), XII, 142). The variants shown in blue (1592) are indicated by fine lines, those in red (1596), by heavy ones.

copy being collated, and the entry number assigned to this edition in the *Short Title Catalogue*. Beginning with the title page, one should then indicate in red all the respects in which the original edition differs from the working copy—all the respects, in this instance, in which Grosart did not follow his basic text.

On the title page one would put the signature—[A], the brackets indicating that the signature does not actually appear on the printed page in the original. The doubling of *"before"* and of "long" in the original are indicated as shown in the illustration opposite; likewise the fact that *"Written"* was originally *"VVritten"* and "publiſhed" was "published". The printer's device is identified as that numbered 299 in McKerrow's *Printers' and Publishers' Devices . . . 1485–1640*. The comma after "Oliue" in the imprint is also shown. The numerals "XII" and "7"—representing signature 7 of Volume XII—belong to Grosart's book and, of course, have nothing to do with the original; hence they are marked for deletion. The fact that the verso of the title page is blank would be indicated on the next page of the working copy (p. [98]): "[A1ᵛ] blank". This page also furnishes convenient space for the recording of running titles: "Greenes (on all verso pp. from A4ᵛ to F1ᵛ); groatſworth of wit. (B1), same with cap G (B2, B4, C1, C2, C4, D1, D2, D3, E1, E2, E3, F1, F2), with wt. instead of wit. (B3, C3, D4, E4)".

One would then go through the book page by page, recording each variant found ("prouided" instead of "promiſed" on C4ᵛ, for example), and mentioning such things as the factotum on A2, the ornamental initial on A2ᵛ, the tailpiece on A3, the catchword "ſurely" for "ſure" on E4ᵛ, and the fact that F2ᵛ is blank. If there are ornaments that cannot be identified, they should be measured and described, or, better still, sketched or traced. Headpieces and tailpieces should be similarly treated, unless they are made up of combinations of type ornaments, in which case it will suffice to give the dimensions. If a leaf is missing from the original, that fact is, of course, to be noted; it may later be possible to collate that leaf in some other copy of the same edition. If a leaf is damaged, the extent of the damage may be indicated by outlining in the working copy that portion of the text which cannot be read in the original because of the damage. Errors in position or alignment of type should be indicated. When the collation has been completed, the date of completion should be noted in red in the working copy. The collation should then be checked for accuracy, preferably by another person. If no other person is available, the editor should allow some time—a few days at least—to elapse before doing this checking; otherwise he is likely to miss on the second occasion the same things that he missed the first time.

Having finished with the 1596 edition, the editor is ready to collate the 1592 edition—either the British Museum copy or the White copy in the Folger Shakespeare Library. Since I used the Museum copy, my collation shows the notation—this time in blue pencil—"92 BM C.57.b.42 (*STC* 12245)"; this is placed above or below the "96 Huntington 61157 (*STC* 12246)" on the page preceding the title page of the working copy. The fact that the first leaf of the original is blank is recorded by a notation in blue, in the upper left-hand corner of the title page: "A1 and A1ᵛ blank". Differences in spelling, in line arrangement, and in type, in the first four lines are shown. "BL" followed by a bracket indicates that the lines so bracketed (lines 5–7 in Grosart) are in Black Letter type. Since the device of the original is not represented in McKerrow's *Printers' and Publishers' Devices . . . 1485–1640,* a sketch or tracing of it must be made, or it may be described: "A snarling mask". Variations in spelling, punctuation, and typography are indicated; and finally the original imprint— "Imprinted for William Wright. 1592."—is given in place of the Creede imprint.

On the verso of the title page, the notation in blue "[A2ᵛ] blank" is put above or below the red "[A1] and [A1ᵛ] blank"; and the 1592 running titles are recorded in blue: "Greenes [small roman] (on versos B1, B4, C2, C4), [large roman] (on versos C1, C3, D1–F3); groats vvorth of vvit. [small roman] (B2–B4, C2, C3), groats-vvirth of vvit. [large roman] (C1, C4), groatſworth of wit. [large roman] (D1–F4)". The collating then proceeds as with the 1596 edition. Wherever the '92 edition varies from both Grosart and '96, the variation is shown by a note in blue pencil; wherever '92 agrees with '96 against Grosart, a tick or check mark in blue placed beside the correction in red will serve to indicate the agreement.

As a specimen page, Grosart's page 142—which contains most of F1 of the 1592 edition and E3 of the 1596—is represented with the necessary corrections. Grosart's variations from his basic text are few and doubtless intentional: in line 6 the word "left" in the original

groatſworth of wit.

gloʒie vnto his greatnes : foʒ penetrating is his power,
his hand lyes heauie vpon me, hee hath ſpoken vnto mee
with a voice of thunder, and I haue felt he is a God that
can puniſh enemies. Why ſhould thy excellent wit, his
gift, bee ſo blinded, that thou ſhouldſt giue no gloʒie to
the giuer: Is it peſtilent Machiuilian pollicy that thou
haſt ſtudied: O peeuiſh follie! What are his rules but
meere confuſed mockeries, able to extirpate in ſmall
time the generation of mankind. Foʒ if Sic volo, ſic iu‐
beo, hold in thoſe that are able to commaund: and if it
be lawfull Fas & nefas to do any thing that is benefici‐
all; onely Tyʒants ſhould poſſeſſe the earth, and they
ſtriuing to exceed in tyʒannie, ſhould each to other be a
ſlaughter man; till the mightieſt outliuing all, one
ſtroke were left foʒ Death, that in one age mans life
ſhould end. The bʒother of this Diabolicall Atheiſme
is dead, and in his life had neuer the felicitie hee aymed
at : but as he began in craft, liued in feare, and ended in
deſpaire. Quàm inſcrutabilia ſunt Dei iudicia? This
murderer of many bʒethʒen, had his conſcience ſeared
like Caine: this betrayer of him that gaue his life foʒ
him, inherited the poʒtion of Iudas : this Apoſtata peri‐
ſhed as ill as Iulian: and wilt thou my friend be his diſ‐
ciple? Looke but to me, by him verſwaded to that liber‐
tie, and thou ſhalt find it an infernall bondage. I knowe
the leaſt of my demerits merit this miſerable death, but
wilfull ſtriuing againſt knowne truth, exceedeth all the
terroʒs of my ſoule. Defer not (with me) till this laſt
point of extremitie; foʒ litle knowſt thou how in the end
thou ſhalt be viſited.

　　With thee I ioyne yong Iuuenall, that byting Sa‐
tyʒiſt, that laſtly with mee together wʒit a Comedie.
　　　　　　F　　　　　　　　Sweet

Page F1 of the 1592 edition of the *Groatsworth*. The readings of this edition are recorded on the working copy in
blue, as shown on the page to the left. Reproduced by
permission of the Folger Shakespeare Library, Washington,
D. C.

was corrected to "felt"; the comma following the parenthesis in line 1
was omitted; and the semicolon in line 16 was changed to a comma.
The only other red marks are those indicating line endings,[25] the
signature "E3", and the indications of irregularity in type.[26] The blue
check marks accompanying the changes of punctuation show that the
original editions both have the comma in the one case and the semicolon in the other; thus Grosart was modernizing punctuation that
he thought might be confusing to a modern reader—as it was perfectly proper that he should. After the words "giuer" in line 9, and
"ſtudied" in line 10, the 1592 edition has the old Black Letter mark
of interrogation, which looks like a colon with an acute accent mark
above it. In line 11, the word which Grosart, misled by his basic text,
took to be a hortatory subjunctive, is discovered to be in the first
edition merely a descriptive adjective, "peeuiſh". Another misreading
due to the compositor of the '96 edition is cleared up by substituting
the '92 reading "brocher" [broacher] for "brother" in line 20.

When all the versions that must be considered—i.e., all those in
which the author may have intervened—have been collated, it should
be possible to decide which of them is to be chosen as the basic or
copy text. No attention is to be paid, in determining the authorita-
tiveness of a text, to such corrections as might easily have been made
by someone other than the author; these include: (1) the correcting
or normalizing of spelling, punctuation, or grammar, (2) the correction of meter, in poetry, by adding or removing syllables, and (3) corrections such as a compositor or proofreader could make by referring
to the context.

It is generally not very difficult to determine whether changes
made in a later edition are an author's revisions or a compositor's
mistakes. In the page just discussed, no one would be likely to take
the substitution in '96 of "puniſh" for "peeuiſh" or "brother" for
"brocher" as the work of the author; of some fifty other changes, not

[25] The fact there is a mark before and one after the word "foole" in line 2 shows
that "foole" is used as the catchword—that is, it is the last word on page E2ᵛ and
the first word on E3.
[26] In most of the Black Letter original editions, roman type is used for proper
names and for expressions in a foreign language. Italic type is generally used for
passages in verse and for prefaces. Grosart substitutes roman for Black Letter and
italic for both roman and italic. Hence the italics of *Iudas* (line 27) and *Iulian*
(line 28) represent roman type in the original, and a note must be made of the fact
that the Latin phrases are in italics.

one can be taken as a likely case of revision, and about half are obvious errors.[27] Hence, there would be no good reason for supposing that Greene had anything to do with the edition of the *Groatsworth* printed in 1596; and the edition of 1592 would be the obvious choice as the basic text.

*   *   *

Let us now see how the problem of choosing a basic text has been approached in some other instances. Dr. McKerrow, in editing the works of Thomas Nashe, was confronted by five texts of *Pierce Penilesse His Supplication to the Diuell,* three of 1592, which McKerrow designated A, B, and C; one of 1593; and one of 1595.

---

[27] The obvious errors include such changes as: (p. 101) "I commend this to your fauourable cenſures, that like an Embrion without ſhape, I feare me will be thruſt into the world." ('92) ". . . cenſures, and like . . ." ('96); (p. 103) "In an Iland bounded with the Ocean, there was ſomtime a Cittie ſituated, made riche by Marchandize, and populous by long peace, the name is not mentioned . . ." ('92) ". . . Iland bound with . . . populous by long ſpace, the name . . ." ('96); (p. 138) ". . . . be deplorde? . . ." ('92) ". . . then deplore? . . . " ('96) [the passage is in verse and the change destroys the rhyme]; (p. 145) "The fire of my light is now at the laſt ſnuffe, and for want of wherewith to ſuſtaine it, there is no ſubſtance left for life to feede on. . . ." ('92) ". . . ſnuffe, and the want of . . ." ('96); (p. 116) "I am very ſorie that our rude entertainment is ſuch, as no way may worke your content, . . ." ('92) ". . . our rude enterment is ſuch . . ." ('96); (p. 129) "What meant the poets in inuectiue verſe, To ſing Medeas ſhame, . . ." ('92) ". . . Poets to inuectiue . . ." ('96). The two cases which look most like revision are these: (pp. 111–12) "You muſt not think but ſundrye marchants of this Cittie expect your company, ſundry Gentlemen deſire your familiarity, . . ." ('92) ". . . thinke but certaine Marchants . . ." ('96); and (p. 138) "My rauiſht ſence of wonted furie reft; VVants ſuch conceit, as ſhould in Poems fit. . . ." ('92) ". . . in Poims fit . . ." ('96). In the first of these instances the problem involves a question of taste or of literary style. I think it would be impossible to show that Greene, having used *sundry* twice, would later have found the repetition objectionable and have substituted *certain*; moreover, the change could have been made, either intentionally or unintentionally, by the compositor. As for the *fit* and *ſit,* although the most recent editor of the work (G. B. Harrison in the Bodley Head Quarto edition, p. 40) takes *fit* to be correct, it seems to me more likely that *ſit* is what Greene wrote; like other Elizabethans he was fond of conceits. However, the chance of confusing *f* and *ſ,* either in type or in handwriting, is so great that the substitution of one for the other in such a case as this cannot possibly be taken as evidence of revision. The story is told of an eminent scholar who once wrote an erudite commentary, citing numerous examples which he had gone to great lengths to discover, to explain a passage in which flaying was mentioned as a means of punishing criminals. The note proved to be superfluous, however, when it turned out that the word in question was not "flaying" but "ſlaying".

McKerrow demonstrated, by the evidence of the Epistle prefixed to all of the other editions, that A was the first. The latter part of B corresponds, page for page, with A and hence must have been printed from a copy of A. Textual evidence [28] shows that C was printed from B, '93 from C, and '95 from '93. There are a good many differences between A and B: *Manibetter* is changed to *Swin-snout, iymiams* to *guegawes, Iack-dropper* to *Inck-dropper, the most Artists* to *all Artists for the most part,* and *musicall* to *misticall.* Some of these changes may represent the printer's corrections, but others show clearly the author's intervention. In C there is even stronger evidence of authorial correction; [29] but the only changes in '93 and '95 are such as might well have been made by the printer. Thus Dr. McKerrow concluded that C was the last text corrected by the author. He continued:

At the same time C is often inferior to A, being much less carefully printed; . . .

There were therefore two alternatives, to print from A, adopting the corrections of C, or to print from C, correcting where necessary from A. I have chosen the latter as being on the whole more consistent; but bearing in mind Nashe's own statement as to the carelessness with which this book was printed (*Have with You to Saffron-Walden,* sig. F1), and the evident truth of it, I have used somewhat more freedom in restoring to the text from earlier editions words which seem to have been merely accidentally omitted in C, than would have been justifiable if we had reason to think that the author himself had read the proofs.[3]

*   *   *

Professor Kaye, in editing Bernard Mandeville's *Fable of the Bees,*[4] Part I, had to consider two editions of 1714, and others of

[28] For example (Nashe, *Works,* ed. McKerrow, I, 189) *frantick* in A becomes *fran-tick* in B, the *fran-* coming at the end of a line, and remains *fran-tick* in C, '93, and '95.

[29] There are two especially interesting examples: (Nashe, *Works,* ed. McKerrow, I, 170) *melancholike course in his gate and countenance, and talke as though* in A becomes *melancholy in his gate & countenance, course & talke, as though* in B, and *melancholy in his gate and countenance, and talke as though* in C; (*ibid.,* p. 174) *wil scarse get a Scholler bread and cheese* in A becomes *wil scarse get a paire of shoos and a Canuas-dublet* in B, and *scarse get a scholler a pair of shoos and a Canuas-dublet* in C. In both instances it seems clear that an attempt to make a change in the reading of A was misunderstood by the printer of B and finally corrected in C.

1723, 1724, 1725, 1728, 1729, and 1732—eight in all. He found evidences of authorial revision in the editions of 1724, 1725, and—perhaps—1732. Of Part II there were editions in 1729, 1730, and 1735. Collation of these various editions led Professor Kaye to make this statement:

The text used in volume one is that of the 1732 edition, which was the last edition during Mandeville's life of the first part of the *Fable*. It is impossible to be sure whether this edition or that of 1725 is closer to Mandeville's final intention. . . . I have preferred the text adopted, because, other things being equal, the last authorized edition[30] seemed to me preferable to an intermediate one and because the orthography of the 1732 edition is more modern.[31] This edition has, moreover, a certain further interest in that it was from this issue that the French translation was made.[32] The text used in volume two is that of the 1729 edition—the first edition of Part II. The only variations in the editions of Part II were apparently, as may be seen from the variant readings, due to the printer, so that the first edition is nearest to Mandeville's text.[5]

*   *   *

Dr. McKerrow's problem in determining the relationship of the *Pierce Penilesse* editions was a comparatively simple one; but to discover the *filiation,* or relationship, of a considerable number of texts —as in the manuscripts of Chaucer's *Canterbury Tales,* for example —is sometimes a matter so difficult and so complex as to be beyond the province of this book.[33] One suggestion as to method that may appropriately be made here, however, is that no reliance is to be placed upon the agreement of two texts in a correct reading as an

[30] "The 1732 edition was authorized; it was by Mandeville's publisher and was acknowledged by Mandeville (*Letter to Dion,* p. 7)" [Kaye's note].

[31] "There is no reason to suppose that this modernity was removed from Mandeville's intention, for the conflicting practices in his various books and the evidence of his holograph (see facsimiles) indicate that he left orthography largely to his printers" [Kaye's note].

[32] "According to the French version, ed. 1740, i.viii; ed. 1750, i.xiv" [Kaye's note].

[33] The *Canterbury Tales* problem is discussed at length in *The Text of the Canterbury Tales,* ed. Manly and Rickert, Vol. II; see also Germaine Dempster, "Manly's Conception of the Early History of the *Canterbury Tales*", *PMLA,* LXI (1946), 379–415. Any one interested in such problems should read: W. W. Greg, *The Calculus of Variants* (Oxford: Oxford University Press, 1927); William P. Shepard, "Recent Theories of Textual Criticism", *MP,* XXVIII (1931), 129–41; and W. W. Greg, "Recent Theories of Textual Criticism", *MP,* XXVIII (1931), 401–4.

indication that one of them is derived from the other; an editor, a compositor, a proofreader—where manuscripts are involved, a scribe —may easily hit upon a right reading in attempting to correct a mistake, and may do so quite independently of any text containing the proper reading. Only when two texts have errors in common—and a convincing number of such errors [34]—can one say with assurance that there is a textual relationship.[35] The fact that A, B, C, and D— whether editions or manuscripts or both—have correct readings in common proves nothing; but the fact that, out of thirty errors in C and twenty-five in D, twenty are common to both C and D, would be significant.

*   *   *

Among problems in textual criticism, the puzzle afforded by the three versions of Shakspere's *Hamlet* has perhaps attracted most attention; a recent contribution on that subject is a book by G. I. Duthie.[6] Similarly, many attempts have been made—without yet completely satisfying everyone—to work out the filiation of the texts of *Henry VI*, Parts II and III, and related plays.[7] Other studies to be mentioned here deal with the texts of *The Twelve Profits of Anger*,[8] the *Sacrificium Cayme and Abell*,[9] the *Canterbury Tales*,[10] *The Taming of the Shrew*,[11] the "Bad Quartos",[12] and *Comus*.[13] There is also a study of the relationship of cancels found in the 1800 edition of *Lyrical Ballads*.[14]

*   *   *

One other aspect of the matter of choosing a basic text should be

[34] When I found two examination papers both containing the rather startling information that Thomas à Becket was a young monk of the seventeenth century whom the pilgrims in Chaucer's *Canterbury Tales* were on their way to Canterbury to kill, I had very little doubt that one of those papers was derived from the other.

[35] Even then one cannot say that A is copied from B or B from A; both may be derived from an earlier text X, or Y may have been derived from A and B from Y, or A may have been derived from X and B from Z, which latter was derived from either A or X. And of course other combinations are possible. Dr. McKerrow suggested (*Prolegomena for the Oxford Shakespeare*, p. 13): "It would, I think, be convenient if we could use some such word as 'monogenous' and 'polygenous' to designate the two groupings of texts . . . : 'monogenous' standing for those which derive from a single extant edition and 'polygenous' for those which have at their head two or more extant editions none of which derives from another—substantive texts, as I have called them . . ."

considered before we leave the subject. In explaining his choice of the second edition of *The Unfortunate Traveller* Dr. McKerrow wrote:

. . . fortunately it is not now considered to be the duty of an editor to pick and choose among the variant readings of his author's works those which he himself would prefer in writings of his own, but merely to present those works as he believes the author to have intended them to appear. Whether, from a literary point of view, the first or the second edition of *The Unfortunate Traveller* is the better, is perhaps open to question. But with this I have no concern whatever, at any rate here, for if an editor has reason to suppose that a certain text embodied later corrections than any other, and at the same time has no ground for disbelieving that these corrections, or some of them at least, are the work of the author, he has no choice but to make that text the basis of his reprint. I have therefore whenever possible, though sometimes, I own, not without regret, followed that edition which was said by the publisher to be 'Newly corrected and augmented'.[15]

In view of this clear statement, I cannot agree with Professor Morize when he writes:

These few examples show:
(1) That it is impossible to give a rule, or even a general suggestion, as to the choice of a text as the foundation for an edition.
(2) That in a great number of cases it is well to choose the first form of an important work.
(3) That, after all, the editor's endeavor should be to select and reproduce the text that has the greatest historical significance.[16]

It seems to me that these statements are at variance, not only with McKerrow, but also with another statement by Professor Morize: "When dealing with manuscripts and printed editions we should choose the text that brings us closest to the author's definitive and complete thought".[17] There may often be difficulty in deciding which of several versions best represents "the author's definitive and complete thought"; but once that version is determined, it is that version which should be presented in a critical edition.[18] That is not to say that there is no room in the world for reprints of other versions; one has a perfect right to print—if he is not purporting to offer a critical edition—one of the stories of Henry James in its unrevised form, or the first edition rather than the fourth of FitzGerald's translation of the *Rubáiyát*. But the editor of a critical edition has done his duty only when he presents the text that best represents the author's final intention, together with textual notes that make it possible for the reader to reconstruct for himself the earlier forms of the work.

III

When a basic text has been chosen, the problem of treatment arises: how closely must the new edition adhere to that basic text? When may the editor depart from his basic text without making note, in the critical apparatus, of that departure, "silently correcting", as editors say? When may he introduce a reading not in the basic text, provided he gives the reading of the basic text in a footnote? There are really two problems involved here: first, the policy to be followed in emending or correcting the text; and second, the policy to be followed in reproducing the typography of the original edition. In solving both problems we are thrown back upon the cardinal principle of all editing: we should strive to present the work as the author wanted it to be read.

*   *   *

Dr. Greg opens an interesting discussion of emendation [19] thus:

The Professor of Latin in the University of Cambridge [A. E. Housman] has said what is perhaps the last word on the subject of emendation, in a passage that runs as follows: 'A textual critic engaged upon his business is not at all like Newton investigating the motion of the planets; he is much more like a dog hunting for fleas. If a dog hunted for fleas on mathematical principles, basing his researches on statistics of area and population, he would never catch a flea except by accident.' [36] I do not believe that this is a fair account of textual criticism in general, but so far as emendation is concerned it comes extraordinarily near the truth. The fact is that there is only one general principle of emendation, which is that emendation is in its essence devoid of principle. At its finest it is an inspiration, a stirring of the spirit, which obeys no laws and cannot be produced to order. In other words, emendation is an art. Yet even as such there should be some conditions which by its very nature it must obey, for it is surely no idle dream of scholars to be 'learned in searching principles of art'. And if we can do nothing to help great critics in making

[36] "A. E. Housman, 'The Application of Thought to Textual Criticism', a paper read before the Classical Association, 4 Aug. 1921: *Proceedings,* xviii" [Greg's note].

brilliant emendations, we may at least hope to discover some rules that should prevent little critics from making foolish ones.[20]

Dr. Greg then goes on to observe that an acceptable emendation is "one that strikes a trained intelligence as supplying exactly the sense required by the context, and which at the same time reveals to the critic the manner in which the corruption arose".[21]

If one were editing Nashe's *Pierce Penilesse,* he would encounter this strange reading in the first edition of that work: "If he be challenged to fight, for his delaterie dye-case, hee obiects that it is not the custome of the Spaniard or the Germaine, to looke back to euery dog that barks". Finding "dye-case" in a context which calls for "excuse", one would naturally investigate Nashe's handwriting to see whether a compositor might have misread "ex" as "dy" and "u" as "a"; [37] fortunately, the necessity for a speculative correction is removed by the fact that the second and later editions all have the word "excuse".

*   *   *

A famous passage that demanded emendation occurs in Shakspere's *King Henry the Fifth* (Act II, scene iii). The Hostess, describing the death of Falstaff, says:

Nay, sure, he's not in hell: he's in Arthur's bosom, if ever man went to Arthur's bosom. A' made a finer end and went away an it had been any christom child; a' parted even just between twelve and one, even at the turning o' the tide: for after I saw him fumble with the sheets and play with flowers and smile upon his fingers' ends, I knew there was but one way; for his nose was as sharp as a pen, and a Table of greene fields.

The comment in Malone's edition of Shakspere on the last phrase in that passage so well illustrates the best and the worst in emendation that it deserves quotation in full:

—and 'a babbled of green fields.] The old copy [i.e., the First Folio] reads—"for his nose was as sharp as a pen, and *a table of green fields.*" Steevens.

These words, "and a table of green fields," are not to be found in the old editions of 1600 and 1608. This nonsense got into all the following editions by a pleasant mistake of the stage editors, who printed from the

[37] I do not mean to imply that the mistake could have occurred only in this way, but such confusion between "ex" and "dy" and "u" and "a" would not have been unlikely in a sixteenth-century hand.

common piece-meal written parts in the play-house. A table was here directed to be brought in, (it being a scene in a tavern where they drink at parting,) and this direction crept into the text from the margin. Greenfield was the name of the property-man in that time, who furnished implements, &c. for the actors, *A table of Greenfield's*. Pope.

So reasonable account of this blunder, Mr. Theobald could not acquiesce in. He thought *a table of Greenfield's,* part of the text, only corrupted, and that it should be read, "he babbled of green fields," because men do so in the ravings of a calenture. But he did not consider how ill this agrees with the nature of the knight's illness, who was now in no *babbling* humour; and so far from wanting cooling in *green fields,* that his feet were very cold, and he just expiring. Warburton.

Upon this passage Mr. Theobald has a note that fills a page, which I omit in pity to my readers, since he only endeavors to prove what I think every reader perceives to be true, that at this time no *table* could be wanted. Mr. Pope, in an appendix to his own edition in 12mo. seems to admit Theobald's emendation, which we would have allowed to be uncommonly happy, had we not been prejudiced against it by Mr. Pope's first note, with which, as it excites merriment, we are loath to part. Johnson.

Had the former editors been apprized, that *table,* in our author, signifies a *pocket-book,* I believe they would have retained it with the following alteration:—"for his nose was as sharp as a pen upon a table of green fells."—On *table-books,* silver or steel pens, very sharp-pointed, were formerly and still are fixed to the backs or covers. Mother Quickly compares Falstaff's nose (which in dying persons grows thin and sharp) to one of those *pens,* very properly, and she meant probably to have said, on a *table-book* with a *shagreen cover* or *shagreen table*; but in her usual blundering way, she calls it a *table of green fells,* or a table covered with *green skin*; which the blundering transcriber turned into *green fields*; and our editors have turned the prettiest blunder in Shakspeare, quite out of doors. Smith.

Dr. Warburton objects to Theobald's emendation, on the ground of the nature of Falstaff's illness; "who was so far from *babbling,* or wanting *cooling* in *green fields,* that his feet were cold and he was just expiring." But his disorder had been a "burning quotidian tertian." It is, I think, a much stronger objection, that the word *Table,* with a capital letter, (for so it appears in the old copy,) is very unlikely to have been printed instead of *babbled*. This reading is, however, preferable to any that has yet been proposed.

On this difficult passage I had once a conjecture. It was, that the word *table* is right, and that the corrupted word is *and,* which may have been misprinted for *in,* a mistake that has happened elsewhere in these plays: and thus the passage will run—"and his nose was as sharp as a pen *in* a table of green fields." A *pen* may have been used for a *pinfold* [a pen for animals], and a table for a picture. . . .

The pointed stakes of which pinfolds are sometimes formed, were perhaps in the poet's thoughts. Malone.

It has been observed (particularly by the superstition of women) of people near death, when they are delirious by a fever, that they talk of removing; as it has of those in a calenture, that they have their heads run on green fields. Theobald.[22]

It may be difficult to decide which is the worst of those proposed emendations, but that Theobald's is the best is proved by its almost universal acceptance. The clause "and 'a babbled of green fields" fits the context perfectly, and thus the emendation satisfies the first of the two criteria; we may look to Dr. Greg for an explanation [23] that satisfies the second: "babbled" would very probably have been written "babld", and "b" and "t" and final "d" and "e" are often difficult to distinguish in an Elizabethan hand.

*   *   *

The editor's attitude with respect to emendations should be a most conservative one. Puzzling passages should be pointed out and discussed, suggestions for emendations should be freely offered in footnotes; but no reading should be introduced into the text unless there is proof, or very strong reason to believe, that the proposed reading, rather than that of the original, represents the author's intention. When an emendation is adopted, the reading of the original should, of course, be given in a footnote.

Dr. McKerrow was wholly justified in changing "running" to "cunning" in the line "It fareth with thē as it did with *Calchas* that running soothsayer, . . ."[24] This emendation fully satisfies the criteria of acceptability: it transforms nonsense—or what approaches nonsense—into good sense; and it explains how the mistake may have occurred, since some forms of "c" are very like some forms of "r" in a sixteenth-century hand. But to insist that "solid" must be "sullied" in Shakspere's famous line

"O that this too too solid flesh would melt" [25]

is, I believe—with all due respect to Dr. Greg and others who have insisted that an emendation is necessary here [26]—going much too far. It may be explained how "sullied" could have been misprinted "solid"; but that is a case of getting the cart before the horse, since there is nothing inherently senseless about the line as it stands. "Sullied" may be right and "solid" wrong, and certainly there should be a note in any edition of *Hamlet* calling attention to this possibility —or probability, if you like; but to substitute any other reading for the "solid" of the Folio would, it seems to me, be going beyond the proper province of an editor.

*   *   *

Emendation is not, of course, the only means of "cleaning up" a text—making it conform with the author's intention. Collation, in addition to enabling one to choose a basic text, may help in the removing of textual errors. Where the basic text is corrupt, another edition may provide the correct reading. Even when two readings are obviously both wrong, in different ways, a comparison of the two errors may enable one to emend with considerable assurance. Thus if one text contained a reference to someone's "flaunting a gray bear", it would be difficult to determine whether the correct reading would be "beard" or "head"; but if there were two texts printed from the same manuscript, and one had "bead" where the other had "bear", it would be reasonable to suppose that the author had made an "h" that looked like "b" and that the correct reading is "head". When a variant reading serves thus to help in correcting the text, it should, of course, be printed in the textual, or collation, notes.

We may, however, collate various editions of a work in the hope of getting help in the interpreting of a passage in which there is no error, no necessity for an emendation. We may have no doubt, for example, that the Queen, in Act V, scene ii, of *Hamlet,* speaks of her son as being "fat"; but we may properly seek variant readings in the hope of getting some light on the meaning to be attached to the word "fat" as the Queen uses it.[38] When such variants are collected merely as possible aids to interpretation, they should be recorded—if at all—in the explanatory notes, not in the collation notes.

At best, however, textual criticism is far from being the "science" that some of its champions would seem to make it. Dr. McKerrow, in

[38] For a possible explanation of this crux, see below, p. 218.

a passage that should be read by every student of literature,[27] points
out that the physical scientist, who can repeat an experiment as many
times as may be necessary, can arrive at a much higher degree of
certainty than can be achieved by the textual critic, for whom experiment is generally impossible:

In most cases all that we can show is that if the parties concerned in the
transmission of a text behaved as we should expect them to have behaved,
the copyist or compositor working with reasonable, but not excessive,
attention to what was before him, the printer's reader bearing in mind,
more or less constantly, that what he read was supposed to make such a
partial kind of sense as could be looked for from poetry, and all other
persons by whom the text could be affected behaving in a similarly
normal manner, then such-and-such a theory of the history of the texts
and their interrelationship is, on the evidence at present available, more
probable than any suggested alternative.[28]

IV

Turning now to the other problem involved in the reproducing
of the text, we shall find many opportunities for choosing one or the
other of two courses, and hence as many decisions to be made. One
might choose to reproduce the original edition with scrupulous exactness, to provide, in other words, a facsimile reproduction. Such an
edition would best serve the purpose of the student who is interested
in bibliography, in printing, in orthography; it would not do for one
who is interested in the paper or the watermarks of old books, and it
would not be convenient for the average scholar. The specialist in
paper or watermarks we need not take into account; for him, nothing
will suffice but the original copy. It is possible, however, to cater to
the needs of the average scholar and, at the same time, meet most of
the requirements of the specialists in bibliography, in printing, and
in orthography.

The principle to be kept in mind in the reproducing of a text is to
follow the basic text exactly.[39] However, an editor may, and should,

[39] Dr. McKerrow, in the "Note on the Treatment of the Text" in his edition of
Nashe's *Works* (I, [xi]–xvi), has a full and excellent statement of correct editorial
practice. Other good statements are to be found in John Archer Gee, *The Life and
Works of Thomas Lupset* (New Haven: Yale University Press, 1928), pp. [201]–2,
and J. C. Ghosh, *The Works of Thomas Otway* (Oxford: Oxford University Press,
1932), I, 89–94.

silently—that is, without in each instance providing a footnote giving the original reading—make such changes as these: (1) correct turned letters which, when turned, do not resemble other letters; (2) substitute letters of the right font when the original has types of the wrong font; (3) shift marginal notes to bring them nearer to the material to which they refer; (4) separate words run together which do not, when run together, form a new word; (5) supply necessary hyphens carelessly omitted in the original; (6) correct such obvious mistakes in punctuation as a comma at the end of a sentence or a period in the middle of one. There should be somewhere preceding the text a statement that such corrections have been silently made.

Certain other changes are to be left to the editor's taste. The substitution of "w" for "vv", of "s" for "ſ", of "from" for "frō", and the adoption of the modern practice in the use of "u" and "v" and "i" and "j" will to some extent destroy the atmosphere present in the original. It may be argued that the gain in ease of reading makes such substitutions desirable, and perhaps it does; but it must be remembered that most of the people who use critical editions are sufficiently familiar with the literature of a period—or should be— that they are not bothered by any archaisms characteristic of that period. At all events, these are matters in which an editor may please himself, though it may turn out to be his publisher whom he will have to please.[40] If it be decided that contractions are to be expanded, another decision will have to be made: Is it to be indicated that there was a contraction in the original? Such indication can be made by printing the letters which constitute the expansion in type of a different font from that used for the rest of the word.[41]

So much for the silent corrections; now for the changes that are to be made, but with a note in each instance acknowledging the change. These errors should be thus corrected: (1) The turned letters *b* and *q*, *d* and *p*, *n* and *u*, and (in Black Letter) *a* and *é*; hence McKerrow, in the second line of Nashe's *The Anatomie of Absurditie*, prints "the

[40] When I asked Dr. McKerrow why he did not use the long "ſ" in his edition of Nashe, he said that Mr. Bullen—who was the publisher of the first four volumes— would never have permitted it; in *Prolegomena for the Oxford Shakespeare* Dr. McKerrow wrote (p. 20, n. 4): "In deference to current (though, I think, wrong) opinion s is substituted for ſ".

[41] See below, pp. 309–10.

Agrigentine Maydes", with the footnote "2 *Agrigentiue* Q".[42] (2) Obvious mistakes in spelling, such as "wich" for "which" (Nashe, *Works,* ed. McKerrow, I, 32), "Setmons" for "sermons" (*ibid.,* p. 270), and "wiehall" for "withall" (*ibid.,* p. 283). (3) Incorrect word divisions which form new words; McKerrow prints: "Thou hast wronged one for my sake (whom for the name I must love) . . .", with the footnote "27 wronge done *93*" (*ibid.,* p. 197). (4) Mistakes in punctuation, changing of which may affect the meaning, as in this passage: ". . . and if so you vnderstand that I alleadge no Author but the Asse, for all Authors are Asses, why I am for you; . . ." where in the original there was a semicolon after "Asse" (*ibid.,* p. 328).

In all changes, silent or otherwise, the editor must keep his guiding principle in mind: he is to present the text as its author wanted it to be read. He should therefore correct any mistake that is obviously the error of a copyist or a compositor, or a *lapsus calami* of the author. Difficult readings that are not the result of obvious errors should be discussed and possible emendations suggested in footnotes; but no change is to be made in the text unless it is practically certain that the change fulfills the author's intention.[43]

V

Having settled all the questions involved in the presentation of the text, we are now confronted by one final problem: How shall the *apparatus criticus* be arranged? There can be no doubt, I think, that the notes giving textual variants should be on the same page with the readings to which they correspond; and some authorities insist [44] that the notes of explanation and interpretation should also be on the same page with the material to which they refer. That would mean that almost every page would be divided into three parts and would have three kinds or sizes of type—one for the text, another for the textual notes, and a third for the other notes. It is, of course, a convenience to the reader if such comment as may be necessary to the understanding of the text is contained on the same page with the

[42] McKerrow used "Q" to indicate that all the early editions—whether actually quartos or not—agreed in the reading given.

[43] An interesting comment by Dr. Johnson is contained in James M. Osborn, "Johnson on the Sanctity of an Author's Text", *PMLA,* L (1935), 928–29.

[44] Professor Morize, for example; see *Problems and Methods,* pp. 57 and 65.

passage to which it refers; and where the text is of such nature that the notes do not out-bulk the text, such an arrangement is most desirable.[45] But where the text is such that the triple division results in many pages containing but one or two lines of text and many lines of annotation—a circumstance which might make the reader think of Prince Hal's complaint: "O monstrous! but one half-pennyworth of bread to this intolerable deal of sack!"—it may be better to put the commentary notes at the end of each text, or, better, at the back of the volume. In an edition which consists of more than one volume, it is likely to be most helpful for the reader if the commentary notes are brought together in one volume, as in McKerrow's Nashe. Then one may keep both volumes—the text and the commentary—lying open before him; and it is just as easy to glance from one volume to the other for an explanation as it is to move the eyes from the top to the bottom of the page.

Textual, or collation, notes may conveniently be put in this form: the number of the line in which the variation occurs; the *lemma* (the word or phrase for which there is a variant, followed by a bracket); the variant, followed by the *siglum* (or *sigla*) of the edition (or editions) containing that variant. Thus we might have:

21 men] man 96

If, in an edition of *Hamlet,* the First Folio has been adopted as the basic text, we should have this note on Act I, scene iii:

115 I, Springes] I *om.* Q1: fprings Q2
Woodcocks. I doe know] woodcocks, Qq: I doe know *om.* Q1 [46]

In a line in which the reading of the basic text is obviously incorrect, we should have a note such as this (*Hamlet,* Act II, scene ii):

442 vallanced] Q1 valanct Q2: valiant F1

The reference in the next line: "Com'st thou to beard me in Denmarke?" makes it clear that *valanced*—"provided with a short,

---

[45] Where an occasional extended commentary is demanded, it is sometimes possible to put such material in an appendix.
[46] We should then be able to reconstruct the lines.
First Quarto: Springes to catch woodcocks,
Second Quarto: I, fprings to catch woodcocks, I doe know
First Folio: I, Springes to catch Woodcocks. I doe know

decorative fringe", as the dictionary says—is the proper reading. The Q2 reading might have been ignored as a mere difference in spelling, and the note might have been:

442 vallanced] Qq: valiant F1

Since, however, the spelling of Q2 may serve to explain the error in F1—the Folio compositor apparently failing to recognize the word and substituting the word most like it that seemed to him to make sense—it seems worth while to record it.

VI

Most of what has been said in this chapter has had to do with the editing of Elizabethan works, though the principles involved are valid for all periods. Professor John Robert Moore points out that the editing of eighteenth-century works is often more difficult than the editing of books earlier than 1642.

There is no Short-Title Catalogue; [47] the bibliography of the period is far less completely worked out, so that the catalogues of even the best libraries are full of errors, and some printed bibliographies are more misleading than informative; and many problems are involved which do not appear so prominently in earlier books.

The increased circulation of some periodicals, or the immediate sale of some books, led to the practice of running off the same work on more than one press, with a great increase in variant readings. The practice of issuing some periodicals in more than one form (like the "imperfects" of Defoe's *Review,* the Edinburgh issues of that journal, and the annual bound volumes of many of the periodicals) led to many more variations. The great increase in piratical publishing confuses our knowledge of some of the more popular works. The fairly common practice of issuing some works in quarto for subscribers and in octavo for the general sale may be a difficulty at times. Likewise the custom of making up new books more or less at random from unsold sheets (sheets perhaps printed on different presses and taken from different warehouses) presents endless possibilities of confusion.

There are, of course, many relatively easy things to edit, for which there are few editions, each clearly related to the others in date and in

---

[47] Since Profesosr Moore wrote, announcement has been made by the Index Society that *A Short-Title Catalogue of English Books, 1641–1700,* compiled by Donald Wing, is to be published in 3 vols., the first of which appeared in 1945. I believe that an eighteenth-century catalogue is also in prospect.

the dependence of one upon another; but such works as *Gulliver's Travels* and *Robinson Crusoe,* with their infinite varieties of "points" and their problems of priority—such things as the controversial pamphlets, in which the title pages were often meant primarily to deceive the reader into reading something very different from what he thought he was getting—such things as *The School for Scandal,* in which the author refused to commit himself to a definitive text—these are enough to drive an editor crazy.[29]

It might be thought that the editing of books written since 1800 would be relatively simple; and in general that is perhaps true. But some of the difficulties just mentioned enter into the editing of more recent works. The existence of a manuscript or more than one manuscript may lead to complications. The greater attention paid by modern authors to the correcting and revising of their works should simplify the task of achieving a definitive text, but it may instead bring about confusion.

In addition to works mentioned previously in this chapter, there are, for the sixteenth century, good critical editions of *The Mirror for Magistrates,*[30] the English works of Sir Thomas More,[31] and the works of Michael Drayton,[32] Christopher Marlowe,[33] and Edmund Spenser.[34] For the seventeenth century there are the plays of Roger Boyle,[35] and the works of George Herbert,[36] Ben Jonson,[37] and John Milton.[38] For the eighteenth century we have Addison's letters,[39] Boswell's *Life of Johnson,*[40] Chesterfield's letters,[41] the critical works of John Dennis,[42] Pope's poems,[43] Swift's poems[44] and prose works,[45] and Walpole's letters.[46] The Romantic Movement may be represented by editions of the poetry of Keats[47] and of Wordsworth.[48] In American literature there are editions of the works of William Byrd,[49] Benjamin Franklin,[50] and Sidney Lanier,[51] the American notebooks of Hawthorne,[52] and the poems of Poe[53] and Melville.[54] This list is, of course, by no means complete.

VII

Among writers for whom critical editions are much needed may be mentioned Nicholas Breton, Samuel Daniel, Robert Greene, Thomas Lodge, Sir Walter Ralegh, Colley Cibber (the plays only), Oliver Goldsmith, and Richard Steele. In American Literature some of the desiderata are editions of Charles Brockden Brown, James Fenimore

Cooper, Jonathan Edwards, Washington Irving, William Gilmore
Simms, and Royal Tyler.

As a final word of advice to prospective editors, let me say what
has been implied throughout this chapter: study McKerrow—you
could have no better master.

❦

CHAPTER TWO

PROBLEMS IN BIOGRAPHY

O F the writing—and the reading—of biographies there is no end. The normal human being is interested in knowing other human beings; and the only way to become acquainted with a person from whom one is separated by time or space is to read biography.

I

If, then, the object of the biographer is to make the reader acquainted with the subject of his work, obviously his writing must be characterized by truthfulness. Dr. Johnson [1]—and after him Boswell —rightly protested against biographies that were all panegyric. As Boswell put it:

And he will be seen as he really was; for I profess to write, not his panegyrick, which must be all praise, but his Life; which, great and good as he was, must not be supposed to be entirely perfect. To be as he was, is indeed subject of panegyrick enough to any man in this state of being; but in every picture there should be shade as well as light, and when I delineate him without reserve, I do what he himself recommended, both by his precept and his example.[2]

It may be that the Doctor and his disciple both lacked the impartiality and the detachment requisite for fulfilling their intention to tell the exact truth; but no one can quarrel with the intention. To the biographer, the saying *De mortuis nil nisi bonum* does not apply.

It is impossible, to be sure, that any individual should ever be able to learn the whole truth about another individual; hence the perfect biography can never be written. All that we can ask of the biographer is that he discover as much of the truth concerning his subject as it is humanly possible to learn, and then present that truth as clearly and as interestingly as possible. But there are different ways of discovering and presenting biographical truth.

*   *   *

One method of writing biography is often considered to be the invention of Lytton Strachey, though credit for it might more justly be given to Gamaliel Bradford, whose *Lee the American* was completed in 1912; whereas Strachey's *Eminent Victorians* did not appear until 1918. In this kind of biography the writer is not greatly concerned with the day-to-day activities of his subject; his object is to convey to the reader an understanding of the subject's mind and personality. Hence the biographer does not hesitate to invent a scene or situation that never happened (or is not known to have happened), or to quote words that may not have been spoken, if such a scene or situation or conversation helps to complete the psychological portrait. The success of such a biography depends, of course, upon the author's ability to achieve rapport with his subject, and no less upon his power to convey vividly and convincingly his impression to the reader.

The weakness of the type is that the reader is at the mercy of the biographer. Fact is so mingled with fiction that the reader is unable to distinguish one from the other, to separate what did happen from what the biographer thinks should have happened or may well have happened. Even when the conversation is taken from the subject's own writings, utterances may be given a false interpretation by being transposed in time or by being deprived of their context.[1] Hence such biographies, though they may serve admirably the purposes of the ordinary reader, are not satisfactory to the scholar, because they give him no opportunity to weigh the evidence, to make use of his knowledge and his judgment; he must take the biographer's word for everything that is said. The student, in his capacity as reader, or even as student of the period, may find both pleasure and profit in the psychographic works of such men as Strachey and Bradford, and in other biographical works in which interpretation carries the author

[1] One could make Pope express an enthusiasm which he may not have felt, for biography or psychology or sociology by quoting "The proper study of mankind is man. . . ." (*Essay on Man*, Epistle II, l. 2) without the concomitant "presume not God to scan, . . ." (l. 1).

far beyond—but not counter to—established fact. But for the student *qua* scholar, the only satisfactory biography is one that is fully documented, one in which a reference—citing chapter and verse—is given to substantiate every fact set forth. Only such biographical studies will be considered in the remainder of this chapter.

II

The student who seeks information concerning the life of an author must look to one or more of five kinds of evidence: (1) data contained in official records; (2) information in records of a semi-official nature; (3) statements to be found in the writings of persons acquainted with the subject; (4) material derived from the subject's own writings; and (5) what may—for want of a better term—be called plastic evidence.

*   *   *

We have a good deal of information about the life of Chaucer. The fact that the poet was connected with the court, that he was ransomed, given pensions, appointed to posts involving fees or salary, even involved in what sounds like—though it may not have been—an unsavory lawsuit: all these things led to frequent occurrences of Chaucer's name in public records which can still be read. All that we know of Chaucer's life we owe to the fact that he was a courtier, nothing—beyond what can be learned from his own writings—to the fact that he was a great poet. And thus it is that we know nothing at all, aside from a dubious name, of Chaucer's gifted contemporary who produced *Piers Plowman*; we do not even know whether "William Langland" was one man or more than one. In earlier times, circumstances involving the receipt or expenditure of money were generally noted, and the record may exist even now; but the writing of a poem or the performing of a play is likely to have gone unrecorded.

It is not surprising, then, that we know no more about Shakspere—despite the fact that he lived two centuries closer to our own times—than we know about Chaucer.[2] If one looks into the evidence for

---

[2] Much of our knowledge of Shakspere's life results from the fact that he, like Chaucer, was connected with the court; there is a difference, however, in that Shakspere's connection with the court was the consequence of his being a writer, or actor.

our knowledge of the events of Shakspere's life, he will find that it
exists in records such as these: various parish registers (for dates of
christenings,[3] marriages, and burials); records of the College of
Arms; inventories, wills, tax-lists, and other records of property;
licenses to carry on the profession of acting; accounts containing
allowance of payment for liveries; and records in various provincial
towns of payments to the company of which Shakspere was a member, for performances given when the actors were on tour.[4] With all
these records of one kind and another dealing with the life of
Shakspere, it may seem that we have abundant knowledge; but such
an impression is erroneous. We do not know where or how Shakspere
was educated, where he lived in London (except that at some time
he lived in St. Helen's parish, Bishopsgate; at another time in the
Bankside, Surrey; and in 1604 at the corner of Silver and Monkwell
streets [3]); or many other things that would help us to know Shakspere, the man, as well as we can know Shakspere, the dramatist and
poet.

If the records concerning Shakspere are scanty and often difficult
to interpret,[4] those dealing with the lives of his contemporaries are
even fewer and frequently more puzzling. For Thomas Nashe we
have a record of a christening in November, 1567 (the day of the
month is not given), and certain college records; [5] aside from the
information contained in these, we know of Nashe only what he tells
us himself in his works and what other people—such as Gabriel
Harvey—wrote about him. Concerning Christopher Marlowe there
is a good deal of material available in various records; [6] many of
these references result from Marlowe's difficulties with the authori-

---

[3] It may be worth noting here that the early records give dates of christenings,
seldom if ever of births. Many scholars have assumed that christening customarily
took place three days after birth, but Sir Edmund Chambers (*William Shakespeare,*
II, 2) casts doubt on this tradition. In view of the belief that baptism was essential
to salvation, and in view, too, of the high rate of infant mortality, we may fairly
assume that parents would take pains to have children baptized as soon after birth
as was convenient; but it seems likely that baptism may have occurred on the
fourth or even a later day as often as on the third. We may assume, too, that a
sickly child who seemed unlikely to survive would have been christened before the
third day, probably within a few hours or even minutes after birth, as in the classic
example of Tristram Shandy.
[4] It should be noted that these last records do not give the names of the actors;
hence we can not be sure that Shakspere was in Oxford on 9 October 1605 just
because the King's Men were given ten shillings for performing there on that day.

ties, few if any are consequent upon his having been a poet and dramatist. What we know of Robert Greene's life—aside from the fact that he produced certain literary works—could be put in three or four sentences.

It is true that many records exist that have not been studied, and from these there may in the future be derived much significant information. Even those that have been published or calendared [5] may contain information that has been overlooked. The records by means of which Professor J. Leslie Hotson cleared up the strange and conflicting notions of the circumstances of Marlowe's death [7] had been available to students for more than three centuries; only the fact that Professor Hotson had a "hunch" when he ran across the name "Ingram Frizer" in a document that had nothing whatever to do with Marlowe—and knew how to follow up his "hunch"—made the discovery possible.

The largest and most important collection of official documents is that contained in the Public Record Office. A guide to these documents exists [8] and is exceedingly valuable; but those who have worked with English records, either in the Public Record Office or in other repositories, are generally agreed that no matter how well equipped one may be, with knowledge of languages, handwriting, English history and government, and all that can be learned from books, one must still learn to use the records by using them—nothing will take the place of such apprenticeship.

In citing official records for purposes of biography one should be on fairly safe ground, though sometimes, because of carelessness or for some other reason, mistakes do occur. The records of Shakspere's marriage, one document giving the bride's name as Anne Hathwey of Stratford and another as Anne Whateley of Temple Grafton, offer a case in point; [9] and the mystery concerning the death of Marlowe remained a mystery for so long a time because the vicar of the Church of St. Nicholas, Deptford, erred in recording the name of Marlowe's slayer as "ffrancis [instead of Ingram] ffrezer".[10]

Let us consider now some pieces of biographical research based

[5] A calendar is "A chronological register of documents with a brief summary of the contents of each, made to serve as an index to the documents of a period." (*Webster's New International Dictionary*, *s.v.* "Calendar" 4a.) For England, the most important calendars are those published by the Historical Manuscripts Commission.

upon official records. Professor A. C. Baugh in 1932 printed a calendar of legal documents [11] pertaining to Thomas Chaucer, thought to be the son of the poet, and brought out in the next year an article on Thomas Chaucer.[12] The latter article is supplemented by a note, likewise based on legal and ecclesiastical records.[13] The same sort of evidence is used in articles that throw new light on Sir Thomas Malory,[14] Sir Thomas More,[15] and the Earl of Surrey.[16] Official documents also form the basis for articles on Spenser,[17] Marlowe,[18] and Emerson.[19] A good deal of information concerning the actors of the first part of the seventeenth century has been gleaned from the registers of the churches of St. Giles Cripplegate [20] and St. Botolph Aldgate.[21] Legal records provide new facts about Andrew Marvell [22] and De Quincey.[23]

*   *   *

In addition to such records of church and state as we have been considering, there are certain documents that might be called "semi-official". They are not public records in the same sense that a parish register and the *Acts of the Privy Council* are, but they are not to be placed in the same category with ordinary letters and personal diaries. The household diary or account book of a family [24] would be a document of semi-official nature, as would the minutes of a society—or a history of the society based on such minutes.[25] Henslowe's *Diary* [26] would also be a document of this class; the information contained in it has been of inestimable value in dating the plays of the period covered by it.[27] Mistakes do occur in these documents, but most of them are of such nature that they can be, and have been, corrected. Anonymous items, such as advertisements, in periodicals might be placed in the same category.[28] The unofficial documents do not, of course, have quite the same credibility as that inherent in the more formal public records. There is even more opportunity for error than is to be attributed to the human fallibility of parish priests and clerks of court. A book is announced as "This day published"; but circumstances unforeseen may delay the actual appearance for days or weeks.[6] Notice is given that a celebrated actress will that night perform in her favorite role; but illness or some other

[6] Moreover, once the book was published, the same "This day published" heading was often used for weeks to come.

circumstance makes it impossible for her to appear, and an understudy takes her place. Nevertheless, the quasi-official nature of this class of documents—the fact that mistakes in accounts may be caught by a steward or auditor, that errors of the secretary may be corrected at the reading of the minutes, and that false statements in a periodical are likely to be the subject of an explanation or apology in a subsequent issue—gives such records more reliability than can be granted to ordinary diaries and letters, which are likely to be colored by the prejudice or the ignorance of the writer.

* * *

Thus we come to the third kind of source of biographical material: what other people have to say about the subject. In using material of this sort we must, as has just been suggested, be on guard against two possibilities: (1) the information may be wrong because the writer was ignorant of the truth and, though he wrote in good faith, was mistaken in his facts; and (2) the writer may make a misstatement with the intention to deceive. With respect to the first of these possibilities, the student must determine as best he can, from his knowledge of the circumstances of the writer's life, whether the writer was likely to know the truth; with respect to the second, it must be determined, if possible, what motive he may have had for an attempt to deceive. Thus in the matter of Kyd's famous letter to Sir John Puckering [29] it may be taken as certain that Kyd knew whether the heretical documents referred to were in his handwriting or not, and as probable, at least, that he knew whether, if not in his hand, they were in Marlowe's. But Kyd was trying desperately to extricate himself from a dangerous situation; as Professor Bakeless puts it:

If we could be quite sure that Kydd was not trying to lie his way out of a predicament, we might regard these notes as genuine examples of Marlowe's own handwriting. But Kydd is so evidently in an agony of anxiety to save himself that his statements are almost worthless. He is telling a good deal of the truth but he is also obviously lying whenever he thinks it likely to be useful.[30]

Perhaps it is going a bit too far to say that Kyd is "obviously lying"; but the fact that, if guilty, he had so much reason to lie, and may have done so, invalidates his evidence.

There has been a good deal of loose thinking, of credulous acceptance of what has been said, about writers in whom we are interested,
especially, I think, those of the Elizabethan period. The older writers
exist for us almost wholly in their works; we are content to leave
them—except for Chaucer—disembodied spirits. We are not likely
to spend much time in speculating on the name or the complexion
of the author of *Beowulf,* or in seeking to invest the life of Cædmon
with more details than Bede gives. Although more information about
such men would be interesting and valuable, we accept uncom-
plainingly the fact that such information is apparently not to be had.
But the Elizabethan age is so vivid, its writers are so colorful, that
we try to know them better than we can; there is a strong tendency
to accept as true every hearsay detail that conforms with the concept of these men that we have gained from their works and from
the little that we do know about them, and to reject whatever does
violence to that concept. Robert Greene provides a good example of
this tendency. Gabriel Harvey's account of the circumstances of
Greene's death [31] has been universally accepted because it fits so well
the popular idea of Greene as a profligate wastrel upon whom poetic
justice was finally visited. Nashe's denial of that account [32] has been
discredited or ignored.

I have already observed that what is known of Greene's life could
be set forth in few words. Grosart quoted Professor J. M. Brown
as saying: "Little is known of Greene's life, and that little we know
only through his enemies and his own too candid confessions. . . ." [33]
Whereupon Grosart proceeded to add enough to what Storojenko
had already written to make something like a hundred pages of
alleged biography!

Of the details in that biography derived from Greene's "own too
candid confessions" we must speak later; let us consider here the
contributions of Greene's enemies—and friends. A single issue will
illustrate the point involved. What Henry Chettle said of Greene has
seldom been questioned. More than forty years ago Churton Collins
wrote: "There is no reason to doubt the truth of what Chettle says,
for, though he was a poor man, he had the reputation of being both
respectable and honest." [34] Twenty years later Professor G. B. Harrison wrote of Chettle as one "who was likely to know the truth
about Greene's affairs, . . ." [35] Henslowe's *Diary* furnishes ample

evidence [36] of Chettle's poverty; but proof of either respectability or honesty—or knowledge of Greene's affairs—is lacking. Harold Jenkins sums up our knowledge of Chettle thus:

> Present-day knowledge of Chettle's life and career is extraordinarily scant for a man so prolific in writing and so closely in touch with most of the important literary personages of his day. He is a stationer's apprentice in London, and passes on to become a printer; he associates with literary men of the town, and gradually abandons the printing for the writing art. He is good-natured and placable, the respected friend of Greene [there is no evidence, aside from Chettle's own assertion, that he had any acquaintance with Greene] and Nashe, of Munday and Dekker. He suddenly comes clearly before us in the records of Henslowe, always miserably poor, struggling against poverty, turning his hand to any sort of hackwork for any meagre reward, resorting to various devices to obtain the most insignificant sums of money, yet repeatedly in trouble and sometimes in prison for debt.[37]

Nevertheless, Mr. Jenkins elsewhere asserts that Chettle's "honesty is not to be called into question . . .".[38]

Certainly it cannot be proved—in the light of present evidence—that Chettle lied when he said of the *Groatsworth of Wit* that *"it was all* Greenes"; [39] but it must be admitted that he may have lied or have been mistaken in his assertion, and in view of that possibility the acceptance of the *Groatsworth* as being everything that Chettle alleges it to be is not sound scholarship. Chettle may have known all about Greene's affairs—and hence have known that Greene wrote the *Groatsworth*—but there is no proof, or even good evidence, that he did. Chettle may have told the truth; but in view of a possible motive for misrepresentation—the desire to make the *Groatsworth* more salable by completing it himself—it is not safe to assume that he did. Consequently the biographical details contained in the *Groatsworth* cannot be accepted as facts in Greene's life unless they are confirmed by something more than Chettle's testimony.

Let us consider now some biographical researches in which information is derived from the writings of persons other than the subject. Professor Tatlock found in several references a number of details concerning an eleventh-century nun, whose own writings have disappeared.[40] Letters form the basis of articles on Swift [41] and

Pope; [42] and letters, in one case, and reminiscences, in the other, provide the basis for articles on Hawthorne [43] and Whitman.[44]

*   *   *

The fourth kind of evidence for biographical research is that supplied by the subject himself. It may be generally assumed that an author knows the truth about the details of his own life; [7] but one may, for one reason or another, indulge in more or less flagrant misrepresentations, as Pope apparently did when he said that he wrote his *Pastorals* at the age of sixteen.[45] Morever, there is always a danger of mistaking for autobiography—especially in works of fiction—that which is not autobiography at all. Even in works allegedly or admittedly autobiographical, it is not safe to assume the truth of every detail. No one could read *Look Homeward, Angel,* by Thomas Wolfe, without realizing that the autobiographical element in that book is very pronounced; but no modern reader would be likely to make the mistake of assuming that every detail in the hero's experience must have had its counterpart in the life of the author. We give the writer credit for having the capacity to imagine details—or borrow them from the experience of someone else—and the power to present those details so realistically that it seems as if they must have been a part of his own life.

The older scholars seem hardly to have been aware of the danger just mentioned. Grosart reveals his attitude in these words: "Storojenko says he has extracted the autobiographical matter of the Works [of Greene]. A quick-eyed reader will easily treble, at least, such autobiographical matter, and often in unlikely places." [46] Every detail in Greene's so-called "repentance pamphlets" is accepted by Grosart—and by many others [8]—as a fact in Greene's life; these "facts" are used to confirm apparently related "facts" in other works, and those to confirm still others in a long chain of sophistical reasoning. Thus Grosart accepts Storojenko's assumption that Greene's wife came from Lincolnshire and was named Dorothy,[47] and assumes

---

[7] However, one writing from memory in old age might easily be mistaken about some of the events of his youth.

[8] I have set forth elsewhere ("Robert Greene and His 'Editors'", *PMLA*, XLVIII (1933), 392–417) reasons for being skeptical of these details; here let it suffice to say that to write in the first person is the most obvious method of achieving realism.

further that her marriage to Greene is not likely to have taken place in London; [48] when, as a matter of fact, there is no valid evidence that Greene was ever married.

It is not, however, professedly or allegedly autobiographical works alone that may convey information about the life of the writer. A man may write a book in which he apparently or obviously identifies himself with one of the characters in that book. If, then, that character in the course of the book makes a trip to Paris, it may be argued—though not without confirmatory evidence—that the author himself must have made such a trip. But the same author may, in a book which is in no sense autobiographical, reveal by describing Paris in terms that could not have been derived from a guide book or from any source other than personal experience, that he had been in Paris.[9] If there were in the novel *Of Human Bondage* no character identified with the author, we should still know that Somerset Maugham must have sojourned in Paris and in Germany.

Let us turn now to some examples of biographical research in which the evidence is drawn from the subject's own writings. Allusions to ecclesiastical music—as well as to the music of the court and the hunt—in the *Pearl* and *Purity* suggest that the author of those poems had been trained in a choristers' school.[49] Differences in the apparent knowledge of law displayed in the three texts of *Piers Plowman* suggest that the author studied law between the writing of the A-text and that of the B-text, or, if there was more than one author involved, that the author of the C-text knew more law than the author of the B-text, and the latter more than the author of the A-text.[50] Skelton's own words are used to support the hypothesis that there was a reconciliation between Skelton and Wolsey before the composing of the poet's last works.[51] A reference to Southampton in one of Heywood's poems suggests that the Earl had lent his name to a company of players, and that the dramatist had at some time been a member of that company.[52] Two articles on Milton make use of the poet's own works: a letter adds to our knowledge of Milton, the public servant,[53] and passages in his published writings—especially the *History of Britain*—are interpreted as

[9] One must, of course, be sure of his ground here; Defoe achieved, in *Captain Singleton,* remarkably accurate descriptions of the interior of Africa, without ever having visited that continent.

indicating that Milton's failure to produce much poetry between
1640 and 1658 was due rather to a disinclination for poetic composition during those years than to lack of time.[54]

Charlotte Brontë's juvenile writings have very generally been
ignored by students, but a good deal can be learned from them that
helps in understanding the author's character.[55] Similarly, light is
thrown upon the young Emerson by a poem which the poet and
essayist wrote during his freshman year at Harvard.[56] It has long
been supposed that Longfellow met Wordsworth on one of his trips
to Europe; but previously unpublished extracts from Longfellow's
Journal make it appear doubtful that such a meeting ever took
place.[57] By the correcting of errors in the dating of a score of letters
written by Browning to Miss Isabella Blagden a good bit is added
to our knowledge of Browning's life between 1858 and 1868.[58]

Other articles using this kind of material deal with the English
writers John Donne,[59] Charles Dickens,[60] Robert Browning,[61] and
Oscar Wilde;[62] and the Americans Washington Irving,[63] Margaret
Fuller,[64] Herman Melville,[65] Samuel Clemens,[66] Bret Harte,[67] H. C.
Bunner,[68] Stephen Crane,[69] and Robert Frost.[70]

A study may be devoted to the minimizing or negativing of such
evidence as we have been considering. Thus an interpretation of
Sidney's sonnets as conventional would make the autobiographical
elements in *Astrophel and Stella* of doubtful significance.[71]

*   *   *

We come now to the fifth and last kind of biographical evidence—
the kind that I have called plastic evidence. If we know that an
author spent a part of his formative years in a certain environment—
a still-existent house, or a college at Oxford or Cambridge—to
achieve some familiarity with that environment will certainly add to
our capacity for understanding the author. To know what books an
author read is an obvious essential to the understanding of him;
to know the copies that he used—their format and their bindings—
adds something more. Thus the suggestion that the *Ayenbite of Inwit*
is not a translation of Cottonian MS Cleopatra Av, but of another
version derived from that and owned by the author of the *Ayenbite*,
will add—if the hypothesis can be confirmed—to our knowledge of
Dan Michel of Northgate; it will stamp him as the owner of a book,

or manuscript, in a time when such a distinction was unusual.[72] Milieu might be thought of as the sum total of plastic evidence; a recent article studied the relationship between Samuel Rogers and his environment.[73]

III

We have been considering articles wholly—or almost wholly— based upon one kind of evidence. It is time now to consider how two or more kinds may be combined to furnish biographical information. Letters and petitions appealing to Queen Elizabeth for rewards for literary labors, and official documents showing that such appeals generally went unheeded, bring out graphically the Queen's nigardliness.[74] Court records and letters are brought together to provide information about Arthur Gorges, information which throws some light upon Spenser and Ralegh, whose friend Gorges was.[75] Similarly, public records and letters provide the basis for an article of interest to students of Pope.[76] Official records of H.M.S. *Chichester,* together with a private journal kept by one of the ship's officers, help us to determine how much of Smollett's *Roderick Random* is genuine autobiography.[77] Official documents and letters are combined in an article on the dates of the birth and the death of Keats.[78] Records also are used in an article on Herman Melville [79] and one involving Lowell and Emerson.[80]

Two studies consider information drawn from public records along with material contained in the subject's own writings: We may learn something about Thomas Bancroft by studying what he wrote, in conjunction with certain records, especially wills.[81] And a study of newspaper notices and Emerson's engagement book makes it possible to compile a list of the dates, places, and subjects of Emerson's lectures in England and Scotland during the tour of 1847–48.[82]

The larger part of our biographical studies, however, combine what others have said or written, with material drawn from the subject's own writings. Thus the writings of Spenser and of Sidney have been examined in an attempt to discover whether or not the two Elizabethans were intimate friends.[83] Communications between Dryden and his publisher, Tonson, make it possible to estimate Dryden's share of the profits from the publication of his translation of the *Æneid.*[84] Letters form the basis for two articles in Congreve.[85]

Two studies concerning Edmund Burke are based on a combination of Burke's own testimony and that of others. In the first of these, a notebook kept jointly by Burke and his friend William Burke, together with some other material, supplies details in a decade of Burke's life about which little or nothing had previously been known.[86] In the other, information from Burke and others is brought together to determine the extent of Burke's contribution to the *Annual Register*.[87] In the first of two articles on Burns, the Burns–Dunlop estrangement is explained by a study of the letters exchanged between the poet and his friend; [88] in the other, the testimony of various people concerning Mary Campbell is compared with Burns's portrait of Highland Mary to bring out the fact that the girl was very different from the poet's conception of her.[89] Letters exchanged between Byron and Coleridge add to our knowledge of both writers.[90] New light is thrown on Keats by a study of references—his own and those of others—to his interest in world affairs.[91] The relations between Charlotte Brontë and George Henry Lewes are revealed in their letters.[92] Other articles making use of this kind of evidence deal with Robert Mannyng of Brunne,[93] Thomas Percy,[94] and Shelley and Southey.[95]

Several studies in this group—all of them based on letters or journals or both—deal with American writers. References in Washington Irving's journal and in Motley's *Correspondence* prove that Irving and Tieck were acquainted.[96] Two studies—presenting conflicting views of the relationship between Hawthorne and Margaret Fuller—are based largely on the writings of the two persons involved; [97] a study of the relationship of Miss Fuller with Emerson depends chiefly upon the former's letters and the latter's *Journal*.[98] Letters provide the material for a discussion of Hawthorne as a critic of poetry [99] and for a study of the friendship between Whittier and Hayne.[100]

*   *   *

Some articles make use of evidence of three kinds. Thus an article on John Cleveland utilizes public records, allusions that Cleveland makes in his own works, and material contained in satiric attacks on him.[101] Similar combinations of material provide studies on George Wither,[102] William Congreve,[103] and Aphra Behn.[104] An article on the life of Smollett is based on the same kinds of evidence,[105] as is one on the publication of Lord Chesterfield's *Letters to His Son.*[106] Other studies making use of more than two kinds of evidence deal with Thomas Morton of Merry Mount,[107] Byron,[108] and Walt Whitman.[109] In an article on Sterne, evidence furnished by Sterne himself and that provided by others is combined with plastic evidence—in this instance bibliographical evidence—to prove that the first edition of *Tristram Shandy* was printed at York by Mrs. Ann Ward.[110]

Despite the difficulty a biographer encounters in trying to collect a sufficient body of established facts to provide material for a complete portrait of his subject, there are numerous biographies in which interpretation and speculation are minimized and always differentiated from fact. Among such biographies of recent years may be mentioned studies of the English writers Spenser,[111] Marlowe,[112] Shakspere,[113] Pepys,[114] Pope,[115] Johnson,[116] Richardson,[117] Gibbon,[118] Sheridan,[119] Shelley,[120] Keats,[121] and Ruskin; [122] and the Americans Jonathan Edwards,[123] Emerson,[124] Bronson Alcott,[125] Hawthorne,[126] Longfellow,[127] Griswold,[128] Thoreau,[129] Emily Dickinson,[130] "Mark Twain",[131] Edward Eggleston,[132] and Lafcadio Hearn.[133] And, of course, there is Carl Sandburg's great work on Lincoln.[134]

IV

By way of recapitulation let it be said that public records, where they exist, are as good evidence in problems of biography as can be had. Thus we have no doubt that Christopher Marlowe was born in Canterbury and William Shakspere in Stratford-on-Avon in 1564, or that Shakspere was married in 1582; but the fact that one record names Shakspere's wife as Anne Whateley and another as Anne Hathwey shows that public records are not infallible. Since Norwich is mentioned by the author himself as the birthplace of Robert Greene, Collins considered [135] that the entry referring to a christening there in 1558 may be taken as establishing the author's birthyear; [10] but the conclusion is only probable, not certain. Robert Greene, unlike Christopher Marlowe, was a common name.

[10] In the entry the infant is spoken of as Robert Greene, the son of Robert Greene, and Collins has an ingenious argument for determining whether the father was Robert Greene the saddler or Robert Greene the innkeeper; but his argument rests upon an assumption which cannot safely be made.

In using public records one must learn to know—if he is to make the most of them—their possibilities. Professor Hotson, when he was balked by finding nothing about Ingram Frezer in the records of Criminal Inquests, or the Queen's Bench Controlment Roll, or the records of the South-Eastern Circuit, still had another string to his bow: he looked for the story of Marlowe's murder in the Patent Rolls of the Chancery, and found it there.[136]

In using the evidence of what others have said about one's subject, one must make sure that the person making any statement (1) was in a position to know the truth, and (2) was certainly telling the truth; if these two things cannot be established, the statement represents at most a probability. The fact that two witnesses agree on a detail does not make it certain, or necessarily more probable; the two may be equally ignorant of the truth, or they may have the same, or an equally pronounced, bias.

Even what a subject says about himself must be treated with care. An individual may actually not know the truth about himself. I have a good deal of doubt that Poe went about the writing of *The Raven* just as he said he did, but I am not at all sure that he was guilty of any conscious misrepresentation when he wrote *The Philosophy of Composition.* Or one may exaggerate, perhaps with intent to deceive, as Pope seems to have done when boasting of his precocity, or jestingly, as perhaps Shaw did when he compared himself with Shakspere, to Shakspere's disadvantage.

It is especially dangerous to put too much stock in apparently or avowedly autobiographical material contained in works of fiction. Critics have said [137] that the autobiographical details in Greene's *Repentance* are so vivid and so realistic that they must be true; that is to say that fiction cannot be so written as to seem like fact. To argue that the Dark Lady of Shakespere's *Sonnets* must have existed in the flesh is to deny Shakspere the power to imagine an emotion and then express it convincingly. One might almost as well say that Shakspere must have had a murdered father and an incestuous mother because Hamlet's emotion seems so genuine.

Plastic evidence is, like bibliographical evidence, perfectly valid if rightly used. It must not be assumed that King's College Chapel at Cambridge, or Magdalen Tower at Oxford, would have had the same effect on an English boy arriving to begin his university studies that it has on one of us coming fresh from twentieth-century America. But if we can come to know that English boy well enough, we may be able to appreciate the effect on him of his Oxford or Cambridge environment, and familiarity with that environment will certainly deepen our understanding of the individual exposed to it.

One must, above all, in biographical studies learn not to force the evidence and then call the result a biographical fact. The biographer should be eternally dissatisfied with what he knows of his subject until he has learned all that there is to know—if such a time can be said ever to come. He should search the records until he has exhausted their possibilities; he should pore over the books written by his subject—and every other scrap of writing that can be attributed to him—until he knows the subject matter almost by heart; he should master the background—literary, philosophical, political, social, economic, and religious—of his subject's period. But let him keep aware at all times of the sharp line of demarcation between that which is established fact, and that which is merely probable, or possible. And when the time comes to write, let him present facts alone as facts, and everything else as probability, or possibility.

Or, if one prefers, let him write fiction. Then he may endow his subject with a wife named Elizabeth or one named Doll, or with no wife at all; with children legitimate or illegitimate; with a house in the country or one in town. So long as he keeps his material true to the psychology of the subject and the atmosphere of the period, and presents it in effective prose, the result will be good—as fiction. It will not be biography.

꒳꒳

CHAPTER THREE

PROBLEMS OF AUTHENTICITY
AND ATTRIBUTION

THERE are those who believe everything they see in print; and an even larger number of persons are but little less credulous. Hence the fourth- or fifth-century *Dares Phrygius* and *Dictys Cretensis* were for centuries accepted as genuine eyewitness accounts of the Trojan war because they contained details that purportedly could have been known only to contemporaries of Helen and Paris and the rest. "How", people said—and among them were some who should have known better—"could any one have known, except through personal acquaintance, that Hector had a squint, or Helen a mole on her right cheek?" What they did not take into consideration are the facts that such details are not known to be true, and, if true, might have been learned in some way other than by personal acquaintance.

It is not ignorant folk alone who are credulous. M. Chasles, a French mathematician of international reputation, paid 140,000 francs to an adventurer named Vrain-Lucas for hundreds of letters from various worthy personages. They bore such signatures as those of Lazarus, Vercingetorix, Cleopatra, and St. Mary Magdalene; but they were all written in modern French on nineteenth-century note paper. Literary men as well as mathematicians may be taken in by the forger. *Trelawney* was accepted as genuine by Scott and Macaulay; and, though the Reverend Mr. Hawker admitted in 1832 that he was the author, the ballad was later printed by J. H. Dixon in *Ancient Poems and Ballads.*[1] Most eighteenth-century collectors succumbed to the temptation to "improve"—without acknowledgement

—the ballads that they printed, thus drawing down upon their heads the vitriolic wrath of Joseph Ritson.[2]

Though problems of authenticity are not altogether the same as those of attribution, the two overlap to such an extent that it will be most convenient to deal with them together. We must keep in mind, however, the fact that a problem of attribution is solved if we can answer the question "Who wrote this work?" But authenticity demands an affirmative answer to three questions: "Was this work written by the person who is purported to have written it? Was it written at the time alleged to be the date of composition? Was it written under the circumstances and for the purpose alleged?"

I

The evidence upon which we must rely in attempting to solve problems of authenticity and attribution may be classified as external, internal, and bibliographical. We could hardly ask for better evidence of a man's authorship of a work than to have a copy of the work in the man's own handwriting; and yet, strictly speaking, such bibliographical evidence proves only that our author wrote the work out in his own hand—not that he was the original composer of the piece. Thus if we had a copy in Chaucer's handwriting of the *Tale of Gamelyn,* the reasons for rejecting that poem from the Chaucer canon would still exist; and we could say only that our manuscript proves— what has already been suspected [3]—that Chaucer had made a copy of an older work, presumably with a view to rewriting it for inclusion among *The Canterbury Tales.*

William Henry Ireland [1] fell afoul of the handwriting test. His imitations of an Elizabethan hand were convincing enough to deceive

[1] William Henry Ireland (1777–1835) forged a great variety of Shaksperean documents—leases, contracts, a profession of faith, and a letter to Anne Hathaway, with an accompanying lock of hair. Many people were deceived; Boswell knelt in rapture and kissed the alleged relics. Becoming more ambitious, Ireland brought forth a Shaksperean play—*Vortigern*—and succeeded in having it produced at Drury Lane with Kemble in the leading role. But Malone had already published evidence that the documents were all forgeries; and, though many people continued to believe young Ireland's protestations, the audience at the Drury Lane performance seems to have been pretty sure that Shakspere had had nothing to do with *Vortigern.* Eventually Ireland published a confession of his guilt. The whole story is well told in John Mair's *The Fourth Forger* (New York: Macmillan, 1939). See also William T. Hastings, " 'The Fourth Forger.' A Supplemental Minority Report," *Shakespeare Association Bulletin,* XIV (1939), 248–51.

the untrained and prejudiced eyes of his father; they were good
enough to impose upon men like James Boswell, Henry Pye (the
Poet Laureate), and the Prince of Wales. But even in the eighteenth
century there were scholars who recognized them for what they were,
and they would not for an instant deceive a modern handwriting
expert. If an inscription consists of only a word or two, there may
be some difficulty in determining its genuineness; [2] but modern experts, with their microscopes, their cameras, their measuring instruments, and all the rest of their scientific equipment, would make
short work of a forgery of any length.

The ink used—or the substitute for ink—may also serve to trap the
unwary forger. As is well known, ordinary ink turns brown with age;
hence one cannot very well execute an allegedly old inscription with
modern ink. Ireland used a combination of marbling dyes; [3] this gave
the proper appearance but would not have withstood analysis.
Collier [4] tried to get around the difficulty by using brown water color
paint, but his stratagem was easily discovered. The appearance of the
ink enters into the controversy between Dr. Greg and Dr. Tannenbaum over the "T. Goodal" inscription in the manuscript of *The*

[2] The genuineness of "T. Goodal" in *Sir Thomas More* was, I believe, still in
dispute between Dr. Greg and Dr. Tannenbaum at the time of the latter's death;
that there should be such a disagreement between experts is as disconcerting to other
scholars as a disagreement among physicians is to their patient.

[3] Colors used by bookbinders in decorating the edges of books or in producing
marbled paper for lining papers.

[4] John Payne Collier (1789–1883) was a brilliant and learned scholar. His early
work is sound; but in 1852 he published *Notes and Emendations in the Text of
Shakespeare,* based on corrections made in a copy of the Second Folio by someone
whom Collier called the "Old Corrector". After some controversy, the entries in the
Folio were shown to be spurious; but Collier, to the day of his death, denied
responsibility for them. One point of significance is the fact that Collier admitted
making certain pencil marks in the Folio, tracing, he said, the inscriptions to see
how the letters were made; it was found, however, on microscopic examination,
that the pencil marks lay beneath, not above, the ink marks. The discovery of other
forgeries attributable to Collier in documents at Dulwich College leaves little doubt
that Collier himself was the "Old Corrector". It is exceedingly difficult to understand
why a mature scholar, with an established reputation, should have stooped to
forgery; the best explanation seems to be that he was so anxious to have certain
readings—many of which had been suggested by earlier scholars—universally
accepted, that he succumbed to the temptation of providing confirmatory evidence.
An account of the affair is given in C. M. Ingleby, *Complete View of the Shakespeare Controversy* (London: Nattali, 1861). See also Hazelton Spencer, "The Forger
at Work: A New Case Against Collier", *PQ,* VI (1927), 32–38; and William Ringler,
"Another Collier Forgery", [London] *Times Lit. Sup.,* October 29, 1938, pp. 693–94.

Booke of Sir Thomas More [4]; the fact that a controversy arose is an indication that evidence of ink, handwriting, and condition of paper —all of which factors are involved—is not always as clear as we might wish to have it.

The paper of which a book or manuscript is composed may provide confirmatory evidence that a work is authentic or positive evidence that it is not. Ireland executed his forgeries upon genuine paper of the period to which the documents were supposed to belong; thus his productions—so far as the paper is concerned—were authentic, and proofs of fraud had to be sought in other directions. It was largely by means of the watermarks in the paper that Dr. Greg was able to show that three Shakspere quartos dated 1600 and two dated 1608 were actually printed in 1619.[5] And when Messrs. Carter and Pollard [5] found that ten pamphlets dated between 1842 and 1858 were printed on paper containing esparto, and thirteen pamphlets dated between 1842 and 1873 were printed on chemical wood paper, they had proof of misdating, since esparto paper was first used in England in 1862, and chemical wood paper was not used for books until after 1873.[6]

It is true, of course, that the paper test cannot always be applied. We have seen in the Ireland case that the paper may be genuine when the work is not; the converse is also true. Most of the manuscripts of Chaucer's *Canterbury Tales* are of the fifteenth or sixteenth century; none can be dated earlier than 1400. Thus, so far as the paper is concerned, the tales now ascribed to Chaucer are no better authenticated than those which have been rejected from the canon.

The type with which a book is printed may furnish evidence bearing on the authenticity of a work. We may be able to determine when a particular font of type was designed and first cast; if a book

---

[5] Some fifty years ago, there began to appear, at one time and another, in the market, editions—seventy or more of them—of various works by Victorian authors; they were of interest to collectors because they were ostensibly earlier than the recognized first editions, and hence they commanded a good price, although they were not particularly rare. It was noticeable that they appeared in what philatelists call "mint" condition; moreover, none of them contained a signature or inscription, though it might have been expected that, if they were what they purported to be, many of them would have been used as presentation copies. The fraud was exposed by John Carter and Graham Pollard in *An Enquiry into the Nature of Certain 19th Century Pamphlets.* See also Roland Baughman, "Some Forged Victorian Rarities", *Huntington Library Bulletin,* IX (April, 1936), 91–117.

printed with that type bears an earlier date, the date must be wrong. In studying the typography of the nineteenth-century pamphlets with which they were concerned, Messrs. Carter and Pollard picked out two letters—in this instance *f* and *j*—which had distinctive characteristics; thus they could determine almost at a glance whether or not a given book was printed with the font in question.[7]

*   *   *

Bibliographical evidence may be negative as well as positive. When one professes to be in possession of some lost or hitherto unknown document, and offers to the world a copy of the document, the world at once insists on seeing the original; failure to produce the document is generally interpreted as inability to produce it, and the whole thing is likely to be dismissed as a fraud. When Macpherson [6] published his English translation of ancient Scottish poetry, every one wanted to see the original manuscript. Macpherson refused to make his manuscript available for inspection; and it was this refusal, more than anything else, that led to suspicions that the *Works of Ossian* were not what they purported to be.

II

When the possibilities of bibliographical evidence have been exhausted, we may look to see what internal evidence of authorship or authenticity the work provides. A work may contain a statement by the author testifying to its genuineness. Such, for example, is Shakspere's reference [7] to *Venus and Adonis* as the "first heir of my invention"; and many like instances might be mentioned. In the absence of any suspicious circumstances that would lead one to doubt the author's words, such evidence is valid, it being assumed, of course, that the style, subject matter, and other characteristics are not incompatible with the alleged authorship.

[6] James Macpherson (1736–1796) published in 1760 *Fragments of Ancient Poetry Collected in the Highlands of Scotland*. This was followed by *Fingal* (1761), *Temora* (1763), and a collected edition, *The Works of Ossian* (1765). Dr. Johnson and others were suspicious of the works and a controversy arose. The exact truth will perhaps never be known. It is now generally believed that Macpherson did have Gaelic, or Erse, originals upon which he built, but that much of his work represents creation rather than translation and is, to that extent, fraudulent. For a concise summary of the controversy, see *Encyclopædia Britannica*, 14th ed., *s.v.* "Scottish Literature".   [7] In the Dedicatory Epistle.

A special form of claim has sometimes annoyed readers. When Defoe asserted that the *Journal of the Plague Year* was written "by a Citizen who continued all the while in London", the real author having been about six years old at the time of the plague, he doubtless hoped that his pretense would promote the sale of the book; and those who bought the *Journal* in the belief that it represented the first-hand observations of a mature observer, had some reason to complain against the author. Likewise, those who were led to believe in Robinson Crusoe, and those who were deceived by Swift's elaborate devices for making Lemuel Gulliver convincing, may have had just cause for complaint.[8] But it is difficult to see how a modern reader, knowing the facts, can find such tricks anything but amusing.[9]

*   *   *

Literary style constitutes another kind of internal evidence, which may contribute to arguments about authenticity or authorship. The older scholars put great reliance—too much, doubtless—in their ability to distinguish one man's style from that of another. Tyrwhitt, mainly on subjective grounds, had by 1778 rejected most of the non-Chaucerian pieces that had previously been accepted as genuine. But, as Professor Crane wrote: "The days of dogmatic attributions grounded merely on a general impression of manner or personality are happily long past." [8] Tyrwhitt's intuitiveness gave Chaucer scholarship a good start; but the Chaucer canon was not truly established until the more scientific efforts of Wright, Morris, Skeat, Lounsbury, Furnivall, and other scholars had borne fruit.

It is perhaps true that some individuals have such a keen awareness to rhythms that they could recognize a literary style as infallibly as the musician possessed of "absolute pitch" can recognize a tone. Unfortunately, that conviction can not be conveyed to other people; and the student who, from the style of a work, makes up his mind as to its authorship, must seek other evidence if he wishes to make his argument convincing.

It is true that there are some writers whose style is so distinctive

---

[8] The ancient mariner who is said to have insisted that he knew Captain Gulliver well was probably a publicity-seeker rather than a victim of deception.

[9] For a violent reaction against all such practices, see H. M. Paull, *Literary Ethics*, pp. 153–59.

as to be almost unmistakable; Professor Balderston argues convincingly, mainly on the evidence of the style, that Dr. Johnson wrote the Dedication for Dr. Burney's *History of Music* and offers an explanation for the apparently deliberate concealment of Johnson's authorship of the piece.[9] Largely on the evidence of style and subject matter certain book reviews in Dodsley's *Annual Register* have been attributed to Edmund Burke;[10] another article assigns three contributions to the *New York Mirror* to Charles Dickens;[11] and a third claims for Walt Whitman three letters printed in the *National Era* in 1850.[12]

Certain enthusiasts, having already proved by tests of style—or something—that Bacon wrote the works of Shakspere, decided to apply their tests to the works of other Elizabethans. To their infinite joy, they discovered that Bacon was also responsible for the works of Lyly, Greene, Marlowe, Nashe, Spenser, and almost any one else you care to mention. Most of us would interpret their findings as proof that their tests of authorship, if they were tests at all, were tests of something else. Professor Manly once said—and he was an expert on cryptograms, ciphers, and all the other paraphernalia of which Baconians are so fond—that by the same tests that were used to prove that Bacon wrote Shakspere, he could demonstrate that Bacon wrote the works of Chaucer. But there are tests that do throw light on authorship.

Given sufficient material—several thousand lines of poetry or as many pages of prose—known to have been written by one person, it would be possible to apply tests that would prove conclusively whether or not another piece of some length could have been written by the same author.[10] It would not be enough, however, to prove that the author in question could have written the piece; for complete proof it would be necessary to apply the same tests to the work of all his contemporaries who might have produced such a work, and thus prove that no one else could have written it. The necessity for such extensive testing brings up a paramount difficulty. There is a subjective element in tests of imagery, of rhythm, of inflection, which makes it doubtful that one investigator could well make use of the results achieved by another. Thus if Jones were working on an

---

[10] A system of tests to be applied to prose is explained in Edith Rickert's *A Scientific Analysis of Prose Style* (Chicago: University of Chicago Press, 1927ᶜ).

analysis of the style of Dickens, and Smith were working on Thackeray, Jones could use some of Smith's results—counting the number of words in a sentence and of sentences to a paragraph, and so on— but some of the tests Jones would have to apply to Thackeray, and not to Thackeray alone, but to George Eliot, and Kingsley, and Reade, and all the rest.

*   *   *

Similarities in language between a doubtful work and the known works of an author may provide a basis for attribution. Inasmuch, however, as an author uses the language of his time, or of a literary tradition (such as Euphuism), or of a school (such as that of Spenser or of Donne) one must be careful not to mistake a common practice for an individual characteristic. Only when a form or construction, which is frequent in the works of our writer and in the suspected work, rarely or never appears in the works of his contemporaries, can we consider that we have any reliable evidence of authorship.

Fraudulent works, however, are often betrayed by their language. Constructions and forms which would not have been used by the historical Phalaris or Æsop provided part of the evidence by means of which Dr. Bentley proved that the *Epistles* and the *Fables* are not what they purport to be.[13] And Thomas Chatterton's [11] handling of Middle English was too crude to deceive any one who had even a slight knowledge of fifteenth-century language or literature.

*   *   *

Verse tests have been relied upon—perhaps too heavily—to determine the share of each collaborator in those Elizabethan plays which are the work of more than one author. When the application of such tests shows a positive and striking result—as when a pseudo-Chaucerian piece contains frequent occurrences of a rhyme that appears nowhere in Chaucer's known works—the test seems valid and is

[11] Thomas Chatterton (1752–1770), beginning at the age of twelve, wrote a great many imitations of fifteenth-century literature, most of which he pretended to be the work of one Thomas Rowley, an imaginary monk of the time of Edward IV. In addition to his pseudo-mediæval works, he produced a great variety of other pieces, brilliantly written in a dozen different veins, which publishers were eager to accept but for which they were little inclined to pay. Facing starvation, the boy committed suicide three months before his eighteenth birthday.

likely to be confirmed by other evidence. Other tests—the number of feminine rhymes, the proportion of run-on lines, and so on—are likely to provide less convincing results; [12] in using them it will be wise to keep in mind the possibility of "individual variation" in poetry as well as in prose.

Professor Jones found that Massinger used *of* and *to* at the end of lines of verse, whereas his contemporaries pretty consistently avoided that practice.[14] But, as Professor Jones observes, "Alone, such evidence can never be convincing; with other metrical tests, qualities of style, ideas, and methods of phrasing, the data of the *of* and *to* test may be found useful as corroborative proof." [15]

* * *

Peculiarities of an author's vocabulary may furnish a means of establishing an attribution. The presence of words found in the works of Tindale and not in those of his contemporaries, led to the suggestion that Tindale was responsible for the 1533 translation of the *Enchiridion* of Erasmus; [16] and the frequent appearance of the word *hath* in *An Apology for the Life of Mrs. Shamela Andrews* is a bit of evidence supporting the attribution of that work to Henry Fielding.[17]

Striking similarities of phrase in a doubtful work and in the work of a possible author may offer a suggestion as to the authorship.[18] Such evidence is usually combined with other signs of common origin; by itself it has merely corroborative value, since it is as likely that one author borrowed from another the phrases that struck his fancy as it is that an author repeated himself.

* * *

Peculiarities in spelling—when there is reason to think that they represent an idiosyncrasy of the author rather than the vagary of a compositor—may provide evidence for attribution. The suggestion that Munday rather than Spenser was the translator of the *Axiochus* was based partly upon spellings thought to be peculiar to Munday.[19] The ascription of the anonymous life of Milton to John Philips, based in part upon the spelling of *their* as *thir,* is objected to on various grounds, the spelling being considered not conclusive.[20]

[12] In such details an author will change as he matures.

Chatterton's spelling was one of the things that gave him away. The orthography of the alleged Rowley is no more characteristic of the fifteenth century than that of Orm is like that of the period *circa* 1200.

*   *   *

Similarities in technique may point to identity of authorship. The use of conceits or of an unusual type of sonnet, a peculiar construction in drama, or a special method of characterization or of plot development in a novel or short story—any of these or other technical devices may help to provide evidence for the attribution of a work. To Godwin, hermit of Kilburn—assuming that he was the author of the *Ancren Riwle*—certain sermons have been attributed because of parallels in technique between them and parts of the *Ancren Riwle*.[21] Technique in plot structure as a test of authorship is discussed in an article on George Peele.[22] A similarity between the organization of the poem *To the Memory of Mr. Congreve* and that of four memorial poems written by James Thomson, leads to the suggestion that Thomson is the author of the Congreve poem.[23]

Literary technique might provide evidence for tests of authenticity. We have a pretty good idea of the date at which various literary devices were introduced into English literature. A work in which some device appears a hundred years or so before it is found in other works would certainly be open to suspicion. We should look askance upon a five-act mystery play, or a Petrarchan sonnet dated 1300.

*   *   *

An article supporting the theory that Spenser wrote the glosses signed "E. K." makes a point of the similarity between the ideas of "E. K." and those expressed by Spenser in the *Shephearde's Calender* and elsewhere.[24] Identity or similarity of thinking must not be counted upon too heavily, however, as evidence of authorship. It is as easy to borrow ideas as phrases. Indeed, friends may be more alike in the way they think than in the way they express themselves.

*   *   *

What has just been said of specific ideas is true of subject matter

in general. The fact that *Mamillia* deals with much the same
material as that of *Euphues,* and deals with it in much the same way,
does not prove that Lyly wrote both pamphlets or that Greene wrote
both of them. But, in view of Greene's habit of using the same kind
of material in more than one work (as in his prodigal son pamphlets),
the fact that the subject matter of the *Defence of Conny-Catching*
is much like that of the other conny-catching works is one reason,
though not the only one, for thinking that Greene wrote the *Defence,*
despite its purporting to be an attack upon him.

A fraudulent work may be betrayed by discrepancies in its subject
matter. If we turned up an alleged mediæval romance and found
that its *historiæ personæ* included Roland, Oliver, and Ganelon
along with Arthur, Lancelot, Gawain, Guinevere, and other dwellers
in Camelot, we might well be suspicious of it. A somewhat similar
confusion in Macpherson's Ossianic poetry was partly responsible for
the doubts that arose concerning its genuineness.[25]

* * *

We come now to textual evidence as a basis for determining questions of authenticity or attribution. Professor Cargill, before offering
William Rokayle as a candidate for the authorship of *Piers Plowman,*
explains away by means of textual evidence the passage in which the
poet apparently gives his name as William Langland.[26] Textual evidence provides the basis for the attribution to Bannatyne rather than
to Lindsay of certain changes made in the *Satire of the Three Estates.*[27] The theory that the actor who played the part of Marcellus
contributed to the pirating of the First Quarto of *Hamlet* rests
largely upon textual evidence,[28] as does Professor Moore's theory
that the songs in Lyly's plays were not in the early quartos from
which the later printed editions were taken, and hence were probably
not by Lyly.[29]

Textual evidence may also furnish proof of fraud. If there should
appear a copy—dated 1587, say—of the lost Ur-Hamlet,[13] and we

[13] Ur-Hamlet: a play no longer extant, of the existence of which there is considerable evidence. It was apparently a pre-Shaksperean version of the Hamlet story
and is generally thought to have been the work of Thomas Kyd. The German prefix
ur- means "that which commences".

should find in it a number of readings which appear in the 1623 Folio version of Shakspere's *Hamlet* but in neither the 1603 nor the 1604 Quarto, we should need a great deal of other evidence to quell our suspicions concerning the "discovery". Similar evidence was helpful to Messrs. Carter and Pollard in some of the nineteenth-century pamphlets they studied. A Ruskin work dated 1852 omits the footnotes written by Ruskin for the publication of the essay in 1852 but contains an emendation made in the edition of 1880 and hence must have been printed after the latter date; [30] a poem by Tennyson, ostensibly printed in 1862, actually follows the text of the *Collected Works* of 1889, and could not have been printed until after that date.[31]

*   *   *

The date of a work—if it can be established—may throw light on its authenticity or its authorship. If a work was written before 1200, it may have been written by some one who died in 1199; but if chronology demands a later date of composition, then the attribution becomes an obviously impossible one. A case was made out for Gilbert Pilkington as the "Wakefield Master"; [14] it depended partly upon the identification of Gilbert as the author of the *Northern Passion*.[32] An objection to the theory insists that the date of the *Northern Passion* (early fourteenth century) makes it impossible that the same person could have written both the *Northern Passion* and the *Second Shepherds' Play*.[33]

The date of composition also enters into the problem of the authorship of the *Owl and the Nightingale*; by presuming a date earlier than 1189, one may argue for one Master Nicholas, who signed as witness to a charter of 1141–71, as the author.[34] But there are objections to so early a date.[15]

The significance of the date in matters of authenticity is, of course, obvious. If a deed is written on paper manufactured in 1620, it cannot have been signed by Shakspere, no matter who witnessed the document, and no matter what the handwriting experts say as to the

[14] The "Wakefield Master": the unknown author who put into their present form the plays of the Wakefield—or Towneley—cycle.
[15] See below, p. 201.

genuineness of the signature. If a volume of poems dated 1865 contains a poem that was not written until 1870, the book is evidently misdated and is, to that extent at least, a fraud.[16]

*   *   *

If one is basing an argument concerning authenticity or attribution on internal evidence, it is, as may well be imagined, an advantage to be able to combine different kinds of evidence. Thus the ascription of a passage in the *Christ* is strengthened by the fact that, in addition to parallel passages, there are similarities in themes and in meter to other works of Cynewulf.[35] Professor Brown, because of Chaucerian rhymes, phrases, and spirit, thinks that *An Holy Meditacioun* is the *Wreched Engendring* mentioned in the Prologue to the *Legend of Good Women*.[36] On the strength of various similarities— moral earnestness, abhorrence of licentiousness, knowledge of the Vulgate, condemnation of the same sins, and parallel examples drawn from the Bible—between the two poems, *The Pearl* has been ascribed to the author of *John of Bridlington*.[37]

On the basis of parallel passages and similarities in ideas and technique, two plays, *The Trial of Chivalry* and *Look About You*, have been claimed for Henry Chettle; [38] but the similarities to Chettle's known works are not convincing.[39] To take a single example: a point is made of the similarity of the Clown in *The Trial of Chivalry* to the clowns in Chettle's *Hoffman,* but the characteristic mentioned would apply equally well to Dogberry in *Much Ado about Nothing*.

Because of their phraseology, themes, and technique, Professor Dunkel has argued for the ascription to Middleton of *Anything for a Quiet Life*,[40] *The Puritan*,[41] and *The Revenger's Tragedy*; [42] Professor Dunkel would also give to Middleton rather than to Rowley the chief share in the authorship of *A Fair Quarrel, The Changeling,* and *The Spanish Gipsy*.[43]

Professor Day, on similar evidence, attributes *Hey for Honesty* largely to Thomas Randolph, and explains the presence of allusions to events that occurred after Randolph's death as due to a collaborator.[44] A controversy arose over another ascription to Randolph.

---

[16] A book which is, and purports only to be, a facsimile reprint, should, and generally does, have that fact made plainly evident.

Professor Day suggested that Randolph wrote *The Drinking Academy*,[45] and Professor Moore Smith accepted the attribution and added more evidences of Randolph's authorship.[46] But after an edition of *The Drinking Academy* was published, bearing Randolph's name as author,[47] Professor Moore Smith changed his mind and suggested Robert Baron as a more likely person to have written the work.[48] Professor Rollins carried on the discussion, championing Randolph and arguing that one so lacking in a sense of humor as Baron was, could never have written a work so humorous as *The Drinking Academy*.[49]

A combination of bits of internal evidence led Professor Ham to suggest that the Dedication to *The Music of the Prophetesse,* though signed by Purcell, was actually written by Dryden.[50] Various similarities to *Falkland, Pelham,* and other of Bulwer's works, make it seem likely that Bulwer was also the author of *Mephistophiles in England.*[51] In the article making that ascription there is, however, a statement that should be challenged. In connection with the fact that *Mephistophiles in England* was attributed to Robert Folkstone Williams, a professor of history and author of a *Historical Sketch of the Art of Sculpture in Wood,* Professor Bangs wrote: "Two works of so great contrast, even in the titles, could not have been written by the same author." [52] If this statement were true, it would imply that Charles Lutwidge Dodgson could not have written *An Elementary Treatise on Determinants* or *Curiosa Mathematica* and *Alice in Wonderland,* and that Stephen Leacock cannot be the author of both *The Unsolved Riddle of Social Justice* and *Behind the Beyond.*

III

We may now consider the third kind of evidence to be used in problems of authenticity or attribution—external evidence. Sometimes historical or biographical circumstances will provide significant data. To take an extreme case, if we knew that a Latin work was written in a certain village at a certain time, the fact that only one person living in the village at that time knew Latin, would be *prima facie* evidence of his authorship of the work. On the other hand, if a work displaying an intimate familiarity with Oxford or Paris purports to have been written by one who was never in Oxford or Paris, we may rightly suspect the attribution, though we must consider whether the knowledge revealed could have been gained in some way other than by direct experience.

If too many works are ascribed to one month or one year of a writer's life, we may suspect either that he is not the author of all of them, or that he did part of the work at some other time. Thus it seems to me unlikely that Robert Greene wrote three—or even two—moderately long pamphlets during the last days or weeks of his life, especially since during some part of that time he must have been too ill to write.

The theory that made Gilbert Pilkington the "Wakefield Master" depended partly upon his being a native of Lancashire and also the author of the *Turnament of Totenham*; to show that the author of the *Turnament* was not a resident of Lancashire would destroy the validity of that line of argument.[53]

The fact that Shakspere and the composer Morley were for a time neighbors in St. Helen's, Bishopsgate, helps to support the suggestion that the songs in *As You Like It* were the result of a collaboration in which Shakspere supplied the words and Morley the tunes.[54] Because a ballad was issued from a certain address, it has been thought that the printing must have occurred more than twenty years before the ballad appeared in Congreve's *Love for Love,* and that the ballad, consequently, was not written by the playwright; the discovery that other books were issued by the same publisher from the old address after 1695 seems to invalidate this argument.[55] An event in the life of Richard Steele provides the basis for the attribution to him of the Prologue and Epilogue to Nicholas Rowe's *Tamerlane.*[56] Similarly, biographical circumstances suggest the attribution of certain sonnets to William Michael Rossetti rather than to his brother Dante Gabriel,[57] and of *Adventures of Alonso* to Thomas Digges.[58]

*   *   *

A second kind of external evidence is a statement by an author in one work that he is also the author of another work. Twice—in the Prologue to *The Legend of Good Women* and at the end of the *Parson's Tale*—Chaucer gives us a list of his writings; neither list is necessarily complete, but for the works mentioned we have Chaucer's own testimony that he is the author. We must be sure, of course, that the "book of Troilus" named in the *Parson's Tale* is the *Troilus and Criseyde* printed under Chaucer's name; but in most instances the identification is unquestioned. In some cases the writer's statement may take the form of asserting or confessing that he is the author of a work attributed to someone else. William Combe is cited as having admitted that he perpetrated certain letters ostensibly written by Laurence Sterne.[59]

Sometimes the author's claim may be implicit rather than direct. When Professor Crane found that the fourth of a series of four essays by "The Indigent Philosopher", which had appeared in *Lloyd's Evening Post* in 1762, was selected by Goldsmith himself to be included in the 1765 collection, *Essays by Mr. Goldsmith,* he was entitled to assume that Goldsmith, by claiming the authorship of one of the essays, was in effect claiming all four.[60]

*   *   *

The form of external evidence most frequently used in matters of authenticity or attribution is a statement by John Doe that the work in question is indeed the work of Richard Roe. I have elsewhere pointed out [17] the danger of accepting such statements blindly, as they have too often been accepted in the past. It is not enough to know—if it can be known—that John Doe was telling the truth as he understood it; it is equally important to prove that John Doe was in a position to know the truth. The attribution to John Halsam of a poem used by Lydgate, on the strength of a statement by the scribe, John Shirley,[61] is made probable by the fact that similar statements made by Shirley have been confirmed by other evidence.[62]

An inscription on the title page of a copy of *George a Greene, the Pinner of Wakefield* [18] was accepted by Grosart as proof of Robert Greene's authorship of the play;[63] a second inscription on the same page [19] was interpreted as evidence that Greene was at some time a clergyman.[20] It may be that Greene was the author of *George*

---

[17] See above, pp. 131–33.

[18] "Ed. Juby faith that yˢ play was made by Ro. Gree[ne]"; there is a facsimile reproduction in Greene, *Works,* ed. Grosart, XIV, [117].

[19] "Written by . . . . . . a minifter, who ac[ted] the piñers pᵗ in it himfelf. Teſte W. Shakeſpea[re]."

[20] Grosart found confirmation for his belief in a reference in *Martine Mar-Sixtus* to "every red-nosed minister", apparently alluding to Greene; but Grosart misread the line, since the word is not "minister" but "rimester" [A3ᵛ]. See Nashe, *Works,* ed. McKerrow, IV, 8.

a Greene; [64] but the attribution cannot be accepted on the strength of the inscriptions. As Professor Gayley pointed out:

> . . . it must be remembered that both inscriptions are hearsay; that both notes are anonymous; that one or both may be fraudulent; [21] that there is no certain proof that they were written by contemporaries; and finally that, unless their contents are shown to be accurate as well as authentic, and to refer to the same author, they do not connect any Robert Greene with the ministry.[65]

The story that Swift acknowledged the authorship of *A Tale of a Tub* by remarking, as he was glancing at a copy of the book, "Good God! What a genius I had when I wrote that book!" has been regarded as probably apocryphal. The discovery of an extract from a letter written by the author's young kinsman, Deane Swift, telling the story in substantially the traditional version, provides new evidence. Deane Swift, as the son-in-law of Mrs. Whiteway, Swift's cousin and companion, was in a position to know what he was talking about. And as he tells the story on the authority of Mrs. Whiteway, who heard Swift's ejaculation, we have better reason than ever before for believing the story to be true.[66]

Another attribution to Swift has to do with *The Day of Judgment*. Lord Chesterfield, in a letter to Voltaire, refers to a poem by Swift called *The Day of Judgment* as being in his possession. In a letter to the Bishop of Waterford the Earl paraphrases a line of the poem as it was later printed, thus, apparently, indicating that the poem in his possession was essentially the same as that which later got into print.[67]

The authors of literary articles that appeared in the *Quarterly Review* between 1826 and 1853 are identified in two articles, in one on the strength of statements in the publisher's "Contributors' Book",[68] in the other by evidence contained in letters by Lockhart, the editor.[69]

IV

A statement by the author and a statement by some one else are combined in an effort to prove that Hogg, rather than Shelley, wrote

[21] See W. W. Greg, "Three Manuscript Notes by Sir George Buc", *The Library*, 4th Series, XII (1931–32), 307–21; S. A. Tannenbaum, *Shaksperian Scraps and Other Elizabethan Fragments* (New York: Columbia University Press, 1933); and R. C. Bald, "The *Locrine* and *George-a-Greene* Title-Page Inscriptions", *The Library*, 4th Series, XV (1934–35), 295–305.

the first draft of *The Necessity of Atheism,* and hence is primarily responsible for the piece. Hogg, in a letter to Shelley, refers to his own "systematic cudgel for Christianity"; and Shelley writes to Hogg of "your little Essay".[70] The case would be strengthened if there were some positive evidence, as there is in the article on *The Day of Judgment* just mentioned, to link these allusions with *The Necessity of Atheism.*

An attack on De Quincey is attributed to Dr. William Maginn largely on the strength of allusions in De Quincey's own writings and references by Carlyle and others.[71]

In connection with a review of Jane Austen's *Emma,* which has long been attributed to Scott, an interesting problem arose. Some allusions in a later review, known to have been written by Whately, to the earlier, gave rise to the suggestion that Whately was the author of both.[72] There is a record of payment to Scott, however, apparently for the *Emma* review.[73] Since the records concerned are somewhat informal and not too clear, that evidence was not wholly convincing.[74] Fortunately, other evidence was forthcoming. A reviewer said in 1835, on what was apparently good authority, that Scott wrote the review of *Emma.* Correspondence between Scott and Murray, the publisher, indicates that Murray suggested that Scott write such a review and that Scott did so and sent the review to Murray. Allusions in Whately's review which make it appear that the same person wrote it and the *Emma* article are explained as being due to Gifford, who seems to have wielded the editorial hand extensively in both articles. Whately himself says that Scott wrote the earlier review.[75]

*   *   *

Many studies involving authenticity or attribution will combine internal and external evidence. A comparison of the manuscript and published versions of Sidney's *Arcadia,* in conjunction with the Countess of Pembroke's expressed attitude toward her brother's writings, throws light on the nature and extent of the Countess's alterations in the work.[76] Another combination of internal and external evidence provides material for an article on *The Life and Death of Hector*; in this instance doubt is thrown on Heywood's authorship by the fact that nowhere in his other works does Heywood refer to *The Life and Death of Hector,* though such allusions were his common practice.[77] In similar fashion, internal and external evidence are both employed to demonstrate that Arbuthnot rather than Swift was the author of *The History of John Bull*.[78]

Internal and external evidence are also combined in the attribution of certain essays that appeared in the *Pennsylvania Journal; and the Weekly Advertiser* in 1768 to John Dickinson [79] and in the identification of Thomas Green Fessenden as the American Munchausen.[80]

V

Let us consider now how one is to set about conducting an investigation into a matter of authenticity or attribution. First of all comes the collecting of every possible bit of evidence. Even if one is privately convinced that Smith is or is not the author, or that the work is or is not what it purports to be (and such convictions, unscholarly though they are, cannot always be shaken off), he must be as careful to collect evidence against his theory as for it. It may go against the grain to be very assiduous in searching for ammunition to destroy one's own case; but it must be remembered that the overlooking of a single detail may be fatal to one's whole argument. Moreover, it is the business of the scholar to seek the truth, and the satisfaction of having found it should be ample recompense for having to give up a cherished but untenable theory.

Having collected the data, one should study it to find which is the stronger side of the case. Let us suppose that the weight of the evidence indicates that Smith is not the author, or that the work is not genuine. One should then set forth, in some logical fashion, all the evidence supporting the attribution to Smith, or the authenticity of the work. Each bit of this evidence must then be explained away, so that the ground is cleared for the presentation of evidence on the other side. If there is some one bit of strikingly conclusive evidence, it may be a good idea to offer that first; the weaker points may have a greater confirmatory effect if a *prima facie* case has already been established. In some instances, however, it may be more effective to build to a climax, starting with the lighter ammunition and reserving the heaviest fire for the end.[81]

The investigator who can find, as Messrs. Carter and Pollard did, evidence that is absolutely convincing, is fortunate indeed. More often one has to do what he can with insufficient data, like a person trying to make bricks without straw. In such circumstances it is almost possible to sympathize with John Payne Collier in his desperate attempt to manufacture the evidence that he lacked. But the true scholar will do the best he can with what evidence he has, and hope that later discoveries, or the reworking of old material in a new light, will at last reveal the truth.

CHAPTER FOUR

✥ ৡ ৡ ✥

PROBLEMS OF SOURCE STUDY

FOR a number of years source study has been in bad repute among scholars. Many pages have been devoted, especially by German writers, to the pointing out of sources which, in many instances, are not sources and, in some instances, are not even parallels. Hence any study based upon "parallel passages" came to be looked upon askance. Nevertheless, source study is important and, rightly carried out, may be extremely valuable. It should not be confined to the discovering of such plagiarisms, conscious or unconscious, as are to be seen in parallel passages; but rather it should involve the analyzing of a piece of literature with a view to discovering whence came the inspiration, the material, and the technique whereby the work came into being.

I

It is, of course, important that plagiarisms should be pointed out wherever they may be found, though at the same time it must be remembered that the attitude of writers and of the reading public toward such borrowings has not always been what it is now. The stealing of Harington's epigrams [1] or of Purcell's songs [2] was undoubtedly looked upon as less reprehensible in the seventeenth cen-

[1] Franklin B. Williams, Jr. ("Henry Parrot's Stolen Feathers", *PMLA*, LII (1937), 1019–30) shows that Parrot "borrowed" epigrams from Sir John Harington and others.

[2] Roy Lamson, Jr. ("Henry Purcell's Dramatic Songs and the English Broadside Ballad", *PMLA*, LIII (1938), 146–61) points out that Purcell's songs were used by writers of ballads, who sometimes expanded the original song by adding new stanzas or used the tune as a setting for a new ditty, sometimes by way of answer to the words of the original song.

tury than we should now regard it, but the fact that such thefts occurred is a matter to be taken into consideration by all students of the period.

The discovery of plagiarism is important to keep us from bestowing admiration upon one author for something that properly belongs to another. We should not, for example, give credit to Goldsmith or to Isaac D'Israeli for ideas that originally appeared in James Ralph's *The Case of Authors by Profession,*[1] or to Thomas Warton for what was taken from Isaac Reed.[2]

*   *   *

Even when plagiarisms are not particularly reprehensible, the fact that they occur may throw considerable light upon the person who is responsible for them. Perhaps Robert Greene had a perfect right to repeat, in a later work, passages—sometimes pages in length— which he had already used in an earlier work,[3] provided, of course, that his readers and his publishers had no objection. But the fact that he did so suggests either that he had a notebook in which he jotted down material for future use and did not always cross off passages as he used them, so that he would not repeat himself, or else that he deliberately copied out passages from works already in print to save himself the trouble of working up new material. In the one case he was certainly careless; and in the other, inexcusably lazy.[4]

Light may be thrown upon an author's erudition—or lack of it— by a knowledge of his borrowings. The euphuistic details that seem a bit surprising when we encounter them in the novels of Thomas Deloney, the ballad-writing silk-weaver, become less anomalous when we learn that they were derived, not from Plutarch, Cornelius Nepos, and Pliny, but mainly from a single book, Fortescue's *The Forest.*[5]

Other borrowings, whether of the nature of plagiarisms or not, may reveal something of the working methods of an author. It has been suggested,[6] for example, that the close parallelism between the earlier sonnets in Sidney's *Astrophel and Stella* and Greville's *Cælica* points to consultation between the two authors and an agreement to write upon the same themes—perhaps in a spirit of friendly competition—rather than to imitation or plagiarism on the part of either poet. If that suggestion represents what happened, we have learned something about the literary practices of Sidney and Greville which we are not likely to have discovered in any other way.

Another detail of literary practice comes to light in connection with Milton's *De Doctrina Christiana*; it is suggested,[7] because of parallel passages, that Milton was indebted to Wolleb's *Compendium Theologiæ Christianæ*. Then this comment is made:

The comparison, moreover, would seem to throw some light on the manner in which Milton wrote his treatise. The appearance of two close parallels in widely separated portions of Book I of the *De Doctrina* from two equally separated places in the *Compendium* suggests notes in a commonplace book. The continued similarity of Book II seems to indicate elaborate notes or constant consultation of the *Compendium* while this portion of the *De Doctrina* was being written.[8]

From a study of the sources of *The Rivals* another interesting fact crops out:

The value of ferreting out these heretofore unnoticed sources is that they focus attention on Sheridan's relations to his contemporaries. . . . Sheridan adopted the broad outline of the main plot for *The Rivals* from Garrick, and that of his sub-plot from Colman. To one familiar with Sheridan's habits of composition, it is significant that he appropriated most from Garrick, the more celebrated of the two managers. . . . Garrick and Colman were not only skilled producers, but were also favorite playwrights. They knew from experience what popular taste demanded of the stage. It is futile, therefore, to ransack Shakespeare or the Restoration Dramatists for sources of *The Rivals*. The more natural approach to a study of Sheridan's plays would be to take first into account his indebtedness to those of his contemporaries who were playwrights as well as managers. Garrick and Colman sensed the type of character and situation which were relished by the diverse, and sometimes contradictory, interests of their audiences; they were also in a position to reject or stage the offerings of a young dramatist struggling for recognition.[9]

II

But it is not in the discovery of plagiarisms and obvious borrowings that the chief value of source study lies. We must learn and then study the sources of a Chaucer [3] or a Shakspere in order to ap-

[3] A most valuable work is *Sources and Analogues of Chaucer's Canterbury Tales,* ed. W. F. Bryan and Germaine Dempster (Chicago: University of Chicago Press, 1940), which supplants *Originals and Analogues of Some of Chaucer's Canterbury Tales* (London: Chaucer Society, 1872–88).

preciate the nature and extent of his originality. If we did not know
the source of *Troilus and Criseyde,* we should in one sense, give
Chaucer more credit than he deserves; for we should attribute to
him all that was his own plus that which was the contribution of
others. But in another sense we should be doing him less than justice; for we should be unaware of the peculiar genius that enabled
him to take a story (which was ready at hand for anybody to use)
and, recognizing its possibilities, to develop them and thus to create
a unique masterpiece. Or if we read *Antony and Cleopatra,* knowing
nothing of Sir Thomas North's translation of Plutarch's *Lives,* we
should not be aware that Shakspere sometimes takes North's very
words and turns them into magnificent poetry; [4] thus we should never
recognize in Shakspere that power which was one of his special gifts.
Let some writers make the plots or invent the techniques, and let
them have full credit for their imagination and their ingenuity; then
let us give to the later writers who used those plots or those techniques, credit only for what they contributed, but full credit for that.

It should be pointed out here, perhaps, that source study may
sometimes have the effect of establishing originality where it was not
expected. William Dunbar has long been classed among the Scottish
imitators of Chaucer; but a study of Dunbar concludes that:

1. The Scottish poet was an original genius who showed a marked
independence of predecessors in all his work. . . .
2. The vast majority of those poems by Dunbar which lack originality
are strongly influenced, if not dominated, by non-Chaucerian elements
in the work of Lydgate.[10]

* * *

We have been looking upon source study as necessary in determining the extent of an author's originality; but it is no less important, to view the matter from another angle, to study the sources of
the literature of a given period in order to discover what that period
inherited from the past. Thus Professor Loomis traces *Gawain and
the Greene Knight,* the *Carl of Carlisle,* and certain episodes in other
romances to Irish traditions of the eighth century.[11] Similarly, the
sleep-walking scene in *Macbeth* is thought to be derived from an oral
tradition going back at least as far as the *Gesta Romanorum,*[12] and

[4] As in the famous passage describing the meeting of Antony and Cleopatra (Act
II, scene ii).

the appearance of a ghost at a feast is a device as old as the Old Testament.[5] It may be shown, too, that however much Smollett drew upon the events of his life as material for his stories, his novels would not have been what they are if the author had not been familiar with Elizabethan drama.[13]

*   *   *

Source study is also important in that it may serve to reveal some obscure writer who acted as the inspirer of a greater writer. Our purpose in such studies should not be to drag anyone from the depths of a well-deserved obscurity, but rather to give credit where credit is due and, more than that, to seek to discover how the perhaps commonplace ideas and pedestrian language of a John Doe or a Richard Roe are transformed into the glorious drama of a Shakspere or the magnificent poetry of a Milton.[14]

*   *   *

Still another value of source study is to be found in the light it may throw upon an author's purpose or upon the real meaning and significance of a work. Robert Greene's pamphlets about conny-catchers—swindlers—have generally been taken for documents of real sociological import. Greene's words have been taken at their face value, and it has been assumed that he betrayed the secrets that had come to him through his intimate knowledge of the underworld in order to put the provincial visitor on his guard and to arouse Londoners against the criminals in their midst. If it should be discovered that Greene's stories were taken from literary sources—and the Stationers' Register contains titles of many works not now extant that might have provided such material—then it might be concluded that Greene had no more knowledge of crime and vice than any of his fellow-writers; and the conny-catching pamphlets would lose their sociological significance. We should then know what now can only be suspected—that Greene's object was entertainment rather than social reform. After the source of Defoe's *The Apparition of Mrs. Veal*

---

[5] This is not, of course, to say that Shakspere got the idea for Banquo's ghost from the story of Belshazzar; that kind of *post hoc, ergo propter hoc* reasoning has been one of the banes of source study. The point is to show that Shakspere need not have invented—hence probably did not invent—a device so old and so familiar.

was discovered, the work could no longer be held the great display of creative imagination that it had been considered; but it looms just as large as an extraordinarily fine piece of reporting of fact, or alleged fact.

An author's purpose may affect his treatment of a source. Herman Melville deliberately altered material that he took from *Life in a Man-of-War* in order to strengthen his attacks on objectionable practices in the United States Navy in *White-Jacket*.[15]

III

Professor Morize rightly calls attention[16] to certain dangers that confront anyone who undertakes the study of sources. These are, first, the danger of assuming that for every passage in a work there is a specific, identifiable source; second, that of succumbing to the "hypnotism of the unique source"; third, that of mistaking a mere resemblance for a direct dependence; and fourth, that of thinking that for every work—or for every passage in a work—there must be a written source.

*   *   *

Of course, in one sense, every line and every word of a piece of literature has its source somewhere in the author's experience, whether it be in his reading, in his conversation with other people, in his emotional reactions, in some other element of living, or in some combination of these things. But that source is, in many instances, so complex or so obscured by the author's treatment of it, that no method of research now available—however diligently or brilliantly applied—will serve to bring it to light. Coleridge furnishes a case in point. Professor Lowes succeeded in tracing, with satisfaction to himself and conviction to most, if not quite all, of his readers, the sources of the *Rime of the Ancient Mariner* and *Kubla Khan*;[17] but he confessed[18] that the problem presented by *Christabel* seemed insoluble.[6]

Another situation which proves baffling to the student of sources is that in which a work is traced to a source now lost or at least

[6] A solution to the *Christabel* problem was offered by Arthur H. Nethercot in *The Road to Tryermaine* (Chicago: University of Chicago Press, [1939ᶜ]). See also Nathan Comfort Starr, "Coleridge's 'Sir Leoline'", *PMLA*, LXI (1946), 157-62.

unstudied. It has been suggested [19] that a lost play, which "was based principally on Hall and revised from Holinshed, was the source of both Folio and Quarto texts" [20] of Shakspere's *Henry VI*. It can be shown that Chaucer's *Melibeus* in some instances follows *Le Ménagier de Paris* and in others MS 1165 in the Bibliothèque Nationale; [21] hence it appears that neither of these versions represents Chaucer's real source. The version that Chaucer followed may be no longer extant, or it may be one of several manuscript versions not yet studied in relation to Chaucer.

*   *   *

The second of Professor Morize's four dangers besets everyone who specializes to any considerable extent in the work of a single author. The student of Gower, Greene, Gay, Gray, or Galsworthy is likely to see the influence of his hero in the work of any or all later writers. Professor Kaye told me that at one time—some ten years before he published his edition of Bernard Mandeville's *Fable of the Bees*—he could see, or thought he could see, Mandeville's influence cropping out here, there, and everywhere in the writings of Mandeville's successors. But, as he broadened his knowledge of the field, he discovered that there were sources other than Mandeville for most of the ideas and expressions in question.

*   *   *

It is the failure to avoid the third danger—that of arguing from a resemblance to a dependence—that makes many articles based on parallel passages unconvincing. In a discussion [22] of Marlowe's translation of Ovid's *Amores* as a source of *Hero and Leander,* nine parallels are mentioned. One of these

> "Beautie alone is lost, too warily kept."
> > (*Hero and Leander,* I, 328)
> "Unmeete is beauty without use to wither."
> > (*Elegies,* II, 3, p. 33)

is a parallel only in idea, and the idea is admittedly a commonplace. Of the four others quoted—not so large a number, surely, as to bar out accident or coincidence—many people would say, on first thought, at least, that there is a resemblance, but no clear evidence of dependence. We should have to know how often and in what other contexts Marlowe used the words "spotless", "youth", "naked", "simplicity", and "truth" in order to feel confident that

> "My words shall be as spotlesse as my youth,
> Full of simplicitie and naked truth."
>   (*Hero and Leander,* I, 207–8)

was necessarily derived from

> "Accept him that wil serue thee all his youth,
> Accept him that will loue with spotlesse truth . . . .
> My spotless life, which but to God gives place,
> Naked simplicitie and modest grace."
>   (*Elegies,* I, 3, p. 4)

Nor are the other parallels quoted much more convincing. This is not to say that the author of the article is wrong in his assumption that Marlowe borrowed from his translation of the *Amores* when he was writing *Hero and Leander*; such a conclusion may very well fit the facts in the case, but it cannot be convincingly demonstrated by the resemblances cited.

Another article involving Marlowe [23] attempts to date a group of Elizabethan plays by showing, through parallel passages, which play is indebted to which; but a reply [24] to that article clearly shows the impossibility in many instances of determining whether Marlowe was the borrower or the "borrowee".

Professor Fred L. Jones claimed *The Trial of Chivalry* for Henry Chettle on the strength of forty-one passages which were cited as being parallels of passages in one or more of Chettle's works.[25] Of this claim Mr. Harold Jenkins wrote:

The attempt is one of the most flagrant examples of the futility of judging by so-called "parallels" of phrase. Not only are parallels drawn extensively with plays of which Chettle is not known to have been sole author and with *Look About You,* a play outside the accepted canon, but the parallels themselves are of the most ordinary kind. Sometimes the resemblance goes no farther than the general idea; in other instances similar phraseology is used in totally different connections. Mr. Jones appears to find special significance in single words like "shallow-witted" or "underlings"; in such ordinary phrases as "close his eyes" or "swelling floods"; in such well-worn notions as those expressed by the meta-

phors "to dim the lustre" and "to nip in the bud". He is especially convinced of Chettle's authorship by references to Tarquin, Tereus, and
Philomel, as if those mythological figures were not among the stock-in-
trade of rhetoric throughout the whole Elizabethan period. . . . An
accumulation of forty-one parallels of no greater consequence than these
can prove nothing. . . .[7]

If one were to judge by the occurrence or non-occurrence of parallel-
isms of thought or phrase, one might safely take the feebleness of those
set forth—presumably the best that can be found—as ample evidence
that Chettle could not possibly have written *The Trial of Chivalry*. And
indeed its style has no very close resemblance to his. . . . In fairness it
should be observed that the quarto has no fewer than five examples of
the dash denoting broken speech which we believe to have been habitually used by Chettle; but texts like *Law Tricks, Humour out of Breath*,
and *The Roaring Girl* are sufficient proof that it wos not Chettle's alone;
while in *The Trial of Chivalry* itself two of the five instances of it occur
in a scene which even Mr. Jones is confident is not by Chettle.[26]

An attempt to prove, by means of parallel passages, that Keats
took various details in *Lamia* from John Potter's *Archæologia
Græca, or The Antiquities of Greece* [27] is likewise unconvincing. It
may very well be that Keats did make use of Potter; some—though
not all—of the details in *Lamia* could have come from Potter. But
the parallels do not prove that these details could not have come
from some other source.

A writer on Shakspere sums the matter up thus:

But . . . to build up an elaborate theory of literary "influence" upon
the evidence of parallel passages alone is unsound unless coincidences in
ideas and wording are unmistakable, and unless such agreements in
thought and phraseology are not to be found in other accessible sources
than the supposed "influencing" author. . . . Ordinarily, to assign
"sources" and to trace "influences" on the evidence of correspondences
in thought and expression is especially unsafe in the Renaissance, and
particularly for matter presumably of classical provenance. The wise
sentences and fitting similitudes of the ancients were in every one's
mouth. Essays, sermons, treatises, the interminably long moral disquisi-

[7] According to Professor Jones this number could be doubled. It should be
observed, however, that little would be gained by increasing the number; the
validity of arguments based on parallel passages depends upon the convincingness
of the parallels, not on their number.

tions so popular in the period, abound in them. The learned no doubt sought this material in the original sources. But educated and half-educated alike could help themselves from those reservoirs of ancient wisdom which were known to all, the books of commonplaces. Certain striking correspondences between Montaigne and Shakespeare do not prove that Montaigne formed Shakespeare's style, nor even that the dramatist used the *Essays* as a store-house of material.[28]

* * *

The fourth danger to be avoided in source study is that of assuming that there must have been a written source for every part of a work. Professor Tatlock's article "St. Cecilia's Garlands and Their Roman Origin" [29] traces an element in Chaucer's "Second Nun's Tale" back to the fourth or fifth century, and shows that the original source probably lies deep in some legend of even earlier date. An article on Synge points out that *The Shadow of the Glen* is based, not on *The Widow of Ephesus,* but on authentic Irish folk-lore.[30]

Even when one has discovered an undeniable written source, there are still pitfalls to trap the unwary. The fact that an author used a literal quotation from another work does not prove that he has read the work; he may be quoting from some intermediary and may know nothing more of Cicero or Quintillian than the passage he quotes. Professor Manly's lecture in 1926 on "Chaucer and the Rhetoricians" [31] was followed by a number of studies of the relationship suggested in the title of the lecture. One of these studies [32] concludes that Chaucer did not know Horace and Juvenal at first hand but took his quotations from them out of Matthieu de Vendome's *Ars Versificatoria* and Geoffrey de Vinsauf's *Documentum de Arte Versificandi.* Similarly, most of the classical "learning" of Francis Meres could have been acquired second-hand from the *Officina* of J. Ravisius Textor.[33]

Even when an author is shown to have been thoroughly familiar with a classical writer or some other source in a foreign language, it is still possible that he has made use of a translation. Thus it is suggested that Chaucer derived his "Clerkes Tale" from an Old French translation of Petrarch as well as from the Latin original; [34] and another writer concluded that Chaucer, in *Troilus and Criseyde* and the *Legend of Good Women,* made use of an Italian translation of

Ovid.[8] Another article expresses the belief that Swinburne used as a source for *Laus Veneris* an English translation of an old German ballad.[35] An article on T. S. Eliot concluded that the poet used Mrs. Garnett's translation of *Crime and Punishment* in writing "The Love Song of J. Alfred Prufrock" and hence must have composed the poem after October, 1914.[36] Mr. Eliot, however, says that the poem was conceived in 1910 and completed by the summer of the following year; his knowledge of Dostoevski was gained through a French translation.[37]

Sometimes the intermediary between an author and his source is an edition rather than a translation. Efforts have been made to determine whether the 1577 or the 1587 edition of Holinshed's *Chronicles* was used as a source for Shakspere's *Henry VI* plays.[38] The importance of such studies lies in the fact that, wherever translations or editions are involved as sources, the translator or editor, rather than the original author, is the real source; hence the user of the source should not be unduly blamed for errors that result from mistranslations or from editorial notes or emendations.

IV

Professor Morize recognizes seven kinds of sources: (1) direct sources, (2) documentary sources, (3) sources of detail, (4) composite sources, (5) oral and indefinite sources, (6) sources of inspiration, and (7) graphic and plastic sources.[39]

*   *   *

Direct sources are what the name implies; but they may be verbatim repetition, such as are Greene's borrowings from himself [9] or Barnabe Riche's from Painter's *Palace of Pleasure*,[40] or they may be borrowings transformed in thought [10] or expression, as are Shakspere's borrowings from Plutarch or Herman Melville's from *The Picture of Liverpool* [41] and from Captain Delano's account of his

---

[8] This article (Sanford Brown Meech, "Chaucer and an Italian Translation of the *Heroides*", *PMLA*, XLV (1930), 110–28) makes an interesting point: "It is a significant testimony to Chaucer's familiarity with Italian that he, the translator of Boethius and certainly a fair Latinist, should have turned to Filippo to help him with Ovid; . . ." (p. 128).

[9] See above, p. 163.

[10] See below, pp. 167, 185.

adventures.[11] Other examples of direct sources are to be found in studies of the author of *Gawain and the Green Knight*,[42] Spenser,[43] Bacon,[44] Edward Taylor,[45] Cooper,[46] and Emerson.[47]

*   *   *

What Professor Morize means by documentary sources he explains thus:

More often than not the source is some reading undertaken by an author to gain information on a detail of his subject, and summed up in a note such as we all make when we are verifying a doubtful point. For a historical work the sources are the documents that the historian discovers, studies, criticizes according to scientific methods, and cites either in his footnotes, appendixes, or bibliography. In the case of a literary work, a work of art, the scaffolding, thanks to which we can follow and 'check up' the investigations of the historian, have been torn down. The documents, the sources, are cleverly absorbed into the texture of the work.[48]

It has been shown that when Chaucer was in need of medical information—as in the description of Arcite's illness in the "Knight's Tale" [12]—he turned to the *Speculum Majus* of Vincent of Beauvais.[49] There is evidence that Drayton went to Speed and perhaps Hall rather than to Holinshed to get material for the *Bataile of Agincourt*; [50] and that Middleton similarly turned to the *Merrie Conceited Jests of George Peele* to get material for *The Puritan, Your Five Gallants,* and *A Mad World, My Masters.*[51]

Dr. Johnson, for all the originality he displayed in devising definitions for his *Dictionary,* must nevertheless have had a number of documentary sources for that work; among them was, apparently, *The Gardener's Dictionary,* by Philip Miller.[52] Before Bulwer-Lytton undertook the writing of *Richelieu,* he seems to have studied Hugo's *Cromwell* and DeLavigne's *Louis XI.*[53] Wilkie Collins is

[11] Harold H. Scudder, in "Melville's *Benito Cereno* and Captain Delano's Voyages", *PMLA*, XLIII (1928), 502–32, wrote: "Captain Delano in this chapter [Chapter XVIII of Amasa Delano, *A Narrative of Voyages and Travels in the Northern and Southern Hemispheres,* . . . (Boston, 1871)] sets down the actual facts of his thrilling and unforgettable experiences in the deserted bay at the island of Santa Maria, February 20, 1805; Melville has transformed them into a Gothic masterpiece." (p. 529)

[12] Ll. 1885–1902.

thought to have made use of the reports of a French criminal case
in his *The Woman in White*.[54] Documentary sources are also pointed
out in articles on Shakspere's *Antony and Cleopatra*,[55] on Jonson's
Alchemist,[56] and on Cooper's *Homeward Bound*.[57]

*   *   *

The details for which sources may be found are, of course, of many
kinds; they may be details of plot, of characterization, of setting,
of description, of figures of speech, even of technique. The source
of a plot detail in Swift's *Gulliver's Travels* may be found in the
voyages of Jacques Massé rather than in Rabelais.[58] The characterization of Tom Jones seems to owe something to Edward Moore's *The
Foundling*.[59] There are details of description in the *Blickling Homilies* that point to a "direct reminiscence" of *Beowulf*; there are also
echoes of *Beowulf* in the *Battle of Maldon*.[60] The solemn anathema
of the Church is thought to have furnished details in Chaucer's *Hous
of Fame* and in the Friar's tale and that of the Wife of Bath.[61] Professor Emerson traced details of symbolism in Chaucer's "Second
Nun's Tale" to St. Ambrose; [62] and another writer thought St. Cyprian
a more likely source.[63] Pindar's seventh Olympian ode is suggested
as the source of a metaphor in Milton's *Epitaphium Damonis*.[64] A
poem ascribed to Friar Nicholas Bozon is thought to be the source
of the allegory of the Christ-Knight in *Piers Plowman*,[65] and a sermon by Bishop Brunton may be the source of the fable of the rat
parliament in the B-text of *Piers*.[66]

Part of Spenser's story of Timias and Belphebe has been traced to
an Old French romance, *Violette*,[67] and some of the details of the
description of Belphebe are thought to have been derived from Virgil.[68] The name Duessa in the *Fœrie Queene* may be a compound
of the Irish *Dub* (black) and *Esa* (a woman's name).[69]

The borrowed detail may be an idea. Shelley is thought to have
taken from Cabanis the notion that a mild and equable climate is
essential to the best development of intellect and morality.[70]

*   *   *

Doubtless the most difficult, and at the same time the most interesting, kind of source study is that which involves composite sources.
A classic example of this kind of work is the study of Coleridge

made by Professor Lowes; [13] and more and more, I think, it is being recognized that other studies should be carried out along the lines laid down in that work. The student of literature, working on the relationship of source to completed work—and keeping pace with the psychologists as they study the way the human mind functions— may eventually learn enough about the operation of the creative imagination to be greatly helpful to those who seek to produce good literature. No such knowledge, no formula, will take the place of experience; but it may be possible to eliminate some of the trial- and-error practices of literary apprenticeship.

The study of composite sources such as lie behind most specimens of great literature is equally valuable as an aid to appreciation; the true merits of a piece, the greatness of an author's work, cannot be realized until all the sources are identified and disentangled from one another.

The Owl and the Nightingale seems to have been derived from a German proverb, the *Fables* of Alfred, and Persian poetry.[71] Pro- fessor Baugh says of the Middle English romance *Athelstan*: "The evidence that has accumulated over the last twenty years sug- gests . . . that the author has made his story out of elements derived from a faint and confused historical tradition, from ballad motives, from the Emma legend, and from the story of the enraged king as told by Walter Map." [72] Chaucer is thought to have used French sources other than the *Ovide Moralisé* in his adaptations from Ovid; [73] and his knowledge of preachers and preaching is thought to combine an acquaintance with preachers' manuals and a keen ob- servation of preachers in real life.[74]

Professor Lowes, turning his attention this time to Keats, points out the composite nature of the sources of a single passage in *The Fall of Hyperion, A Vision*; [75] and the composite source of a bit of symbolism in Shelley's *Ode to the West Wind* is discussed by another writer.[76] Professor Bradner calls attention to the composite source of *Wuthering Heights*; [77] and Swinburne's *The Leper* is found to contain details drawn from a number of mediæval stories.[78]

An article on Washington Irving [79] shows how milieu, language, folk-lore, and literary sources combined during his travels in Ger- many to influence Irving; and a study of Hawthorne mentions a

[13] See above, p. 167.

whole galaxy of sources, including Cotton Mather, Increase Mather, Felt, Sewall, Winthrop, Spenser, Milton, Shakspere, Bunyan, Scott, Southey, Browne, Beckford, Maturin, Walpole, and others.[80] Two articles deal with the origin of *The Turn of the Screw*.[81]

A comment on the sources of Spenser's Red Cross Knight may serve to conclude this discussion of composite sources:

The stanzas which tell the story of the infant George are full of reminiscences of often-recurring romantic enfances—the shreds and patches gathered by an eclectic imagination and fused, as was Spenser's habit, into a new whole, coherent, convincing, true, yet none the less suggestive of those tales of other foundlings—from Romulus and Remus, Valentin and Orson, down to Libeaus Desconus and the young Perceval —which were Spenser's unrealized literary inheritance. It is only as we are aware of this unconsciously eclectic temper that such considerations as these have any importance in the study of a poet's 'sources'. For if by that may be implied only the conscious adaptation, into a consistent parallel, of material carefully scrutinized and deliberately selected,— only the making over of a *Rosalynde* into an *As You Like It*,—if 'sources' may include that process only, then indeed we must admit *this* sacred river to be flung up momentarily from no source whatever. But there were caverns through which it ran, and though perhaps they are, to our sorrow, measureless to man, they are, after all, surely worth our remarking.[82]

*   *   *

The next category of sources is that made up of oral and indefinite sources, which are likely to have a considerable part in any literary work. Who can doubt that much of the inspiration and not a little of the subject matter of the Elizabethan drama were derived from convivial conversations, whether in the Mermaid—as tradition has it—or in some other tavern? Or that Fielding altered, from time to time, his plans for Tom Jones as he learned, presumably from his sister Sarah, what Richardson had in store for Clarissa? [83] Unfortunately, these sources are, by their very nature, difficult if not impossible to demonstrate conclusively. However, if one can make himself master of a period, steeping himself in its background and exploiting to the fullest degree such letters, journals, periodicals, and other ephemerides as may exist, he may hope to achieve reasonably satisfactory results in the study of oral and indefinite sources.

Professor Smith suggested that the river names which Spenser is generally thought to have invented, were actually derived from Irish place-names.[84] It has been plausibly argued [85] that the fake beheading in the *Arcadia* was suggested by Sidney's witnessing such a trick at Bartholomew Fair in 1582 rather than by reading of the device in Reginald Scott's *Discoverie of Witchcraft.*

Among the interesting studies which point to sources in life rather than in literature is that of Professor Kathryn Huganir,[86] who shows that the fine of £100 levied against the knight in *The Owl and the Nightingale* was not excessive in view of the fact that in punishing his wife, the nightingale, by quartering, the knight was usurping the king's "highest prerogative; i.e., use of equine quartering to dispatch a traitor." [87] Professor Nichols sees in Fielding's attacks on Pantomime in *Pasquin* the literary man's reaction against the popularity of such performances; [88] and it can be shown that Smollett's own experiences are reflected in the naval scenes in *Roderick Random.*[89] Another study of an author's life as a source is that of Ruth C. Wallerstein, "Personal Experience in Rossetti's *House of Life*".[90] The milieu of eastern Tennessee is thought to contribute much to the setting, characters, and plot of Sidney Lanier's *Tiger-Lilies,*[91] as does that of London to *The Dynasts.*[92]

Such studies as these may, of course, lead to the opposite conclusion, i.e., that the source is in literature or literary tradition rather than in personal experience. Thus Professor Banks studied *Astrophel and Stella* and concluded:

Astrophel and Stella is a series of Petrarchan love sonnets. Sidney's purely artistic impulse was the chief motivating force, the emotion of joy in the creation of a thing of beauty. I read the series as a Renaissance production which follows the fashion of the time. I think that it was accepted by contemporaries without question simply as an unusually skillful example of courtly compliment; and I think that this very skill of Sidney's in dramatic imagination, and the fact that the Petrarchan convention has become obsolete, have misled some critics into judging *Astrophel and Stella* by the standards of the twentieth rather than of the sixteenth century.[93]

If one might, without being considered irreverent, reach the same conclusion concerning Shakspere and his sonnets, the enigma of the Dark Lady would cease to be the puzzle that it long has been.

Public opinion often operates as a source. An author, unless he be as strong-minded as Samuel Richardson, gives a novel a happy ending—though he may have preferred to write a tragic one—if the reading public insists on happy endings. *Romeo and Juliet* and *Macbeth*—to name two plays among many—were butchered to make a Restoration holiday. In the eighteenth century Garrick and Colman were guided in their revisions of Shakspere by the desire to give the play-going public what it wanted; and it often happened that the versions which did the most violence to their originals were the most popular.[94]

Time was when an American author could characterize his villain by the mere mention of cigarette-stained fingers; in these days abstinence from tobacco might be more suspicious. The writer of a moving picture scenario follows a code—whether written or unwritten—which is designed to keep film plays from giving offense to public taste, not only in the United States, but in any country in which the film may be shown.

In Gascoigne's *Adventures of Master F. J.* public opinion operated as a source in two ways. The story was first published anonymously, with an English setting; then it was republished as a translation from "Bartello", with Italian names for the characters. Gascoigne's pretense that his story was a translation was no doubt prompted by the fact that in its original form the work was libellous; and the choice of Italian—rather than French or German—names was dictated by the popularity, in the age of Elizabeth, of Italian stories.[95]

Details in three of Shakspere's plays have been explained as having their origin in public opinion. Thus Iago is interpreted, not as an inherently wicked villain, but as an Elizabethan who is compelled by conventional standards to seek revenge for a supposed wrong in the only way open to him, according to his code—which was also the code of Shakspere's audience.[96] Similarly, Shakspere's variations from Bandello and Belleforest in the characters of Hero and Claudio are explained as necessary to make the Hero–Claudio plot conform with Elizabethan ideals.[97] The secret of the hostility of most of the characters in *Twelfth Night* toward Malvolio is found in his aspiring to wed his mistress, rather than in his puritanism. The entertaining of such an ambition and the mere possibility of achieving it "represented a fundamental change in Elizabethan life, a change that swept thousands into want and evil courses; and Shakspere makes him [Malvolio] express this change in particularly blatant and offensive form".[98] Hence, the source of the attitude of Maria, Sir Toby, and the rest—one might almost say the source of the comic underplot— is to be found in part at least in public opinion. A force somewhat analogous to public opinion—the Christian doctrine of atonement— is taken to be the source for Shakspere's revision of *Promos and Cassandra* in *Measure for Measure*.[99]

Sometimes the main source of a work—or of details in a work— is an individual. If his influence is exerted through his writings, we should classify the source as a direct one, or perhaps a documentary one; if through conversation, we should call it an oral source. But there are undoubtedly instances in which the influence is exerted through sheer force of personality and can hardly be classified in any other way. We know something about the influence—much of which seems to have been personal as much as literary—of Jonson upon the Cavalier poets; and it can hardly be doubted that Shakspere was indebted to Jonson—and Jonson to Shakspere—in ways that we shall probably never discover. A great many instances of sources in the personality of an individual must exist. The influence of Dryden, of Pope, and of Dr. Johnson upon their contemporaries is to be seen in many ways; but there are doubtless as many more that have not been traced. The influence of Wordsworth upon Coleridge— and, even more, of Coleridge upon Wordsworth [100]—cannot be fully known, or that of Browning and Tennyson or of Dickens and Thackeray upon one another.

Sometimes the source of a detail in a work is to be found in the requirements of the *genre* or type of literature to which the work belongs. The writer of a detective story might wish to make the footman or the gardener the villain of the piece—as might very well happen in life; but he will probably, on second thought, heed the injunction expressed by almost everyone who has written on the subject: Do not have the murder committed by a servant or other presumably unimportant character.[14] Every literary technique—

[14] Dorothy L. Sayers had one of her characters say (*Suspicious Characters* (New York: Modern Age Books, 1931ᶜ), p. 260): "See here, Wimsey, you're not going to turn round now and say that the crime was committed by Mrs. Green [the charwoman] or the milkman, or somebody we've never heard of? That would be in the very worst tradition of the lowest style of detective fiction."

from that of the sonnet to that of the picaresque, or heroic tragedy to sentimental comedy—acts to some extent as a source of any work written in that form.

According to one writer, Marlowe made his Tamburlaine more likable than his prototype in Mexia and Perondinus because, in keeping with the requirements of the kind of drama he was writing, he wanted the protagonist to be admirable; [101] hence the *genre* is the source for the change in characterization. It has been argued that Malvolio and the other characters in the sub-plot of *Twelfth Night* were inspired by Jonson's comic method in *Every Man in His Humour* and *Every Man out of his Humour*.[102] Professor Nethercot argued that Royall Tyler's *The Contrast* owed much to eighteenth-century English comedy; [103] and Byron's Manfred is thought to have been shaped, in certain respects, by the Gothic drama.[104]

*   *   *

The sixth class of sources to be considered involves the source of inspiration, whether it be inspiration for the initial idea, for subject, for characterization, for setting, for plot, for ideas, for technique, or for other details. Spenser's *Veue* is thought to have been the source of inspiration for Wordsworth's *View of the State of Ireland*.[105] An "old yellow book" provided the inspiration for Browning's *The Ring and the Book*.[15] Doubtless *Les Trois Mousquetaires* had some share in prompting Kipling to write his stories of Mulvaney, Learoyd, and Ortheris; and either Dumas or Kipling, or both, very probably had something to do with the genesis of the *Three Soldiers* of John Dos Passos. It has been suggested that Bacon was inspired by Campanella's *Civitas Solis* to write the *New Atlantis*; [106] that the opening lines of the last satire in Marston's *Scourge of Villanie* inspired Milton's *L'Allegro*; [107] that Shadwell's dedication to the Duke of Buckingham in his *The History of Timon of Athens, the Man-Hater* inspired *MacFlecknoe*; [108] that William Gilpin's *Observations* led Wordsworth to write *The Borderers*; [109] and that the

[15] The book would also properly belong in the next category—that of graphic and plastic sources, although it might be argued that it was really the story in the book rather than the physical book which constituted the source of Browning's inspiration.

prison scenes in Reade's *It's Never Too Late to Mend* owe much to Harriet Beecher Stowe.[110]

The inspiration for the initial idea may at the same time suggest the subject; the classic example of such a source of inspiration is that which prompted Milton to write *Paradise Regained*—the chance remark of young Thomas Ellwood: "Thou hast said much here [in the manuscript of *Paradise Lost*] of *Paradise Lost,* but what hast thou to say of Paradise Found?"[111]

It would be interesting to know how much the Tabard Inn of Chaucer's day had to do with the choice of the setting for the opening of the *Canterbury Tales,* or the surroundings of Ludlow Castle with the setting of *Comus.* There can be little doubt that Fielding's familiarity with the west country—particularly the Great West Road —dictated the setting of much of *Tom Jones*; another instance of inspiration for a setting that leaps to mind is the house of Hawthorne's *The House of the Seven Gables.*

An article on Chatterton and Coleridge [112] points out that the atmosphere of the *African Eclogues* is much like that of *Kubla Khan,* and raises the question "Could Chatterton have used a source that Coleridge also used?" The author examines parallels between Chatterton's work and the Reverend Alexander Catcott's *Treatise on the Deluge* and concludes that the geological elements, which give Chatterton's poems their "magic", are largely drawn from Catcott. A study of the prose fiction of the early nineteenth century demonstrates that the realistic oriental settings are derived from travellers' tales.[113]

A number of studies of the sources of inspiration for plots have found these sources in real life. It has been said that the plot of Fielding's *The Letter-Writers: Or, A New Way to Keep a Wife at Home* was suggested by a wave of terrorism that swept England in 1730 and 1731.[114] "Incendiaries and murderers had flooded the country with threatening letters, and had succeeded in extorting considerable sums of money from the easily intimidated."[115] The plot of *The Modern Husband* is traced to the case of Abergavenny *v.* Lyddel;[116] and *Eurydice Hiss'd* is shown to have a double relation to life: "it applies equally well to a playwright's endeavor to make a farce succeed in the theatre [referring to Fieldings' own unsuccessful *Euridice, or the Devil Henpeck'd*] and to a minister's attempt to push an unpopular bill through the House of Commons [Walpole's Excise Bill of 1733]".[117]

Another suggestion that actual events furnished the inspiration for a plot has to do with Hardy's "The First Countess of Wessex" in *A Group of Noble Dames*. The early part of Hardy's story closely parallels the marriage, in 1584, of Douglas Howard, the thirteen-year-old daughter of Viscount Binford, and Arthur Gorges, aged about thirty. Other details of Hardy's tale are based upon the marriage of Stephen Fox and Elizabeth Horner in 1736.[118]

It is generally assumed that two of the plot details in *She Stoops to Conquer* were inspired by incidents in Goldsmith's life. It has been pointed out,[119] however, that a trick similar to that played by Tony on Mrs. Hardcastle is related in one of the *Spectator* papers (No. 427) and the mistaking of a palace for an inn occurs in another (No. 289). Even though the ultimate source of these details in the play may be found in Goldsmith's life, the reading of the *Spectator* may have recalled the events to the dramatist's mind, or may have suggested their literary possibilities; hence, the *Spectator* may have served in a way as the source of inspiration for part of the plot.[16] Another case in which a written work may have served as a vehicle for material from real life is found in a study of Reade's *Put Yourself in His Place*.[120] An actual event, and various accounts of it, are taken to be the source of parts of Melville's *Moby Dick* and *Clarel*.[121] Another example of a plot inspired by real life, with a literary intermediary, is brought out in an article [122] dealing with Campion and Middleton. The plot of the latter's *Chaste Maid in Cheapside* is traced to one of Campion's epigrams; then we are reminded that Mr. Bullen, the editor of Campion, regarded the epigram as one referring to an actual event.[17]

[16] The autobiographical element in Fielding's *Amelia* is often overemphasized; Professor Cross pointed out (*The History of Henry Fielding*, 3 vols. (New Haven: Yale University Press, 1918), II, 312 ff.) the significance as a source for the novel of Fielding's own *An Enquiry into the Causes of the Late Increase of Robbers*.

[17] Thomas Campion, *Songs and Masques with Observations in the Arte of English Poesy* (London: A. H. Bullen, and New York: Scribner's, 1903), ed. A. H. Bullen, Eighth Epigram (p. 252) and Note: "In spite of Campion's assertion that 'though sometimes under a known name I have shadowed a feigned conceit, yet it is done without reference or offence to any person', this epigram plainly refers to Barnabe Barnes and Gabriel Harvey". (p. 288)

Much scholarship has been devoted to the pointing out of literary sources of inspiration for plots; such sources have been found for Chaucer's *Rime of Sir Thopas*,[123] for Greene's *Pandosto*,[124] for Jonson's *Epicœne*,[125] for Beaumont and Fletcher's *Philaster*,[126] and for *The Tryall of Chevalry* [127]—to mention only a few.

As with plot, so with characters the source of inspiration may be found in life itself or in literature. A study of *Hudibras* [128] concludes that Butler's satiric attack on Sir Paul Neile in 1664 was originally directed against William Lilly. Other studies have found in real life the sources of Columella and Parson Pomfret in *Columella*; [129] of Mr. Clare in *Caleb Williams* and the Solitary in Wordsworth's *The Excursion*; [130] of the Poet in Shelley's *Alastor*; [131] of Becky Sharp in *Vanity Fair*; [132] and of Feathertop in Hawthorne's tale of that name.[133]

What might be called a combination of real life and literary source is brought out in an article on Heywood's *A Woman Killed with Kindness*; [134] the anomaly in the characterization of Mrs. Frankford —the ease with which she fell into the sin of adultery—is traced to the Jane Shore tradition, which, as it came to Heywood, was doubtless a blend of historical fact and legend. That the source of inspiration for a characterization is sometimes to be found, neither in life nor in literature, but solely in the author's imagination is interestingly brought out in an article on Mary Campbell.[135]

One of the many studies of literary sources of inspiration for characterization argues that the character details in which Shakspere varies from Brooke in the Romeo and Juliet story would indicate that Shakspere knew in some way the *Giulietta e Romeo* of Luigi da Porto, of which no English or French translation is known to have existed in the sixteenth century.[136] (The author of the article seems inclined to the opinion that Shakspere read da Porto in the original Italian; it should be pointed out that there are other possible explanations, e.g., that Shakspere made use of an English version no longer extant.) Marlowe's Dr. Faustus has been explained as a combination of the Faustbook hero and the legendary Simon Magus.[137] The Yahoos of Swift's *Gulliver's Travels* may have been inspired by Tyson's *Orang-Outang, Sive Homo Sylvestris*; [138] the character Rima in Hudson's *Green Mansions* is traced to Lady Morgan's *The Mis-*

sionary.[139] The character of Gawain is thought to have been derived from Chuchulinn, not directly but through the intervening character, Gwri.[140]

More and more, in recent years, scholars have been directing their attention to studies of an author's ideas, rather than his plots, or his characters, or his technique. In the nature of things, the sources of ideas are likely to be literary sources; but one article finds the source of inspiration for ideas in life: Goldsmith's views—especially his championing of the English middle class—are ascribed to the circumstances of his upbringing in Ireland.[141] Swift's attitude toward the Puritans is traced to a tradition rather than to any specific literary source.[142] A study of the background of Howells' social criticism mentions Laurence Gronlund and Björnson.[143]

There have been numerous contributions [144] to a controversy as to the sources of Spenser's ideas, in which Plato, Lucretius, Empedocles, Bruno, and others have been mentioned. Some of Sidney's ideas have been traced to Plutarch's *Moralia.*[145] In two articles [146] Schiller, Spinoza, and Kant are discussed as having inspired Wordsworth at different stages in the development of his philosophy. James A. Herne is thought to have been inspired in some of his work by Ibsen.[147]

Sometimes a study of a possible source of ideas has the negative—but nevertheless valuable—effect of demonstrating that the ideas, wherever they may have come from, did not come from the source in question. Non-academic people have sometimes found great amusement in this sort of thing, poking fun at scholars for proving that an influence does not exist when no one ever suggested that it did. If the ideas of Jones cannot possibly be the source of Smith's ideas—as, to take an extreme case, when Smith was dead before Jones was born—to write an article or a book to prove the fact would be absurd. But if there is some likelihood that Jones served as a source for Smith, then to prove that he did not may be just as important a contribution to knowledge as would be proof that he did.

It has been generally assumed that the *Færie Queene* was an important source for *Pilgrim's Progress*; but a study of Spenser and Bunyan led to this conclusion:

Into the imaginative synthesis, which is the real source of *Pilgrim's Progress,* diverse elements entered in permanent union, . . . elements which include the Bible, the popular romances, the commonplaces of theological phraseology, as well as the men that Bunyan knew and all that he had seen, heard, or experienced. If *The Faerie Queene* had a part in this synthesis, this part, it is clear, can not have been large. Both as a romance and as a religious allegory, it was but one among many.[148]

Other studies of literary sources of ideas include an article dealing with Hermetic philosophy and Henry Vaughan,[149] one concerning Shaftesbury and Henry Needler,[150] and one on Chapman and Keats.[151] Sometimes the source of ideas is to be found in a misinterpretation—intentional or unintentional—of the views of a predecessor.[152] One may interest himself in the source of a detail of allegory, as does the author of an article on *Piers Plowman*.[153]

The last of the sources of inspiration to be considered are the sources of an author's technique or details of technique. One article argues that the technique of the *Book of the Duchess* was derived from Guillaume de Machaut rather than from Matthieu de Vendome, Geoffrey de Vinsauf, and other mediæval rhetoricians.[154] Professor Gerould suggests that the author of *Gawain and the Green Knight* may have been inspired in his choice of dialect by Dante's praise of the vernacular in *Il Convivio*.[155] Euphuism, according to another article,[156] had its source in the Latin orations of John Rainolds, which Lyly and others could have heard at Oxford in the 1570's and read in print in the 1580's. Several articles deal with the sources of the style of one author or another.[157] Of Synge, for example, it was said: "In this play [*Deirdre of the Sorrows*] he was attempting to adapt his peasant dialect to the heroic people of the sagas. He did not live long enough to prove that Yeats' conception of a peasant Grania was unsound, but he did show that it would be difficult to achieve." [158]

*   *   *

We now come to the seventh and last kind of source—what may be called graphic or plastic sources. Many examples of literary works, or details in such works, that were inspired by paintings or statues can easily be called to mind. That Markham's *Man with a Hoe* was inspired by one of Millet's paintings is well known, and Browning's *Eurydice to Orpheus* was admittedly suggested by one of Leighton's pictures. A picture is thought to be the source for

Poe's "The Island of the Fay".[159] Specific pictures may also have
contributed to such of Browning's poems as *Old Pictures in Florence,
My Last Duchess,* and *Andrea del Sarto.* We need not speculate
upon the relation of sculpture to Hawthorne's *The Marble Faun*
or to Keats's *Ode on a Grecian Urn*; and it may very well be that
an actual bust—whether or not of Athena—played a part in the
composition of Poe's *The Raven.* One attempt to find sources in art
produced negative results; no evidence was found to indicate that
Shakspere made use of statues or paintings as sources.[160] (Professor
Manly, however, once suggested [161] that a scene in *The Rape of
Lucrece* had its source in a painting.)

Illustrations and maps may likewise be used as sources. It might
be difficult to determine whether George Seymour or Dickens deserves the greater credit for the origin of Mr. Pickwick and his in-
comparable companions.[162] We know that in intention, at least, the
pictures came first, the narrative being meant merely to accompany
and elucidate the drawings. That a map had something to do with
the genesis of *Treasure Island* we are told both by Lloyd Osborne
and by Stevenson himself.[163] It has been suggested [164] that a map
such as "Tabvla Asiae VIII" in the 1540 (Basel) edition of Ptolemy's
Geography was the source of the passage in *Othello* [18] in which the
Moor relates his adventures among the anthropophagi.

When we think of architecture as a source of literary inspiration,
we may be reminded of the influence of mediæval castles on the
Gothic novels; the influence of Moorish architecture on Washington
Irving is equally obvious. We know that a castle inspired Byron
to write *Sonnet on Chillon* and *The Prisoner of Chillon,* and houses
had something to do with Hawthorne's *The House of the Seven
Gables* and *Mosses from an Old Manse.* Architectural remains influenced Bulwer-Lytton in the writing of *The Last Days of Pompeii,*
and it can hardly be doubted that the Tower and the Cathedral had
much to do with Ainsworth's *The Tower of London* and *Old St.
Paul's.*

Music inspired Milton to write *At a Solemn Music,* and music—of
a sort, perhaps—prompted Noyes to write *The Barrel-Organ.* In a
somewhat different way, music was responsible for Browning's *A
Toccata of Galuppi's* and *Abt Vogler.* If we admit to the category of

[18] Act I, scene iii, ll. 140–45.

works inspired by music those in which the song of a bird was the source of inspiration, we may go back to the thirteenth century to mention *Sumer Is Icumen In,* with its "Lhude sing cuccu". Among others we should also name the skylark poems by Wordsworth and Shelley, and the *Ode to a Nightingale* of Keats.

Nature in various forms and aspects is, of course, an inexhaustible source for writers. We have spoken of the songs of birds as an inspiration; sometimes the bird itself provides a source, as in Bryant's *To a Waterfowl,* Tennyson's *The Eagle,* and Masefield's *The Wild Duck.*[19] Animals, too, may serve as sources, as in Gray's *Ode on the Death of a Favorite Cat* and Burns's *To a Mouse.* We should mention also Blake's *The Lamb* and *The Tiger,* and, even, hesitantly perhaps, Lamb's *A Dissertation upon Roast Pig.*

The garden of the Duchess of Somerset provided Shenstone's inspiration for *Rural Elegance,* and landscapes more cultivated than wild prompted Dyer's *Grognar Hill* and Pope's *Windsor Forest.* Landscapes were also the inspiration for Hawthorne's *The Great Stone Face* and for Lanier's *The Marshes of Glynn.* Poems with similar sources might be Burns's *Ye Flowery Banks o' Bonnie Doon,* Wordsworth's *I Wandered Lonely as a Cloud,* Arnold's *Dover Beach,* and Housman's *Loveliest of Trees, the Cherry Now.*

Flowers have been a frequent source of inspiration; one thinks off-hand of Herrick's *To Daffodils,* Waller's *Go, Lovely Rose,* Burns's *To a Mountain Daisy,* Wordsworth's daisy poems, Freneau's *The Wild Honey-Suckle,* Tennyson's *Flower in the Crannied Wall,* Bryant's *The Yellow Violet* and *To the Fringed Gentian.* As many more could easily be listed.

Among other characteristics of nature that have served as sources are winds (Shelley, *Ode to the West Wind*; Emily Brontë, *The Night-Wind*; Masefield, *The West Wind*; Bryant, *The Evening Wind*; Robinson Jeffers, *Gale in April*), clouds (Shelley, *The Cloud*; Amy Lowell, *Night Clouds*), rain (Maugham, *Miss Thompson*), snow (Emerson, *The Snow-Storm*; Whittier, *Snow-Bound*), night (Shelley, *To Night*; Robinson Jeffers, *Night*), stars (Blake, *To the Evening Star*; Keats, *Bright star, would I were stedfast as thou art*), the sun

---

[19] A parrot—transformed by poetic license—may have had something to do with Poe's *The Raven*; see J. H. Whitty, "A Parrot", *Colophon,* new series, I (1935), 189–90.

(Whitman, *Give Me the Splendid Silent Sun*), rivers (Burns, *Afton Waters*; Emerson, *Musketaquid* and *Two Rivers*; Lanier, *Song of the Chattahoochee*; Joaquin Miller, *The Missouri*), and seasons (Shakspere, *When icicles hang by the wall*; Keats, *To Autumn*; Bryant, *June*; Millay, *I know I am but summer to your heart*).

Other objects of nature that have inspired literary men would include the butterfly and the glowworm of Wordsworth, the honey bee of Freneau, the chambered nautilus of Holmes, and the spider of Whitman. And we should not forget the louse that inspired Burns.

Any number of literary works inspired by human beings might be cited; Defoe found inspiration in Alexander Selkirk, Wordsworth in Napoleon and in Toussaint l'Ouverture, Whitman and Sandburg in Lincoln. Members of the Royal Society seem to have served as sources in Shadwell's *The Virtuoso*.[165] There are certain classes of poems in which persons provide the fundamental inspiration; among these are love poems—such as Mrs. Browning's *Sonnets from the Portuguese*—written in honor of the one beloved; and elegies—like Milton's *Lycidas,* Shelley's *Adonais,* and Arnold's *Thyrsis*—inspired by the person whose death is lamented. Individuals may also serve as sources for caricature; in many of the Victorian novels, for instance, well-known personages are portrayed in one guise or another, generally for purposes of ridicule, as Thackeray is thought to have portrayed Sir Martin Archer Shee.[166]

One more thing should be mentioned and, I think, merely mentioned: that two or more of these sources may be combined, as in Cowper's *The Dog and the Water-lily* or Hardy's *Rain on a Grave*; such combinations might, of course, be classified as composite sources.

V

It is time now to consider how one should enter upon research in source study. The first step is to discover, if possible, what books the author owned. Unlike a collector, whose interest in books may lie in their bindings or their price, a writer is likely to read the books that surround him from day to day. It is not to be assumed, of course, that an author had read every book he owned, much less that he was so familiar with each of them that he used it as a source. But to know the contents of an author's library will provide a starting point.

For the older writers we can not hope to get satisfactory information as to books owned. A number of books exist that, because of a trefoil mark in the margin of some pages, are thought to have belonged to Ben Jonson; whether they constitute the whole of Jonson's library or, as is much more likely, are but a small part of it, would be difficult if not impossible to determine. With more recent writers we may hope for better luck. A diary may contain notes of the purchase of books; there may be in letters or other documents a record of the borrowing of books or the lending of them to friends. Sometimes there is a printed or manuscript catalogue of the writer's library, which will be helpful if used cautiously; most catalogues of this sort are unsatisfactory: they do not list all the books the author owned, and they are likely to include some books that the author never possessed and perhaps never even saw.

*   *   *

The second step—where it may be applied—is to determine what periodicals the author regularly received and read during what period of time. To be sure, few individuals read every article in every magazine to which they subscribe; but if there is in a periodical an article which could have served as a source, and we know that our author was, at the time when the article appeared, a subscriber to the periodical, we are justified in considering the article a likely source, provided we have canvassed the situation and have found no reasonable alternative. It might sometimes happen that an author, though not a subscriber, made a practice of reading a certain journal at his club, or at a friend's house; if he refers to an article in a certain issue in such a way as to indicate that he has read the article, we know that he saw the issue and may have read other articles in it.

*   *   *

The third step is to compile, from whatever clues the author has provided us, a list of the books he is known to have read. We may find help here in the curricula of the schools attended; [20] we know that in the days before elective courses were invented, every boy was

[20] Students of the sixteenth century will find helpful George A. Plimpton, *The Education of Shakespeare. Illustrated from the School-books in Use in His Time* (New York: Oxford University Press, 1933). The same author has written a similar book on Chaucer, *The Education of Chaucer* (New York: Oxford University Press, 1935).

at least exposed to all the authors in the curriculum. Books mentioned in the author's works, books from which he obviously borrowed,[21] books which his friends were reading, books which were "all the rage"—all these are to be considered; some of them it may be possible to include among the books read, others will have to be relegated to the next category: books probably read.

*   *   *

Study of the list of books certainly read may throw such light on the author's habits as to enable us to assume with a considerable degree of probability that he read certain other works. We might find that he made a practice of reading popular novels as soon as they appeared; unless we found some reason for the omission, it would be unlikely that one work in this class would be discriminated against. If we found that he had a passion for Shakspere, we might assume that he had read *Hamlet,* even though we could find no proof that he had. We might learn that he made use of the library of a friend; if that library contained copies of works that we could be sure would have interested him, we may be justified in including them among the books probably read. If we know that he read French only with difficulty and habitually read French works in English translations, we may consider it probable that his knowledge of Molière came through a translator. One thing should be kept in mind in making up the list of books probably read: The statement that "everyone" has read this or that work may be almost—but is never quite—literally true; there are even now people who have not read *Gone with the Wind* or *The Grapes of Wrath* or *Forever Amber.*[22]

The last category of literary sources is made up of books possibly read. For all but the earliest periods such a list would be too long to record, and it is not likely to include many determinable sources. But it is important to keep in mind the fact that some books our author may have read, whereas others he cannot have read. Among the latter

---

[21] The warning given above (p. 171) against assuming that because an author mentions a book or quotes from it, he must therefore have read it, is, of course, to be kept in mind.

[22] Gabriel Harvey wrote in a letter to Spenser (*Works,* ed. Grosart, 3 vols. (London: privately printed, 1885), I, 69) that this is one of the conditions prevailing at Cambridge in 1580—the time of the Ramus controversy: "*Aristotle* muche named, but little read: . . ."

would be works of which no copy at any time was accessible to him and works not to be had in his lifetime in a language which he could read. Such books can be disregarded in a search for direct sources.

* * *

Having learned all that he can about his author's reading—and that should include, whenever possible, the determination of the time in his life at which each work was read—the student of sources should study all the other elements of the author's life that may have served as sources in his works. The author's family and his friends, his habits and his hobbies, the various environments to which he was subjected—all these should be examined as possible sources.

* * *

The next step is more than a step—it is a life's work. Before one can hope to do anything in source study beyond the obvious and the superficial, he must have achieved a thorough familiarity with the period in which his author lived. He must know well not only the works of the author in whom he is chiefly interested, but also those of that author's contemporaries and predecessors. Only through such knowledge can one determine whether a parallel is significant or commonplace, whether a similarity is evidence of dependence or merely a resemblance, or which of a dozen possible sources is the certain or most likely one.

When all the sources that can be identified have been discovered, the most important part of the student's work still remains to be done. It is interesting and it may be significant to show that Author X took one thing from A, another from B, and still another from C; but the really important thing is to show—if it can be shown—how Author X treated those sources. Those who pointed out that Shakspere was indebted to the *Il Pecorone* of Ser Giovanni Fiorentino, the *Gesta Romanorum,* and *The Jew of Malta* made valuable contributions to knowledge; but the one who can show how those and perhaps other sources became *The Merchant of Venice* will have done much more. Conceivably, he will have made possible another Shakspere. Perhaps such epochal studies are not yet within the scope of our abilities; but devoted and intelligent effort may make it possible to achieve them. They will not be achieved by those whose conception of source study is limited to searching for parallel passages.

CHAPTER FIVE

❦

PROBLEMS IN CHRONOLOGY

THE word *chronology,* as used in connection with research in literary history, has two distinct meanings. The first of these involves the knowledge of dates and time relationships. Thus, if we say that an individual has mastered chronology, we mean that he knows the dates of all the events that have any significant connection with literature; or, to bring the matter more nearly within the scope of human accomplishment, to be expert in chronology implies having a knowledge of the dates of the most important events of literary significance in all periods and of all the dates in the period in which one is specializing.

I

So far as one's general background is concerned, there is no particular magic in knowing exact dates. To devote one's efforts to the memorizing of a long list of dates is for two reasons an absurd waste of time and energy, both of which might be much better applied. In the first place, knowledge so acquired is seldom long retained; and in the second, one with the proper knowledge—or even a rudimentary knowledge—of reference books can easily look up any known date that he may have occasion to require. What is more important for the graduate student is the ability to place events within the proper half-century or quarter-century, and to associate readily those events that belong together in time.

Few things make a worse impression on an examining committee than to have a candidate, when called upon to name the prose writers of the first part of the seventeenth century, mention Defoe, Swift, Addison, Steele, and Arbuthnot instead of Bacon, Ralegh, Donne,

Burton, Browne, Fuller, and Milton; but it would be an unreasonable examiner indeed who would insist that the student who is specializing in Victorian literature should know that Lyly lived from 1553 to 1606, Lodge from 1558 to 1625, Chapman from 1559 to 1634, and Nashe from 1567 to 1601.

As has been suggested, chronology is not a subject to be studied; it is rather, as Professor Morize pointed out,[1] a habit of mind. But how is the student to acquire this eminently desirable habit of mind? First, he must accustom himself to thinking of the past in terms of the proper century, until the thirteen hundreds are as readily thought of as the fourteenth century, or the sixteen hundreds as the seventeenth century, as the present is thought of as the twentieth century. The student who wrongly assigned Swift and his associates to the seventeenth century was probably simply confusing the centuries; if he had been asked to name the prose writers contemporary with Bacon, he doubtless would have made the proper response.

Another thing that the student should do in attempting to master chronology is to practice constantly the establishing in his mind of chronological associations. Mention of poets of the first part of the nineteenth century should lead him instantly to think of Wordsworth, Coleridge, Southey, Scott, Byron, Shelley, and Keats. The novel of that period should bring to mind Maria Edgeworth, Jane Austen, Scott, and Bulwer; the essay, Lamb, Hazlitt, De Quincey, and Hunt. One should be reminded, too, of the critics Jeffrey and "Christopher North".

A few exact dates, easily remembered, will help in the establishing of these associations. For most of us it is a matter of no consequence that the date of Chaucer's death is 1400 rather than 1399 or 1401; but 1400 is an easy date to remember, and remembering it enables us instantly to assign Chaucer—along with his contemporaries Gower and the author, or authors, of *Piers Plowman*—to the latter part of the fourteenth century. In the same way Dryden's death in 1700 may serve as a chronological landmark once the proper associations have been established. Remembering that Shakspere was born in 1564 and died in 1616 will help to remind us that his greatest work belongs to the seventeenth century rather than to the sixteenth, that his real contemporaries are not Marlowe and Greene, but Jonson and Beaumont and Fletcher.

Many chronological charts and tables have been published; one of these may be a useful thing for the student to own, but he will find it much more valuable to construct one for himself. A sheet of paper should be devoted to each century, half-century, or quarter-century, depending upon the extent of the individual's interest in the period represented. Each sheet should be ruled into columns. In the first column may be put the names of the authors, with dates of birth and death; their literary works are listed in adjoining columns. Works by the same writer may be grouped together next to the author's name, or all the works of the period may be arranged chronologically. There should be a column for each type of literature important in the period. Sometimes prose, poetry, and drama will be the natural divisions; but generally the prose should be divided into fiction and non-fiction. In some periods it may be appropriate to devote a column to history, or biography, or criticism, or to some other special type. Another column should be devoted to political events, and still another to such achievements as works of art and architecture and musical compositions. It will be best not to do too much of this charting of events at one time. One should take a single period—it would be logical to start with the earliest—and fill in a column or two, then turn to other work; the next day, perhaps, another column may be added, and so on until the first chart is finished and a second one can be started. After the charts are all completed, one should get them out and glance at them from time to time, not with the idea of memorizing them, but rather to keep their appearance fresh in mind. Then, if one has—as many of us do have—a visual memory, he may find, when he wishes to recall a date or a group of titles, that he can visualize in his mind's eye the proper chart and read from it, as it were, the desired information.

I have suggested that for the period in which the student specializes he will need to know exact dates and many of them; but this fact need cause no one concern. By the time a person has studied a man or a period sufficiently to regard himself as anything of a specialist, he will find that the dates he needs to know have become as familiar to him through repetition, through working with them, as the important dates of his own life. For the period in which he specializes, the student does not need to study chronology; he simply absorbs it.

II

So much for the first meaning of the word *chronology*. In the second sense, the word, as used by students of literature, means the science of determining the dates of events of literary significance. The evidence upon which we must rely in problems of chronology is of three kinds: bibliographical, external, and internal.

*   *   *

Bibliographical evidence is that which is inherent in the physical material of which the manuscript or book is composed. It is often possible to date a piece of paper. Obviously a manuscript or book cannot be older than the material of which it consists. Three things should be noted, however. First, establishing the date of manufacture of the paper gives one only the *terminus a quo* (date after which something must have happened); paper once made may be written upon or printed upon at any later date. Second, determining the date of the paper provides evidence only for the date of a particular copy of a work; the date of composition may be much earlier. Third, if one is dealing with a book, the date of manufacture of each sheet of which the book is composed must be determined, if possible; paper of rather widely different dates was sometimes used in the making of a single book.[2]

The chief evidence upon which we must rely in attempting to date a piece of paper is the watermark;[3] but in recent investigations use has been made of another kind of evidence. Messrs. Carter and Pollard showed[4] that in several nineteenth-century pamphlets the paper was manufactured after the alleged date of publication. We know with some exactness when esparto was first used in paper-making, when chemical wood paper and mechanical wood paper were first used for books. Without a watermark we cannot date any piece of paper exactly; but for any manuscript or book composed of esparto, chemical wood, or mechanical wood paper, we have at least a *terminus a quo*.

The handwriting of a manuscript, or of an inscription in a book, may be dated with some exactness by experts in palæography; thus it may furnish evidence of the date of the manuscript or provide a *terminus ante quem* (date before which something must have happened) for the printing of the book. In using handwriting as evidence, it is to be remembered that an old man's hand will resemble that which was in vogue some years earlier rather than that popular at the date of writing.[1] It may be noted also that fashion in handwriting tends to be more advanced in the metropolis than in the provinces; thus a provincial writer will use a style which had been in vogue in London or Philadelphia some time previously.

In a book—especially an early one—the printer's technique may provide evidence for dating. Thus in Caxton's early books the lines are irregular in length, leaving the right-hand margin of the page uneven; after 1480 his books have the lines spaced out to make an even margin. We may say in general, then, that books with the lines spaced out to end evenly are later than books in which the line-endings are irregular.[2] It is the evidence of the printer's technique that has taken away from Oxford the honor once claimed for that city—that of having produced the first book printed in England. A book entitled *Expositio S. Hieronymi in Symbolum Apostolicum,* which was printed at Oxford by Theodoric Rood, bears the date 1468; if that date were correct, it would mean that Rood had anticipated Caxton by nine years. But there is no other book printed by Rood earlier than 1479, and books of that date show exactly the same level of typographical achievement as the *Expositio.* Since it is inconceivable that a printer, at so early a stage in the development of the craft, should have made no technical progress in eleven years, scholars are agreed that the *Expositio* is misdated, that it was actually printed in 1478 rather than 1468.[3]

Bibliographical evidence of date is often furnished by woodcuts used as illustrations or for ornamental initials. Such woodcuts may develop wormholes; obviously a book in which the impression of a woodcut shows wormholes is later than one in which the cut appears

[1] Given sufficient material with which to work, a handwriting expert can determine, approximately at least, the age of the writer, although physical conditions, such as illness, may make the writing of a young person resemble that of one much older.

[2] For exceptions see McKerrow, *Introduction to Bibliography,* pp. 55–56.

[3] The book bears a colophon: M.CCCC.lxviii. xvij die Decembris. Probably an *x* was pulled out of the forme in the process of inking; there are exact parallels for that sort of error. See Esdaile, *Student's Manual of Bibliography,* p. 23.

maynteyne them and there may noo wele be in a royame
withoute it be habitraunt of people / for the decay of a royam
is fawte of people. And if they with drawe hem / the prince
is left lorde alone and therfore remembre wele thy dedis
and eftsones thinke on thy saule and put in that garison
all that thou shalt haue nede of in the other world. And
yf it happen that thou must goo in the werre in thyn owne
persone. beware wele that thyn ennemyes surprise the not
by slowthfull soiournyng. And when thou goost to
bataile loke that first thou solicite and exorte thy people as
corageousely as thou can. and loke that alle thyn habil-
mentis of werre be redy. and euery man set in hys warde
and appointed howe they shal fight and sette oute.

    ¶ And beware wele that thou be not supprised by thyn
ennemyes. for lakke of wache and good espial. ther
fore multiplie thy scoute wache and thyn aspies so that
thou mayst alwaye knowe the gydyng of thyn ennemyes
and loke that thou be sure they dkcyue the not. And
whan thou shalt commaunde thy folkes to do eny thyng
loke secretely whether they haue obserued it after theyr
charge or nat. whiche shall make them drede the more
to offende the. ¶ And whan thou shalt commaunde eny
lettres to thy klerke to be made / signe nor seale them not
til thou haue ouerseen thaim. for many haue ben discey-
ued therby. ¶ Ware thou be not to familyar with them
that thou knowes not. vttre not the secretes of thy hert
but to them that thou haste preued. and knowest true
vnto the. ¶ Gouuerne the so wysely. that thy knygh-
tes. and thy people may haue pleasir of the. and gladde

in its perfect state. Cracks may appear in a woodcut, and they tend to increase in length and breadth with age and use. A book showing a woodcut with a short and narrow crack will have been printed earlier than one in which the crack is comparatively long and broad. It should be remembered, however, that the length and breadth of a crack may depend upon the degree of compression exerted upon the cut by the chase; if the type page was very tightly wedged in the chase, the crack might appear in the impression to be shorter than it really was, or might not appear at all.[5] Likewise the appearance of an impression might be affected by the amount of moisture present; paper used in printing was dampened before being put in the press, and moisture transferred from the paper to the woodcut and to the wooden furniture might, by causing the wood to expand, make the compression greater toward the end of a printing than it was at the beginning. Thus the last book to come from the press might show an impression that seemed to come from an earlier condition of the woodcut than that represented in the first copies. Moreover, variations in the shrinkage of the paper as it dried might affect the appearance of a woodcut.

With metal ornaments, as well as woodcuts, certain portions—especially borders—may break or wear down so that they fail to print. Of course a book in which such an ornament appears without any imperfection is earlier than one showing a break; but again one needs to be sure of his ground. If there is only a single copy of a book showing the break, it may be that the apparent defect is due to faulty inking or to the presence on the paper of a bit of lint rather than to a damaged cut. Evidence of this sort is used by Professor Bradner to prove that Henry Cheke's *Freewyl* was printed before 1577.[6]

Engraved plates used for illustrations or decorations also show the effect of use; and experts may be able to determine the order in which different editions or different copies of a work were printed by examining the engravings for evidences of wear.

It is to be remembered, however, that many of the ornaments found in books—especially factotums—were produced by casting, i.e., pouring type metal into a mold; these, of course, will provide no evidence of the sort we have been considering, since perfect copies can be turned out as long as the mold remains intact. In order to derive any chronological information from two impressions of a cast ornament, we should have to determine somehow that both impressions were made by the same specimen of the ornament.

An analysis of the ink, or of the pigment used in illuminations, may furnish evidence of date. Forgers have sometimes used brown water color paint, or something similar, to simulate faded writing, and have consequently betrayed themselves.[4] An illuminated manuscript in which one of the pigments proved to be an aniline dye would necessarily have been produced—or at least tampered with—after 1856, when aniline dyes were introduced.

*   *   *

If we turn now to external evidence for dating, we shall find that the most obvious instance is that in which a dated—or datable—work contains a reference to another work, thus providing a *terminus ante quem* for the latter. As is well known, Francis Meres, in his *Palladis Tamia* (1598) mentions several of Shakspere's plays; thus we know that the plays included in this list were in existence by 1598. Since the list appears to be exhaustive, we may argue—though with much less assurance—that plays not mentioned by Meres were written after 1598.

Entries in the *Stationers' Register* are also used as evidence for dating, though they offer some difficulties. In the first place, the author's name is frequently not given, and the title often appears in a form quite different from the published title; thus one must be quite sure that an entry actually refers to the work with which he is concerned. Moreover it is possible that a work might have been entered in the *Register* before it was written; if an author had told a bookseller that he intended to write a piece on a given subject, the bookseller might have entered the work at once by way of forestalling a rival project.[5] All we can say of an entry in the *Register* is that it indicates that the work referred to was in existence or in prospect at the time of the entry; it does not prove that the book was then written, or, indeed, that it was ever written.

Allusions in letters that are dated, or can be dated, may also pro-

[4] See above, p. 144.

[5] The entry would not, of course, have given any legal protection against a competing book; but if another publisher proposing to bring out a book on the same subject, saw by the entry that he had apparently been anticipated, he might in all likelihood abandon the project.

vide evidence for chronology. An argument [7] for dating the composition of Spenser's Cantos of Mutability in 1579–80 rests upon allusions in a letter written at that time by Gabriel Harvey; however, the case rests upon an interpretation which some scholars are unwilling to accept.[8] October or November, instead of March (1581) is suggested as the date of the marriage of Penelope Devereux to Lord Rich on the strength of references in a letter, written by Richard Brakinbury to the Earl of Rutland and dated September 18, 1581, in which the marriage is referred to as still in prospect. Since other details in the letter are demonstrably correct, it may well be that the writer was telling the truth about the wedding.[9]

The date of Waller's *Panegyric to My Lord Protector* is indicated by a dated edition and also by a reference in a dated letter.[10] An article on Congreve uses two statements and a letter by Congreve, a statement by a contemporary, and other bits of evidence to establish the probability that a first draft of the *Old Bachelor* was written in the spring of 1689 and that the play was still being revised as late as August, 1692.[11] A study of Shenstone reveals that a letter may contain an allusion to an event that can be dated by an announcement in a contemporary publication; or a letter may be dated by the fact that it contains an allusion that can be connected with some reference in a dated letter.[12]

Sometimes we may discover the *terminus ante quem* of a literary work by the fact that a reply to it exists and can be dated; thus Milton's *Of Prelatical Episcopacy* must be earlier than May 31, 1641, since a reply to it is so dated.[13]

Other external evidence for dating a work may be arrived at through our knowledge of an author's life. If we know that a man was seriously ill during a certain week or month, we may take it as unlikely that he did any extensive writing at that time. If an author, in one of his books, says that he has always enjoyed perfect health, we might take the date of a serious illness as the *terminus ante quem* for that work; if another book contains an allusion to the illness, the date of the illness provides a *terminus a quo* for that book.

An argument for 1374 or 1375 as the date of composition of Chaucer's "Monk's Tale" is based on a theory as to the way in which the material for part of the tale came to Chaucer.[14] The period 1568–72 is suggested as the date of composition of Henry Cheke's *Freewyl* on the ground that (1) on being graduated from Cambridge in 1568 Cheke might well have wished to do something to make a name for himself, and (2) after 1572 he was too much occupied with politics to have had time for writing.[15]

Circumstances other than those in the life of the author may also contribute evidence for dating. Knowledge of the practices of the Restoration theatre leads one author to suggest some time during Lent in 1677 as the date of the first performance of *Wits Led by the Nose*.[16] Similarly, external evidence helps in the dating of two of Dryden's plays. It is indicated that *Marriage à la Mode* was written before July 13, 1671, since there is evidence that the King read the play at Windsor and the most likely time for that reading is the period from May 26 to July 13, 1671. Moreover, since the *Rehearsal* —which appeared in December, 1671—contains satire directed against *Marriage à la Mode,* it seems likely that the latter play was performed long enough before December for audiences to have become familiar with it; otherwise, the satire would lack point. Similar evidence would date *Amboyna* before June, 1672.[17]

* * *

Let us now turn to internal evidence of date. The most common instance of internal evidence is the occurrence in a work of an allusion to a datable event. The death of a monarch, the birth of an heir, a new title of nobility, a notable storm or earthquake or famine or plague—an allusion to any of these may provide a *terminus a quo* for the writing (or revising) of the work in which the allusion occurs. Some question has been raised in connection with an allusion of this sort in *The Owl and the Nightingale*; does the prayer for the king's soul necessarily imply that the king is dead, and hence date the poem as having been written after 1189?[18] The fact that Henry Cheke's *Freewyl* is dedicated to Lady Cheyne—who did not become Lady Cheyne until 1572—proves that the work was printed,[19] though not necessarily composed, after that date.[6]

Similarly, arguments based on allusions to contemporary events have been advanced in connection with attempts to date the *South*

---

[6] Another study based on the same kind of evidence is Acton Grisom's "The Date of Composition of Geoffrey of Monmouth's *Historia*: New Manuscript Evidence", *Speculum,* I (1926), 129–56.

English Legendary and the *Legenda Aurea*,[20] two of the *Piers Plow-man* texts,[21] the sermons of Bishop Brunton,[22] the Wakefield cycle,[23] Skelton's *Speak, Parrot*,[24] and others of Skelton's poems.[25] In addition to the evidence already given for the dating of Cheke's *Freewyl*, there is the fact that the religious controversy which prompted the work became less violent after 1570; hence the work was probably com-posed in or before that year.[26]

We shall often find, as in some of the instances just mentioned, that the significance of an allusion as evidence of date depends upon the interpretation placed upon the allusion; thus the student's prob-lem becomes a matter of bringing together evidence to support his interpretation. If the interpretation can be established, the correct-ness of the dating follows as a matter of course. Thus, if Spenser's *Veue of the Present State of Ireland* was written, as one scholar argues, in support of the plan of the Earl of Essex to lead a conquer-ing army into Ireland, it may have been composed in the summer of 1596.[27] And if Shakspere's Sonnet CVII, in the lines

> The mortal moon hath her eclipse endured,
> And the sad augurs mock their own presage;
> Incertainties now crown themselves assured,
> And peace proclaims olives of endless age. . . .

refers to the death of Elizabeth and the peaceful accession of James I, the poem must have been written on or after March 24, 1603.[28] Evidence of the same sort has also been used in arguing that Marston wrote *Antonio's Revenge* late in 1601.[29]

Professor Pound very properly calls attention to some common misconceptions concerning English and Scottish popular ballads.[30] She points out that students are likely to think of the ballads as being much more ancient than they actually are; and the makers of anthologies have contributed to the error by lumping all the ballads together in the time of Chaucer or earlier. Thus we find "Mary Hamilton" assigned by implication to the thirteenth or fourteenth century, when as a matter of fact, the heroine of that ballad was a contemporary of Mary of Scotland.[31] It is true that some ballads are very old and some cannot be dated; but as Miss Pound shows there is evidence for dating that is often overlooked. Thus a ballad in which Robin Hood is represented as being a Roman Catholic was pretty certainly composed before the break between Henry VIII and the Pope; and one in which Robin Hood is satirized must be of comparatively late origin. A ballad celebrating a specific event must naturally be later than the event itself, unless it is merely an adaptation of an older ballad, with a substitution of names. Although the date of the event gives us merely the *terminus a quo,* it will, in most instances, provide an approximate limit in the other direction; for, generally speaking, the ballad will have been composed while the event was still fresh in the public memory. Several years ago the name of Floyd Collins, who was trapped for days in a cave, was in all the headlines; and long before the case ceased to be news, ballads about Floyd Collins were being composed and sung. That was little more than a generation ago, but we can hardly imagine any one's being inspired to write a ballad about Floyd Collins' misadventure now.

Allusions in undated letters may furnish evidence of the date of writing when they are compared with allusions in letters—whether by the same author or another—that can be dated. If an undated letter is clearly a reply to one that can be dated, the latter provides us with a *terminus a quo* for the date we are seeking. If the letter we wish to date alludes to an event mentioned in a dated letter, we may again be provided with a *terminus a quo*; but if the author speaks of an event in prospect—if an author, for example, tells us that he has just started a new novel—the culmination of the event (in this case, the publication of the novel) would furnish a *terminus ante quem* for the writing of the letter.[32]

Another kind of internal evidence of date is to be found in borrowings. It goes without saying that a work containing a borrowing must be later than the work from which the borrowing comes. Some of the York plays contain borrowings from the *Gospel of Nichodemus,* which fact would date the composition—or revision—of the plays about 1400 or later.[33] It is not always easy, however, to determine which is the source and which the borrowing. Thus an argument establishing the chronology of certain Elizabethan plays by the assumption that they contain borrowings from Marlowe [34] will collapse if it should turn out that Marlowe was himself the borrower rather than the lender.[35] A study of the relationship between *The Taming of the Shrew* and Greene's *Orlando Furioso* leads to the con-

clusion that the folio version of *The Shrew* was composed as early as
A Shrew.[36]

An author may, intentionally or unintentionally, furnish us with
evidence for dating a work if we can link it up with events of his life.
The fact that *Lord Jim* is written in English—to take an extreme
case—would be sufficient, even if we had no other evidence, to prove
that it was written after 1878; not until then did Conrad begin to
learn the English language. If an author gives evidence in one of his
works of having read a certain book, and we can discover when he did
that particular bit of reading, we have provided ourselves with a
terminus a quo for the writing of the book. If he shows in one of his
works that he has visited a certain city or country, and we can date
the visit, again we have a *terminus a quo* for the work.

Evidence for the dating of a letter may be derived from the fact
that it was written at a certain place or addressed to a certain place.
A letter written by Spenser from New Abbey would very probably
have been written between 1582, in which year he leased the place,
and 1586, when he wrote to Harvey from Dublin. If from New Abbey
he wrote a letter to Harvey in London, and we knew that Harvey
had made a London visit of some length only in 1583, we should have
brought within fairly narrow limits the date of the letter. Evidence
of this sort was helpful in establishing the chronology of Congreve's
letters.[37]

Sometimes a knowledge of social history will enable us to make use
of allusions to customs as evidence for dating. If we know that a
certain style of feminine head-dress was introduced in a certain year,
that fact gives us a *terminus a quo* for any work in which such a
head-dress is referred to as being worn. If we can determine the date
at which this vogue was replaced by some other, we have evidence
toward a *terminus ante quem*. Thus the date of *Cambyses* has been
put at 1550 or even earlier on the strength of a reference to embroid-
ered guards as a new fashion already passé.[38] Another reference to
costume—this time to millinery—has been used in attempting to
establish the date of the authorship of the Wakefield plays.[7]

We come now to the internal evidence of date provided by the

---

[7] The article referred to (Mendal G. Frampton, "The Date of the Flourishing of
the 'Wakefield Master' ", *PMLA,* L (1935), 631–60) also makes use of another detail
of social history—the number of gilds in Wakefield and their size.

technique of a work. It is well known that an author's technique changes as he develops in experience; the early work of a poetic dramatist may differ in the proportion of run-on lines, of feminine rhymes, and of prose to verse, from that of his mature and later years. If we make an analysis of the work we wish to date,[8] and analyze in the same way the other works of our author, we may reasonably suppose that the work in question was written at approximately the same time as the works which in technique it most resembles. Although evidence of this kind is exceedingly valuable when it is used to confirm other evidence, it is not always convincing when used alone. The application of tests of technique to the Wakefield plays in an attempt to date them [39] immediately evoked a reply [40] in which the same kind of evidence was used to point to a different result.

Similarly inconclusive have been studies of the technique of Spenser's "Cantos of Mutability". Professor Padelford found [41] that on the evidence of the feminine rhymes the Mutability Cantos were written after Cantos I–III. Tests of the compound words and the run-on lines indicated that the Mutability Cantos preceded Canto VI; the weightier evidence points to their having been written after Canto VI. Using other tests of the same kind, however, Professor Purcell arrived at the opposite conclusion: that the Mutability Cantos represent early work. Then he very sensibly observed: "From these various studies analyzing Spenser's style—Padelford's, Fletcher's, and the present article—it is safe to draw only one conclusion: that is, that the counting of words in a partial analysis of a vocabulary is not satisfactory evidence for determining the dates of composition of portions of *The Færie Queene*." [42] He observes also that the difference in style between two parts of a work may be deliberate and "not the result of a weary or flagging imagination".[43]

Technique is used as evidence in an argument that Spenser had written parts of the *Shephearde's Calender* before the idea of producing a unified work occurred to him and that these parts were incorporated in the larger work.[44] The evidence of technique is also used to support the argument that *Waverley* is not the first-written of Scott's novels.[45]

[8] A very elaborate analysis, which may be applied to prose as well as to poetry, is worked out in Edith Rickert's *New Methods for the Study of Literature* (Chicago: University of Chicago Press, 1927).

The last kind of internal evidence of date to be here considered is that provided by the language of a work. Expert philologists can date a piece of writing—if it is long enough to provide a fair test—within fairly narrow limits by determining what state of the language it represents, judging by the presence or absence of inflectional endings, by the grammatical constructions used, and so on. It is largely on the basis of such evidence that *Beowulf* is believed to have been written, in the form in which we now have it, in the first half—or perhaps the middle—of the eighth century.[9] Linguistic evidence is, of course, most valuable in the dating of Old English and Middle English works; grammatical change is so slow in modern English that it is doubtful whether linguistic evidence would be very helpful in the dating of works written since 1500, especially since better evidence for dating is generally available for such works.

With all the kinds of evidence that have been discussed at our service for use in dating literary works, it is still unfortunately true that there are some pieces that cannot be dated. A ballad, handed down by oral tradition, provides no manuscript to be tested by bibliographical evidence; such a work as "Lord Randal" or "The Twa Sisters" alludes to no datable event; and the linguistic evidence is vitiated by the fact that, at best, it may provide a date only for a particular version, which version may be a relatively late one. Nevertheless, with most works we are on rather surer ground in problems of chronology than in some other fields.

[9] The one extant manuscript of *Beowulf* is assigned, on the evidence of the handwriting, to about the year 1000.

CHAPTER SIX

꧁ ꧂

PROBLEMS OF SUCCESS
AND INFLUENCE

PERHAPS it is obvious that success and influence are by no means the same thing and do not necessarily go together. Doubtless no book and no writer can be greatly successful without exerting some influence, but the influence may not be at all proportionate to the success. Conversely, a book might enjoy small success and at the same time be greatly influential. Plutarch and Holinshed would have left their impress on Elizabethan drama if they had been read by no one other than Shakspere, and Horace Walpole might still have inspired the Gothic novel if Mrs. Reeve and Mrs. Radcliffe had been the only readers of *The Castle of Otranto*.

I

It should be fairly easy to determine the success of a modern work. The publisher can testify as to the number of copies sold; [1] this is not an absolute gauge, since some copies may remain for years on a bookstore shelf, but taken together with library circulation figures, should make possible a fairly accurate estimate of the number of readers. It is more difficult to determine the success of a work in times past. The number of editions is one test; obviously a work of which there were many editions must have enjoyed a greater success than one of which there were few. Unfortunately there is no way of telling how many copies of an edition were printed; [2] one edition may have

[1] The number of copies printed is not a reliable guide; sometimes a considerable number is left on the publisher's hands, to be disposed of eventually as "remainders".

[2] Dr. McKerrow gives (*An Introduction to Bibliography*, pp. 131–33) such figures on the size of editions as are available.

consisted of anything from one hundred to thousands of copies. During the latter part of the sixteenth century there was a provision of the Stationers' Company that not more than 1250 copies (later changed to 1500 and then to 2000) be printed from one setting of type; but that figure gives us only a maximum limit, and we have no assurance that the regulation was strictly enforced. For the period 1475–1640 the *Short Title Catalogue* will give the number of editions of a work of which copies are known to exist; [3] and the number of editions as compared with the number achieved by a work of similar type and appeal is a fairly good measure of success. When a book contains a list of subscribers, the length of the list and the importance of the names would also furnish some evidence. [1]

The number and nature of contemporary allusions to a work provide still better testimony of success. Thus the discovery of previously unnoticed references to Middleton's *A Game at Chesse* gives additional information as to the play's popularity. [2] The popularity of Shelley's *The Cenci* has also been studied. [3] A study of Edward Fairfax prompted this comment:

We may see the author admired by his contemporaries for his Italianate richness of description, praised by the seventeenth century for his smoothness and heroics, neglected by the eighteenth for his lack of elegance and rime (i.e., of couplets), revived by the romantics for his touching passages of emotion, and left on the shelf today because, perhaps, we have other things to think about. [4]

An article on Crashaw shows that his poetry had little vogue during the eighteenth century, but became increasingly popular in the nineteenth. [5] Similar studies have been made of Fielding, [6] of Samuel Butler, [7] of Ruskin, [8] and of the nineteenth-century American humorists. [9] Literary critics and reviewers may give us some idea of a book's success, though it must be remembered that the reading public does not always see eye to eye with the experts; Congreve's *Mourning Bride* offers a case in point. [10] The existence of a parody testifies to the success of the work parodied; a parody has no point unless the original is well known. [11]

[3] As has elsewhere been observed, the *STC* is not perfect; a good many editions are not noted, and sometimes variant copies or issues have been mistaken for editions. In a given work, however, such errors can generally be discovered without great difficulty. Moreover, a new edition of the *STC* is in progress.

Sometimes the study of an author's popularity reveals the fact that his success was non-existent, or at least was less extensive than had been supposed; the reputation in England of the German romanticist, Hoffmann, is greater in the twentieth century than it was throughout the nineteenth.[12] A study of the popularity of Pope in the United States [13] showed one piece of evidence to be false, but brought out other indications of success.

One may study the success of a *genre* rather than that of a writer or a specific work; such a study has been made, for example, of the *roman de longue haleine*—the long-winded romance.[14]

Studies of success may be limited either geographically or chronologically, as are some of those already mentioned; others with geographical limits include articles on the fame of Byron in France,[15] and that of Longfellow,[16] Whitman,[17] and Melville [18] in England. Studies with chronological limits include articles on Shakspere's sonnets in the early nineteenth century,[19] and on the contemporary popularity of Defoe's *Review*.[20] Both geographical and chronological limits are applied in an article on Melville's *Typee* and *Omoo* [21] and in *Keats' Reputation in America to 1848*.[22] One might profitably direct his attention to the type of reader attracted to a certain work or to an author.

II

Let us consider now the matter of influence as distinct from success. Questions of influence are much like the problems of source study considered in an earlier chapter; indeed, the difference is largely, if not wholly, one of attitude. The student of Marlowe thinks of the relation between Shakspere and Marlowe as an instance of Marlowe's influence; to the student of Shakspere it is a matter of Marlowe's being one of Shakspere's sources. One of the most interesting things to consider in any question involving influence is the reason for it. Why does one man—like Chaucer, say—exert so strong and so lasting an influence, while another—like Pope—whose influence was for a while even greater, loses his hold on his fellows in a relatively short time? And why is one age, like that of Elizabeth, so avidly receptive to new ideas, while another is, by comparison, smug and self-satisfied? To answer these questions one must invade the fields of psychology and social history; such an excursion would hardly come within the province of this book.[4] We are concerned here rather with the questions "What kinds of influence may one study?" and "How is one to proceed in such studies?"

The most obvious kind of influence is that of one author upon another. When the latter frequently alludes to the work of the former, or directly quotes from him—as Walt Whitman quoted Shakspere [23] —we have proof of influence; but the influence may be much broader and deeper than the quotations and allusions alone would indicate. Professor Clark found that the influence of Shakspere on Shelley is proved by various bits of evidence, among them "parallels in thought, phrase, imagery, symbolism [in the work of Shelley] to passages in the plays of Shakspere . . ." [24] An article based on similarity of ideas and an allusion brings out the influence of Voltaire on Thoreau; [25] similarly, references and parallel passages show the influence of Mary Tighe on Keats.[26] Other studies bring out the influence of Virgil on Spenser; [27] of Beaumont and Fletcher on Shakspere; [28] of Burton on Keats; [29] and of Swift on Keats [30] and Franklin; [31] of Milton on Freneau; [32] of Keats on Shelley,[33] Rossetti,[34] and William Morris; [35] of Shakspere on Scott; [36] of Maurice Morgann on Hazlitt; [37] of Roger Fry on Virginia Woolf; [38] and of Ibsen on James Joyce.[39]

The influence of a writer or a work may also be shown by pointing to imitations, replies, or attacks; evidence of this sort brings out the relation between Charles Churchill and various minor eighteenth-century satirists.[40]

Sometimes personal acquaintance or friendship may be evidence of influence almost sufficient in itself. Even if we knew nothing more than that Wordsworth and Coleridge were intimate friends for years, we should be very sure—each being the sort of person that he was— that they must have profoundly influenced one another. Examples of less famous literary friendships are those of Markham and Garland [41] and Trowbridge and Whitman.[42]

It may happen that investigation of the influence of one writer on another achieves the negative result of proving that no such influence existed; that is the conclusion of a study of the influence of Boling-

[4] Professor Morize has an excellent discussion of these matters in *Problems and Methods,* pp. 225–62.

broke on Voltaire.[43] As I have elsewhere suggested,[5] people are sometimes contemptuous of negative results; but in some studies a negative result may be just as interesting and just as important a contribution to knowledge as a positive one.

Sometimes in studying the influence of one man upon another we may be particularly concerned with the effect on the latter's thinking —as was the author of an article on Bacon's influence on Hall [44]—or on his life as well as on his works—as was the author of an article on Socrates and Byron.[45] Or the interest of a study may be centered in a changing or developing influence, such as that of Wordsworth on Emerson.[46]

We may profitably interest ourselves in some instances with the way an influence was exerted. Thus it is said of the influence of Bacon on Shelley that it was indirect rather than direct, that "It was the *spirit* of the great philosopher that influenced Shelley. . . . They were, in fact, kindred spirits, for Bacon treated philosophy poetically, and Shelley treated poetry philosophically." [47]

An influence may be discovered in certain of an author's works, but not found in others; thus the influence of Charles Brockden Brown is thought to be strong in Shelley's work before 1817 but not evident in his later writings.[48] A study of Arthur Hugh Clough's *Mari Magno* concludes that the work shows in its themes the influence of Crabbe, and in its form, that of Chaucer.[49] The influence of an author on one aspect of another's work is brought out in an article on Virgil and Dryden; [50] and an influence exerted on a group of works is studied in a paper on the influence of Beaumont and Fletcher on Restoration drama.[51]

Sometimes an influence may exist in one detail or one respect. Thomas Vaughan is thought to be responsible for the interest in Hermetic philosophy shown by his brother, Henry,[52] and also for the latter's ideas concerning God in nature.[53]

One may study an influence upon style or technique.[54] In one article Lydgate is blamed—I think the word is permissible here—for the "aureate" language of the Scottish Chaucerians; [55] in another the influence of Virgil upon the forms of English verse is brought out.[56]

The influence of a single writer may be seen throughout a *genre,* as

[5] See above, p. 184.

Lyly affected Elizabethan prose fiction or Poe the short story. A study of Prévost concludes that much of the sentimentalism of the English novel in the second half of the eighteenth century can be traced to the author of *Manon Lescaut*.[57] It may happen that the suspected influence can be disproved; thus it is denied that the type represented by Chaucer's "Monk's Tale"—the collection of tragic "falls"—is traceable to Boccaccio.[58]

A study may be made of the influence of a single writer upon two or more writers, or upon a people, or an age. Blake is shown to have influenced "A.E." and, even more deeply, Yeats.[59] Conversely, one may disprove such an influence. The pessimism of later nineteenth-century England is attributed, not to Schopenhauer—as might well be supposed—but to "certain social causes which clearly had begun to operate before Schopenhauer was known, . . ."[60] Similarly, Rousseau is found to have been less influential in eighteenth-century England than he is generally thought to have been.[61]

The influence of several writers upon a period may be studied, though to analyze and disentangle the separate influences would be an almost, if not quite, insuperable task. Allusions would indicate, according to one article, that the writers most influential in the last decade of the eighteenth century were Shakspere, Milton, Thomson, Collins, Thomas Warton, Burns, Southey, and Gray.[62]

Attention may be directed to the influence of a single work, as that of Ovid's *Metamorphoses* on Spenser's Mutability Cantos.[63] A whole host of works with titles ending in "-iad" are to some extent at least imitations of Pope's *Dunciad*.[64]

The interest of a study may lie in the means by which an influence is exerted by one work upon other works. Whether the Platonic element in the heroic drama of the Restoration came from French sources or from earlier English drama is the question discussed in a series of articles.[65]

The influence of a work upon a type of literature may be studied, as in an article on the influence of *Ivanhoe* upon the writing of history.[66] Or one might study the influence of a work—such as *Uncle Tom's Cabin* or *The Descent of Man*—upon a people or a period.

An influence—even a literary one—is not necessarily that of a writer or a work; it may derive from a literary form, or a style, or a convention. Thus we might study the influence of the ballad on Scott, or the drama on Browning; we might seek to trace the influence of Euphuism on prose style, or of conceits on poetry; we might examine the effect on literature of such stock characters as the braggart soldier or the clever servant, of such devices as disguises or asides. Professor Baldwin shows in Chaucer a reaction against the conventional popularity of rhetorical "colors"; [67] a study of the "vice" and "parasite" shows the influence of a type character on a *genre*.[68]

Influences other than literary ones may be studied; there are articles on the influence of painting on F. Hopkinson Smith [69] and Theodore Dreiser,[70] for example.

The circumstances of an author's life exert an influence that may be studied. Scott's lameness made it necessary for him to indulge his interest in military exploits by writing about them instead of living them. The poverty-stricken boyhood of Dickens is reflected throughout his humanitarian novels, and the seafaring experiences of Joseph Conrad color everything he wrote. Without having known M. Heger, Charlotte Brontë could hardly have written *Villette*; and *Wuthering Heights* undoubtedly owes much to Emily's relations with her brother Branwell.

One may study—if he has sufficient background in history as well as in literature—the influence of one period upon another. There can be no doubt that much of the laxity of the Restoration was caused by the strictness of the Commonwealth; and much of the literature of the *fin de siècle* was written in protest against another era of puritanism. One study of this sort involves the influence of Old English poetry upon a Middle English author.[71]

The last kind of study of influence to be mentioned here deals with the influence of the literature of one country upon that of another. Three articles have to do with the influence of Irish literature upon English.[72]

III

In undertaking a study of the success of a writer, one must first determine as accurately as possible the number of people who have read his work in the period under consideration. Publisher's sales figures and library circulation have already been mentioned as guides available for recent works; for more remote periods one must rely upon the number of editions (if that can be determined), references and allusions, quotations, and unacknowledged borrowings. The inclusion of a work in the curriculum of a school or college will also give us information if we can discover how many individuals submitted themselves to that curriculum. The fact that the reading was required makes the success of such a work a little different from that of one which is read voluntarily; nevertheless its being required represents a kind of success that must be taken into consideration. If we could compare the number of people who, during the past forty years, have read Dickens, with the number of readers of Thackeray, there would undoubtedly be a large plurality in favor of Dickens; but is the true measure of success of the two novelists to be determined by these figures in view of the fact that Dickens, far more often than Thackeray, is "required reading"? Similarly, *David Copperfield* has perhaps far more readers than any other of Dickens' novels; is it, therefore, the most "successful"? These are questions that must be considered by one who attempts to solve problems of literary success.

Another kind of qualified success is that achieved by a work when the reading of it comes to be a sort of *tour de force*. For a number of years Professor William Lyon Phelps printed in *Scribner's Magazine* the names of all correspondents who testified to having read Spenser's *Færie Queene,* and the *American Legion Magazine* included in a "roll of honor" the names of those who had read Gibbon's *The Decline and Fall of the Roman Empire.* Such part of the success of a work as is due to readers who wish to see their names in print or to boast of their accomplishment is surely to some extent a spurious success. Another anomaly is presented by *Émile*; as one writer put it: "Although *Émile* stands at the head of Rousseau's works in point of eighteenth-century English diffusion, and although this is no mean position, its reputation was predominantly unfavorable." [73]

Another circumstance which may serve to qualify the success of a work is popularity as a gift book. In the latter part of the last century and the first years of this, graduates and celebrators of anniversaries were likely to find among their presents *The Idylls of the King* or *Lucile*—or both. A copy of one of these works, generally in a colorful if not lavish binding, was to be found on many a parlor table; but it was there largely, if not solely, as an ornament. There were certainly many people who owned copies of *Lucile* but never read it, knew nothing of "Owen Meredith's" other works, did not know that "Owen Meredith" was the Earl of Lytton; hence an estimate of Lytton's success based on the number of copies of *Lucile* sold would be a fallacious estimate.

*   *   *

In attempting to study the influence of a writer or a work one's problem is even more difficult. It first must be determined that an influence was exerted, for it is possible to read a book without receiving from it any stimulus, any effect. Perhaps, strictly speaking, there is always an effect, since a bit of reading—like any other experience—inevitably contributes something to one's life; but the effect may be much too slight to constitute an influence that can be studied. A jesting remark of Stephen Leacock concerning the influence of Greek or Latin upon the disciples of the classics contains an element of truth:

My friend the Professor of Greek tells me that he truly believes the classics have made him what he is. This is a very grave statement, if well founded. Indeed I have heard the same argument from a great many Latin and Greek scholars. They all claim, with some heat, that Latin and Greek have practically made them what they are. This damaging charge against the classics should not be too readily accepted. In my opinion some of these men would have been what they are, no matter what they were.[74]

To show that an author or a work exerted an influence upon John Doe, we must, then, first prove that Doe read the work or works in question and, second, show that he was affected by his reading in some discernible and demonstrable fashion.

For an author to admit his indebtedness to a predecessor or a contemporary is of course helpful to the student interested in tracing the latter's influence, but such admissions must not be pushed too far. An author might honestly think himself influenced by something which did not actually affect him, or might think the influence greater than in fact it was. Or one might think that he should have been influenced by Shakspere or Milton, and say that he was from fear of being thought unappreciative. Even when an author is telling the exact truth, we can make little of his statement unless we find evidence to confirm it. A writer like Lord Dunsany, for example, might conceivably be perfectly unaware of the influence of the Old Irish language and literature upon his style; he might tell us that the strongest influence on his work is that of the Bible. That the Irish influence is there, whether or not the author is conscious of it, could easily be demonstrated; how strong the Biblical influence is could be determined only by a study of the diction, imagery, ideas, and rhythms.

The warnings previously given [6] in connection with the study of sources apply also to the study of influences. Parallels must be real parallels, explainable only on the ground of a source-and-influence relationship. One must not make the mistake of allowing a knowledge of a certain writer, or an interest in him, to delude one into discovering his influence in all of his successors; few men have been so influential as their champions are likely to think them. It must be remembered, too, that influences may be indirect; they are still influences, to be sure, but with a difference. A book written under the stimulus of *All for Love* would represent the influence of Shakspere, and of Plutarch, for that matter; but the primary influence—and in certain respects the only one that counts—would be that of Dryden. A work inspired by the cinema version of *Gone with the Wind* or *Of Mice and Men* would represent the influence of Margaret Mitchell or of Steinbeck only indirectly.

It must be remembered, too, that—as the last illustration suggests—there are influences other than literary ones. Radio, music, art—all of the things, in fact, that can serve as sources—may exert influences, some of which would be difficult, if not impossible, to trace.

One who seeks to solve problems of influence must have an extensive background, in order that he may not mistake one influence for another; he must be open-minded to the point of skepticism, lest he should discover an influence that does not exist. In publishing his results let him suggest influences where he finds good reason to suspect them, but confine more positive assertions to those that can be proved.

[6] See above, pp. 167–71.

⋘ ⋙

CHAPTER SEVEN

PROBLEMS OF
INTERPRETATION

IT is the objective of the student of literature to appreciate what
he reads; in order to appreciate, he must interpret, and interpret
rightly. A Hottentot or an infant might derive a certain pleasure
from hearing Shaksperean verse or Biblical prose well read. An adult,
ignorant of English, might be able to tell, just from hearing a reading of *L'Allegro* and *Il Penseroso,* which of the two poems expresses
the meditative mood and which the light-hearted. But true appreciation demands understanding, and understanding often involves
problems of interpretation.

One who reads Spenser's *Mother Hubberds Tale* without thinking
of Burghley and Elizabeth's court, or *Gulliver's Travels* without
reference to its political and social background, or *Joseph Andrews*
without having read *Pamela,* will gain something, no doubt; but he
will miss what is most important in each work. Sometimes the essence
of a work is its allegory or symbolism, as in Melville's *Mardi;* [1] without interpretation, there can be neither appreciation nor understanding. Even where there is no appearance of allegory, or symbolism, or
satire, one must still be on his guard; Defoe's *The Shortest Way
with Dissenters* deceived everyone for a time. Moreover, those works
that have no secondary or hidden meaning must, to be fully appre-
ciated, be read in the spirit of their times. Long though it is, *Clarissa*
must be read entire for its full flavor to be savored; one must realize,
too, that eighteenth-century readers, brought up on "long-winded
romances", did not find long books either tedious or tiresome. Without an understanding of the author and of those for whom he wrote,

one cannot know all there is to be known about any literary work.

I

Sometimes a problem of interpretation involves only a part of a work—a single word, or a phrase, or a short passage. Professor Gerould corrects a misapprehension concerning Chaucer's Franklin by citing evidence that the word implied, not a parvenu, but a member of the gentry.[2] Another scholar is concerned with the meaning of the word *burdoun* in Chaucer.[3] The word *favours* had various meanings in Elizabethan times; its use in *King Henry IV, Part I* (V, iv, 96) has been interpreted to mean that Prince Hal takes the plumes from his own helmet to cover the face of his dead foe.[4] A famous crux in *Hamlet* (V, ii, 298) might be solved by interpreting the word *fat* to mean *sweaty*; the author of the suggestion points out that the word is still so used in Wisconsin.[5] A difficulty in *L'Allegro* is removed if we consider the word *hoar* as meaning *misty* or *dewy* rather than *frosty*.[6] Sometimes the word involved constitutes an allusion; thus the identification of the name *Letitia*, in one number of *The Rambler*, with Letitia Pilkington, leads to the suggestion that in that reference Dr. Johnson was making a bid for popularity.[7] Other articles in which interpretation depends upon the identification of characters deal with Spenser's *Faerie Queene* [8] and *Shepheardes Calender*,[9] Nashe's *Pierce Penilesse*,[10] and Pope's *A Receipt to Make an Epic Poem*.[11] An autobiographical interpretation of Shelley's *Alastor* rests mainly upon the connotation of the word used as the title.[12] Suggestions concerning Browning's *A Grammarian's Funeral* depend upon two words used in the poem; *comment* is interpreted as meaning, not the commentary printed with the text, but one that the grammarian intended to write, and the Latin word *tussis* is given a double meaning.[13] Sometimes the problem is one of translating from a foreign language; taking the Latin *alter* in one of Gabriel Harvey's letters as *changed* rather than *another* makes it possible to infer that Spenser's wife was the "Rosalind" of the *Shepheardes Calender*.[14] Sometimes it seems possible to interpret a word only by emending it, as in the reference to Falstaff's death cited in another chapter;[1] a

---

[1] See above, pp. 114–16.

suggested emendation of a single word clears up a difficulty in the Exeter *Harrowing of Hell*.[15]

*   *   *

It may be that the interpretation of a word involves another word, or the context. In Shakspere's Sonnet CVII, if we take the "Mortal Moon" to be Queen Elizabeth, and "eclipse" to mean death, the other allusions fall into place and the poem becomes a celebration of the peaceful accession of James I.[16] The fact that Malvolio refers to a drinking song—"Please One, and Please All"—as a "true" sonnet is taken to indicate that he was not so much a puritan as is generally supposed.[17] That Shakspere's conception of the balcony scenes in *Romeo and Juliet* (II, ii, and III, v) was quite different from the modern staging of them is suggested by Tom Coryat's difficulty in attempting to explain Italian architecture to Elizabethan readers.[18] The proper interpretation of the word "Yis"—in the light of the passage that precedes it—brings out the point of the joke in Chaucer's *Hous of Fame* (Book II).[19]

*   *   *

Sometimes interpretation involves a phrase rather than a word—a line in *Beowulf* (l. 1231)[20] or an expression in the *Canterbury Tales* (Prologue to the "Reeve's Tale").[21] Several of Shakspere's expressions have called forth explanations: "partridge wing" in *Much Ado about Nothing* (II, i, 155); [22] "standing water" in *Twelfth Night* (I, v, 168); [23] "star-crossed lovers" in *Romeo and Juliet* (Prologue, l. 6); [24] and "miching Mallico" in *Hamlet* (III, ii, 147) [25]—to name only a few. Two of Milton's phrases have aroused considerable discussion: the "two-handed engine" of *Lycidas* (l. 130)[26] and the "golden Compasses" of *Paradise Lost* (Book VII, l. 225).[27] An interpretation of *Endymion* is based upon the meaning of the phrase "fellowship with essence",[28] and the implication of "no voyager e'er puts back" is taken by one writer to be the crux of Melville's *Mardi*.[29]

An interpretation of a passage—this time a scene in a play—involves Webster's *Duchess of Malfi*; objection is made, because of the attitude expressed by other characters in the play, to the idea that

the Madmen's Scene (IV, ii) provided any comic relief.[30] Other
articles are devoted to the interpretation of parts of works by
Milton,[31] Shelley,[32] and Coleridge.[33]

Sometimes the part of a work to be interpreted is not a scene or a
passage but a character or a type of character recurring in several
works. One article deals with the Green Knight in *Gawain and the
Green Knight*,[34] another with a character in *John Brown's Body*; [35]
studies of recurring characters concern Melville,[36] Edwin Arlington
Robinson, [37] and Robinson Jeffers.[38]

II

Coming now to problems of interpretation involving whole works
rather than parts of works, we may consider first those in which an
interpretation is arrived at by consideration of the work itself. A
unity otherwise lacking may be found in *Beowulf* if the poem is
thought of as essentially a pageant-drama.[39] Inconsistencies and con-
tradictions in the character of Criseyde—which have long bothered
readers of Chaucer's *Troilus and Criseyde*—are explained by the fact
that the heroine is a static character, that the requirements of the
story make her what she is.[40] (It has sometimes been suggested that
a similar view would provide the true solution of the *Hamlet* problem; Hamlet must act as he does to furnish material for a five-act
play.) A reconsideration of the text itself gives explanations for *Piers
Plowman*,[41] *Gorboduc*,[42] and for *Hamlet*.[43] Another writer finds,
largely within the work itself, material for an interpretation of *The
Marble Faun*.[44]

*   *   *

Sometimes an interpretation of a work can be achieved by a consideration of the relation between a part of the work and the whole,
by establishing a consistency between the two. It has been thought
that the last stanza of Chaucer's "Envoy to Scogan" contains an
appeal for help from Scogan; an interpretation which makes this last
part consistent with the remainder of the poem seems much more
convincing.[45] The incongruity between the epilogue of *Troilus and
Criseyde* and the poem itself might be accounted for as due to the
conflict between the two natures of the author—the pure artist and
the religious man.[46] A study of *The Rime of the Ancient Mariner*

provides an interpretation that brings the rather obtrusive moral into harmony with the poem as a whole.[47]

* * *

Sometimes to determine the authorship of a work enables one to make the proper interpretation. If James Thomson wrote "To the Memory of Mr. Congreve", the character "Cenus" is easily identified as Thomson's enemy, Joseph Mitchell.[48]

* * *

We may find our best opportunity to interpret a work by drawing upon our understanding of the author's psychology at the stage in his career represented by the work in question. Three articles on Drayton's *Sirena* [49] and two on Shakspere's *The Tempest* [50] are based on evidence of this kind, as is a study of Melville's "Benito Cereno".[51] The whole body of a man's work may be studied in the same way, as in articles on Richardson [52] and E. E. Cummings.[53] Unfortunately, we lack objective standards for measuring the minds of others; [2] hence, interpretations based on one's view of the author's psychology will not carry conviction to a person who has a different conception of the author.

* * *

We have evidence somewhat more concrete when we turn to other works by the same author in seeking to interpret a piece of literature. Making due allowance for technical and intellectual development, and allowing, too, for changes of mind and human liability to error, we should be able so to interpret any literary work as to bring it into harmonious relationship with the rest of the author's work. By an interpretation which implies a reconciliation with Wolsey, Skelton's last work is brought into harmony with his earlier poems.[54] Students have drawn upon the whole canon of Keats, and upon that of Shelley, to confirm interpretations of various poems by one or the

[2] See, however, Caroline F[rances] E[leanor] Spurgeon, *Shakespeare's Imagery, and What It Tells Us* (New York: Macmillan, and Cambridge: Cambridge University Press, 1935); an earlier work by the same author is "Shakespeare's Iterative Imagery", *Proceedings of the British Academy*, XVII (1931), 147–78. See also Lillian Herlands Hornstein, "Analysis of Imagery: A Critique of Literary Method", *PMLA*, LVII (1942), 638–53.

other of those two writers.[55] And Melville's other works provide a
basis for an interpretation of "Daniel Orme".[56] The whole body of an
author's work may be studied in the light of the inter-relationship of
the various works.[57] Often the author himself may provide an interpretation.[58]

*   *   *

The work of other writers may also help us to interpret an author
in whom we are interested. By bringing together references in Scandinavian accounts as well as in Old English versions, Professor
Malone throws light on the story of Hrethric—and hence on *Beowulf,*
in which poem Hrethric is mentioned.[59] An interpretation of the first
part of *Beowulf* is based, to some extent, on references in Tacitus.[60]
The study of many writers of Tudor and earlier times provided a
basis for an interpretation of Marlowe's *Edward II.*[61] The theory of
courtesy expressed in *The Fœrie Queene,* Book VI, is found to be a
blend of Renaissance courtesy book ideas and the ideals of Christian
knighthood.[62] The same method of study is used in several other
studies of Spenser,[63] and in an article on Marston's *Fawn* and Beaumont's *Woman Hater.*[64] Wordsworth provides the basis for an interpretation of Coleridge's *Ancient Mariner,*[65] and Maxwell Anderson's
Winterset has been interpreted in the light of Jewish apocalyptic
literature.[66]

*   *   *

Historical events—whether those of national importance, like the
invasion of an armada, the rise of a new favorite, or the death of a
monarch; or those of purely personal concern, such as the gain or loss
of a wife or child—may provide the key for an understanding of a
literary work for which they constitute the background. Such evidence is brought to bear in articles on *The Owl and the Nightingale* [67]
and *Guillaume de Palerme* ; [68] in the latter study Professor McKeehan
suggests that the author purposely emphasized parallels to contemporary events as a means of stimulating interest in his story. Interpretations in the light of history have been made of the "Tale of Sir
Thopas" [69] and of the *Parlement of Foules.*[70] Similar historical evidence is used to support the suggestion that *The Pearl* was intended
as an elegy in honor of Margaret, granddaughter of Edward III.[71]

One article on *Piers Plowman* would connect the A-Text with the Good Parliament,[72] another, with the Norman Wars.[73]

An article on Malory finds historical significance in *Le Morte d'Arthur*,[74] one on Skelton, in *Speak, Parrot*.[75] Several studies of Spenser look to contemporary events to provide the clues to the meaning of the poet's works. Thus one interpretation of *Muipotmos* makes the poem an allegory of Sidney, involving Penelope Devereux and others of Elizabeth's court; [76] and a reply to that view takes the position that it is Sidney's wife rather than Penelope who is portrayed.[77] Another objection to the identification of Spenser's Asterie as Penelope Devereux makes the point that there is no contemporary evidence that the marriage of Penelope to Lord Riche caused any such commotion among Sidney and his friends as has often been assumed.[78] An interpretation of Spenser's *Veue of the Present State of Ireland* is based upon references to contemporary events contained in letters in Spenser's hand.[79] Historical evidence is also used in another article on Spenser's *Veue*.[80] The fact that there was in Spenser's day a reaction against Italianate influence makes the large proportion of classical coinages in *The Fœrie Queene* of possible significance in the understanding of the poem.[81] Two more articles on the Elizabethan period are based on historical evidence; Greene's *James IV* is interpreted in the light of the contemporary state of affairs in Scotland,[82] and Shakspere's *Timon of Athens* is taken to be a defense of the Earl of Essex.[83]

Knowledge of Manso leads to the suggestion that the "cups" referred to in the *Epitaphium Damonis* [3] as having been given to Milton by Manso were actually books, copies of Manso's works.[84] Professor Moore finds in the political background of Otway's *Venice Preserved* evidence that the play is a satiric attack on Parliament in its conflict with Charles II.[85]

Social history is utilized in an interpretation of *Nights with Uncle Remus*.[86] Uncle Remus, Brer Rabbit, the other characters, and the author himself are studied in the light of Joel Chandler Harris's understanding of the situation in the South following the Civil War and his desire to interpret that situation to readers in the North.

*   *   *

[3] Ll. 181–83.

Differences between the Folio version and other texts of Shak-spere's *Henry V* prompted the interpretation that the Folio text is one designed for a special performance before courtiers on the eve of the return of the Earl of Essex from Ireland.[87] Wherever different versions of a work exist, whether the differences are to be accounted for as due to interference by church or state or to a change of heart on the part of the author, the fact that there are variations must affect any attempt at interpretation.

*   *   *

If a writer, in borrowing from some other writer, makes a change in the material borrowed, we may find in the nature of the change a clue to help in understanding the later work. Thus when Robert Greene takes from Thomas Bowes' translation of Primaudaye's *French Academie* several stories illustrative of the strange operation of fortune, and omits the story of Tamburlaine—which is the best of the lot—we may find in the omission a bit of evidence that Greene was jealous over the success of Marlowe's play and had no wish to give his rival free publicity.[88] Such evidence—but involving changes rather than an omission—has been used in an attempt to interpret Spenser's *Muipotmos*.[89] Other interpretations in the light of sources involve works of Bacon,[90] Fielding,[91] Keats,[92] and Yeats.[93]

*   *   *

A reply to a work may throw a great deal of light on the work itself. The theory that Spenser's letter to Harvey (now lost) expressed no great hope of going abroad in 1579 [94] is challenged on the strength of Harvey's reply.[95]

*   *   *

It is obvious that the date of a work has a vital bearing on the interpretation of it. If a work was written before an event occurred, it cannot—except by way of prophecy—refer to that event. If Shak-spere was known to his contemporaries in the summer of 1592 as a rising young playwright, then the attack on the "upstart Crow, beau-

tified with our feathers" contained in *Greenes Groatsworth of Wit* [4]
may very well be—as is universally asserted—an attack upon Shakspere. But if Shakspere was known to Greene only as an actor, or not
known at all—and there is no proof that Greene had ever heard of
him—then, whatever may be the significance of the famous letter
(assuming that Greene wrote it), it cannot be an attack on Shak
spere.

Or, if a work is proved to have been written so long after an event
that allusion to the event would have lost point, we must take that
fact into consideration in any interpretation of the work. Professor
Lawrence uses evidence of this sort in attacking Professor Manly's
theory [96] that Chaucer's "Sir Thopas" is a satire directed against the
Flemings.[97]

*   *   *

It is also obvious that interpretation depends upon punctuation.
In the classic example in the old play, Udall's *Roister Doister,*
changes in punctuation turn a most insulting document into a love
letter.[98] It must be remembered that the punctuation in the older
literature was scanty and careless and frequently confusing; the
punctuation in the texts that we read today was supplied by modern
editors, and may, consequently, misrepresent the author's intention.
The punctuation of *Beowulf* was discussed by Professor Emerson.[99]
An article on the character of Chaucer's Criseyde is based in part
upon a proposed change in punctuation.[100] The passage involved
reads, in Professor Root's text:

> The morwen come, and, gostly for to speke,
> This Diomede is come unto Criseyde;
> And shortly, lest that ye my tale breke,
> So wel he for hym selven spak and seyde,
> That all hir sykes sore adown he leyde.
> And finally, the sothe for to seyne,
> He refte hire of the grete of all hire peyne.[5]

[4] Ed. Bodley Head Quarto, p. 45; ed. Grosart, XII, 144.
[5] Geoffrey Chaucer, *The Book of Troilus and Criseyde,* ed. Robert Kilburn Root
(Princeton: Princeton University Press, 1926), p. 366 (Book V, stanza 148).

By changing the semicolon after "Criseyde" to a period, Professor Graydon would emphasize the break between lines two and three, and make the "shortly" rhetorical:

The line:
                    And shortly, lest that ye my tale breke,
is not direct narrative continued, but parenthetical comment upon the poet's intended method. "To speak briefly so as not to interrupt the story too much, Diomede did console her and relieve her of her pain"; but neither this statement nor the immediately succeeding stanzas should be read without bearing in mind St. 156, which warns us concerning the time intervals and sequences of the incidents.[101]

Thus Professor Graydon would have us understand that Diomede broke down Criseyde's resistance not shortly after his arrival, but only after an indefinite but much longer time.

                          *   *   *

Sometimes a correction may involve something more than punctuation. Several passages in Nashe's *Pierce Penilesse* are quite unintelligible in one or another of the old editions.[6] An argument assuming a corruption in the text of Shakspere's *Henry IV, Part I,* would eliminate Gadshill from the famous tavern scene in the second act, on the ground that Gadshill, being a "setter", would not have had—and nowhere else achieves—such social equality wth Falstaff and the rest as is implicit in his presence with them at the Boar's Head Tavern.[102]

                          *   *   *

Graphic or plastic evidence may in some instances contribute to our understanding of a passage or an entire work. I have mentioned in a previous chapter [7] the crux in *Beowulf* that was explained by the discovery of a bronze plate upon which a pair of Viking warriors were portrayed. A new significance is attached to the Round Table, famous in Arthurian legend, by the fact that many specimens of mediæval art show a round table as a detail of Christian symbolism.[103] Unlike

---

[6] For examples see Nashe, *Works,* ed. McKerrow, I, 144–47. Some of these difficulties are removed by what appear to be Nashe's own corrections in later editions.
[7] See above, p. 91.

the typical rectangular table of the Middle Ages, with its head and foot, its places above and below the salt, the round table provided no means of indicating the feudal rank of the diner by his position at the table. An attempt to discover just what sort of garment Shylock means by his "Jewish gaberdine" is aided by pictures of Jews in prescribed costume.[104] Illustrations also provide evidence in a study of the Dark Lady of Shakspere's *Sonnets*.[105] Another use of graphic evidence occurs in Professor Moore's study of Middleton's *Game at Chesse*.[106]

* * *

The article just cited illustrates another method of interpretation —the application to a literary work of special knowledge involved in the work. Professor Moore made use of his knowledge of the game of chess; similarly, one must know astrology to understand certain passages in Chaucer, or mediæval medicine to interpret the lines telling of Arcite's death.[8] An article on Middleton's *Fair Quarrel* furnishes another instance of the use of special knowledge.[107]

* * *

As might be supposed, many articles devoted to problems of interpretation—including some of those already mentioned—must depend upon combinations of different kinds of evidence. An article on the *Crist* makes use of bibliographical evidence mainly, but other evidence is also involved.[108] An article on Chaucer combines the evidence of history with that provided by other authors.[109] An interpretation of *Piers Plowman* depends upon the three versions of the poem and upon other writers.[110] That the theology of a passage in *Paradise Lost* is Arminian is argued on the basis of a comparison of the Calvinism of the *Westminster Confession* with Milton's views as expressed in *De Doctrina*.[111] A study of Thomas Hardy depends upon a comparison of his poetry with his other works and with the works of other authors.[112]

* * *

I have left for consideration together a series of articles on Shakspere's *Richard II* and the Essex conspiracy.[113] Not only do these

[8] *Canterbury Tales*, "The Knight's Tale", ll. 1885–1902.

articles afford an opportunity for following through the details of
two opposed lines of argument, and noting how the same words, the
same facts, may be differently interpreted; but also one of them—
it is not necessary to specify which one—is an illustration of what a
scholarly article should not be. It is no part of a scholar's business to
deal in personalities or invective; real scholars are equally anxious to
arrive at truth, and progress in that direction was never made in
anger.[9]

Indeed, the scholar should go beyond merely restraining his anger;
he should at all times display the tolerance and courtesy that are
the invariable marks of true gentility. Professor Manly once suggested that ideal to me in rather subtle fashion. I had submitted for
his consideration a paper which contained this sentence: "Finally, it
should be said that all students find much for which to be thankful
and much to condemn in the editions of Dyce, Grosart, and Collins."
When he had finished reading the paper, Professor Manly had only
one suggestion to make: "I think it would be better if you said
'something to condemn and much for which to be thankful.' "

*   *   *

What is there to say, in conclusion, of interpretative research?
First, perhaps, that it is not the kind of research to be undertaken by
a graduate student. To bring to bear all the resources of linguistics;
of history—political, social, and economic; of psychology—as applied
to the author and his contemporaries; and of textual criticism—all
this will generally require the full equipment of a mature scholar.
But if a student should, through a "hunch" or a sudden ray of
illumination, hit upon a new interpretation, he is not debarred by his
youth from taking advantage of his good fortune. Instead, let him
amass all the evidence he can find. Let him set down, in orderly
fashion, all the arguments in favor of his interpretation, and then,
with equal or greater scrupulousness, all those against. Let him study

[9] It may be remarked that Nashe is generally conceded to have got the better of
Gabriel Harvey in their quarrel—which, to be sure, was not a matter of scholarship,
though otherwise a case in point—not because he called Gabriel more names and
more ridiculous ones than were hurled at him, but because, aside from name-calling,
he wrote more effectively. I think anyone who reads the contributions to that famous
controversy will feel that Nashe is often merely amused and nowhere loses his
temper; whereas Gabriel is frequently incoherent with fury.

the evidence, giving full value to every argument; for it may very well happen that a single bit of *contra* evidence will make the piling up of *pro* arguments like the adding together of zeros: whether there are twelve or twenty, the total is still zero. Having assured himself that he has a case, let the student then present his hypothesis, not as a revolutionary discovery that must supplant the quaint notions of his predecessors, but as a tentative suggestion for the consideration of those who may be able to bring further evidence to bear on the matter.

CHAPTER EIGHT

❦

PROBLEMS IN TECHNIQUE

ALL literature is characterized by manner as well as matter; an investigation of the former is a study in technique, just as the investigation of the latter is a matter of interpretation or of the history of ideas. We may in general assume that content is more important than form; but studies of technique are often of paramount value, especially as they may be made to throw light on the meaning of a work or to contribute to our understanding of an author. Such studies may confine themselves to a consideration of a single device, such as the dream-vision in mediæval literature, or the soliloquy in Elizabethan drama, or the surprise ending in O. Henry's short stories. They may deal with a type of literature—a *genre,* such as the novel, the heroic tragedy, or the ode—either throughout its history, or, more often, in a specific period and region. Or they may concern themselves with the technique of a single writer, or with some part of that technique.

I

Sometimes we are interested in the source or origin of an author's technique. We may find the answer to our problem in the existence of a definite theory of the art of literature, such as the "rules" religiously observed by Pope and his followers, or the convention that the author of an orthodox detective story must eschew all traces of a love interest. Or the source may lie in public opinion or current taste —the demand for happy endings instead of tragic ones, for prose instead of poetry, for short stories rather than long ones. Again we may find the secret of an author's technique deep within himself, in his experience or his personality.

A study of Middleton's early London comedies finds that the technique of those plays represents an attempt to cater to public taste.[1] The technique of Sir Thomas Browne is found to have its basis in the author's personality.[2] In another study, Milton's ability to compose by dictation is attributed to a method of work developed before the necessity for dictation arose.[3] Still another study traces Emerson's theory and practice of poetry to Coleridge's criticism and Wordsworth's poetry.[4]

We may study an author's technique as an aid to discovering the nature and extent of his originality, as in articles on Chaucer,[5] Shakspere,[6] and Vanbrugh.[7]

*   *   *

It is on the basis of the technique displayed that paintings are ascribed to one artist or another; perhaps in time we may have tests as conclusive to apply to literary works. Even now we may make use of our knowledge of an author's technique to provide part of the evidence for determining the authorship of a given work. A study of *Piers Plowman* [8] brings out the fact that the increase in the number of legal references in the later versions of the poem is more than proportional to the increase in the length of the B and C versions over that of the A. The study concludes that this evidence is not sufficient to prove that the three versions are not by the same author; but it does suggest that, if there was only one author, he added to his knowledge of the law between the composition of the first and that of the succeeding versions, or, if multiple authorship is involved, that the authors of the B and C texts were more expert in the law than was the author of the A.

*   *   *

The evidence of technique may help in the dating of a work, though generally as contributory rather than determining evidence. A study of Spenser's technique in the *Shepheardes Calender* led to the suggestion that some of the poems in that work were written early, before the poet had any idea of putting them together in a unified work.[9] Professor Gaw decided, largely because of the technique, that *Much Ado about Nothing* does not represent a revision of an older play.[10]

Another study of technique led to the conclusion that Scott wrote four of his other novels before he wrote *Waverley.*[11]

*   *   *

Sometimes our interest in an author's technique may be centered in the use he makes of his sources. Thus it is Chaucer's technique in the handling of the *Filostrato* that led Professor Young to regard *Troilus and Criseyde* as romance rather than novel.[12] Another Chaucer article deals with his treatment of the *Teseide.*[13] A study of Sidney considers the relationship between the *Arcadia* and *Orlando Furioso.*[14] Spenser's alterations of current ideas lend significance to one of the episodes in the Second Book of the *Færie Queene.*[15] A similar study deals with James Mabbe's handling of the Spanish *Celestina* in his translation of that work.[16] Other studies involving the author's treatment of his sources include one on Munday's *John a Kent and John a Cumber,*[17] two on Wordsworth's *Descriptive Sketches* and *The Prelude,*[18] and one on Herman Melville and Redburn.[19]

*   *   *

In many instances our purpose in studying an author's technique may be to discover—for whatever value the knowledge may possess —the artist's practices in such details as plot construction or characterization. One study deals with characterization in Scott, Balzac, Dickens, and Zola.[20] An article on *Beowulf* [21] and one on *Piers Plowman* [22] express the view—which is contrary to the usual opinion— that those poems are essentially well-constructed. A study of *Sire Degarre* [23] reveals a mediæval hack writer's methods. Peele's technique in plot structure has been studied as a possible test of authorship.[24] Professor Thaler concluded, partly on the evidence of Shakspere's usual practice in plotting, that it was unnecessary to suppose that any scenes of *Macbeth* have been lost.[25] Other studies deal with the dramatic technique of Ben Jonson [26] and of Middleton.[27] An article on *Tristram Shandy* [28] suggests that the book is not to be dismissed as formless but may be regarded, in one sense, as a carefully planned historical novel. Another author discusses *Peregrine Pickle.*[29]

Studies have been made of the technique of Robert Browning,[30] Charles Reade,[31] Herman Melville,[32] and Thomas Hardy.[33]

*   *   *

An author's habits in revising and rewriting may throw a considerable light on his technique; studies dealing with such practices include two each on Chaucer [34] and Conrad [35] and single articles on Chapman,[36] Lovelace,[37] Crashaw,[38] Bryant,[39] Mark Twain,[40] Henry James,[41] and George Moore.[42]

Studies in versification, being to a large extent objective, are often very valuable; they may provide tests of authorship or of date, and they may contribute to one's understanding of a work. One study of *Paradise Lost* deals with rhythm,[43] another with rhyme.[44] Studies have been made of the versification of such writers, among others, as Campion,[45] Donne,[46] Shelley,[47] Rossetti,[48] Emerson,[49] and Poe.[50]

*   *   *

A good many studies have dealt with diction or with figures of speech—or both. An article on Spenser's language concludes that there is less artificiality in Spenser's diction than has generally been supposed.[51] Miss Spurgeon's studies of Shakspere's imagery [1] show that a thorough understanding of one detail of a poet's technique may greatly enlarge our knowledge of the writer. A study of Poe's use of color words [52] concludes:

The analysis reveals a predilection for black, for white and gray, and, to a lesser degree, for red, much as the general reader might have expected. It is found that a small group of descriptive, landscape tales stress the greens; that a few popular colors are used more freely in the humorous tales; that the tales of ratiocination make less use of color than the others; that the tales of horror are characteristic of Poe's total work; and that Poe's poetry follows his general work except for a decrease in blacks, and a rise in the conventional "golden" of poetry.[53]

As the writer recognizes, the results here presented are just what might have been expected; but such analytical studies may lay the foundation for a psychological study which would discover the reason

[1] See above, p. 221, n. 2.

for the poet's practice in choosing color words, or, more important, the part such words play in the effectiveness of the work in which they appear. Other studies of diction involve William Morris,[54] J. M. Synge,[55] and James Joyce.[56]

A device which is almost, if not quite, a figure of speech is discussed in a study of John Donne's use of dissonance.[57] Starting from Johnson's comment that the characteristic of metaphysical poetry is the *discordia concors*, the author suggests that this device is found not only in the imagery of Donne's poetry, to which Johnson and most others have apparently limited it, but also in its diction, versification, language, and general plan. After examining the poetry for examples of dissonance, the author concludes that "in general, . . . the dissonance is an expression of underlying temperament. . . ."[58] Milton's use of figures of speech is discussed in an article on the Miltonic simile [59] and in one on the animal simile in *Paradise Lost*.[60] There are studies of figures of speech in *Moby Dick* [61] and in *Leaves of Grass*; one article on the latter work finds that, despite Whitman's protestation to the contrary, there are many poetic devices in *Leaves of Grass*,[62] and another holds that the reiterative devices in the poem are a method of tying it together.[63]

Miscellaneous studies of details of an author's technique deal with such subjects as the style of *Beowulf*,[64] dramatic irony in Chaucer,[65] characterization in the "Knight's Tale",[66] Jonson's literary methods,[67] Hooker's prose,[68] the punctuation of *Comus*,[69] the verses used as chapter-headings in the Waverley novels,[70] and irony in Hardy and Conrad.[71]

*   *   *

Studies of an author's technique may deal with his work in a single *genre*; thus there are articles on Dekker and prison literature,[72] on the rhetoric of Donne's sermons,[73] on the handling of the couplet by Donne [74] and by Gay,[75] on Milton's work in satire,[76] and on the work of Bulwer-Lytton [77] and of Mrs. Catherwood [78] in prose fiction.

The technique of an author may be studied as evidence of artistic development, as in articles on Chaucer [79] and on Synge; [80] it is often possible to trace a writer's growth toward maturity more clearly through improvement in technique than in any other element of literary art.

II

In studies of technique we need not, of course, confine ourselves to the work of a single writer; it is interesting and often valuable to study a detail of technique throughout its history, or, more often, within a given period. Sometimes such studies may be directed toward the discovering of the origin or the purpose of a technical device. Studies of this sort have been made of understatement in Old English poetry,[81] of the visit-to-the-perilous-castle theme,[82] and of rhetorical balance in Chaucer.[83] A study has been made of low comedy as a structural element in mediæval and Elizabethan drama.[84] Another study traces the Elizabethan villain to the vice and the parasite of the older drama.[85] A question arises concerning Shakspere's use of the unhappy happy ending: are the conclusions of *Love's Labors Lost, The Two Gentlemen of Verona, Measure for Measure,* and *A Winter's Tale* careless and conventional or are they psychologically sound and artistically right? [86] Other studies of the origin or purpose of details of technique include articles on conventions in Restoration tragedy,[87] on music in the cycle plays,[88] on the descriptions of costume in the mediæval romances,[89] and on Dickens and the evolution of caricature.[90]

Sometimes our interest in a detail of technique may lie in its importance or significance; such a study may involve several writers, as does an article on theories of poetic diction in Wordsworth and others [91] and one on particularity in characterization,[92] or a single writer—in one instance, Thomas Hardy.[93] Studies in technique need not be confined to the technique of writing; studies of the technique of acting, for example, may constitute a valuable contribution to literary history.[94]

III

Instead of studying details of technique separately, we may study the combination of techniques which constitutes a literary type or *genre*. Professor Zucker traced the origin of the genealogical novel, as it appears in the work of Thomas Mann, Galsworthy, and others, primarily to Zola.[95] A *genre* may be studied for the purpose of seeking to define it, differentiate it from other types,[96] or to discover the relationship between types.[97] We may study a *genre* attempting to discover the origin, not of the *genre* itself, but of specimens of the *genre*.[98] The history and characteristics of a type, such as that represented by Chaucer's "Monk's Tale", may be well worth study.[99] Such studies have been made of the Romanesque lyric,[100] the framing-tale, [101] the school drama in England,[102] the Elizabethan jig,[103] the Elizabethan elegie,[104] the Elizabethan lyric,[105] bilingual dictionaries in Shakspere's time,[106] the seventeenth-century essay,[107] the songs in Restoration tragedy,[108] female prologues and epilogues.[109] English magazines for ladies,[110] the eighteenth-century formal eclogue,[111] the comedy of manners,[112] the dramatic monologue,[113] contemporary biography,[114]—even, of all things, the dime novel.[115]

Often, as is true of some of the articles just mentioned, studies of a *genre* are definitely limited in time: "Animal Actors on the English Stage before 1642",[116] "English Burlesque Poetry 1700–1750," [117] "Whig Panegyric Verse, 1700–1760",[118] "Neo-Classical Criticism of the Ode for Music",[119] "The Metrical Tale in XVIII-Century England",[120] and "The Beginnings of the American Poetical Miscellany".[121] Sometimes the limiting element is a geographical one; as well as the broad limit set in confining a study to a country or part of a country, we may have a narrower limit, as in a study of drama in Lincoln Cathedral.[122]

*   *   *

In many instances a study of a *genre* attempts an analysis of the technique of that *genre*; perhaps the analysis is offered just as a thing of interest to scholars, or it may represent an attempt to aid those who wish to write specimens of the *genre*. In the former category would be placed an article on the technique of saints' legends [123] and one on the "Parson's Tale" as a mediæval sermon; [124] here, too, would be placed a study of epistolary fiction [125] and perhaps one of sonnets and sestinas.[126] Many studies of the novel [127] and of the drama [128] would belong to the other category.

One may study a *genre* within a *genre*—for example, the lyric in Elizabethan drama.[129] Something interesting might be done in studying the whimsical chapter heading found in some eighteenth-century novels, including *Tom Jones*, and, more recently, in the books of Jeffery Farnol. One might study the sonnet in sonnet sequences, though the suggestion may raise the question whether the sonnet sequence constitutes a *genre*.

IV

The procedure to be followed in a study of technique will, of course, depend upon the type of study involved. If it is to be a study of the technique of an individual, one will turn first to similar studies of other writers. Thus he will learn what characteristics are to be considered. He must discover for each of these characteristics what might be called the norm for the kind of writing that his author practised and for the period in which his author lived. Then he will be able to determine the extent to which his author deviated from the norm. In a study of versification, for example, one would consider the forms and meters used, the proportion of feminine endings and of run-on lines, the number and nature of figures of speech, and so on. For a writer of fiction, there must be an analysis of practices in plot-construction, in setting, and in characterization. In the field of characterization, the characters may be studied in the light of their function or their importance in the story, their sex, their social status, their vocations; the author's method of treatment of his characters must also be considered—whether his characterization is achieved by means of direct exposition, through what the character does or what is said about him by other characters, or by some combination of these methods.

In studying an author's technique, one should not overlook the element of creative power or genius. Great literature is not produced merely by the application of an acquired technique to borrowed material. It has already been pointed out [2] that the difference between a passage in Shakspere's *Antony and Cleopatra* and the counterpart of that passage in North's translation of Plutarch cannot be wholly explained by saying that the former represents the application of the poetic—or dramatic—technique to the latter. And yet it may be that the study of Shakspere's technique—the attempt to learn how some of Sir Thomas North's prose became some of the poetry of *Antony and Cleopatra*—will not only lead to a fuller appreciation of Shakspere's drama, but may even enable another writer to perform a similar miracle of transmutation.

There is great danger that one who chooses to study a detail of technique may lose consciousness of the fact that it belongs to the

[2] See above, p. 165.

work of which it is a part. Falstaff is unquestionably linked with the *miles gloriosus* tradition, and it may be very interesting and worth while to study him as a part of that tradition; but he is, at the same time and perhaps even more importantly, an integral, an essential part of the Henry IV plays and of *The Merry Wives of Windsor*. The student should not allow himself to forget that taking a character or any other detail out of a work for study is likely to change the significance of the part and that of the whole. Keeping that fact always in mind, the student may safely proceed with his dissection.

If one should attempt a study of a previously unexplored *genre*, an original analysis would have to be worked out; it would be much wiser for the graduate student to choose a subject that will permit him to use a model—a good study of a similar problem—as a guide. One word of warning in this connection may not be amiss. The fact that a number of works have an element—or several elements—in common does not, *ipso facto*, unite them in a *genre*. There would be little point in studying collectively poems about bluebirds or barefoot boys, or novels involving a damsel in distress, a disguised aristocrat, and a witty peasant. To constitute a *genre*, works must have in common elements of literary significance, elements that tend to shape and give character to the finished work. The *genre* will almost certainly determine whether the work be long or short, in prose or in verse. A poem of twelve or sixteen lines, or one without rhyme, is not a sonnet; a long poem may be labeled by its author, or by publisher or critics, "A novel in verse"; but it is not a novel. The *genre* may also specify the mood, the style, and—to some extent—the subject matter. The seventeenth-century *character* is a short piece of prose, generally in a light vein, describing a type of person more or less familiar to the reader—a man about town, a retired sea captain, a coquette, a country squire. A "Character of a Babylonian Warrior" or a "Character of the Emperor of China" would have been an anomaly.

All students of technique should keep constantly in mind the fact that technique is not the most important element in literary art. To know how to write is worth little unless one has something to say. The value of studies in technique lies in the contribution they can make to a fuller understanding on the part of the reader and the help they can give to the potential author.

CHAPTER NINE

◦ᴇᵹ ᵹᴇ◦

PROBLEMS IN THE HISTORY
OF IDEAS

IT is the function of the philosopher to discover new ideas, and, according to Matthew Arnold,[1] that of the literary critic to make the best ones prevail. But we are concerned here with neither philosophy nor literary criticism. We are concerned rather with ideas in their relation to literature and to literary history. There are exponents of art for art's sake who may argue that literature need not concern itself with ideas; and it is undoubtedly true that some poets—Swinburne, in *The Forsaken Garden,* and Poe, in *The Bells,* for example—have achieved their effects through sound rather than meaning. In most poetry, however, and most plays, and in all novels [1] and essays, writers use words for their content rather than their sound; and the result desired is achieved—when it is achieved—through the meaning, that is to say, through the ideas expressed.

Literature overcharged with ideas may easily become propaganda, and propaganda is seldom, if ever, great literature. Even short of propaganda there is such a thing as too much content or too little

---

[1] There are, perhaps, exceptions; but to them a remark in a review (J. M. Lalley, "On Collaboration", *The Washington Post,* January 31, 1944, p. [10]) of Professor Elmer Edgar Stoll's *From Shakespeare to Joyce: Authors and Critics; Literature and Life* (New York: Doubleday, Doran, 1944) may well be applied: ". . . the main basis of Professor Stoll's quarrel with such contemporaries as Mr. T. S. Eliot and the late James Joyce is in the difficulties they have deliberately and disdainfully interposed between themselves and their readers. And since the meaning or purpose, when laboriously deciphered with the help of keys, codes, commentaries, and glosses, turns out to be something less than wonderful—in *The Waste Land* a mere statement that our civilization is ugly and sterile; in *Finnegan's Wake* a complete disassociation of language and sense—such writers cannot wholly escape a suspicion of charlatanism."

art. Whatever Milton and his contemporaries may have thought of the more didactic passages of *Paradise Lost,* it is certain that later generations have found some of the lines in which the poet explains his theological ideas less admirable than other parts of the poem. Nevertheless, the study of ideas is an important part—and, judging from the number of books and articles in the field, an increasingly important part—of the study of literary history. We are not thinking now of efforts to comprehend a work; such study is a matter of interpretation. We are concerned here with terms and concepts as they appear in the literature of a given time and place, with an author's thinking as he expressed himself in one or all of his works, and with intellectual movements that represent the thinking of many people.

I

In his article in the first number of the *Journal of the History of Ideas* and in the introductory chapter of *The Great Chain of Being* [2] Professor Lovejoy set out to define the until then rather amorphous subject of the history of ideas. It developed, he suggested, as scholars [2] learned how far afield it was necessary to go to understand even simple literary documents.

Lovejoy recognized, as some have not, the great danger that students of literature might venture so far afield as to find themselves at last lost in research for which they were equipped neither by training nor by temperament. Here is a real problem. By the nature of his work, a literary scholar is likely to think of ideas only in the crystallized form in which they are found in books, and perhaps to overemphasize the importance of purely intellectual relationships. And this seems a perfectly natural emphasis for one whose entire training has been in the interpretation of literary documents rather than in the recognition and understanding of historical conditions.

In a review of several works, including *The State in Shakespeare's Greek and Roman Plays,* by James Phillips, Jr.,[3] and *Drama and Society in the Age of Jonson,* by L. C. Knights,[4] Professor Malcolm Ross wrote:

[2] Professor Lovejoy uses literary scholars as an example, perhaps for obvious reasons, since literary expression, which involves ideas of all sorts, requires for understanding a broader knowledge than other forms, say in the physical sciences or in economics.

The literary man, impelled by the ruling passion of his age to seek in social history the explanation of cultural phenomena, often approaches the task nervously, conscious of the frown of his less adventurous colleague, 'the safe scholar,' conscious, too, of the social scientist's quizzical smile as, contemptuous and unafraid, he observes his province invaded by the rank amateur. Perhaps for safety's sake, the literary scholar clutches the hand of the tallest stranger he can find in the strange new land. Dr. Phillips will not so much as tip-toe without Professor Allen at his side. Mr. Knights marks the footsteps of Professor Tawney. Nor are they to be criticized for their deference to the authority of the historian and the political economist. The trouble is not that they have jilted Kittredge and Bradley for a pack of outlanders—some transference of allegiance was necessary. The danger lies rather in the mechanical divisions which still beset the social sciences themselves. It may indeed serve the interests of the academic curriculum to separate politics from economics. But it is unsafe for the literary scholar to adopt these curricular divisions in reaching out for a new synthesis of social and cultural values. The sociological criticism of literature, to be valid, must recognize and analyse the fluent interrelation of all discernible social and cultural factors in the given historical moment. Nor must that moment be detached and isolated from its context in time. The imposition of a sharply-defined method derived from one or the other of the social sciences may needlessly suppress or exclude or distort elements relevant to the solution of the scholar's problem. . . .

The sociological critic, then, must do more than seek in the literature of the period direct evidence of political and economic ideas. It is not enough to know what Shakespeare and Spenser and Jonson thought. This is only the first step for the scholar, though an important one which he too often hesitates to take. Nor is it enough to understand the economic motivation of the age—although without such understanding the sociological critic will be helpless, and his work, at best, will be one-dimensional. The sociological critic must investigate not only ideas and 'forces,' but also the subjective manifestations of these ideas and forces in the cultural climate as a whole. . . .[5]

Lovejoy has also noted that any practitioner in the history of ideas needs a special skill. Mere reading of the philosophical and historical texts is not sufficient for an understanding of how ideas work—"a certain aptitude for the discrimination and analysis of concepts, and an eye for not immediately obvious logical relations or quasi-logical affinities between ideas"[6] are indispensable.

From what he says later on in his essay, when he lays down the objectives of the history of ideas, Lovejoy would apparently have these dangers recognized by scholars, and the bounds of the history of ideas respected by those not specially trained in its discipline. For, though he speaks of the breaking down of the fences between subjects, he apparently does not mean that scholars should range at will on the greener side. His solution seems to be instead some sort of scholarly co-operation, in which a literary scholar would not try to do work for which a historian, a philosopher, or an economist is better fitted, but would avail himself of pertinent work in the other fields. The graduate student in English who wishes to work in the history of ideas will need to know, to mention only a few, such writers as Durkheim,[7] Beard,[8] Becker,[9] Barzum,[10] Curti,[11] Bernard Smith,[12] and Mannheim,[13] as well as Lovejoy, Parrington, Perry Miller, Van Wyck Brooks, Hardin Craig, and others who will be mentioned later in this chapter.

Lovejoy suggests four broad areas of knowledge for the historians of ideas to investigate:

1. The influence of classical on modern thought, and of European traditions and writings on American literature, arts, philosophy, and social movements.

2. The influence of philosophical ideas on literature, the arts, religion, and social thought, including the impact of pervasive general conceptions upon standards of taste and morality and educational theories and methods.

3. The influence of scientific discoveries and theories in the same provinces of thought, and in philosophy; the cultural effects of the applications of science.

4. The history of the development and the effects of individual, pervasive, and widely ramifying ideas or doctrines, such as evolution, progress, primitivism, diverse theories of human motivation and appraisals of human nature, mechanismic and organismic conceptions of nature and society, metaphysical and historical determinism and indeterminism, individualism and collectivism, nationalism and racialism.[14]

The graduate student in English should approach the study of the history of ideas humbly and with trepidation. Though investigating the meaning of words like "nature" and "reason", as they are used by particular authors, may at first seem not so exciting as compiling a documentary history of, say, romanticism, it is much the safer bet. It will use a skill for which, presumably, the student will have trained himself: the understanding of literary texts. In the long run it may also be very useful, for it will provide information for a more fully equipped historian of ideas.

II

As we have just seen, a study in ideas may involve a single word; such would be the attempt to convey to English university students the meaning of "apple-polisher" or "pipe course", or to American students the meaning of "buller" (which is something quite different from what the American student might imagine). It may seem that these are properly matters of interpretation. So they would be if it were a question of the word's use in one passage or even, perhaps, in a single work. But when the word appears in several or many works, the study of its meaning is a contribution to the history of ideas.[3] Meanings change so during the course of the life of a word— as a glance at a few entries in the *NED* will clearly show—that, more often than not, some historical change or development is involved. One might think that a dictionary such as the *NED* would make unnecessary the studies to which I have reference; but no dictionary can or should attempt to reveal all the nuances and connotations that may attach themselves to a word. Professor Lovejoy found some forty meanings for the word *romanticism*;[15] and, although there may not be many words of such almost infinite variety, there are few that do not reveal some changes depending upon time and circumstances. To know just what the word *elegie* meant in the sixteenth century requires more than a dictionary can tell us in two or three definitions, with illustrations; it requires that we should know all the ways in which an Elizabethan might—or did—use the word.[16] Professor Lovejoy, in an article which serves as a sequel to the one just mentioned, discusses the meaning of *optimism* and *romanticism*.[17] There are also studies of the terms *imagination*,[18] *invention*,[19] *beauty*,[20] *nature*,[21] and the *comic*.[22] An accurate knowledge of the meaning of certain words is necessary to the understanding of

[3] Such studies are actually, of course, studies in semantics.

Shaftesbury,[23] or Emerson,[24] or Masefield,[25] or Jonathan Edwards and William Godwin; [26] and the same may be said of many another writer.

Sometimes these studies of a term deal with the history of an expression as well as its meaning; one such article deals with the word *sentimental*,[27] and another with the expression *moral sense*.[28]

III

When we turn our attention to the thought of an individual writer, we may again find the meaning of specific terms important, as the words *reason* and *understanding* are in a study of Coleridge and Maurice,[29] or the word *novelty* in an article on Addison.[30] Generally, however, when we study a writer's thinking, we are concerned, even if we limit ourselves to a specific topic, not with words, but with concepts, such as Spenser's views on friendship [31] Shakspere's ideas on love and honor,[32] Wordsworth's conception of grace,[33] or Shelley's thoughts about love.[34]

* * *

Studies still limited, but dealing with larger fields than those we have been considering, include articles on the literary interests of Sir Francis Bryan; [35] Shakspere on style, imagination, and poetry; [36] Mulcaster's view of the English language; [37] Ralegh and natural philosophy; [38] Defoe and modern economic theory; [39] Swift and immortality; [40] Steele and the status of women; [41] evolutionary thinking in Akenside [42] and Henry Brooke; [43] Mrs. Radcliffe and the supernatural in poetry; [44] Keats and world affairs; [45] science in Clough [46] and Matthew Arnold; [47] Pater and æsthetics; [48] and Browning and higher criticism.[49] In the field of American literature, there are studies of the religious ideas of Franklin [50] and Channing,[51] the political ideas of Orestes A. Brownson [52] and Walt Whitman,[53] the social philosophy of Ellen Glasgow,[54] and the humanism of Irving Babbitt.[55]

* * *

Still more general studies would take in even larger aspects of a writer's thinking; among these might be mentioned articles on Hall,[56] Traherne,[57] Wordsworth,[58] Tom Paine,[59] Prescott,[60] William James and Emerson,[61] Tourgée,[62] Hart Crane,[63] and Theodore Dreiser,[64] and books on Milton,[65] Sir Thomas Browne,[66] Keats,[67] Hawthorne,[68] Melville,[69] and Emily Dickinson.[70]

* * *

It is interesting to study the views on literature of literary men, not only because such study contributes to our ability to interpret the works of those men, but also because the literary opinions of creative writers are as important a part of the history of ideas as are those of literary critics. Thus we have more than one reason for being interested in knowing why Milton gave up the idea of using an Arthurian story as the subject of his *magnum opus*; [71] what Fielding thought of critics and criticism [72] and of heroic romance; [73] to what extent Goldsmith was a sentimentalist; [74] and what were the views of Bulwer-Lytton [75] and of Charles Reade [76] on the novel, of Browning [77] and Swinburne [78] on poetry, and of Maxwell Anderson [79] on the drama. Many of the ideas of Coleridge and of Wordsworth are brought out in a review of Lowes's *The Road to Xanadu*.[80] Other studies deal with Burke's theory concerning words, images, and emotions; [81] the literary opinions of Charles Brockden Brown [82] and Hawthorne; [83] and the criticism of Richard Grant White [84] and Henry James.[85]

Some men have been known equally—or almost equally—for their criticism and for what may be called more creative work. Studies involving such men include articles on Coleridge's criticism of Wordsworth,[86] Lowell's criticism of romantic literature,[87] and Hazlitt's criticism of Shakspere.[88] Mention may also be made here of articles on Thoreau,[89] Henley,[90] Pater,[91] and Meredith.[92]

One may study the ideas expressed in a single work, as, for example, the political ideas in Sidney's *Arcadia* [93] or the philosophical background of *Gulliver's Travels*.[94] Other studies of this sort deal with Richard Taverner's *Proverbes or Adagies*,[95] Coleridge's *Religious Musings*,[96] and T. S. Eliot's *The Hollow Men*.[97]

A study may be made of changing or developing ideas in a writer. "Chaucer's Changing Conception of the Humble Lover",[98] "Coleridge's Scheme of Pantisocracy and American Travel Accounts", [99] "The Religious Evolution of Darwin",[100] and "The Three Stages of Theodore Dreiser's Naturalism" [101] are examples of this type of study; others deal with Mary Wollstonecraft,[102] Emerson,[103] and Henry James.[104]

Or one may study the ideas of an individual writer in an attempt to discover his relation to current or conventional thought. One article deals with Spenser's handling of a psychological problem in the light of Elizabethan views on the subject; [105] another treats the friendship theme in Orrery's plays; [106] still another studies the "Art for Art's Sake" creed in Saintsbury.[107] When such studies of a writer trace his thinking—or certain aspects of it—to another, they are, of course, studies of influence or source and might have been mentioned in Chapter Four or Chapter Six of this work; so far as they concern ideas, however, they may appropriately be included here. There are such studies of, among others, John Donne,[108] William James,[109] and Edwin Arlington Robinson.[110]

IV

Perhaps the most interesting of the studies in the history of ideas are those which trace through decades or through centuries the thinking of a people—or of that part of a people which is articulate—upon more or less specific topics, revealing the attitude of such people upon subjects literary, philosophical, social, or æsthetic, and showing how each attitude evolved from a preceding one and in time gave way to a later. The studies of a literary movement may deal with a large subject, such as Platonism in English poetry,[111] or a small one, such as the attitude toward fables.[112] In the former category would be placed Professor Baldwin's work on mediæval rhetoric and poetic,[113] and Professor Lowes's *Convention and Revolt in Poetry*; [114] the work of Professor Mills on the friendship theme, though a smaller subject, assumes large proportions because of the amount of material studied.[115] Studies more limited in scope include *Elizabethan Psychology and Shakespeare's Plays*,[116] "Ritson's Life of Robin Hood" [117] (bringing out the attitude of the public toward the ballad hero), "Native Elements in English Neo-Classicism",[118] "Changing Taste in the Eighteenth Century: A Study of Dryden's and Dodsley's Miscellanies",[119] *The Noble Savage: A Study in Romantic Naturalism*,[120] "The Nature of Romanticism",[121] *The Gloomy Egoist: Moods and Themes of Melancholy from Gray to Keats*,[122] "Mad Shelley: A Study in the Origins of English Romanticism",[123] and "Muckraking

in the Gilded Age".[124] Two articles deal with the American periodicals *Putnam's Magazine*[125] and the *North American Review*.[126]
Studies treating a more specific type of literature include "Antiquarian Interest in Elizabethan Drama before Lamb",[127] "Prose Fiction and English Interest in the Near East, 1775–1825",[128] *The History, from 1700 to 1800, of English Criticism of Prose Fiction,*[129] and,
perhaps, "The Beginnings of Nature Poetry in the Eighteenth
Century".[130]

Studies more purely philosophical deal with humanism,[131] pessimism,[132] primitivism,[133] enthusiasm,[134] optimism,[135] and puritanism.[136]
Other works to be mentioned in this category would include Professor Tinker's *Nature's Simple Plan*,[137] "The Survival of Mediæval
Intellectual Interest into Early Modern Times",[138] and "The Perfect
Prince: a Study in Thirteenth and Fourteenth Century Ideals".[139]
Such philosophical movements as are treated in these studies, since
they find frequent and often important expression in literature, are
properly of concern to the student of literary history as well as to the
philosopher.

Many intellectual movements have a social basis; they represent
what people think as members of the body politic, the social group.
Among studies of such movements are discussions of the spread of
ideas in the Middle Ages,[140] middle-class concern over learning in
the Renaissance,[141] and middle-class culture in Elizabethan England.[142] Another study shows that Swift's attitude toward puritanism
was in line with a social tradition of some standing.[143] The attitude
toward fiction just before and just after 1800 is discussed in another
article.[144] Professor Tinker studied the influence of the salon on
English letters.[145]

The attitude toward fiction, both in America and in England, has
often—perhaps usually—had a social rather than a literary or æsthetic origin. Fiction in general, or a type of fiction, or an individual
work, has been praised or denounced on moral or ethical, not on
artistic, grounds. One study deals with the American attitude toward
fiction during the period 1789–1810; [146] another concerns itself with
English views, almost a hundred years later, on realism in fiction.[147]
A third shows that Victorian criticism dealt much more leniently
with the realism of the Russians than with that of the French; [148]
and a fourth reveals that the American reaction to French naturalism

in the latter part of the nineteenth century was more liberal than the English reaction of that period.[149] In still another article, the Victorian objection to Swinburne's *The Leper* is ascribed to the taste of the era rather than to any fundamental moral or æsthetic judgment.[150]

Some intellectual movements have involved ideas primarily æsthetic. Such a movement is discussed in an article on harmony of the senses.[151] Professor Bredvold studied the tendency toward Platonism in Neo-Classical æsthetics.[152] Three articles[153] on eighteenth-century taste, or views about taste, would also belong in this category, as does a study of the attitude toward naturalism of certain Victorians.[154]

V

Another group of studies in the history of ideas is made up of investigations of a tradition—a tradition concerning a personage, such as that by which Virgil underwent a strange evolution from poet to prophet to magician; or a character, such as that in which Cressida went from Court of Love heroine to Elizabethan villainess; or a type, such as the braggart soldier or the artful servant; or a form of literature. Studies of Joseph,[155] Herod,[156] and Judas[157] may be thought of as belonging either in the first or in the second group; a historical individual closer to our own time—such as Prince Hal[158]—is more definitely a personage. Studies of characters involve Lorenzo and Jessica,[159] Diomede,[160] and the devil.[161] Among the types that have been studied are the vice,[162] the parasite,[163] the rebellious lover,[164] the gentleman,[165] the Quaker,[166] the country booby,[167] the besieged lady,[168] the sailor,[169] the bestial man,[170] and the country squire.[171] An example of a study of a form of literature treats the Utopian novel in America;[172] and two articles of the same sort are devoted to the Indian captivity narrative.[173]

VI

The last group of contributions to the history of ideas to be discussed here is made up of studies of a people—a race, a nation, or the inhabitants of some specific part of a country. There is generally a chronological limitation as well as a geographical one. The emphasis may be literary, political, social, economic, religious, military, æsthetic, or philosophic; or there may be a combination of emphases. A study may be the work of one writer, or it may represent a collaboration or symposium, the product of several minds. The influence of one people upon another may be the subject of study.

Examples of works that concern themselves with a race are *The Negro's Morale: Group Identification and Protest;* [174] *The Story of the American Negro;* [175] and *Race Relations in a Democracy.*[176] Perry's *The American Mind* [177] and Commager's more recent work with the same title; [178] Parrington's *Main Currents in American Thought;* [179] and Cargill's *Intellectual America* [180] deal with a nation. Van Wyck Brooks' *The Flowering of New England: 1815–1865* and *New England: Indian Summer, 1865–1915* [181] and Wesley Frank Craven's *The Southern Colonies in the Seventeenth Century, 1607–1689* [182] are sectional in scope.

Sometimes the chronological limitation is a broad one, as in Hardin Craig's *The Enchanted Glass,*[183] a study of Elizabethan England, or Perry Miller's *The New England Mind: The Seventeenth Century;* [184] studies more narrowly limited include *The Disruption of American Democracy,*[185] which covers only a few years in the middle of the nineteenth century, and *The Revolutionary Generation, 1763–1790.*[186] Frequently the emphasis is indicated or suggested in the title, as in *The Origins of American Critical Thought, 1810–1835* [187] and *American Criticism: A Study in Literary Theory from Poe to the Present;* [188] *History of American Political Thought;* [189] *Are Men Equal? An Inquiry into the Meaning of American Democracy;* [190] *Government and the American Economy, 1870–Present;* [191] *Popular Freethought in America 1825–1850,*[192] *American Freethought, 1860–1914,*[193] and *The Forming of an American Tradition: A Re-examination of Colonial Presbyterianism;* [194] *Lincoln Finds a General: A Military Study of the Civil War;* [195] *Æsthetic Experience and the Humanities;* [196] and *The Political and Social Growth of the American People* [197] are examples. Co-operative efforts are represented by *Changing Patterns in American Civilization* [198] and *Years of the Modern.*[199] The influence of one people upon another is studied in *The Atlantic Civilization: Eighteenth Century Origins* [200] and *The American Spirit in Europe.*[201]

VII

We have seen, then, that studies in the history of ideas may concern themselves with the meaning of a term or the history of a term, or both; they may be devoted to the specific ideas of an individual, or his philosophy in general, or his views—implied or expressed—on literature or any other subject that merits study; they may trace the development of an intellectual movement of literary, philosophical, social, or æsthetic nature; they may show the evolution of a literary tradition involving a person, a character, a type, or a literary form; or they may deal with the ideas of the people of a certain region—in general, during a given time, or in one field.

The difficulty in drawing a line of demarcation between the history of ideas and other fields, such as social history, or the history of philosophy, or of religion, or of science can readily be understood. *The Journal of the History of Ideas* in its second volume (1941) classified the books received for review under three headings: "History of Literature and Art", "Social and Political History", and "History of Religion, Philosophy, and Science". In the first group are included two works [202] which might equally well be classified under "Social and Political History"; two other works assigned to the "History of Literature and Art" group might seem to be as properly classified under the heading "History of Religion, Philosophy, and Science".[203] A work listed under the second heading should come also under the first and third.[204] And two books assigned to the third group belong quite as much to the second.[205]

The graduate student who is tempted by the history of ideas must remember that in no other type of literary research is there the necessity for such broad reading and such extensive note-taking as few graduate students have time to achieve. Keeping this warning in mind, a graduate student may attempt a study, on a small scale, in the history of ideas; the method to be followed will depend upon the type of problem selected.[4]

If the problem is the investigation of the meaning or the history of a term, the time covered should be limited to a fairly brief period—perhaps only ten years, perhaps twenty-five, certainly not more than

---

[4] Before beginning such a project the student should by all means read Morize, *Problems and Methods,* pp. 263–88.

fifty. Dictionaries and concordances will provide a start; from them should be taken all the illustrations that fall within the period selected. One should then begin to read all the authors who are likely to have used the word or phrase in question, or at least those whose use of the term will be significant. It goes without saying that, even if the period involved is only a decade, a great deal of reading must be done if the study is to be anything more than a superficial *essai*. It will be found, however, if one is pressed for time—as graduate students generally are—that one can skim rather rapidly through a book and still discover any occurrences of the word or phrase in which he is interested. Of course he will get little else from the reading; and it is better, if time permits, to read more slowly and more thoroughly, and let the collecting of data be secondary to the digesting of the thought. Wherever one finds the term used, he should put in his note, not only the sentence in which the term appears, but also enough of the context to make the meaning of the term—as there used—perfectly clear. The date of the usage should be indicated on the note; particularly if one is concerned with the history of the term, he should be careful to determine, if possible, that the date is that of composition, not that of publication. Once the reading is completed and all the notes are taken, all that remains is to put the material into some logical arrangement.

If one is attempting to study the ideas of an author, the first step is to acquire a thorough familiarity with the author's works; only when one has a command of the entire body of a man's writings, can one be sure of the significance of a single work, or of a passage in a work, or even of a single idea. It will not be enough, however, to master one author; in order to do any very thorough work, one must know well the author's background—his environment, his sources, the work of his contemporaries. Thus it is easy to see that a good piece of work in the history of ideas, even if it be confined to the ideas of one writer, is likely to require years of study.

When one extends the scope of his work to include many men instead of one, and makes it cover centuries instead of a generation, he obviously increases enormously the amount of work to be done; indeed, he is likely to have taken in more territory than can be covered in one lifetime. Hence it is permitted that he be less thorough —less detailed, but not less careful—in his covering of the ground than the person whose study takes in a smaller territory. If one is interested in a certain philosophical problem, and he finds what attitude toward that problem is expressed by the first- and second-rate writers, it is certainly not necessary that he should know and set forth the attitude expressed by all the fourth- and fifth-rate writers, whose name is legion. He should, perhaps, cite some of the lesser fry, to show that their attitude is or is not the same as that of their betters; but to exhume from a merited oblivion a host of trivial, and doubtless dull, writings and give them careful study would be a work of supererogation.

In a study in the history of ideas, how is one to know when to stop collecting data? The question is not easy to answer. As long as one continues to turn up anything—ideas, expressions, whatever it may be—new, anything different from what he already has in his notes, he must go on searching and studying. But when one has made what seems a reasonably intensive and comprehensive survey of the field, and for some time has failed to find anything new, and has come to feel sure that there is nothing new or different to be found, then he is entitled to stop collecting and begin the organization and presentation of his material.

There is, I am sure, no kind of research in English literary history more difficult than that in the history of ideas, nor is there one which pays better rewards—both in self-satisfaction and in recognition by others—for conscientious and intelligent effort.

CHAPTER TEN

∾⧉∾

PROBLEMS IN FOLKLORE

by Stith Thompson

Professor of English and Folklore,
formerly Dean of the Graduate School, Indiana University

NO field of research open to the student of literature shows wider
variety than folklore. Many aspects of the subject take him
entirely away from ordinary literary pursuits and carry him well over
into the materials of the social sciences, and even sometimes into
the methods and techniques of the biological sciences. It is a
marginal subject, which has never attained an equilibrium in the
scholastic scheme.

I

Our concern in this chapter is with folklore only as it touches on
literary expression. And yet the folklorist must not ignore the other
boundaries of his field. He must always recognize its affinity to history and realize the light that folk customs, superstitions, weather
and agricultural lore, not to speak of local traditions, may throw
upon the cultural history of an area. Nor can he disregard its close
connection at many points with anthropology. If one reads anthro-
pological literature, he will find that a very large proportion of the
studies devoted to primitive peoples is concerned with their æsthetic
life, their myths, songs, dances, ceremonies, and tales. When we are
dealing with the folktale and considering its function in the life of
the people who tell it, is our problem really one of literature or

anthropology? Even the folklorist with interests primarily literary must be something of a student of society, and of local or national history.[1]

II

The literary scholar is usually interested in the individual contribution of a particular author. Literary history is largely a series of studies of authors or of movements dominated by them. But the individual expression of these authors takes place in a common milieu, interesting to the scholar not so much because of its differing manifestations as because of the uniformity observable throughout. This common milieu, the chief concern of the folklorist, is of two kinds. The subject of any author's work must be in large degree the life of man, and even in the most individualistic persons or groups a surprisingly large part of life is purely traditional and conventional. Moreover, when the author comes to treat his subject, he finds that he is not a free agent but that his work is conditioned by the literary habits of his time and place. Folklore, therefore, which is essentially the study of tradition, may concern both materials and literary forms, usually involved in such a way that they can hardly be separated.

For an understanding of this common background which we call folklore, the following forms are of particular interest to the literary student: (a) riddles; (b) proverbs; (c) charms (folk medicine); (d) festivals and their celebration; (e) ceremonials; (f) local legends; (g) folktales (both oral and literary); (h) ballads; (i) folk lyrics (both secular and religious).

The study of folklore requires two complementary processes. The material must be assembled and then it must be interpreted. Individual scholars usually specialize in one of these aspects of the subject, or indeed in some small subdivision of one. Unless one is to be superficial, he cannot take all folklore for his province.

III

Many folklorists spend all their time and energy in collecting. Such scholars may turn over whole libraries to find data already published,

---

[1] Only folklore as a subject for scholarly investigation is considered here; otherwise we should have to invade the realms of public entertainment, such as stage and radio presentation of folk material.

or they may go out into the field and record tales or songs from the lips of informants. The task of the former type of scholar is not essentially different from that of any other literary student, but the collector of oral folklore must develop quite another method. Though it is true that the best collectors are born and not made, some definite suggestion as to procedure cannot fail to be helpful.

The field worker's first problem is the discovery of good informants from whom he can hear old songs or tales or other folklore. He will naturally be attracted toward areas which have already yielded first-rate material of the kind which he seeks. Such areas are by no means always in isolated districts. Usually one of two conditions is necessary to produce good traditional material. The social stability that results from geographical isolation or stagnation, or else that is produced by common cleavage in speech with the surrounding district, is the most important element in preserving those manifestations of the practical and æsthetic life which interest the folklorist. Foreign language groups in large cities (the French in Canada and Missouri, the Spanish in New Mexico, and the Swedes in Minnesota), isolated mountaineers and hill folk, rural communities near but quite separate from cities, pioneer groups, cowboys, Indians, Negroes, lumbermen, miners, or indeed, any of the millions who carry in their memory what they have learned from older generations—all of these beckon the folklore collector. In addition to these naturally fertile fields, one may receive clues as to good informants by the careful reading of folklore journals, by attendance at meetings of folklore societies, or through interested students in schools and colleges. The latter means is only now being properly realized. In Ireland, for example, all school children have the collecting of some folklore as a regular task. Though they are sending in to Dublin over a half million pages of folklore annually, their principal service is in calling attention to men and women from whom trained collectors can later recover rich traditional lore. Aside from these two obvious methods of obtaining clues, the most generally employed is that of following the suggestions of informants themselves. They can nearly always call attention to some friendly rival in the same neighborhood.

Informants may be possessed of a rich store of tradition, and yet an unskillful approach by the field worker may fail utterly to bring it to light. Because of the apparent simplicity of both the informant and the material he has to give, many amateurs make the mistake of attempting to collect without adequate preparation. One of the reasons for the relative failure in so many states of the Folklore Division of the Federal Writers Project was that although the workers were plentiful and were paid for collecting folklore, they had little idea as to what they were seeking. A good collector goes into the field with a rather accurate knowledge of the material he hopes to find. He has acquainted himself with collections from neighboring areas; he has at his finger tips a great store of songs, tales, and other lore which he has good reason to expect to find. The best way to collect ballads is to know ballads. By suggesting a ballad plot, "a song about such and such", or the humming of a tune he stimulates the memory of his informant. The best ballad collectors have been able to sing their ballads and to enter into a song exchange which breaks down all reserve. The same background of thorough acquaintance with the field is necessary for all other types of collecting. Perhaps the person who specializes in the collecting of tales has the most difficult task, for though he can usually succeed with a relatively few typical stories in discovering whether his informant knows folktales at all, he should, in addition, know many hundreds of plots and must have some idea as to the occasion and type of raconteur appropriate for each.

Much use has been made in recent years of questionnaires; and when they are properly employed they are of great value. It is usually unwise, however, to take a questionnaire into the field and make inquiries from it as if one were filling out a tax report. Perhaps the chief function of these lists is the preparation of the collector himself. Questionnaires serve as memoranda of things he must look for while he is in the field. Among the most successful users of questionnaires are the collectors working in connection with the Irish and the Swedish Folklore Archives. In Ireland a complete questionnaire is furnished the collector, but he is urged to master a small part of the list and to carry on his interview without referring to it. In Sweden essentially the same method is used, except that a relatively small group of questions on a particular subject is sent out at stated intervals. It seems important for maintaining the proper psychological attitude in a folklore collecting interview that the questions appear to be spontaneous, and that they arise from the situation itself and from the normal give and take of conversation.

How long should the folklore collector remain in the field? If life were not short and if there were a large number of persons engaged in recovering popular tradition, it would be desirable that he should spend his entire life in reasonably close contact with the people he has chosen to study. Especially if this group is primitive, a long period of years is necessary for a real acquaintance. The late James Mooney, who spent most of his life among the Cherokees, was particularly scornful of those who hoped by a sojourn of a mere year or two to get at the heart of native tradition. There is no doubt that certain types of folklore—particularly ceremonial songs and tales— yield only to long and oft-repeated efforts. On the other hand, the student with a small amount of time should not despair. Frequent revisitings are almost as good as unbroken residence. Given a proper attitude toward his work, a good knowledge of his subject, reasonable tact and kindliness, he is not likely to encounter insurmountable difficulties. Some of our greatest collectors have been able to go into a new community and secure a huge amount of material in a single week. But such success comes only to that rare man or woman who has genius.

Until the last few years all recording of folklore from informants has been by dictation. And, indeed, for most purposes, this is still the only practicable means. Ballads must be sung in a natural way so as to show the tune and the manner of singing. A recorder must learn to abbreviate and to record as fast as possible. Dictation also seems to be reasonably successful for tales, descriptions of customs, celebrations, and the like. An animated teller of a story may find the delays incident to dictation so annoying that his whole style is spoiled. For such a man, and for singers in general, phonographic recording is particularly effective. The exact tune and the exact narrative style can be preserved in this manner. In spite of several difficulties to be mentioned, the making of records is being more and more widely adopted by collectors. The equipment necessary is fairly expensive and heavy, and sometimes it is impracticable because of the lack of electric current in isolated communities, or because, especially in Canada, one often encounters unusual frequencies in the current. But these two latter handicaps are gradually being overcome. Lighter equipment with wire or tape is taking the place of the heavier disc machines. Some collectors find it difficult to train their informants to speak into the machine without self-consciousness, but usually if they have habituated themselves to giving dictation they can easily learn to use the microphone. Even in such a conservative community as the Gaelic-speaking section of western Ireland, the ancient tale-tellers have become expert in speaking to the phonograph. None of them can resist the urge to hear his own voice played back to him. In passing it may be said that such re-playings may easily become a great waste of time for the collector who is in a hurry, and that with discs an original record should not be played oftener than once because of wear.

No matter how much proprietorship the collector may feel in the results of his labors, he will always wish in one way or another to make them available to the rest of the world. His first thought will doubtless be to publish. Sometimes he has visions of large royalties from the sale of these folklore collections. He will almost certainly not receive them, and it may well be that he will find no one to sponsor his publication, much less reward him for his work. If the practical matter of securing publication, either as a book or in some periodical, has been arranged, the material must be properly prepared for the press. If it is possible to do so, all variants of songs or tales, even from the same informant at different times, should be printed, so that the scholar can get a true picture of the tradition. Material should be furnished for studies of variation in folklore. A conscientious scholar will by no means concoct versions out of a combination of variants. If he may publish only one, he should select a typical one and make proper notes as to other versions he has, but not try to improve the story or song he publishes. If the collection includes songs or ballads, it is of the first importance that the tune be given. Music doubles the value of any ballad book.

The publication of folklore material may be either with or without comparative notes. Both forms are valuable; but it is not necessary that all collections include distribution studies. If the notes are attempted, they should be done with the utmost care, for inaccurate or badly arranged notes have little value. If it is at all possible, publication should be done either in a book or in one of the folklore journals which have at least national circulation. One of the greatest difficulties with folklore material is the fact that it is so scattered about and inaccessible.

Publication of one's collections may be quite out of the question. Sometimes the mere bulk of the material makes the expense prohibitive. But the collector should not be content to keep his songs and tales to himself; he should make them available at least to the earnest scholar. It is for the preservation of such materials that folklore archives are founded. In Europe a number of countries have established national bureaus of this kind where manuscript material and records are preserved, analyzed, and kept open to scholars. In America the Library of Congress has made a good beginning with its Folklore Section, now rapidly being expanded to include all types of traditional material. Such archives copy the collector's work, either photostatically or phonographically, without interfering with any proprietary rights he may claim. It would be wise for any collector who desires the best use to be made of his work to see that in one way or other copies of his material are made a part of this archive. The time is rapidly coming when the Library of Congress will be the natural clearing-house for all folklore collecting in America.

Up to this point in our discussion we have been concerned with oral folklore. Before coming to grips with the wider problems of folklore study, it is well to remind ourselves that a large part of tradition, especially the widely-known tales, have already become a part of literature. Every competent folklorist should become thoroughly acquainted with a few of the great monuments of such written tradition.

*   *   *

The most important literary collections of tales have come from India. Not all of them are easily available to the western student. Best known is perhaps the *Panchatantra,*[1] five books of fables serving as a manual of instruction in the wise conduct of life. This work has gradually spread westward under the title of *The Fables of Bidpai,* or *Kalila and Dimna,* or, as known in the Latin middle ages, *Directorium Humanœ Vitœ.* An abbreviated form of the *Panchatantra* is included in the huge collection, *Kathā Sarit Sāgara* or *Ocean of Story,*[2] now available in a very elaborate ten-volume edition in English. Four other important works in the same general sphere are the *Hitopadesa,*[3] the *Śukasaptati* (or *Seventy Tales of a Parrot*),[4] the *Vētālapañcavimśatika* (or *Twenty-five Tales of a Vampire*),[5] and

Vikram's Adventures (or *Thirty-two Tales of a Throne*).[6] Less interesting, but nevertheless important for comparative study, are the
traditions of Buddhism which appear under the title of *Jātakas*,[7] and
purport to give stories of events in the former lives of the Buddha.

Much of this Indian material early spread into Persia. The *Panchatantra* was translated by the sixth century of our era. Most important for the folklorist is the *Tútí-námeh*,[8] which contains a considerable amount of the Indian *Tales of a Parrot* and which had wide
influence in Europe during the middle ages because part of it was
taken over into the *Seven Sages of Rome*.[9] The great tale collection
from the Arabic world shows many points of dependence on Persia
and India. This is the *Thousand and One Nights*.[10] Although some of
its individual tales were known earlier in Europe, it began to influence western literature and folklore only at the beginning of the
eighteenth century. Another oriental stream in our written tradition
is Hebrew. Besides such folklore from this source as is found in the
Bible, a large number of Hebrew exempla and of pious traditions
were current in mediæval Europe.[11]

The folklorist has need of a good classical background, not only
for such well-known authors of good stories as Homer and Ovid, but
also for many less prominent writers whose works give us an insight
into the traditional tales current in the ancient world. Particularly
valuable are such men as Apollodorus [12] and Apuleius.[13] The former
tells many myths that are off the beaten path, and the latter gives us
a beautiful folktale in his "Cupid and Psyche". For a comparative
stylistic study of the folktale in the modern world and in the ancient
a classical background is indispensable.

The European middle ages were particularly fond of story telling.
This tendency is seen in their romances and ballads and also in their
huge collections of prose tales. Of the latter there were several kinds.
The clergy used illustrative anecdotes to give point to their sermons,
and these narratives (originating, it may be, in India or Palestine or
Rome) were brought together in large compendiums, often arranged
alphabetically under the Latin name of the virtue or vice illustrated.
The greatest of these collections of exempla are *Gesta Romanorum*,[14]
probably of English origin and the most popular of the whole *genre*;
The Exempla of Jacques de Vitry; [15] *Scala Celi;* and the *Summa
Predicantium* [16] of John Bromyard. The two latter works are par-

ticularly full, each containing a thousand or more illustrative stories. Most of these collections ceased to be of influence after the end of the middle ages; but their individual stories frequently lived on, sometimes in literature, and sometimes, with utter ignorance of their scholarly origin, in the mouths of the ignorant and lowly.[17]

The student of the folktale must acquire a knowledge of several other cycles of narratives besides these exempla. The Æsop tradition [18] will take him rather far, because he must become conversant with collections of fables in ancient Greece and Rome and try to master their relationship with first, the Hindu collections, second, the animal tales of northeast Europe, and, finally, the mediæval retellings in France, England, and Germany. At some point in his dealings with mediæval story the student will certainly encounter the romance of the *Seven Sages of Rome*. The popularity and influence of this group of tales can hardly be exaggerated, although a few of the stories have little interest for the modern reader. This collection takes the student immediately back to some of the Persian and Indian collections already mentioned.[2] One of the European redactions is the *Dolopathos* by Johannes de Alta Silva, an example of the importance of the Christianized Jew in bringing Oriental tradition to the west.

In the later middle ages three literary forms helped to popularize tales. One of these, the *fabliau*,[3] a short, poetic form which received its principal development in France, dealt primarily with risqué situations and marital infidelity. Such famous literary stories as Chaucer's "Miller's Tale" undoubtedly go back to one of these racy poems. In Italy the characteristic story collection was in prose and was called the *novella* (plural *novelle*). Best known of these is Boccaccio's *Decameron*, though several other authors, notably Bandello and Straparola, have played a large part in the enrichment of European fiction.

Borrowing much of its material from the *fabliau* and the *novella*, and taking much from popular tradition, the jestbook came into its own with the invention of printing in the fifteenth century. In the origin of this form the Italian Poggio is the leader, but it was in Germany that it received its most vigorous development. Perhaps the

[2] See Campbell's edition cited in note 9.
[3] See J. Bedier, *Les Fabliaux,* 2nd ed. (Paris, 1895).

most representative collection of these *Schwänke* is Pauli's *Schimpf und Ernst,* really a combination of exempla and jests, for the author always carefully announces whether the story is "Schimpf" or "Ernst". Through the work of the great folklore scholars, Johannes Bolte and Albert Wesselski, these jestbooks have received careful and intelligent editing. The student will certainly wish to have some acquaintance not only with Poggio and Pauli, but also with Bebel, Frey, Schumann, and Wickram in Germany, with Arlotto in Italy, with the Oriental *Hodscha Nasreddin,* and with the English jestbooks of the sixteenth century.[19]

These English jests appeared in fugitive publications known as "chapbooks". They were cheap pamphlets and small volumes which treated all kinds of subjects, among them jests, anecdotes, and real folktales. This field has not been well explored, though some of the older collections of English folktales took much of their material from these sources. A similar type of cheap publication was the broadside ballad.[20] In these printed sheets have been preserved not only tens of thousands of quite worthless pieces of doggerel, but also some of the most important versions of really traditional ballads.

Such are some of the purely literary productions with which the student of folklore, particularly one interested in the tale or ballad, must be acquainted. This is, of course, a counsel of perfection, but the more nearly the ideal can be attained, the better.

As mentioned earlier in this sketch, the folklorist may be either a collector or a student of material already collected. Some of the special problems of the field worker have already been discussed. We will now assume that an investigator, reasonably well equipped with the literary background which has just been outlined, and with a good folklore library at his disposal, wishes to undertake a serious study of some problem involving the ballad, the folktale, the proverb, the riddle, or another of those aspects of folklore interesting to the literary student. His first task, obviously, is to assemble the materials with which he is to work. For this purpose he needs some acquaintance with folklore bibliographies and some knowledge of how to make use of the various archives. The machinery for using the latter is indispensable when we have to deal with unpublished material.

*   *   *

Certain periodicals are so important for the field that nothing short of a thorough examination of the complete files will suffice to assure one of even reasonable bibliographical completeness. If one has decided upon the study of one particular song or tale or some *genre* or motif, it would be wise to look through the following sets: *Volkskündliche Bibliographie* (annual, 1929–   ); Annual Bibliography in *Publications of the Modern Language Association of America, s.v.* "Folklore"; *Journal of American Folk-lore; American Anthropologist; Southern Folklore Quarterly; Folklore* (English); *Journal of the Folk Song Society* and its successor *Journal of the English Folk Dance and Song Society; Zeitschrift für Volkskunde; Hessische Blätter für Volkskunde; Folkminnen och Folktankar.* The four latter journals are especially good for their reviews and notices of new books.

For the special field of the ballad, the complete edition of Child's *The English and Scottish Popular Ballad* (five volumes in ten) should be constantly consulted for its bibliographical references. This work may well direct the student into the Scandinavian field, and most good folklorists find that they must sooner or later learn the Scandinavian languages. For these northern ballads, Grundtvig's *Danmarks Gamle Folkeviser* (nine volumes, 1853–1923) is indispensable, since it acts as a guide into the whole field. The American ballad student may well wish to secure access to the enormous collection of ballads and folksongs made in this country, sometimes of the same material as the Child ballads, and sometimes of quite new types. For this purpose he will find the notes in the following ballad collections especially valuable: H. M. Belden, *Ballads and Songs Collected by the Missouri Folklore Society* (Columbia, Missouri: 1940); Barry, Eckstrom, and Smyth, *British Ballads from Maine* (New Haven: 1929); A. K. Davis, *Traditional Ballads of Virginia* (Cambridge, Massachusetts, 1929); Sharp and Karpeles, *English Folk Songs from the Southern Appalachians* (New York: 1932); Lomax, *American Ballads and Folk-Songs* (New York: 1934). For a more general bibliography of ballads, and for excellent treatment of the whole subject, see Gerould, *The Ballad of Tradition* (Oxford: 1932) and Entwistle, *European Balladry* (Oxford: 1939).

The field of the proverb is opened up for the student by Archer Taylor in his *The Proverb* (Cambridge, Massachusetts: 1931). This

work is supplemented by an index published in *FF Communications*
No. 113 (Helsinki: 1934). Taylor also has an excellent treatment of
scholarly problems concerning proverbs in the *Journal of American
Folk-lore*, XLVI (1933), 77–88.

Perhaps the most difficult bibliographical field for the folklorist
is that dealing with the folktale. The scholar must seek some guidance, not only into the extensive field of the traditional literary tale
but also into the worldwide collections of oral stories from every
people and every rank. And he must learn how to approach the latter
whether they are in print or still in manuscript.

By far the most important bibliographical aid for the whole field
of the folktale is Bolte and Polívka's *Anmerkungen zu den Kinder-
und Hausmärchen der Brüder Grimm,* five volumes (Leipzig: 1913–
31). In this work the authors have annotated such tales as appear in
Grimm so thoroughly that there is no likelihood of the book's ever
being superseded. The general bibliography at the end of volume
three and the classified lists in volume five are indispensable. Thompson's revision of Aarne's *Verzeichnis der Märchentypen* (*The Types
of the Folk-tale,* Helsinki: 1928) and his *Motif-Index of Folk-Litera-
ture,* six volumes (Helsinki and Bloomington, Indiana: 1932–37)
offer bibliographical guidance for particular folktale types and
motifs. Beginning in 1911 there have appeared—largely in the most
important of all folklore publications, *FF Communications* (Helsinki: 1907–)—a series of surveys, each concerned with the tales
of a particular country or district. These are arranged in accordance
with Aarne's classification of tales, and, in later years, with Thompson's revision. Lists of these surveys will be found in the end sheets
of *FF Communications* No. 106. They are constantly being added to,
and not always in this series, so that one must be on the alert not to
overlook an important contribution. A convenient survey of scholarship on the folktale will be found in Thompson, *The Folktale* (New
York: 1946).

Certain bibliographies give access to the folklore of particular parts
of the world. Among these may be mentioned the following: DeVries,
Volksverhalen uit Oost Indië, two volumes (Leiden: 1925–28);
Thompson, *Tales of the North American Indians* (Cambridge, Mas-
sachusetts: 1929); Dixon, *Oceanic Mythology* (Boston: 1916);
Warner, *African Mythology* (Boston: 1925); Chauvin, *Bibliographie*

des Ouvrages arabes (Liège: 1892–1922); and Eberhard, *Typen chinesischer Märchen* (*FF Communications* No. 120).

* * *

The folklorist would be happy if the assembling of his materials were as simple a task as the making of a bibliography. But whether his data is largely to be found in the pages of printed books, as with the proverb, fable, and riddle, or whether he must attempt to explore large unpublished collections, the actual bringing together of his material may become so formidable a labor as to discourage him utterly. The number of libraries which pretend to even reasonably good folklore collections is very small, both here and abroad. Most of them are, however, generous in lending their books to serious scholars. Perhaps the outstanding folklore collections in the United States are in the Widener Library at Harvard, the White Collection of the Cleveland Public Library, and the Library of Congress.

If one is working with unpublished sources, whether in manuscript or on phonographic records, his work is not easily defined. Let us assume that he wishes to secure the data for a thorough comparative study of a widely distributed folktale. He will, of course, use the bibliographical aids which we have already mentioned. He will find that many of the special surveys refer to manuscript collections in various archives. Practically all of these archives have their folktales arranged according to the Aarne–Thompson classification, and it is quite possible to find all versions of a particular tale with great ease. Under normal world conditions the archivist can arrange, at a very reasonable cost, to have the desired material copied, and, if necessary, translated into one of the better known languages. Archives that should certainly be approached for the study of any item of folklore are: Finnish Academy of Sciences (Soumalainen Tiedeakatemia), Helsinki; Landsmålsarkivet, Uppsala, Sweden; Folklore Archive, Nordiska Museet, Stockholm; Hyltén-Cavallius-Institution for Swedish Folklore-research, Lund, Sweden; Västsvenska Folkminnesföreningen, Göteborg, Sweden; Dansk Folkemindesamling, Copenhagen; Norsk Folkeminnesamling, Oslo; Irish Folklore Commission, Dublin; Musée des Arts et Traditions Populaires, Trocadero, Paris; Deutsches Volksliedarchiv, Freiburg im Breisgau; Folklore Section, Library of Congress, Washington, D. C.

Besides these regularly established archives, a number of private scholars have material which they are willing to make available for research. A good list of these private collections in the field of American folksong is to be found in the report of the Committee on Folksong of the Popular Literature Section of the Modern Language Association of America which appeared in the *Southern Folklore Quarterly* in June, 1937.[21] American scholars have often received great help from several internationally famous folklorists of Europe. A good roster of names of such scholars is to be found in current numbers of *Saga och Sed*, the annual publication of the Royal Gustav Adolf Academy of Sweden.

*   *   *

After recording folklore in the field or ransacking libraries or bringing together copies from archives over the world, the scholar may reach a point where he feels certain that he has before him such a large proportion of the available data that he is justified in studying his material. If he has not already solved it, he is now faced with the problem of what use to make of these tales or ballads which he has assembled with so much labor. What kinds of investigation, he may well ask himself, are suggested by the nature of folklore material?

Since folklore is transmitted by oral tradition, it offers scholarly problems essentially different from those of literary history. Items of folklore must be studied with much the same technique as other items of cultural history, so that folklore research in some of its aspects has close resemblance to studies undertaken by the ethnologist or sociologist. Folklore is usually found to have rather continuous geographical distribution. One of the most important questions, therefore, with every traditional item, concerns the exact nature of the distribution. Scholars of the nineteenth century usually tried to reach large generalizations about the direction of folklore dissemination. But we know now that these generalizations were entirely premature and that we can only hope to approach the truth about this problem after hundreds of intensive studies have been made of particular songs, tales, riddles, and other items of folklore.

The methods of distribution study have been more thoroughly considered and more extensively practiced in connection with the folktale than with any other form, but most of the principles involved would appear to be at least partially applicable also to all kinds of traditional literature. Though the historical-geographical method of folktale study has been attacked by some scholars in some of its important details, there is no doubt that, if used with good judgment and with a proper consideration of historical and literary influences, it is the most fruitful method for studying the dissemination of a story, especially if it exists in oral tradition in many versions and if the tale itself has a certain complexity of structure.

The practitioner of this method hopes by assembling and arranging geographically and, where possible, historically all the versions of a tale, and by a thorough analysis of these versions to discover approximately the original form of the tale, its place of origin, and its subsequent vicissitudes. It will pay the student to take care with his initial arrangement of the tales and to work out a brief way of referring to each version. The usual method is to have a conventional system of abbreviation. If, for example, there are six versions from Norway, they are usually referred to as GN_1, GN_2, GN_3, etc.[4]

The tale is now analyzed into its component parts and the versions are examined with this analysis in mind. This process can be better illustrated than explained. Walter Anderson studied the story of *Kaiser und Abt* in which a ruler propounds to his enemy three questions which must be answered within a given time on pain of death. A humble man substitutes and answers the questions, thus discomfiting the king and saving the life of the intended victim. This story presents the following traits: (1) the number of persons concerned; (2) the question giver; (3) the man questioned; (4) the answer giver; (5) the number of questions; (6, etc.) the various questions and answers. The handling of the second trait will be illuminating. Anderson goes through all his versions and lists the various men who propound the questions. The result is given in the following form:

Emperor. [There follows reference to eleven literary documents arranged chronologically; then the oral:] GG 32, 44, 45, 48, 54, 55,

---

[4] For this conventional scheme, see any of the monographs which have appeared in *FF Communications*. Perhaps the best is Walter Anderson's *Kaiser und Abt*, *FF Communications* No. 42. In the above reference G = Germanic, N = Norwegian, and the figure represents the number of the version. The scheme is carried throughout the world: C = Celtic, R = Romance, S = Slavic, etc.

GV 1, 2, 4–7, GD 22, GN 1, Lit 1, SR 1–9 [10], 11–20, 23, 24, . . .
(121 variants = 25.5% of the whole).

King. [Reference to twenty-eight literary versions; then:] CB 1,
RP 1, RF 2, 4, 5, RW 1, 4, 5, . . . (254 variants = 53.6% of the
whole).

After this are considered the versions which mention President,
Pope, Bishop, Other Clerical Person, Priest, Miscellaneous Officials,
Nobleman, Professor, Wise Man, Magician; and then at last comes
the heading "The Trait is Lacking".

For each possible way of handling a particular item in the story
the scholar lists all available versions both written and oral, and he
works out percentages for each one. At the end of each section of the
tale he attempts to interpret the percentages in order to see whether
they give an unequivocal indication of the predominant form of the
tale. Usually he finds that the solution is not altogether simple, and
that a proper interpretation of the data involves much weighing of
evidence. But on a basis of the percentages the scholar will at least
construct a theoretical form as a trial archetype. It is likely, however,
that this purely mechanical construction will not actually represent
the original form of the tale, if indeed such an original form can
ever be attained. Re-examination of the tables must be made to see
whether special developments of the story may be characteristic of
particular geographical areas or of particular literary traditions.
After his careful statistical examination of the tale mentioned above,
Anderson eventually distinguished eighteen such redactions, which
differ enough among themselves to have established separate traditions. Now, with these special redactions established, it is possible by
analysis to attempt the construction of a real archetype which could
have produced all of these redactions or subtypes. One of the errors
made by some scholars using the historic-geographic method is that
they have attempted to work immediately from their percentage
tables to the construction of an archetype without consideration of
these local special developments. The proper procedure here is
analogous to that used by the student of Indo-European linguistics.
He arrives at his theoretical Indo-European form, not directly from
the English, the Russian, and the French forms, but rather from the
primitive Germanic, the old Slavic, and the Latin forms which represent the archetypes for their respective linguistic groups. Even when

arrived at by the most carefully guarded methods, the theoretical form of the tale which we posit as the archetype may be only a vague approach to the original form. But it is the best we can do, and no other method than that of strict analysis is likely to arrive nearer to the goal.

The close scrutiny which the scholar must have given a tale by the time he reaches the construction of the archetype will undoubtedly have afforded him some indication as to the time and place of origin. No exact methodology can be suggested for arriving at this result. There are some obvious principles. If the story of the Grateful Dead Man appears widely in oral tradition and is also in the Book of Tobit, we can be quite sure that the story was known at least two thousand years ago in the part of the world where Tobit was composed. But one should be very careful about the criteria he accepts. It is not always true that because a story is spread over great geographical distances it is therefore very ancient. Nor is it necessarily true that the place of origin is within the present area of distribution. Generally these principles are valid, but the exceptions are frequent.

With at least an approximate archetype established, the scholar now attempts to explain how the various special developments and the multitude of versions attained their present form. The changes that take place in tales as they pass from person to person involve certain very simple psychological principles. Although these processes have been rather thoroughly analyzed,[22] they are all concerned in some way with omissions resulting from forgetfulness, with additions, or with substitutions. Of the latter, some may come from misunderstandings, some from pure lack of skill, some from inventiveness, and some from a change of geographical background. At any rate, the goal of the folktale scholar is to trace the vicissitudes of his story and to make a reasonable explanation of all changes.

The theory on which the study of dissemination is based is that a story proceeds from an original center and the dissemination may and frequently does occur in a wave-like motion in all directions. But for any one of a number of reasons a major change in the story may occur and set up a new center of dissemination. The waves spreading from this new center meet and complicate the original waves and those proceeding from still other centers. For the interpretations of these waves, the folktale scholar has used suggestions from some of the biological sciences. A widespread trait, for example, which entirely surrounds the area of another form of the trait is likely to be the older, and the element in the smaller area is likely to represent a special development. This is only one of the criteria used in the establishment of subtypes or special redactions.

The criticisms leveled against the historic-geographic method are important, but they rather suggest improvement in technique than abandonment of the entire plan of work. C. W. von Sydow of Sweden is impressed with the importance of long established racial or national boundaries in the development of subtypes. These he calls *ekotypes,* since they seem to be "at home" in one country and not in another. This tendency must certainly be considered by the thorough investigator, but as an addition to, rather than a substitution for, a rigorous study of all versions. The late Albert Wesselski rightly insisted upon the importance of the literary tale and went so far as to state that the printed page had made a real study of oral tradition impossible. This dogma should be examined in the light of actual studies of the relation of the literary tale to the oral in Europe. Moreover, pure oral folklore should be studied whenever possible. One of the values of the investigation of such tales as those of the North American Indian is that we are dealing entirely with the spoken word and that the chance of literary influence is all but out of the question. Such comparative treatments of primitive tales as have been made would seem to show the validity of the historic-geographic method.

For the study of the diffusion of any item of folklore, whether it be a tale or not, some adaptation of this method would seem possible. It is clear that the item to be studied must be sufficiently complicated to permit of analysis, so that an objective investigation can be made of its different manifestations. Those folktales which consist of a single motif may be too simple for proper analysis, though it is true that some single motifs have enough complexity of structure to permit a thorough analytical treatment. Most tales, most ballads, many local traditions, and most riddles would seem to fit themselves to such study. The application of the method to ballads, though it is only in its beginning,[23] gives promise of clarifying their distribution and of making it possible to map out the main lines of their history. Such beginnings have also been made with a comparative study of riddles,[24] and of children's games,[25] and cumulative tales.[26]

The student of the dissemination of a folklore item may be interested in its history for its own sake, or he may feel that he is adding one more monograph which will help in arriving at some general laws. Our older scholars were interested in answering the leading question, "Where do folktales come from?" We are still interested in such problems, but we realize that it is only when we know about specific tales that we can hope to come to any conclusions. Dogmatism about diffusion, or independent origin, as a universal principle is entirely premature. We must learn what kinds of material diffuse, what kinds arise independently.[27] With the thirty or forty monographs which have already been written, it is possible even now to re-examine some of the older theories and to give consideration to others. Does our data already indicate currents which have given direction to oral tradition? What relation have these currents with migrations and other well-established historic facts? How are they correlated with racial, cultural, or linguistic boundaries? Is there, for example, a typically Indo-European folklore? For an objective study of the latter question, the American Indians again afford an unusual opportunity, since racial and linguistic boundaries on the American continent have little correspondence.

Such are some of the problems arising from the fact that folklore obeys certain laws of oral transmission, that it proceeds from centers of distribution and not from document to document, like literary material.

We have seen that folklore as well as literature has developed its special *genres*.[28] The scholar must be sure that any differentiations of such forms as he makes should have actual validity. Much of the hair-splitting which has taken place in trying to differentiate between various kinds of folktales is futile from any point of view. It is convenient, however, to recognize the difference in intent and subject matter between a *Sage* (a local tradition) and a *Märchen* (a tale like Cinderella). And sometimes an analytical study which attempts to make minute subdivisions of recognized *genres* brings out interesting facts about regional, racial, or other differences in treatment of material. A type of interesting study with which very little has been done would seek to apply the differentiations of European folklore *genres* to the traditions of primitive people, and see how far they have validity in the very nature of the material and how far they would seem to be a result of a particular place and age. One of the most difficult of these studies would undoubtedly be with the myth. How much of the speculations of nineteenth-century mythologists would be left when one has finished?

The relation of folk literature to the people from whom it is recovered should be interesting to the literary student as well as to the sociologist. How do tales or folksongs actually function in their lives? Certainly their feeling toward them is different from that of a collector to whom they are dictated. Can we not learn from the attitude of the simple folk whose lore is still alive some of the essential principles of æsthetics—why people tell tales and sing songs and why other people listen to them?

The study of literary style in folklore is almost untouched, and even the methods would have to be invented by the student who would undertake to explore the field. Such pioneer works as Professor Hart's *Ballad and Epic*,[29] with the excellent method of literary analysis suggested there, have not been followed up as they should be. Objective analyses of the folktale styles of various countries and periods, for example, have hardly been attempted. How shall the student even begin such an analysis?

Certain detailed studies can surely be undertaken that have their bearing on the question of style. The beginning and end formulas of certain kinds of tales or ballads, the kinds of material favored by particular *genres* or by particular peoples or ages can be easily studied and their influence on narrative style observed. Why are the tales of some American Indian tribes uninteresting to the white reader and those of the next neighboring tribe filled with all the qualities we are used to associating with good narrative art? Do the Iroquois, for example, really enjoy their long-winded and repetitious tales? If so, what elements in their culture, religious or social, have brought about this result?

A combination of the methods proper to oral literature and those of ordinary literary history must be employed whenever we attempt to study the relation of written literature to folk tradition. Unless one confines his study to primitive peoples, even the investigation of the folktale itself must be partly a question of the relation of literary documents. Tales have been recomposed by writers of prose or verse, and these literary retellings in turn have profoundly affected the purely oral tradition. It would be an interesting thing to know just how much influence the particular version of Cinderella composed by Basile in Italy in the early seventeenth century and that of Perrault sixty years later in France have had on the Cinderella as recorded from the people in western Europe. Such a study would include both style and content, and its feasibility would depend primarily upon the thoroughness with which the versions could be assembled.

What of the folktale and the ballad as the origin of sophisticated literature? The European ballad is a distinct *genre* whose origin does not go back more than a thousand years. The literary imitations and borrowings from these ballads have been rather thoroughly studied, though further relationships may well be discovered. As to the narrative songs in Europe before the advent of the present ballad form, we know so little that we are reduced to guesswork. In the absence of sufficient historic data scholars may speculate as to the heroic songs that may have been current at the court of Hrothgar or of Alcinous. Generally the attempt to explain the great epics themselves as artistic amalgamations of such songs has been abandoned. A somewhat analogous problem, indeed, is presented by the relation of the Finnish heroic folksong and the literary epic, the *Kalevala*. The great number of these Finnish heroic songs has made possible good technical studies of their distribution and mutual influence.[30] But conditions making possible these Finnish studies are probably unique.

Folktale enthusiasts have undoubtedly overstated the influence of the popular tale on literature. The scholar should try to consider every problem of this kind as an individual question not to be solved by the application of any general laws. Too many studies were made in the last century on the assumption that folktales are broken down myths or in some other way the debris of literature. When the fallacy of this position became clear, the reaction was strong; and the folktale became the favorite hunting ground of the seeker for literary sources. The only advice that can be given the student in this regard is to insist that he approach his problem with the proper scholarly attitude. Before he examines his data thoroughly and interprets it to the best of his ability, he has no right to arrive at conclusions. All scholars must now recognize the mutual give and take which has occurred between the folktale and literary narrative.

One point that has been very confusing in the study of the relation just mentioned is the fact that scholars have seldom differentiated sufficiently between entire folktales and the motifs out of which these tales are made. Many motifs combine freely in almost any kind of narrative, and the student must beware of concluding that because a particular romance or epic contains a certain folktale motif it has therefore borrowed that motif from a particular folktale. Some of the studies of *Beowulf* and other monuments of Germanic legend [31] have been subject to this fallacy. Anyone who looks into the folk material in Homer, for example, must be especially careful to distinguish between tale-type and motif. The same caution must be given for the study of the puzzling relation of the mediæval romances with the folktale. There was undoubtedly much mutual influence, for many undoubted tale-types constitute either an entire romance or a part of one. Comparative studies of most of these have been made with fair thoroughness, though some further historic-geographic monographs on tales with romance variants should be worth while.

For a long time various attempts have been made to classify folklore material. It is only after some satisfactory classification has been contrived that it is possible to make a proper sorting of the data of any scholarly activity. Not until Aarne's *Verzeichnis der Märchentypen* appeared in 1910 was it possible to begin surveys of the folktale repertories of various countries. Even though the system there exemplified is not perfect, it has been so widely adopted that the part of wisdom would seem to lie in improvements and modifications rather than in contriving another. For the individual incidents and traits in all kinds of popular narrative literature, Thompson's *Motif-Index* seems to offer a satisfactory basic classification. But in both the type-index and the motif-index there is much opportunity for improvement by individual scholars who wish to undertake thorough revisions of particular sections. Moreover, the motif-index is now serving as a common basis for an analytical treatment of whole *genres* or literary traditions, such as the Italian novelle, the French fabliaux, and the like. Every study of this kind serves to expand the classification in certain directions, and it is only by some such practical co-operative effort that the scholarly world can gradually approach a more complete view of the enormous variety of narrative motifs.

The present index of tale-types is made primarily to fit the tales of Europe and adjacent lands. Surveys of folklore material from other parts of the world, such as Africa, Oceania, or the American continent, raise the question of new classifications for each area or the possibility of expanding one scheme to cover the world. Work is already being done in some of those fields, but there is room for many analytical studies and classifications of this kind.

A satisfactory ordering of ballads and folksongs is much to be desired. More than a mere list of titles is necessary, for songs are variously known. It will take some ingenuity to devise a scheme which will include Sir Patrick Spens, Old Joe Clark, Git Along Little Dogies, The Jam on Gerry's Rock, and the songs of Lead Belly, not to speak of even more diverse types. It may be that the plan will recognize certain well-established groups, such as the Child ballads, the play party songs, etc.; or it may be made purely on a basis of subject matter. But however it is devised it should make easier the work of the collector in the field and the scholar annotating his material.

Classification of folk music is a problem so special that it must be left to the musicologist, but it is to be hoped that some generally acceptable system may be made available that is not beyond the understanding of the literary student.[32] The Deutsches Volksliedarchiv uses a system which seems to give satisfactory results with German folklorists.

Should special classifications of other *genres* be undertaken? It is possible that separate indexes of *Sagen* and riddles and myths should be constructed, or it may be that the same end will be served by a great extension of a general motif-index, with special finding-lists for each *genre*.

In this summary treatment of the methods and problems of folklore research it has been made sufficiently apparent that the field is not nearly so well explored as those dealing with pure literature. One has not only the sense of adventure belonging to the pioneer but also the disadvantages. He must do many tasks and assume a variety of duties. For example, he must not let the mere fact that a text or discussion is in a foreign language deter him. He must learn something of anthropology, and perhaps of music or dancing. He must undertake many fields of knowledge, but he must have a strong will not to follow the broad road of dilettantism. He must strive to keep up with the real scholars in all the fields he tries to cultivate. Too many literary folklorists are still using methods of study that serious anthropologists abandoned fifty years ago. The serious student will find that it is not impossible to cultivate literary folklore as both an art and a science. At least it is a challenge.

Part IV SUGGESTIONS ON THESIS-WRITING

I DO not propose in this section to tell any one how to write a thesis in English literary history. Of all things, literary research is one that must be learned by doing, not by reading or listening. No one, however learned he may be, however good a teacher and scholar, can be of much help to the graduate student with a thesis to write, except by way of suggesting methods of procedure and criticizing results achieved. Even this help some graduate schools used to neglect or minimize; it was their practice to assign a thesis subject to the student and then allow him to seek his own salvation according to his ability—his intelligence and initiative. Perhaps those who emerged triumphant from such an experience were the better scholars for having been left so much to their own devices, but I doubt that such aid as might have shortened and lightened the task—such aid as can be given—would have been particularly injurious to the student. Every individual who completes a thesis, unless he has such help as amounts to having his work done for him, will have experienced the training and discipline that constitutes the value of thesis-writing.

I

The first problem that confronts the student faced with the necessity of preparing a thesis is the choice of a subject. This is an important matter and one which is too often carelessly or haphazardly settled; but it is, I think, less important than many students suppose. To have a good subject is not a guarantee of a successful thesis; conversely, an apparently dull or unpromising subject may lead to a vitally interesting and important piece of research. The first step, as has previously been suggested,[1] is to select a field in which one is, or can make himself, competent. It would be a capital mistake for one whose language equipment is weak to undertake a study which might involve comparative literature. It is desirable, though not necessary, that the field chosen be one which holds some natural attraction for the student; it will be found that working in a field, becoming acquainted with it, generally creates an interest where none formerly existed. An important consideration in the choice of a field is the faculty of the institution in which the student expects to do his work; if it includes an individual of special note, the student may do well to choose the field which will bring him under that individual's direction.

In actual practice, I suppose, the typical graduate student, after gaining some acquaintance with the professorial staff, selects the member of the staff under whom he wishes to work, which choice automatically determines the field. If the person thus chosen is one who will give serious and thoughtful consideration to the assigning of a subject, who will discuss the problem at some length, seeking to discover the student's interests and abilities, there is every prospect for a successful thesis. Unfortunately, there are in most graduate schools some scholars who have more interest in their own research than in the training of students; these individuals are likely to assign projects that they wish to have studied, not bothering to determine whether the student has any interest in the research assigned, or, indeed, whether he has the ability to carry it out successfully. Such persons the graduate student will do well to avoid.

Having chosen a field and a director for his thesis, the student will want to formulate a definite problem on which to work. For a master's thesis, which the student may wish to complete within an academic or a calendar year, a specific topic should be chosen as soon as possible; but for a piece of research which may extend over a longer time, the subject may at first be very general. If I may mention my own experience as a case in point, I started to work on the suggestion from Professor Baskervill that Robert Greene would be a good subject for study. For a long while—too long, at times, for my peace of mind—I studied without arriving at a more

[1] See above, p. 92.

specific subject; eventually there emerged not one topic, but four. In view of the fact that they all had to do with the latter part of Greene's life and his work during that period, I was able to achieve some sort of unity by treating the four problems under the rather unacademic title *Greene's Last Years.*

One advantage of delay in choosing a specific subject is that such delay encourages the student to keep an open mind until he has sufficiently mastered his material and can take an intelligent position. Too often the student who is given a subject such as "The Influence of Spenser on Bunyan" is unconsciously predisposed to find an influence rather than to seek the truth. To encourage open-mindedness the University of Chicago, in company with other universities, has long favored the use of the word *dissertation*—with its connotation of thoroughness and exhaustiveness—instead of the word *thesis,* which suggests an attempt to prove a point.

Before making a definite choice of a subject, either specific or general, the student must make sure that the materials—books and manuscripts—necessary for the study are available to him. The individual or the committee directing the thesis should be able to advise the student as to the availability of material, and the student is entitled to rely upon such advice; but he may save himself from later grief by conducting his own investigation and determining, as soon as he is in a position to know what materials are necessary, whether the resources of local libraries are adequate. Some materials may be secured by means of inter-library loans, but it would be a great inconvenience to have to depend much upon such borrowings. Of course if the student is financially able to travel to New York or Chicago, to Harvard or Yale or Texas, to the Folger Library or the Huntington, or to buy books and photostats or microfilms, he need not worry about local resources. But few graduate students are so happily situated as to be able to buy much more than the textbooks required in their courses.

Another factor to be considered in the choice of a thesis-subject is the time element. One who expects to finish a thesis in ten months must select a subject which, without superhuman industry and with no more than ordinary good fortune, can be completed within that length of time. If one cannot be reasonably certain that a subject in

question can be finished in the time proposed, he must either choose
another subject or resign himself to the possibility of having to spend
more time on the project than he had intended.

Still another consideration is the value and importance of the
results to be achieved. It is not always possible to determine, until
after a piece of research is completed, how important its conclusions
will be; but it can not be denied that many theses have been written
which any one might have known from the beginning would be of
interest and value to no one except the person who assigned the
subject and the student who did the work—perhaps not even to
them. This is not to say that all theses, and especially master's theses,
must represent "discoveries"—original and strikingly important contributions to knowledge.[2] I remember that some years ago a student
apologized to Professor Manly for the fact that his work did not
involve a discovery. Professor Manly replied that no apology was
necessary, and added that he had read a good many doctoral dissertations in his time and could remember only two or three that
constituted discoveries. Nevertheless, it is possible to find, even for
a master's thesis, a subject that has interest and significance. The
training received from writing on a dull and lifeless subject is no

[2] Articles which may be said to represent "discoveries" of greater or less importance include: Edythe M. Backus, "The MS Play *Anna Bullen*", *PMLA*, XLVII
(1932), 741–52; F. M. Salter, "Skelton's *Speculum Principis*", *Speculum*, IX (1934),
25–37; T. H. Vail Motter, "A 'Lost' Poem by Arthur Hallam", *PMLA*, L (1935),
568–75; William Von Lennep, "Three Unnoticed Writings of Swift", *PMLA*, LI
(1936), 793–802; DeLancey Ferguson, "Some New Burns Letters", *PMLA*, LI
(1936), 975–84; George Reuben Potter, "Unpublished Marginalia in Coleridge's
Copy of Malthus's *Essay on Population*", *PMLA*, LI (1936), 1061–68, and Kenneth Curry, "A Note on Coleridge's Copy of Malthus", *PMLA*, LIV (1939),
613–15; Irving L. Churchill, "Shenstone's Billets", *PMLA*, LII (1937), 114–21;
Bertrand Harris Bronson, "Ritson's *Bibliographica Scotica*", *PMLA*, LII (1937),
122–59; Alan L. Strout, "James Hogg's Forgotten Satire, *John Patterson's Mare*",
PMLA, LII (1937), 427–60; Bernard Mathias Wagner, "New Poems by Sir Philip
Sidney", *PMLA*, LIII (1938), 118–24; Rossell Hope Robbins, "The Gurney Series
of Religious Lyrics", *PMLA*, LIV (1939), 369–90; Willa McClung Evans, "To
Splendora", *PMLA*, LIV (1939), 405–11; John Edwin Wells, "Wordsworth and
De Quincey in Westmoreland Politics, 1818", *PMLA*, LV (1940), 1080–1128; Thomas
O. Mabbott and Rollo G. Silver, "Walt Whitman's ' 'Tis But Ten Years Since' ",
AmLit, XV (1943–44), [51]–62; Helen E. Sandison, " 'The Vanytyes of Sir Arthur
Gorges Youth' ", *PMLA*, LXI (1946); Rollo G. Silver, "Whitman in 1850: Three
Uncollected Articles", *AmLit*, XIX (1947–48), [301]–17; and Robert Shafer, "Paul
Elmer More: A Note on His Verse and Prose Written in Youth, with Two Un-
published Poems", *AmLit*, XX (1948–49), [43]–51.

better than that resulting from work on a good subject. Why, then, should one not choose a subject that gives promise of leading to a thesis of value to others than the writer?

Before starting to work on a subject one should make sure that what he proposes to do has not already been done. It may be said that this is a responsibility which should rest with the director of the thesis or the candidate's committee. That is undoubtedly true; a subject which has previously been treated should not be suggested or approved unless there is a reason—such as the fact that the first treatment was unsatisfactory or that new material has become available—for a second treatment of it. But thesis-directors and graduate committees sometimes err; and when they do, it is generally the candidate who suffers for the mistake. To be safe, then, one should make sure for himself that his work will not be a duplication of previous efforts. For a master's thesis, it will probably suffice to search the available catalogues and the *MHRA Bibliographies*; but if one is preparing to work on a doctoral dissertation he should by all means consult the *List of American Doctoral Dissertations Printed* (published by the Library of Congress annually from 1912 to 1938) and Donald B. Gilchrist (and others; see below, p. 321, n.51), *Doctoral Dissertations Accepted by American Universities* (annual since 1934). One should also consult *Works in Progress . . . in the Modern Humanities,* published annually by the Modern Humanities Research Association; and the section "Research in Progress" in each issue of *AmLit*; and it may be wise to write to several of the leading scholars in the field—especially those who are connected with productive graduate schools—to inquire whether they know of anyone's being at work on the proposed subject. One of the greatest of academic tragedies is to have a piece of research well under way—perhaps almost finished—and then to be anticipated in publication by someone else.

One more suggestion and we shall have done with the matter of choosing a subject. More and more people are taking doctoral degrees; in many positions, where formerly a master's degree or even a bachelor's degree was sufficient qualification, a doctor's degree is now an inexorable requirement. Consequently, many a student now working on a master's degree and expecting to be satisfied with the attainment of that goal, may find himself later working for the

more advanced degree. It will be wise for those who may eventually
have to write a doctoral dissertation, as well as for those who expect
to do so, to choose as the subject for the master's thesis one that
will lead to work which will provide a basis for, or will be related
to, future research. One may write his master's thesis on one phase
of a question, leaving others for future investigation, or on one
author of a group, or one work of several, or a short period out of a
longer one.

II

The subject having been chosen or assigned, the student is ready
to proceed to work. Mention has previously been made of the equipment required.[3] What is much more important than the size and kind
of note slips and filing devices is the quality of the notes taken. Much
excellent work was produced from notes copied into bound notebooks, and we shall have profited little if our improvement in
matériel is counteracted by carelessness or inefficiency in note-taking.
Professor Dow, in his *Principles of a Note-System for Historical
Studies,* has worked out an arrangement which may be desirable or
even necessary for students of other kinds of history, but which
seems to me unnecessarily elaborate for students of literary history.
Instead of the ten or twelve kinds of notes recommended by Professor Dow, I should suggest three kinds: bibliographical notes,
critico-bibliographical notes, and subject notes. It may also be helpful to distinguish subject notes representing primary sources from
those representing secondary sources and also from those containing
one's own ideas.[4]

Since the first step in the solution of a research problem is the
compiling of a bibliography, the first notes to be taken will be bibliographical notes. A bibliography is, of course, a list of documents—
books, articles, pamphlets, manuscripts—dealing with a common subject. To be of any value, a bibliography must be accurate, and it
should—so far as is humanly possible—be complete. That is not to
say that a bibliography for a thesis on Shakspere's knowledge of
botany, or of medicine, or of law should contain everything written
on Shakspere; but it should contain everything that may contribute

[3] See above, pp. 86–88.
[4] See below, Appendix B.

to a discussion of Shakspere and botany, or medicine, or law. Unfortunately, such completeness is generally an impossible ideal. A bibliography is likely to be out of date as soon as it is completed; perhaps even before it is completed a book or an article will have appeared that should have been included and would have been included had the compiler of the bibliography known of it. Moreover, significant material often lurks in out-of-the-way places, in books which—to judge from their titles—might be expected to have nothing to contribute; and it would be an obvious impossibility for the student to read everything that has been written on Shakspere to make sure that he has included everything that touched on his specific subject. But he should make the utmost endeavor to include all those works that by their titles give promise of being helpful.

We are considering now the working bibliography—a collection of slips, preferably 4″ by 6″—containing the titles of all the works that seem likely to have, or may have, something to contribute to the thesis. Such notes are primarily for the student's own use; but they form the basis for the thesis bibliography, which may be consulted by others. Hence they must contain all the information necessary to enable the user to locate, with the minimum expenditure of time and effort, any work represented; all other information, however interesting it may be to a librarian or a book-collector, is confusing to the student and should be omitted. Data concerning the size of a book, the number of pages, the presence of illustrations, have nothing to do with making it easy to locate the book, and hence have no place in a thesis bibliography. But the following facts must be given: For books, the name of the author; the title of the book; the facts of publication; [5] the name of the editor, or translator, or compiler

---

[5] These, of course, consist of the place of publication, the publisher, and the date. In many bibliographies the name of the publisher is not given, the assumption being, I suppose, that the place and date are sufficient to identify the edition, since two or more publishers would not be likely to bring out different editions in the same place during the same year. That may be true; but it seems to me that the publisher's name should be given in view of the fact that the user of the bibliography may wish to purchase the book, in which case the publisher's name is the first thing he will want to know. However, the student will in this matter, as in all matters of form, naturally follow the advice of the director of the thesis. If place and publisher are both given, it matters little which item is placed first; probably the commoner practice is to put the place first.

(if there is one); the number of the edition, or the fact that it is a revision of a previous edition; [6] the number of volumes or, as in a work like the *Cambridge History of English Literature,* the numbers of the volumes pertinent to the study at hand; and the name of the series to which the work belongs, such as *Indiana University Studies,* or the "Modern Readers' Series". For periodical articles, the name of the author; the title of the article; the name of the periodical; the volume number; the date; and the pages covered by the article are necessary. Most of the entries with which one has to deal in a thesis in the field of English literary history will clearly belong to one of these two categories and can be treated according to the formula given [7] for that category. Occasionally an entry—a government bulletin, an advertising pamphlet, an article in an encyclopædia or a dictionary, an unpublished manuscript—will cause trouble. [8] In treating such anomalous entries, one must keep in mind the necessity for completeness, clearness, and consistency.

To begin the compiling of the working bibliography, the student may consult a reference work, such as the *Encyclopædia Britannica* or, if the subject is a person, a biographical dictionary such as the *DNB,* and take down the titles given at the end of the appropriate article. Or one may find in a library catalogue or in Clark S. Northup's *Register of Bibliographies* the most recent book that contains a bibliography covering or relating to one's subject. It may be possible to assume—with the consent of the director of the thesis— that such a bibliography was complete for the date of its publication,

---

[6] If different editions are involved, one must use the same edition as that given in the bibliography, to be sure that the page numbers will agree; one may, however, use a copy with a date different from that given in the bibliography if it represents merely a different printing or impression. In the latter case, however, the possibility of corrections or revisions on the page in question must be considered.

[7] See below, pp. 286–89.

[8] Serial publications of universities and learned societies are frequently troublesome. When such publications are put out in volumes with two or more studies bound together and consecutively paged, it would seem best to treat them like periodicals, putting the title of the study in quotation marks and italicizing the name of the series, thus: Merrit Y. Hughes, "Virgil and Spenser", *University of California Publications in English,* II (1929), 263–418. When each study is issued and paged separately, it might be better to italicize the name of the study: Germaine Dempster, *Dramatic Irony in Chaucer,* in *Stanford University Publications, University Series, Language and Literature,* IV (1932), No. 3.

or approximately that date.[9] For the period since that time, one should then consult one's own library catalogue and any other catalogues available, for the titles of books, and the *Readers' Guide to Periodical Literature* and the *International Index to Periodicals,* for articles in magazines and learned journals. The *MHRA Bibliographies* will give both books and articles for the years 1919–1938; but one should consult all possible sources of information, even at the cost of considerable duplication of effort, to make sure that no promising title is overlooked. If one keeps his bibliographical notes always at hand, and in alphabetical order, it will take but an instant to determine whether a newly-discovered title is already included in the notes. One should never assume, because a title seems familiar, that he has made a note of it. It is much better to go to the trouble, if one's notes are not at hand, of making a duplicate note; otherwise, the work thus inadvertently omitted will invariably prove to be the one that should, above all, have been included. Nothing gives critics more joy than such lapses.

Since the notes for the working bibliography are for the student's own use, he may please himself in the way he arranges the information on the slip; common sense would suggest that he use essentially the same form that he will be required to use in the bibliography that will accompany the finished thesis.[10]

The student may find it helpful to keep the slips representing periodical articles separate from those for books; but it is the usual practice to put all entries into one alphabetical arrangement in the final form of the bibliography, and there is little reason for not doing the same in the working bibliography.

We come now to the matter of bibliographical form. Unfortunately, there is no uniform standard in such matters; the information that follows represents what seems to me the commonest and best practices, but the student may find that some of my recommendations

[9] It must be remembered that bibliographies are sometimes completed months before the date of publication; one should begin his independent search for material at a point three or four years before the publication date, thus making sure that he will discover anything that may have appeared too late for inclusion and at the same time establishing a check on the completeness of the bibliography.

[10] It may be convenient, however, to put the items on different lines, as in Appendix B.

will be overruled by the director of his thesis or by the requirements
of his graduate school.

It is usual in a bibliographical entry to put the author's surname
first,[11] in order to emphasize the alphabetical arrangement and make
it easy to find a given entry. Works written by two or more authors
jointly should be entered in full under the name that comes first on
the title page, but there should be a cross reference for each collaborator.[12] In determining where to alphabetize names beginning
with prefixes such as De, La, and Von one may well follow the practice of a good model such as the biographical section of *Webster's
New International Dictionary*. Such portion of an author's full name
as does not appear on the title page of his work should be enclosed
in square brackets: "H[erbert] G[eorge] Wells". It used to be a common practice to group together works of unknown authorship under
the heading "Anonymous"; it is now considered better to alphabetize
such titles under the first important word contained in them. Thus an
unsigned article, "A First Edition Forgery", would follow "Finch"
and precede "Frost". Encyclopædia articles are frequently signed
with initials which can be identified by referring to a table at the
beginning of the volume; thus part of the article on "Shakespeare"
in the *Encyclopædia Britannica* (14th edition) is signed "E.K.C.",
representing, of course, Sir Edmund Chambers, and should be entered
"C[hambers], [Sir] E[dmund] K[erchever]". If an article—such as
an editorial—has no title, the name of the periodical in which it
appeared would determine its position in the alphabetical arrangement. An unsigned, untitled review of a book or a play might be
alphabetized according to the name of the work reviewed; but for the
sake of consistency it would be better to alphabetize it according to
the name of the periodical in which it appeared, with a cross reference under the name of the book or play.

The American Library Association has made popular the practice
of capitalizing in a title only those words which would be capitalized
if they were not part of a title—i.e., proper nouns and proper adjectives. The older and more conventional practice is to capitalize the
first and last words and all nouns, pronouns, adjectives, adverbs, and
verbs. Unless the director of the thesis or someone else in the depart-

[11] For the practice in footnotes, see below, p. 303.
[12] See below, Appendix A.

ment has strong feelings about italic capitals, the student may adopt whichever system he prefers; he should, however, be consistent in adhering to the system he chooses.

As soon as one has looked up a title in his library catalogue, he should put on the note-slip the call number of the work represented by the note, so that he need never again take time to consult the catalogue for that entry.[13]

Titles of parts of publications are enclosed within quotation marks; the title under which a whole work is published is underlined in long-hand or typewriting, to be set in italic type if printed.[14] Thus the titles of short stories, articles in magazines, essays, and short poems are quoted; titles of books and plays and names of periodicals are underlined. An exception to the rule is sometimes made in favor of works that are regarded as classics; one may legitimately underline instead of quoting the title of Keats's sonnet "On First Looking into Chapman's Homer" or Stevenson's "An Apology for Idlers", even though neither work may ever have been published separately. When a title that would normally be italicized occurs within an italicized title, it is sometimes enclosed within quotation marks, sometimes set in roman type. One may see either: "*A Study of* Hamlet *as a Senecan Tragedy*" or '*A Study of* "Hamlet" *as a Senecan Tragedy*'. When a title that is to be italicized forms part of a larger work—as in a collection of plays—it is convenient to use the word "in" to bring out the relationship: "John Fletcher, *Rule a Wife and Have a Wife,* in *Representative English Comedies,* ed. Charles Mills Gayley (New York: Macmillan, 1914), III, 215–300." In a bibliography in which roman type is used instead of italic for titles, the word "in" in such entries should be italicized. In references involving page numbers, the concluding page should always be represented by two digits unless the first of the two is a zero. Thus we may have "pp. 107–9" or "pp. 113–19" but not "pp. 113–9". This rule, like most apparently arbitrary rules, has good sense back of it. If one forms the habit of giving only the last digit, he is very likely to write "117–9" when he means to write "117–29"; but one who is accustomed to write "117–19" is not

---

[13] Call numbers are not, however, included in the final form of the bibliography, since they are not the same for all libraries.

[14] Roman type is often substituted for italics in printed bibliographies, apparently for no better reason than that modern printers are not fond of italics; the practice is, however, one which can in some instances create a good deal of confusion.

likely to substitute another numeral for the "2" when he means to write "29".

When a reference includes a volume number and a page number, it is unnecessary to use any abbreviation for volume or page; it is understood that the Roman numeral [15] represents the volume and the Arabic numeral the page. When the reference contains only one of these items, an abbreviation must be used: "*Cambridge History of English Literature* . . . Vols. V, VI". Or, assuming that Volume II has nothing to contribute to the thesis, we might have "Smith, G. Gregory, *Elizabethan Critical Essays* . . . Vol. I". If only certain pages of a book are pertinent to the inquiry, the fact may be indicated in the bibliography: "Spencer, Hazelton, *The Art and Life of William Shakespeare* (New York: Harcourt, Brace and Co., 1940c), pp. 89–102".[16]

If the name of an editor, translator, or compiler is to be given, it may be placed either before or after the facts of publication.

In an entry relating to a periodical article it is usually necessary to give only the year of publication, ignoring the month and day. One might ask why any date need be given, since the volume number alone is sufficient to enable the user of the bibliography to locate the article; but there are at least two good reasons for including the year. In the first place, when periodicals are bound, the binder may put on the backstrip of the bound volume the date rather than the volume number; of course both should appear, but one sometimes finds only the date. In such a case one must, if he has only the volume number, take down a volume at random, find the volume number for that year, and then perform an arithmetical calculation in order to discover the volume for which he is looking. The other reason is that giving both year and volume number gives the user something to go

[15] Some authorities permit the abandonment of the Roman numeral and the substitution of the system used in the *Readers' Guide*; thus we should have: 'D[eWitt] T[almadge] Starnes, "Bilingual Dictionaries of Shakespeare's Day", *PMLA,* 52: 1005–18 (1937)' instead of '. . . . *PMLA,* LII (1937) 1005–18'. The use of Arabic numerals may be necessary in such a work as the *Readers' Guide* to conserve space and lessen expense; but in thesis-writing the use of Roman numerals for volume numbers is so universally practised that one can hardly abandon them without laying himself open to the suspicion that he is unable, rather than merely unwilling, to handle them.

[16] The superior *c* accompanying the date in this reference indicates that the date is that of the copyright, there being no date of publication given.

on if one of the items happens to be incorrect. Suppose one is looking up a reference in which only the volume number is given and that, he discovers, is wrong; no such article as he seeks is to be found on p. 47 or any other page of Vol. LIX. He may try LXI and XLI and various other combinations; but he might conceivably save time by starting at the beginning and looking on page 47 of every volume; and with a journal like *The Athenæum,* which began publication in 1828, or *The Edinburgh Review,* which began in 1802, the task would be an arduous one. When both volume and year are given, it is most unlikely that both will be wrong; if the article sought is not in the volume indicated, the searcher finds that the date of that volume does not correspond with the date given. Turning then to the volume indicated by the date, he finds the article he is seeking.

In handling dates and volume numbers one must be alert to notice any irregularities. Some periodicals began publication in March or July and carried the first volume into the succeeding calendar year. Others publish two volumes in one year. Still others may have one volume bound as two or more, or two volumes bound as one.

Most of the older periodicals are paged consecutively from beginning to end of each volume; and when the volume is bound, any distinction between issues disappears. Hence there is no point in giving the number or the date of the issue in which an article is to be found. However, some of the more recently established journals, and popular magazines generally, follow the practice of paging each issue separately; in referring to such periodicals the month and year must be given for monthly and quarterly publications, and the day, month, and year for weeklies and dailies. If one is taking down a reference and finds the month or month and day given, he should of course copy that information, unless the page number is so large as to prove that the volume is consecutively paged.

The compiling of a working bibliography is a long and arduous task and one that the student should not attempt to complete before beginning the next stage of his work. Indeed, it will not be possible for him to complete his bibliography until he has almost finished his thesis; for again and again as he reads, new bibliographical items will keep appearing and must be added to the working bibliography if any degree of completeness is to be achieved.

We have so far been considering purely bibliographical notes;

these should, as quickly as possible, be turned into critico-biblio-graphical notes by the adding of information as to the nature and value of the work represented by each note. Such comments may be in part the student's own reactions, recorded after a study of the work involved; but the student will do well, before making his own evaluation, to read and consider the reviews of the work in literary and learned journals.[17] He may find it desirable to quote statements from a review on his note; in such a case the borrowed opinion should, of course, be enclosed in quotation marks, and the source of it should be given, so that there will be no confusion between the student's opinion and that of some reviewer, and so that the source of the quotation may easily be found if occasion for consulting it should arise.

III

As soon as the working bibliography is well under way, the student will naturally be eager to begin taking the third kind of notes—the subject notes. But here a difficulty arises. The student cannot tell just what piece of information he should take down—much less how it is to be classified—until he knows, in a general way at least, what the form and content of the thesis is to be; but the form and content of the thesis he cannot determine until he knows a good deal about the material with which he is to work—not, in other words, until he has taken a good many notes. Thus the student who begins a piece of research is thrust into what may well seem a vicious circle: he does not know what notes to take until he has taken a good many, and he cannot take notes—efficiently, at least—until he knows what notes to take. It might seem that the only solution is to start taking down haphazardly whatever information appears as if it might be relevant, and then, after acquiring some command of the field of investigation, to discard the notes already taken and start over again. But the solution is not quite that bad.

---

[17] The *Book Review Digest* will be helpful in locating some of these, but reviews of works published between 1919 and 1938 may be most conveniently located through the annual bibliographies of the Modern Humanities Research Association. It must be remembered that reviews, especially in learned journals, do not always follow promptly upon the publication of a work. If a book was published in the latter part of the year 1930, most of the reviews will be found in 1931, and some in 1932 or possibly later.

There are two things that one may do to make sure that his note-taking will be done with some degree of efficiency. First, he should do a good deal of reading in the field which he proposes to examine, taking no notes other than bibliographical ones. When he has sufficiently oriented himself, the problem should begin to take such shape as will enable him to determine, of any piece of information he encounters, whether or not it is relevant to his investigation, and, also, if it is relevant, what place it occupies in the solution of his problem. How much of this orientation reading will be required will depend, of course, upon the student's background and upon the nature of the problem. Most of the materials used in this preliminary reading will have served their purpose when the background reading is finished and will not be cited in the thesis itself, because the student will have found more authoritative sources for any information derived from them that he may have occasion to use. For example, one might well read Sir Edmund Chambers' article in the *Encyclopædia Britannica* as part of the background for a study involving Shakspere; but he would probably find that the details in that article also appear either in Chambers' *William Shakespeare: A Study of Facts and Problems* or in his *The Elizabethan Stage,* and one would naturally cite the book rather than the article.

In the course of the preliminary reading, the problem that is to be solved by the thesis should begin to take shape, and certain topics— destined to be the main headings of the discussion—should begin to make themselves apparent. As such points of interest arise, the student may find it helpful to put them in the form of questions— whenever possible, questions that can be answered "Yes" or "No"; "Did Spenser exert an influence on Bunyan?" "Is that influence to be seen in *Pilgrim's Progress*?" "Did it come from Bunyan's reading of Spenser's works?" "Could it have come instead from the neo-Spenserians or some other source?" And so on. When these questions are arranged in logical order, the thesis topic has been formulated and an outline can be planned; the finished outline will consist of the answers to the questions.

IV

At this point the student may avail himself of the second means of insuring efficient note-taking referred to above. By adopting a sufficiently flexible note-system one may be able to do a good deal of reorganizing of material, as a need for reorganizing becomes apparent, without having to make any changes in the notes already taken. Suppose that one writing on Milton had decided to organize his material into the following main divisions: I Life, II Character, III Works, IV Criticism. To save time he might label all the notes pertaining to Milton's life "I", those having to do with his character "II", and so on. If it should later seem best to deal with the poetry and prose separately, the student must go through all his notes changing "III" to "III-A" or "III-B". But if the notes representing works had been labeled *Lycidas, Paradise Lost, Of Prelatical Episcopacy, Comus, Areopagitica*—they could be rearranged without any change of labels. Conversely, if it should be decided that "Life" and "Character" belong in the same main division, those notes can be put together without having to change "II" to "I". Arbitrary labels—based on the position the material represented in the note will presumably occupy in the finished thesis—have to be changed with every change in organization; logical headings—based on the subject matter of the notes—do not.

As the note-taking proceeds, the need for subheads and sub-subheads will generally appear. Thus a note for a Chaucer study may be labeled "*P*[*arlement of*] *F*[*oules*]—allegory—political" or "*C*[*anterbury*] *T*[*ales*]—Man of Law—Source". As the need for such subheads develops, the notes already taken should be examined and the proper labels added wherever necessary.

Every subject note consists of three parts: heading or topic, subject matter, and bibliographical reference. The heading or topic, as we have just seen, indicates the section of the thesis to which the information on the note pertains; the subject matter is, of course, the information for the sake of which the note was taken; and the bibliographical reference gives the source of that information. It would be logical to arrange these three items in the order just used—label, material, and source; but it may be good discipline to put source before subject matter. One is so likely to feel a sense of completion when he has taken down the information he wants, that he may grow careless in recording the source, or worse—forget to record it. And a note containing the most valuable information to be had is almost worthless if it does not give the source of the information.

The most important rule in note-taking, however, and the one which probably causes students the most trouble, is to put on each note one, and only one, unit of information. The rule is easily stated and easily learned, but to apply it is a different matter. Learning to recognize what constitutes a unit of material requires discrimination along with, sometimes, good guessing. A unit of material is that amount of information—whether it be paragraph, sentence, phrase, or word—which will stand by itself in the finished thesis, within which no intervening information, except, possibly, a comment by the author of the thesis, is properly to be placed. In the early stages of one's research it is frequently impossible to be sure whether one sentence from a given source should appear in the thesis immediately following its predecessor in that source, or whether a sentence or several sentences should come between them. If the student knows that a passage of, say, six sentences is to appear as a unit in his thesis, then those six sentences properly belong on one note-slip. But even when a detailed outline has been worked out, there are often occasions when one cannot be sure whether or not he should put two pieces of information on the same slip; in such cases of doubt, the safe thing is, of course, to use two slips. Suppose, however, that one has already put a passage of six sentences on one slip and finds later that a sentence from some other source should come between the third and fourth of those sentences. He may copy sentences four, five, and six on another slip and cross them out on the first one; or—and this procedure saves time and probably does just as well—he may fasten the new note with its one sentence to the old one with a paper clip, and put an asterisk between the third and fourth sentences to show where the appended material belongs.

It is sometimes suggested that different colors be used for different kinds of notes; I see little to recommend such a scheme, but if it appeals to one—if the use of colored note-slips will lessen the drudgery involved in all research—let him by all means use as many hues of the rainbow as he can find excuse for.

On all notes, of whatever kind or color, there should be a margin of about an inch at the left of the slip. In this space should be set down, in abbreviated fashion, the date on which the note was taken. To have a record of the date of each of several notes may make perfectly plain the history of the evolution of an idea, over which one might otherwise puzzle his head in vain. The marginal space on the note may also be used for afterthoughts (each of which should also be dated), for cross references, and for any other jottings which it may be desirable to link directly with the material of the note.

Some authorities urge the use of one's own language in taking notes, rather than that of the source. Such advice is undoubtedly to be followed in undergraduate term papers, but I think that the writer of a thesis will do well to take many notes verbatim. Certainly he should take down the exact words of his source whenever there is a possibility that he may want to use a direct quotation in his thesis. He should then enclose the subject matter of the note—or whatever part of it is in the words of the original—in quotation marks. He should, of course, be extremely careful to copy everything, including spelling and punctuation, accurately.[18] If the original contains a mistake, in spelling, perhaps, or in grammar, which the note-taker is afraid someone may impute to him—he may disclaim responsibility by using the conventional device—*sic* within brackets: ". . . his freinds [*sic*] all knew . . ."

In taking down on a note-slip a quotation that extends from one page to another, one should indicate on the slip where one page ends and the other begins: "*The Comedy of Errors* is based on Plautus; it is an artificial thing, really a / farce, which mildly pleases by adroit manipulation of plot." (Hazelton Spencer, *The Art and Life of William Shakespeare,* pp. 38–39.) If one decided later to use only the last clause, the slanting stroke would tell him that the proper reference is "p. 39".

When the copying of a quotation is completed, the note should be collated with the original; then, if the student is satisfied that his note exactly reproduces the source, he may add a check mark or some such symbol as evidence that he is free to quote from his note without again consulting the original. In what I have just said, I do not, let it be understood, mean to suggest that there should be too lavish a use of direct quotations in a thesis; but it is much easier to turn a note into one's own language at the time of incorporating it into the

---

[18] If there is any chance that the student may wish to reproduce in his thesis the typographical peculiarities of the original—such as the long s (ſ), mā (for *man*), yᵉ (for *the*), or the Elizabethan usage in the matter of *i* and *j* and *u* and *v*— he must of course be careful to indicate those peculiarities in his notes.

thesis than it is to get out the source of the note if a direct quotation should prove to be desirable.

In taking notes one must constantly keep in mind the difference between primary and secondary sources. A primary source is the original, the direct source. Thus for the date of Shakspere's christening the primary source is the register of the Church of the Holy Trinity in Stratford-on-Avon; if that date is quoted from Sidney Lee, or J. Q. Adams, or Sir Edmund Chambers, or Hazelton Spencer, one is making use of a secondary source. The primary source for one of Shakspere's plays would be Shakspere's manuscript; but since we do not have the manuscripts, we are accustomed to think of the various quartos and the First Folio as primary sources, as, indeed, they are for the printed versions of the plays, which may, or may not, differ materially from what Shakspere actually wrote. It may be said, then, that a primary source is that beyond which it is impossible to trace a piece of information. For all practical purposes, Arber's *Transcript of the Stationers' Register* and Greg's *Henslowe's Diary,* accurate as they are, serve as primary sources; but strictly speaking, the Register itself, and the Diary, are the primary sources, the editions of Arber and Greg being secondary.[19] Primary sources are not necessarily more valuable to the student than secondary ones, but should be used whenever possible. Second- and third-hand sources may furnish ideas and suggestions, and it is perfectly proper to use them, so long as they are presented as second- and third-hand sources; but the student should trace all information back toward its origin as far as it is possible for him to go.[20]

Likewise, the student must keep himself at all times aware of the difference between fact and opinion. If we read that in the First Folio version of *Hamlet* there are a certain number of run-on lines, or rhymed lines, or feminine rhymes, the statement—assuming the count to have been correct—represents a fact. But when we read that

[19] A perfectly clear photostat of a primary source is equivalent to the source and may be cited as if one were citing the original.

[20] Professor T. Atkinson Jenkins told a story on himself ("An Inaccurate Quotation from Dr. Johnson", *PMLA*, XLIV (1929), 313) that resulted from failure to observe this rule. He quoted Dr. Johnson as defining a novel as "a smooth tale, generally of love". He was quoting his source (Walter Scott, *Essays on Chivalry, Romance, and the Drama*) correctly, but the source was wrong; what Dr. Johnson really said was "a *small* tale, generally of love".

Shakspere attended the local grammar school at Stratford, we are dealing with an opinion. If the records of the school for the period of Shakspere's boyhood were extant and showed Shakspere's name on the attendance roll, we might accept his membership in the school as a fact, just as we may accept the date of his christening as a fact. But lacking such evidence, the assumption that Shakspere was educated at the Stratford school is only an opinion, however probable it may be. Opinions, like secondary sources, may be exceedingly valuable; and the student may make free use of them so long as he never forgets, or allows the reader of his thesis to forget, that they are opinions, not facts.

In taking notes, since they are for his own use and need not be understood by anyone else, the student may feel free to use such contractions and abbreviations [21] as will make for economy of time and labor. But this license is one to be used cautiously. Many a student has taken a cryptic note, the meaning of which was perfectly clear to him at the moment, only to find that, after the passage of weeks—or perhaps only days—it has become a baffling enigma. One must be sure, then, to employ only such abbreviations as he will always understand; he must not make the mistake of condensing beyond the point of comprehensibility. Indeed, it is a good idea, I think, to make a practice of taking notes in complete sentences. A sentence may not have, a year later, all the connotations that it has as one writes it, but it will still convey a basic meaning; whereas a truncated sentence may, after a lapse of time, cease to convey any meaning at all, and serve only to make one wonder what on earth he could have meant.

Any difficulty in understanding one's notes will be largely obviated if one uses them as he should—keeps reading them, poring over them constantly. Only by thus living with his notes can the student hope to bring out their full possibilities. Trained scholars need not work at such heat, though many of them do; but the average graduate student, while he is working on his thesis, ought to become so absorbed with his subject, so unable to talk about anything else, that he becomes, for the time, a nuisance to his friends.

One more word on taking notes: take plenty of them. The more

[21] In taking down verbatim quotations it will be best to abbreviate only where there is an abbreviation in the original; then there will be no question later whether an abbreviation in the note stands for an abbreviation or a full word in the original.

notes one has, the better his chance, by selecting the best of them, to achieve a brilliant result. Everything that may possibly be helpful should be taken down. When a second source repeats something that has already found its way into one's notes, the repetition should be recorded. The subject matter of the note need not be recopied if it is identical; the second reference can be added to the original note. It may later prove that the second authority is a much better one to cite than the first; it may be worth something to have two sponsors for the opinion, or two confirmations of the fact. But, having taken a multitude of notes, one should not allow himself to be betrayed by his affection for them or by his pride in their bulk. One should ruthlessly discard, no matter how much it may hurt to do so, every note whose contribution turns out, after all, to be neither significant nor particularly interesting. By such Spartan methods are good theses produced.

V

Little that would be helpful can be said here concerning the problem of organizing the material for a thesis; [22] effective organization depends upon the nature of the problem. A biographical problem or a study of a movement will lend itself to a chronological arrangement; many studies demand analysis or synthesis or a combination of those two methods. When one comes to feel that he has accumulated all the notes necessary for the thesis, he should sort them out into piles, putting together those bearing the same main heading; those he will again sort and divide, until he has brought together in separate piles the notes representing the smallest sub-topic in his outline. Each such group should contain not more than fifteen or twenty notes, so that they can be spread out before the student's eyes and their contents digested almost at a glance. It will then be easy to decide that a certain note will provide a good climax for that section of the thesis and hence should come last; that another will furnish a good opening; that still another leads up to the last, or naturally follows the first, or makes a good transition somewhere. When the notes for each smallest subdivision are so arranged, and the subdivisions themselves are put in logical order, and finally the main divisions are disposed so as to lead up to and provide a climax, one has what is in effect a rough draft of the thesis. What yet remains to be done is important;

[22] Some suggestions have been made in the various chapters in Part III.

many a thesis has been ruined in the final stage. But if the preliminary work—the compiling of the bibliography and the collecting
and arranging of the notes—has been well done, the actual writing of
the thesis should be almost, if not quite, a pleasure.

VI

Every graduate student in English should be able to write com-
petently; nevertheless, a good handbook should be kept available for
solving those problems of grammar, sentence structure, and punctuation that are forever rearing their ugly heads. Some students may still
have the handbook used in their freshman days, and that will doubtless serve the purpose; if a new one must be secured, Porter G.
Perrin's *Writer's Guide and Index to English,* revised edition (Chicago: Scott Foresman, 1950) will be found especially satisfactory
because of its dictionary arrangement and its eminently sane point of
view.

It is not enough, however, for a thesis to be written in correct
English; it should have what many students—and many thesis-directors, too, for that matter—overlook: an attractive style. That does
not mean that there should be "purple passages" or "fine writing". It
means simply that the sentences should be pleasingly varied in structure and that the diction should achieve the golden mean between
stiltedness and familiarity. It is sometimes said that a thesis must be
written in the third person, and that is doubtless generally true. But
I think that with some subjects and by some writers the first person
can be used without any loss of the objectiveness and the impartiality
that every good piece of research must have.

Before one starts to write, he may profitably examine, being especially mindful of their literary style, several examples of scholarly
writing of more or less the same sort that he is undertaking. Some
will doubtless be found to be lifeless and dull; whereas others, no less
scholarly, have all the charm and interest of a good novel. Without
playing too much the sedulous ape, the student may well adopt the
latter as models for style.

VII

I have, in this discussion, of necessity separated the comments on
the writing of the thesis from those on documentation. In practice, of

course, writing and documentation go along together. One puts in the footnotes as he writes; indeed, for the first draft, at least, it is best to put each footnote immediately below the line of text in which the reference occurs, with a line above the footnote and one below it to separate the note from the text.[23] In some graduate schools the thesis may be submitted in this form; more often the student is required, in the final draft, to collect the footnotes for each page at the bottom of that page. The advantages of inserting the footnotes in the text in the first draft are: first, one copies the reference from a note as soon as he has finished using the material from that note and hence is in little danger of forgetting the necessity for giving the source of his information; and second, in typing out the reference, the student learns how many typewritten lines each footnote requires and can make proper allowance for it at the bottom of the page when putting the manuscript into final form.

Unacademic people—together with, perhaps, some graduate students—sometimes have queer ideas about footnotes. I have heard the story of an individual who submitted a doctoral dissertation to one of our leading universities only to have it rejected. Without making any change in it "except to stick in a few more footnotes", he resubmitted the dissertation, whereupon it was promptly accepted. The story is told as a reflection upon the university; and perhaps the university was at fault, either in overlooking the merits of the work in the first place, or in accepting it later. It is much more likely, however, that the addition of the proper footnotes turned a piece of bad scholarship into a satisfactory dissertation; for the difference between a good piece of research and a bad one may easily lie in the footnotes. Material presented on the authority of no one but the writer may become a real contribution to knowledge when it is properly confirmed and attested. That is not to say that one should strive for a great number of footnotes; there is no more merit in a mere multiplicity of footnotes than there is in a multiplicity of pages. There should be a footnote wherever one is needed and nowhere else. But how is one to know where these places are?

Footnotes are sometimes classified as being of three or four kinds; but fundamentally they serve two purposes: to give the source of a bit of information contained in the text, and to supplement or

[23] See below, Appendix C.

amplify the text. There should be little difficulty about the first kind. Once the student realizes that he is expected to provide a footnote for every idea and every bit of language [24] that did not originate in his own mind, all that is necessary is to put down the source of every bit of information based on reading as soon as it has been transferred from the note-slip to the text. The other kind of footnote causes a little more trouble. It may often happen that an illustration of a point just made or the expansion of an argument would be helpful to the reader of the thesis, but to provide the illustration or extend the argument would confuse the main line of discussion. In such a circumstance the student may be well advised to put the illustration or the extension of the argument in a footnote, first being careful to satisfy himself that the additional information is really helpful to the reader and that it does not properly belong in the text. There are footnotes that have neither interest nor value for the reader and serve only to display the erudition of the writer; no matter how proud he may be of some bit of esoteric knowledge picked up in the course of his reading, the graduate student should resist the temptation to indulge in a footnote that is not germane to his text.

What might be considered a third kind of footnote is the cross reference, which calls attention to the fact that a point touched on in the text is developed elsewhere in the thesis in more detail.

Footnote form is a little more nearly uniform than is bibliographical form, but again the important thing is that one be perfectly consistent in adhering to whatever form he decides to adopt or has forced upon him. It used to be the practice to number footnotes page by page, labeling the first footnote on each page number one. It is generally considered better form now to number the footnotes consecutively throughout a work or a chapter or section of a work. A master's thesis might have the numbering consecutive throughout; but if there are more than one hundred footnotes, numbering by sections or chapters will be better. A doctoral dissertation should almost certainly have the notes in each chapter separately numbered.

[24] An exception may be made in favor of expressions so well known as to be almost proverbial; thus it seemed unnecessary to cite a reference to Robert Louis Stevenson for the phrase "sedulous ape" used a few lines above, and "temper the wind to the shorn lamb" is often used without being credited to Laurence Sterne, even though most people take it to be from the Bible.

The advantage of consecutive numbering of footnotes is that it makes it possible for a reader to correct an error. If I am reading a thesis and find myself directed to "p. 17, n. 2", and, turning to the designated page, I find that the second note has nothing to do with the thing for which I am looking, I know that something is wrong. Looking at the other notes on p. 17 I find that they are no more relevant than note two; hence the page number must be a mistake and I must look to some other "n. 2". But on what page? Which one of perhaps two or three hundred note two's is the one I am looking for? With consecutive numbering there is no difficulty. I turn to page 17 and find that the notes on that page bear numbers from 16 to 19; note 2 is on page 7 and proves to be the one I am seeking. Even in a poor thesis, page number and note number are not likely both to be wrong in the same reference.

The reference number in the text should follow the material in the text taken from the source indicated in the footnote to which the number refers. Students sometimes wonder how far back the influence of a footnote extends, how much of the text preceding the reference number is to be taken as coming from the source indicated. Theoretically, unless the text indicates that part of the material is original with the writer of the thesis, it might be assumed that all of the information contained between two reference numbers is taken from the source indicated by the latter; actually that seldom amounts to more than one paragraph.[25] If the writer wants the reader to know that the beginning of a paragraph is entirely original, though the latter part comes from someone else, he must show the fact by the language of the text.

The reference number in a typewritten manuscript may be put on the line with the text and a proofreader's mark (like a broad V—ᵛ) put below it to indicate that it should be a superior number or superscript. It is just as easy, however, and considerably neater, to turn the platen or roller of the typewriter toward one slightly and hold it

[25] With direct quotations, of course, the scope of the reference is shown by the quotation marks. If a quotation should contain more than one paragraph (for the usual treatment of long quotations, see below, p. 309), it is customary to repeat the quotation marks, when quotation marks are used, at the beginning of each paragraph and to show that the quotation is continuous by omitting the quotation marks at the end of each paragraph except the last.

in place with the left hand while striking the proper key or keys with the right. The corresponding number preceding the footnote should be indented slightly; generally the indention is the same as for the beginning of a paragraph. The number may be raised, or marked for raising, like the reference number, or it may be left on the line unmarked; since it comes at the beginning of a line and is preceded by an indention, there is no likelihood of confusion. If the footnote requires more than one line, the lines should be single-spaced; there should be a double-space between footnotes.

In papers that are not accompanied by a bibliography, it is customary to give full bibliographical details concerning a work in the first footnote in which the work is referred to. Since every thesis is presumably accompanied by a bibliography, it is not necessary to give the facts of publication of a book in the first or in any other footnote; the reader is expected to use the footnotes in connection with the bibliography. The usual form, then, for a footnote referring to a book would be: author's name, title of book (underlined for italics), volume number (if the work contains more than one volume), and page number. Some thesis-directors consider that the author's surname alone is sufficient, unless the bibliography contains two or more authors with that surname. The title of the work may be shortened; no one would think of using the full title of one of Defoe's novels in a reference footnote. One may use the first words of the title, or the first and last part of it, with marks of ellipsis to indicate the omission. Thus McKerrow's *A Dictionary of Printers and Booksellers in England, Scotland, and Ireland, and of Foreign Printers of English Books 1557–1640* might appear: *A Dictionary of Printers . . .* or, better, perhaps, as more informative, *A Dictionary of Printers . . . 1557–1640*. If more than one edition of a work is included in the bibliography, a footnote referring to that work must indicate the edition involved.

Footnote form for periodical articles is the same as the bibliographical form, except that the page reference will generally be to a single page or perhaps two pages: author's name, title of article (in quotation marks), name of periodical (underlined for italics), volume number (in Roman numerals), date (in parentheses), and the page or pages (in Arabic numerals).

An author's name need not be repeated in the footnote if it is given in the text;[26] the footnote then begins with the title of the work. If the author's name and the title of the work both appear in the text, the footnote contains only the page number ("[11] P. 30."), or the volume and page ("[12] IV, 17–21."); for a periodical reference, if the author's name and the title of the article are given in the text, the footnote would begin with the name of the periodical.

It was formerly the common practice to put the author's surname first in footnotes as in bibliographical entries; it is now considered better to use the natural order, with the surname last. A footnote beginning "Horace Howard Furness, Jr., . . ." is much more sensible than the awkward "Furness, Horace Howard, Jr., . . ."

For information taken at second hand one should give both sources. If one wished to quote Amos Cottle on the Teutonic ideas of heaven and hell, and could not gain access to a copy of Cottle's *Icelandic Poetry,* one might take the quotation from another source. The text would then read: "The Teutonic nations, on the contrary, held that there was a fixed Elysium, and a hell.[3] . . ."; and the footnote: "[3] Amos Cottle, *Icelandic Poetry, or The Edda of Sæmund Translated into English Verse* (Bristol, 1791), p. ix, as quoted in Arthur H. Nethercot, *The Road to Tryermaine,* p. 132".

If one wishes to use a quotation for which there is a footnote in the original, he should reproduce the footnote if it is a reference note; he may disclaim responsibility for any error it may contain by attributing it to the original author: "The attempted description of the early press which follows is based principally on Moxon,[2] . . ." with the footnote: "[2] *'Mechanick Exercises,* the second volume (Printing), 1683' [McKerrow's note]". The writer should substitute for McKerrow's reference number the number that would be called for if the note were his own. The words quoted from McKerrow should be enclosed in quotation marks. An explanatory footnote may be reproduced or not, depending upon its nature and importance. If the writer decides not to reproduce it, no notice is taken of its presence. If I should wish to quote:

He [the printer] must let the ink of the first printing dry before he attempts to print the sheet on the other side. This necessary interval

---

[26] If, however, the author's name is separated from the quotation or the reference number by several lines of text, so that it may not be immediately clear to the reader, it will be best to repeat the name.

between the printing of the two sides of a sheet is, as we shall see later, of great importance in connexion with variations between copies of the same edition of a book. (McKerrow, *An Introduction to Bibliography*, p. 21),

I am under no obligation to point out that there is a reference number following the first sentence, and a footnote: "There are ways of avoiding this trouble by the use of 'setting-off sheets', but it is unlikely that the sixteenth-century printers were often sufficiently pressed for time to make such expedients worth while." If, however, I were to quote: "Eventually they [Baskerville's types] seem to have been dispersed and the whereabouts of the punches and matrices is not known. . . .", I should think it desirable if not absolutely necessary to give the accompanying footnote: " 'Cf., however, Updike [*Printing Types, Their History, Forms, and Use, a Study in Survivals*], ii. 114. It appears that some of these types have recently come to light in French printing-houses.' [McKerrow's note]".

Students are often puzzled over the use of the abbreviations *ibid.* (for the Latin *ibidem*, i.e., in the same place), *op. cit.* (for *opere citato*, in the work previously cited), and *loc. cit.* (for *loco citato*, in the same place—passage—previously cited); and there is some confusion in the matter. *Ibid.* is used instead of repeating a footnote when the reference is the same in every respect as that in the immediately preceding footnote. If the second reference is to the same author, work, and volume, but to a different page, the footnote should read "*Ibid.*, p. 79."; if the second reference is to a different volume, we should have "*Ibid.*, II, 118." When another reference intervenes —as when a work by Smith is cited, then one by Jones, and then the one by Smith again—one can still avoid repeating the full reference by using "Smith, *loc. cit.*" if the reference is to the same passage as that cited in the first note, or "Smith, *op. cit.*, p. 19" if the reference is to a different part of the work.

The difficulty comes not so much in the rule itself as in the exception to it. I have read theses in which the writer used the title of a work only in the first footnote in which the work was referred to, and used *op. cit.* or *loc. cit.* thereafter. That is hardly just to the reader. Of course one can presumably find the title of the work in the bibliography; but the reader hates to have to keep turning back to the bibliography, and it is not fair for a writer to cater to his own convenience at the expense of the reader. Moreover, there are times when the bibliography will not solve the problem. Suppose that I am reading a thesis on Dickens; if the writer has used a set of the collected works of Dickens—as he most naturally would—the footnote might have a volume number that would tell me, after I had looked it up in the bibliography, which novel is involved.[27] But if separate editions were used, then, unless I can tell from the text which novel the writer is discussing, I must, when I come to a "Dickens, *op. cit.*, p. 197" turn back through the preceding pages of the thesis until I find the footnote giving the title. I once had the curiosity to pursue such a reference through thirty-seven pages, but few theses would reward one for the time and effort involved in running down many such references.

The best practice in printed books is, I think, to use *ibid., op. cit.,* or *loc. cit.* only in such circumstances that the abbreviation is explained on one of the two pages that one can see as the book lies open before him. One may use such an abbreviation on a recto page if it is explained on that page or on the preceding verso page, but not on a verso page if the explanation is on its recto side—not, in other words, if the reader is required to turn a page in order to learn the meaning of the abbreviation. If the principle here involved be applied to a typewritten manuscript, it would seem to me logical to require that abbreviations be used only where the explanation of them occurs on the same page, so that the reader need not turn back even one page in order to identify the work involved.

There are a good many other abbreviations, many of them coming from Latin words, that a graduate student should know and understand, however much or little occasion he may have to use them.[28] Some of these are:

ante—before (used to refer to pages of a work preceding the page on which it occurs; *supra,* or "See above" is better)

art.—article; plural, arts.

cf. (*confer*)—compare

chap.—chapter; plural, chaps.

---

[27] Generally, however, the bibliographical entry would give merely the number of volumes in the edition; it would not tell which volumes contain which novels.

[28] The abbreviations of the names of learned journals are given elsewhere; see above, pp. 73-75.

circa or *ca.*—approximately (used with dates when exact date is not known, as *"circa* 1500")

col.—column; plural, cols.

del. (*delineavit,* he drew it)—on an engraving indicates the artist from whose work the engraving was made

ed.—edition, editor, edited by; plurals, edd.—editions, eds.—editors

e.g. (*exempli gratia,* for the sake of example)—for example

et al. (*et alii*)—and others

et seq. (*et sequens*)—and the following; "pp. 10 *et seq.*" would mean pages 10 and 11, though in practice the abbreviation is often used when the following one should be used—to indicate more than two pages

et seqs. or, preferably, *et sqq.* (*et sequentes* or *sequentia*)—and the following (plural); thus "pp. 10 *et sqq.*" would include an indefinite number of pages but at least three, beginning with p. 10

f.—and the following; plural, ff.; this corresponds in usage to the preceding; "pp. 10 f." includes pages 10 and 11, "pp. 10 ff." means from page 10 to page 12 or some page beyond 12

fig.—figure; plural, figs.

fl. (*floruit*)—flourished (generally applied to an individual when the approximate date of his work is known but not that of his birth or death; e.g. "Orm, *fl.* 1200)"

idem, sometimes *id.*—the same (used instead of *ibid.* when referring in a footnote to another work by the author of the work cited in the immediately preceding footnote)

i.e. (*id est*)—that is

infra—below (referring to a subsequent part of the work in which it is used); used with *supra*

l.—line; plural, ll.

MS—manuscript; plural, MSS

n.—note; plural, nn.

n. d.—no date (used in giving facts of publication when the date of publication is not given, or, better, not known; if the date does not appear on the title page but can be determined, putting the date in brackets—[1869]—will serve to indicate the date and at the same time will show that it does not appear on the title page. Similarly, giving the date of the copyright—1904^c—is an indication that the date of publication does not appear in the work itself)

no.—number; plural, nos.

n. p.—no place (used in giving facts of publication when no place of publication is indicated; if the place is not stated but can be determined, it should be put in brackets. This same abbreviation is sometimes used to indicate that no publisher's name is given; but the absence of a publisher's name generally means that the book was privately printed and is better so described. If a work bears no information as to its publication, we should have "(n. p.: privately printed, n. d.)" as the facts of publication).

p.—page; plural, pp.

passim—here and there (throughout the work or portion of a work cited; used when the detail alluded to is repeated so frequently that citing each instance would be too laborious and would serve no good purpose)

pinx. (*pinxit*)—he painted it (used, like *del.* to indicate the artist from whose work an engraving was made)

post (after)—below (referring to a subsequent part of the work in which it is used; "*infra*" or "below" is to be preferred); used with *ante*

pt.—part; plural, pts.

q.v. (*quod vide*)—which see (used following the title of the work to which it is intended to refer the reader; corresponds to "cf.", which precedes the name of the work to which reference is made)

sc. (*scilicet*)—that is to say, or namely

sculp., or *sculpt.* (*sculpsit*)—he carved it (used on an engraving to indicate the engraver; the abbreviation follows the name)

sec.—section; plural, secs.

sic—thus (used within brackets to indicate that an error in a quotation appears in the original and is not the fault of the person using the quotation)

s.n. (*sub nomine*)—under the name (used occasionally instead of *s.v.* when the reference is to a personal name in a dictionary or encyclopædia; the name follows the abbreviation)

supra—above; opposite of *infra*

s.v. (*sub verbo,* under the word, or *voce,* title)—see under (followed by the heading of an entry in a dictionary or encyclopædia)

trans. or *tr.*—translation, translator, or translated by

v.—verse; plural, vv.

vid., sometimes *v.* (*vide*)—see ("cf." and "see" are now more commonly used)

viz. (*videlicet*)—namely, to wit

vol.—volume; plural, vols.

It should be noted that some abbreviations, although they represent foreign words, are not italicized; this group includes cf., e.g., etc., i.e., and viz. The difference in the formation of plurals should also be observed. The plurals of art., chap., col., fig., no., pt., and vol. are formed by adding *s*; others—f., l., n., p., and v.—have the plural formed by doubling the letter. Ed. has two plurals: eds. for editors, and edd. for editions. The plural of *et seq.* may be *et seqs.* but *et sqq.* is preferred. Some of these expressions are complete words and need no period: such are *ante, circa, idem, infra, passim, post,* and *sic. Del., pinx., sculp.* and *sculpt.* should have periods following them but often do not.

If one uses "See above" to refer to an antecedent portion of the work in which the abbreviation occurs, "See below" should be used to refer to a subsequent portion; similarly "*ante*" and "*post*" go together, as do "*supra*" and "*infra*".

In using *f., ff., et seq.,* or *et sqq.* one should always use—if no volume number is given—the plural abbreviation for pages: "pp. 19 f." (or "pp. 19 ff."), never "p. 19 f." It is better to avoid the use of ff. and *et sqq.*; presumably the writer knows, as he puts down the reference, where the passage ends as well as where it begins, and it is only fair to the reader to let him know whether it will take him two minutes or two hours to consult the passage referred to.[29]

Many students are careless in the use of the abbreviation "etc." They set down two or three members of a group or series and then, without stopping to think whether all are included that should be included, they throw in an "etc." to take care of possible omissions.

---

[29] There are situations, of course, in which the indefinite reference is wholly justified, as, for example, in referring to a discussion only the first part of which would be of interest to some readers; whereas other readers will wish to pursue the matter further, and others still further.

One should first determine whether there are "others" that need to be included and, if so, whether they should not be included specifically. Even when it seems best to make the inclusion indefinite, an expression such as "and the like" is generally better than the abbreviation.

When one of the abbreviations we have been discussing stands at the beginning of a sentence, the first letter of it should, of course, be a capital letter. Thus if the author and title of a one-volume work are mentioned in the text, the footnote would read: "P. 18."

In the abbreviations for *manuscript* and *manuscripts*, the letters are always capitals and no periods are used.

There is no space between the letters in the abbreviations "e.g." and "i.e."; "q.v.", "s.n.", and "s.v." are sometimes found with a space, sometimes without.

VIII

I do not propose to take up such matters as the formula to be used on the title page of a thesis, or the number of spaces to be used for indentions, or other things that are purely details of typing. Most graduate schools have their regulations about such matters, and most theses are typed, in their final form, by professional typists who understand those regulations and know how to conform with them. There are, however, two or three matters of form that the writer of a thesis should observe even in the preliminary drafts.

In using direct quotations, the rule is that short quotations are run into the text and set off by quotation marks; long quotations—generally those of five lines or more—are indented and single-spaced, without quotation marks.[30] The indention is usually the same as paragraph indention. Some difficulty arises when a short quotation has quotation marks within it; one must then substitute single quotation marks for the double marks of the original.[31]

In quoting a passage containing contractions [32] one may wish, for the sake of clearness, to print contracted words in full. That a word represents an expanded contraction may be indicated by underlining

[30] For examples, see below, Appendix C.

[31] Some books use single quotation marks regularly instead of double ones; see McKerrow, *Introduction to Bibliography* as an example. In quoting from them, one can reproduce a quotation within the quotations exactly as it appears.

[32] See above, p. 119.

(for italics) the letters not present in the original, if the original is in roman, or *vice versa*. Thus mā would be represented by man, m̄a by <u>man</u>, and ſcus ſpūs by ſanctus ſpiritus or sanctus spiritus.

Ellipsis marks need not ordinarily be used to indicate that something precedes or follows a passage quoted, unless the first part of the opening sentence or the last part of the closing one is omitted. If something is omitted within a quotation, the fact that there is an omission must be indicated. Some publishers use four periods [33]—in addition to whatever punctuation precedes the omission—to show that something is left out, but the more common practice is to use three. Thus we might have: " 'A world without vice! . . . without immorality!' cried Asem, in a rapture; 'I thank thee, O Alla! . . . this, this indeed will produce happiness, . . . and ease. . . . Oh, for an immortality, to spend it among men . . . incapable of ingratitude, . . . and a thousand other crimes that render society miserable!' " [34] Or, the fourth omission (after *ease*) might be represented by five periods and the others by four each. It is unfortunate that there should be lack of uniformity in this matter; as it is, one cannot be sure in a given work—unless he knows the publisher's practice or can determine, by finding an omission indicated by five periods or by only three—whether a sentence preceding an omission indicated by four ellipsis marks is complete and ends with a period or was broken off incomplete.

Another detail of punctuation concerning which there is a difference of opinion has to do with the position of a period or a comma used with a quotation mark. The practice in England has been to put the period or comma inside the quotation mark when the quotation marks enclose the sentence element to which the period or comma belongs, but to put the quotation mark inside the other when the quotation involves only the latter part of the sentence element. This is, of course, logical: "You don't have to 'cram', do you? Let's go to

---

[33] Asterisks were formerly used to indicate omissions but are not often found so used in modern printing.

[34] The passage in full: " 'A world without vice! Rational beings without immorality!' cried Asem, in a rapture; 'I thank thee, O Alla! who hast at length heard my petitions: this, this indeed will produce happiness, ecstasy, and ease. Oh, for an immortality to spend it among men who are incapable of ingratitude, injustice, fraud, violence, and a thousand other crimes that render society miserable!' " (Oliver Goldsmith, *Works,* Globe ed. (London: Macmillan, 1923), p. 291).

the 'Gym'." But apparently American printers so object to the appearance of a period or a comma following a quotation mark that they have sacrificed logic to æsthetics in laying down the rule that a period or a comma must always be placed within the quotation mark. Thus the University of Chicago Press insists:

The period is placed inside the quotation marks for appearance' sake. Put it inside the parentheses or brackets when the matter enclosed is an independent sentence forming no part of the preceding sentence; otherwise outside . . . :

Tennyson's "In Memoriam."

Put the period inside the quotation marks. (This is a rule without exception.)

When the parentheses form a part of the preceding sentence, put the period outside (as, for instance here).[35]

And for the comma:

The comma is always placed inside the quotation marks, but it follows the parenthesis if the context requires it at all . . .

See the sections on "Quotations," which may be found elsewhere in this volume.

Here he gives a belated, though stilted (and somewhat obscure), exposition of the subject.[36]

It seems to me that the appearance of

Tennyson's "In Memoriam".

or

See the sections on "Quotations", which . . .

is not so alarming as to justify insistence on a treatment of the period and the comma different from that accorded to the semicolon, the colon, the exclamation point, and the interrogation point, all of which are put inside or outside the quotation mark as logic demands. I am glad, therefore, to see the more logical practice carried out in at least one book published by the University of Chicago Press; there may be found:

Here in the midst of his [Coleridge's] allusions to Dr. William Hunter, Plato, and Thelwall's own recent essay on "Animal Vitality", he re-

[35] *Manual of Style*, ed. 1949, p. 88.
[36] *Ibid.*, p. 104.

marked: "Ferriar believes in a soul, like an orthodox churchman." This remark would not be important except for the fact that the third volume of the *Memoirs* also contained another article by the Manchester virtuoso—"Observations concerning the Vital Principle".[37]

*   *   *

When the thesis itself is completed, it is time to put the bibliography into its final form. With the working bibliography at hand, one should go through the thesis, footnote by footnote, taking from the working bibliography each slip representing a work referred to in the thesis. The resulting pile of slips represents a selected bibliography which includes the titles of all the works that lent material to the thesis. There may be other works included in the working bibliography which the writer considers to have been helpful, even though they were not cited in the thesis; with the permission of the director of the thesis, such works may be added to the bibliography, perhaps in a separate list or in some other way distinguished from the works cited.[38] When the bibliographical slips have been arranged in alphabetical order and copied in the approved form,[39] and all the pages of the thesis have been put in order, the work is at last com-

[37] Arthur H. Nethercot, *The Road to Tryermaine*, p. 61. The period after *churchman* is put inside the quotation marks presumably because it is taken as serving primarily to punctuate the sentence beginning *Ferriar* rather than that beginning *Here.*

[38] It should be noted that the bibliography—especially if it includes the comments contained on the critico-bibliographical notes, so that it becomes a critical bibliography—may well be the most important and most valuable part of a thesis. Articles that are essentially bibliographies include J. N. Douglas Bush, "English Translations of Homer", *PMLA*, XLI (1926), 335–41; Alfred Harbage, "Elizabethan and Seventeenth-Century Play Manuscripts", *PMLA*, L (1935), 687–99; *idem*, "Elizabethan and Seventeenth-Century Play Manuscripts: Addenda", *PMLA*, LII (1937), 905–7; *idem*, "A Census of Anglo-Latin Plays", *PMLA*, LIII (1938), 624–29; Franklin P. Rolfe, "On the Bibliography of Seventeenth-Century Prose Fiction", *PMLA*, XLIX (1934), 1071–86; Sybil Rosenfeld, "Dramatic Advertisements in the Burney Newspapers 1660–1700", *PMLA*, LI (1936), 123–52; R. W. Babcock, "Eighteenth-Century Comic Opera Manuscripts", *PMLA*, LII (1937), 907–8; Edgar M. Branch, "A Chronological Bibliography of the Writings of Samuel Clemens to June 8, 1867", *AmLit*, XVIII (1946–47), [109]–59; and Eunice C. Hamilton, "Biographical and Critical Studies of Henry James, 1941–1948", *AmLit*, XX (1948–49), [424]–35. Good examples of critical bibliographies are those in the various learned journals mentioned above; see pp. 72–73. See also Morize, *Problems and Methods*, pp. 70–81.

[39] In typewritten bibliographies the names of the authors are often written in capital letters; when there are two or more works by the same author, a long dash is generally used for the second and subsequent entries to avoid repeating the name.

pleted; and the writer, doubtless with a sigh of relief and satisfaction, may congratulate himself on having surmounted the first major obstacle in the way of becoming a scholar.

A few words of general advice to the graduate student in English may be appropriate here. First, as to the length of the thesis. I have known candidates for degrees in English who complained bitterly because candidates for degrees in mathematics or chemistry, perhaps, could satisfy the thesis requirement with a work of some twenty or thirty pages; whereas a thesis in English must contain a hundred pages or more. It is sometimes felt that English departments pay more attention to quantity than to quality in theses. But the situation is not quite what it may seem offhand to be. In some fields, particularly in the sciences, a student may be able to demonstrate in a few pages that he has accomplished an amount of research such as a thesis is supposed to represent; but in English the amount of work involved is at least roughly commensurate with the length of the thesis. A paper of three thousand words may constitute an important contribution to knowledge, it may serve admirably as a term paper in some course, but it can hardly be accepted as a thesis. It will not show that the writer has learned to locate a wide variety of materials with which to work. It may have an impressively extensive bibliography; but the impressiveness of the bibliography disappears unless the accompanying work proves that the materials listed have been studied and used. Unless there are a good many footnotes, the thesis will not show that its writer has learned how to handle various forms of documentation; and such knowledge is important not only to enable the student to use that knowledge himself in future work, but also to make intelligible to him the work of other scholars. A short thesis—one of less than twenty thousand words, say—will not serve as proof that its writer has experienced the training that thesis-writing is expected to provide.

The student who fancies himself a creative writer is sometimes irked because he is not permitted to submit a novel or a play in lieu of a thesis. There is some merit in this complaint, and some graduate schools are permitting their students to fulfil the thesis requirement by doing creative writing. On behalf of the more conservative institutions, however, those that still insist upon the orthodox type of thesis, this should be said: Most of the candidates for advanced degrees in

English are, or will be, teachers of English. Few of them will spend all their time in teaching creative writing. It is not enough, therefore, that their graduate training should make them competent novelists or dramatists or teachers of the art of writing; it must also provide them with the knowledge of literary history and the training in scholarship that are part of the equipment of every good teacher of English.

In addition to the writing of a thesis, most graduate schools require the completion of a certain number of hours of course work, and the passing of an examination, either written or oral. It is seldom possible for the candidate to take all the courses offered in his department; hence it is of the first importance that he choose his courses wisely. Too many students succumb to the temptation of taking all the work offered by a favorite professor; or they take courses of relatively little value to them because those courses are reputedly easy, or because they are given at convenient hours. Such students will find themselves at the end of their course work woefully ill prepared for the final examination. It is best, of course, for the prospective graduate student in English to begin his preparation at the beginning of his undergraduate work—even earlier, if possible. Then he can build an adequate background that will later stand him in good stead. The person who, as a child, has read Scott and Dickens will have done a good deal toward grounding himself in nineteenth-century literature; it will be easy, when the time comes, for him to refresh his memory of those novels. As soon as one has decided that eventually he will be a graduate student in English, he should begin to choose his courses with that aim in view. That is not to say that he should overload himself as an undergraduate with English courses; work in other fields, particularly the social sciences, is just as important a part of the equipment of an English scholar as is a knowledge of English literature. In graduate school, only such courses should be taken as will fill definite gaps in the student's background. One will doubtless wish to take some intensive courses in the field in which he specializes, the field of his thesis; aside from those, it will generally be best to cover as much of the history of English literature as possible by taking period or survey courses.

Such systematic preparation as has been suggested, covering a considerable period of time, will lessen the agony of preparing for the final examination; nevertheless, some special study for the examination is generally necessary. The student will do well to learn as much as he can—and graduate schools are usually teeming with such information—about the idiosyncrasies of the various examiners. Having some idea of the type of question likely to be asked and the kind of answer expected gives the candidate poise and confidence. Examiners generally insist that students should know important works from having read them, rather than from having read about them. Some study of a work such as Moody and Lovett's *A History of English Literature* (New York: Scribner's, 1930ᶜ) may not be amiss; but the bulk of one's time should be spent in reading the classics which constitute English literature. (I once knew a student who prepared for his doctoral examination by outlining the fourteen volumes of the *Cambridge History of English Literature*; I think he would be the first to dissuade anyone from repeating the experiment.) Two kinds of important information graduate students are likely to overlook in their preparation: Every graduate student should know the significance of such names as Skeat, Kittredge, Manly, McKerrow, and Greenlaw, and those of other scholars, living and dead; he should know the institution with which each was, or is, connected and know something, too, about the nature and importance of each one's contribution to scholarship. Graduate students should also know what are the best editions of various classics, especially those that may at this time be said to be definitive editions.

One more word of advice to examinees: Don't "bluff". A single wrong guess may lead the examining committee to suspect that all the previous answers were likewise guesses. No candidate is expected to know all the answers; an occasional "I don't know" does no irremediable damage.

The achieving of a master's or doctor's degree is at best a laborious affair; but those who survive the ordeal generally feel that the discipline and training received—to say nothing of the satisfaction of being the possessor of the degree—make the experience wholly worth while.

BIBLIOGRAPHICAL REFERENCES

PART I

THE MATERIALS OF RESEARCH

1 R[onald] B[runlees] McKerrow, *An Introduction to Bibliography for Literary Students,* 2nd Impression, with corrections (Oxford: Clarendon Press, 1928), p. 350.

2 Ed. W[alter] W[ilson] Greg (London: Oxford University Press, 1932), 2 vols.

3 McKerrow, *op. cit.,* p. 98.

4 Arundell Esdaile, *A Student's Manual of Bibliography* (New York: Scribner's, 1931), p. 37.

5 Edward Heawood, "The Position on the Sheet of Early Watermarks", *The Library,* 4th Series, IX (1928–29), 38–47.

6 Esdaile, *op. cit.,* p. 47.

7 The [London] *Times Printing Number* (September 10, 1912), p. 5.

8 McKerrow, *op. cit.,* p. 284.

9 Esdaile, *op. cit.,* p. 120.

10 McKerrow, *op. cit.,* p. 11, n. 3.

11 *Ibid.,* p. 50.

12 *Ibid.,* pp. 46–48.

13 *Ibid.,* pp. 102–6.

14 Esdaile, *op. cit.,* p. 236.

15 Robert Greene, *Planetomachia* (1585).

16 *Idem, Arbasto* (1584).

17 *Idem, Gwydonius, the Carde of Fancie* (1584).

18 *Idem, Euphues, His Censure to Philautus* (1587).

19 *Idem, Perimedes the Blacke-Smith* (1588).

20 *Idem, The Spanish Masquerado* (1589).

21 *Idem, A Quip for an Upstart Courtier* (1592).

22 *Idem, Penelope's Web* (1587).

23 *Idem, The Mirrour of Modestie* (1584).

24 McKerrow, *Introduction to Bibliography,* p. 82.

25 Argosy Book Stores, New York, Catalogue 170, Item 53.

26 Henry Young and Sons, Ltd., Liverpool, Part 569 (April, 1939), Item 52.

27 Frank Hollings, London, Catalogue 218 (1939), Item 20.

[317]

PART II

THE TOOLS OF RESEARCH

1 Henry Bartlett Van Hoesen and Frank Keller Walter, *Bibliography, Practical, Enumerative, Historical* (New York: Scribner's, 1928), p. 1.

2 *Ibid.*, p. 3.

3 Arthur Garfield Kennedy, *A Concise Bibliography for Students of English, Systematically Arranged,* 2nd ed. (Stanford University, California: Stanford University Press, 1945).

4 John Webster Spargo, *A Bibliographical Manual for Students of the Language and Literature of England and the United States,* 2nd ed. (Chicago: Packard and Company, 1941ᶜ).

5 Tom Peete Cross, *Bibliographical Guide to English Studies,* 8th ed. (Chicago: University of Chicago Press [1943]).

6 Theodore Besterman, *The Beginnings of Systematic Bibliography,* 2nd ed. (London: Oxford University Press, 1936).

7 See above, n. 1.

8 Charles Victor Langlois and Charles Seignobos, *Introduction aux Études Historiques,* translated by G. G. Berry (New York: Holt and Company, 1912).

9 Gustave Lanson, *Méthodes de l'Histoire Littéraire* (Paris: Société d'éditions "Les Belles Lettres", 1925).

10 Martha Connor, *Practical Bibliography-Making with Problems and Examples* (New York: H. W. Wilson Company, 1931).

11 André Morize, *Problems and Methods of Literary History with Special Reference to Modern French Literature: A Guide for Graduate Students* (Boston: Ginn and Company, 1922).

12 Vivian Hunter Galbraith, *An Introduction to the Use of Public Records* (London: Oxford University Press, 1934).

13 Margaret Hutchins, Alice Sarah Johnson, and Margaret Stuart Williams, *Guide to the Use of Libraries: A Manual for College and University Students,* 5th ed. (New York: H. W. Wilson Company, 1936).

14 Johann Georg Theodor Grässe, *Trésor des Livres Rares et Précieux* (Dresden: Kuntze, 1859–69), 7 vols.

15 Louis Gustave Vapereau, *Dictionnaire Universal des Litteratures* (Paris: Hachette, 1893); supplement, 1895.

16 Robert Watt, *Bibliotheca Britannica* (Edinburgh: Constable, 1824), 4 vols.

17 Van Hoesen and Walter, *op. cit.*, p. 239.

18 William Prideaux Courtney, *Register of National Bibliography* (London: Constable, 1905–12), 3 vols.

19 Julius Petzholdt, *Bibliotheca Bibliographica* (Leipzig: Englemann, 1896).

20 Henri Stein, *Manuel de Bibliographie Générale: Bibliotheca Nova* (Paris: Picard, 1897).

21 A[ksel] G[ustav] S[alomon] Josephson, *Bibliographies of Bibliographies Chronologically Arranged,* 2nd ed. (Chicago: Bibliographical Society of America, 1910-13).

22 Clark S. Northup, *A Register of Bibliographies of the English Language and Literature* (New Haven: Yale University Press, 1925). Other works that may be useful are: Theodore Besterman, *A World Bibliography of Bibliographies* (London: privately printed, 1939-40), 2 vols. (Vol. I of a 2nd ed. appeared in 1947); *The Bibliographic Index: A Cumulative Bibliography of Bibliographies* (New York: H. W. Wilson Company, 1938–   ); and Lawrence Heyl, *Current National Bibliographies: A List of Sources of Information Concerning Current Books of All Countries,* rev. ed. (Chicago: American Library Association, 1942).

23 Isadore Gilbert Mudge, *Guide to Reference Books,* 6th ed. (Chicago: American Library Association, 1936) and *Reference Books of 1935–1937* (Chicago: American Library Association, 1939); Constance M. Winchell, *Reference Books of 1938–1940* (Chicago: American Library Association, 1941), *Reference Books of 1941–1943* (Chicago: American Library Association, 1944), and *Reference Books of 1944–1946* (Chicago: American Library Association, 1947). The "British Mudge" is John Minto, *Reference Books* (London: Library Association, 1929-31), 2 vols.

24 *London Catalogue of Books in All Languages . . . Printed in Great Britain since 1700* (London: 1773). There was a second edition in 1786; and others, by various publishers, at intervals throughout the first half of the nineteenth century. The last (London: T. Hodgson, 1855) covered the period 1831-55.

25 *British Catalogue of Books Published from October 1837 to December 1852* (London: S. Low and Son, 1853); the main catalogue (1837-49) was followed by annual catalogues for 1850, 1851, and 1852. It was merged with the *London Catalogue* in the *English Catalogue,* published annually since 1837.

26 *United States Catalogue* (New York: H. W. Wilson Company, 1899, 1902, 1912, and 1928).

27 *Cumulative Book Index* (New York: H. W. Wilson Company, 1898–   ).

28 British Museum *Catalogue of Printed Books* (London: W. Clowes and Sons, Ltd., 1881-1900), 95 vols.

29 British Museum *Catalogue of Printed Books Supplement* (London: W. Clowes and Sons, Ltd., 1900-1905), 15 vols.

30 British Museum *General Catalogue of Printed Books* (London and Beccles: W. Clowes and Sons, Ltd., 1932–   ).

31 Bibliothèque Nationale *Catalogue Générale de Livres Imprimés: Auteurs* (Paris: Imprimerie Nationale, 1900–   ).

32 *A Catalogue of Books Represented by Library of Congress Printed Cards Issued to July 31, 1942* (Ann Arbor, Michigan: Edwards Brothers, 1942-46), 167 vols. A *Supplement,* in 42 volumes, covers the period from

August 1, 1942 to December 31, 1947. The Library of Congress has continued the project by publishing three volumes for 1948, three for 1949, and
three for 1950; quarterly and monthly parts are being issued for the current
year.

   33   Robert Alexander Peddie, *Subject Index of Books Published before
1880* (London: Grafton and Company, 1933); *idem, Subject Index of Books
Published up to and Including 1880, Second Series* (London: Grafton and
Company, 1939).

   34   *The Wordsworth Collection Formed by Cynthia Morgan St. John
and Given to Cornell University by Victor Emanuel* (Ithaca, N. Y.: Cornell
University Press, 1931); *Supplement* (1942).

   35   Cornelius Patton, *The Amherst Wordsworth Collection* (Amherst,
Mass.: Trustees of Amherst College, 1936).

   36   *Catalogue of the Harriss Collection of American Poetry with Biographical and Bibliographical Notes by J. C. Stockbridge* (Providence, R. I.: Brown
University Library, 1886); *Catalogue of the John Carter Brown Library in
Brown University* (Providence, R. I.: Brown University Library, 1919–31), 3
vols.

   37   A. G. S. Josephson, *List of Books on the History of Science* (Chicago:
John Crerar Library, 1911–16), 2 vols.

   38   Ruth Lapham, *Check List of American Revolutionary War Pamphlets
in the Newberry Library* (Chicago: Newberry Library, 1922); Pierce Butler,
Check List of Incunabula in the Newberry Library (Chicago: Newberry
Library, 1919); *idem, Check List of Books Printed during the Fifteenth
Century* (Chicago: Newberry Library, 1924); *idem, Check List of Fifteenth
Century Books in Newberry Library and Other Libraries of Chicago* (Chicago:
Newberry Library, 1933); Mae I. Stearns, *Check List of Books Printed in
English before 1641* (Chicago: Newberry Library, 1923); Jane D. Harding,
The Arthurian Legend: A Check List of Books in the Newberry Library
(Chicago: Newberry Library, 1933); *idem, Supplement* to preceding (Chi-
cago: Newberry Library, 1938); Gertrude L. Woodward, *English Books and
Books Printed in England before 1641 in the Newberry Library* (Chicago:
Newberry Library, 1939); and Virgil B. Heltzel, *Check List of Courtesy
Books in the Newberry Library* (Chicago: Newberry Library, 1942).

   39   *Check List or Brief Catalogue of the Library of Henry E. Hunting-
ton—English Literature to 1640, Compiled under the Direction of George
Watson Cole* (New York: privately printed, 1919); *Supplement* (1920). See
also Cecil K. Edmonds, *Huntington Library Supplement to the Record of the
Books in the Short Title Catalogue of English Books 1475–1640* (Cambridge,
Mass., 1933), Huntington Library Bulletin No. 4.

   40   Herman Ralph Mead, *Incunabula in the Henry E. Huntington Library*
(San Marino, California: Huntington Library, 1937). Other catalogues of
American incunabula include: *A List of Incunabula in Ann Arbor* (Ann Arbor,
Michigan: University of Michigan Press, 1940); Ada Thurston and Curt F.
Buhler, *Check List of Fifteenth Century Printing in the Pierpont Morgan
Library* (New York: Pierpont Morgan Library, 1939); and Olan V. Cook,

Incunabula in the Hanes Collection of the Library of North Carolina (Chapel Hill, N. C.: University of North Carolina Library, 1940). A short title catalogue of the Chapin Library at Williams College was compiled by Lucy Eugenia Osborne (New York: privately printed, 1924).

41 Seymour de Ricci and William Jerome Wilson, *Census of Medieval and Renaissance Manuscripts in the United States and Canada* (New York: H. W. Wilson Company, 1935–40), 3 vols. See also M. B. Stillwell, *Incunabula in American Libraries: A Second Census of Fifteenth Century Books Owned in the United States, Mexico, and Canada* (New York: Bibliographical Society of America, 1940).

42 Ernest C. Richardson, *An Index Directory to Special Collections in North American Libraries* (Yardley, Penn.: F. S. Cook and Son, 1927).

43 Johann Samuel Ersch and Johann Gottfried Gruber, *Allgemeine Encyklopädie der Wissenschaften und Künste* (Leipzig: Gleditsch and Brockhaus, 1818–89), 99 vols.

44 The Catholic Encyclopedia (New York: Robert Appleton Company and Encyclopedia Press, 1907–1917^c), 16 vols.; *The Jewish Encyclopedia* (New York: Funk and Wagnalls Co., 1925^c), 12 vols.; and *Encyclopædia of Religion and Ethics*, ed. James Hastings (New York: Scribner's, 1925–32), 13 vols. The last is particularly good for mythology and folklore.

45 The Century Dictionary and Cyclopedia (New York: The Century Company, 1911^c), 12 vols.; Vol. XII is the *Century Cyclopedia of Names*.

46 Encyclopædia of the Social Sciences, ed. Edwin R. A. Seligman and Alvin Johnson (New York: Macmillan, 1937), 15 vols.

47 Grove's Dictionary of Music and Musicians, ed. H. C. Colles (London: Macmillan, 1940), 5 vols.; there is also an American supplement, ed. Waldo Pratt and C. N. Boyd (New York: Macmillan, 1928).

48 For America, Paul Monroe, *A Cyclopedia of Education* (New York: Macmillan, 1911–13), 5 vols.; for England, Foster Watson, *The Encyclopædia and Dictionary of Education* (London and New York: Pitman and Sons, 1921–22), 4 vols.

49 Sir William A. Smith, *A Dictionary of Greek and Roman Antiquities*, 3rd ed. (London: J. Murray, 1890–91), 2 vols.; Harry Thurston Peck, *Harper's Dictionary of Classical Literature and Antiquities* (New York: American Book Co., 1923^c); Sir Paul Harvey, *The Oxford Companion to Classical Literature*, 2nd ed. (Oxford: Clarendon Press, [1940]).

50 Richard S. Bowker, *Publications of Societies: A Provisional List of the Publications of the American Scientific, Literary, and Other Societies from Their Organization* (New York: Publishers' Weekly Office, 1899), and J. David Thompson, *Handbook of Learned Societies and Institutions* (Washington: Carnegie Institution, 1908).

51 Doctoral Dissertations Accepted by American Universities (New York: H. W. Wilson Company, 1934–). The earlier volumes in this series were compiled by Donald B. Gilchrist; those for 1939–40 to 1943–44 by Edward A. Henry; and those for 1944–47 by Arnold H. Trotter. See also *List of American Doctoral Dissertations Printed*, published by the Library of Congress annually from 1912 to 1938, and Thomas R. Palfrey and Henry H. Coleman, *Guide to Bibliographies of Theses, United States and Canada* (Chicago: American Library Association, 1940). *American Literature* published in Vol. XX (1948–49), [169]–230, "Doctoral Dissertations in American Literature, 1933–1948".

52 Helen Hefling and Eva Richards, *Index to Contemporary Biography and Criticism* (Boston: F. W. Faxon and Company, 1929).

53 Phyllis M. Riches, *An Analytical Bibliography of Universal Collected Biography, Comprising Books Published in the English Tongue in Great Britain and Ireland, America and the British Dominions* (London: The Library Association, 1934).

54 John Venn and J. A. Venn, *Alumni Cantabrigienses: a Biographical List of All Known Students, Graduates, and Holders of Office at the University of Cambridge from the Earliest Times to 1900* (Cambridge: The University Press, 1922).

55 Anthony à Wood, *Athenæ Oxonienses* (Oxford: Ecclesiastical History Society, 1848).

56 *Who's Who in America: A Biographical Dictionary of Notable Living Men and Women of the United States* (Chicago: A. N. Marquis Company, 1899–). There is also *Who Was Who in America* (Chicago: A. N. Marquis Company, 1942ᶜ), Vol. I of which covers the period 1897–1942. For England there are *Who Was Who, 1897–1916*; *Who Was Who, 1916–1928*; and *Who Was Who, 1929–1940*, published in London by A. and C. Black in 1920, 1929, and 1941, respectively.

57 *Dictionary of American Biography Published under the Auspices of the American Council of Learned Societies* (New York: Scribner's, 1928–). Twenty volumes had appeared by 1936; an index to these volumes appeared in Vol. XXI (1937). A *First Supplement* (1944) brought the work down to December 31, 1935.

58 *Current Biography: Who's News and Why* (New York: H. W. Wilson Company, 1940–); there are a cumulative index and annual bound volumes.

59 Stanley J. Kunitz and Howard Haycraft, *American Authors, 1600–1900: A Biographical Dictionary of American Literature* (New York: H. W. Wilson Company, 1938); *Authors Today and Yesterday* (New York: H. W. Wilson Company, 1933); and *Twentieth Century Authors* (New York: H. W. Wilson Company, 1942). Kunitz and Haycraft are also responsible for *British Authors of the Nineteenth Century* (New York: H. W. Wilson Company, 1942).

60 Samuel Halkett and John Laing, *A Dictionary of the Anonymous and Pseudonymous Literature of Great Britain* (Edinburgh and London: Oliver and Boyd, 1926–34), 7 vols.

61 *Readers' Guide to Periodical Literature* (New York: H. W. Wilson Company, 1900–). There is also the *Nineteenth Century Readers' Guide to Periodical Literature 1890–1899, with Supplementary Indexing 1900–1922*, ed. Helen Grant Cushing and Adah V. Morris (New York: H. W. Wilson

Company, 1944), 2 vols. "Poole's Index" has been reprinted: *Poole's Index to Periodical Literature, 1802–1907* (New York: Peter Smith, 1938), 6 vols. in 7.

62 International Index to Periodicals Devoted Chiefly to the Humanities and Sciences (New York: H. W. Wilson Company, 1907–). See also *Articles on American Literature Appearing in Current Periodicals 1920–1945*, ed. Lewis Leary (Durham, N. C.: Duke University Press, 1947).

63 Some of the more popular magazines, such as the *Atlantic Monthly*, and newspapers such as the *New York Times* and the *New York Herald Tribune* publish noteworthy book reviews. There are also the *Book Review Digest* (New York: H. W. Wilson Company, 1905–) and the *Review Index: A Quarterly Guide to Professional Reviews for College and Reference Libraries*, ed. Louise Kaplan and Clarence S. Paine (Chicago: Follett, 1940–).

64 The Cambridge History of English Literature, ed. A. W. Ward and R. W. Waller (Cambridge: The University Press, 1919–30), 15 vols.

65 John G. O'Leary, *English Literary History and Bibliography* (London: Grafton and Company, 1928).

66 Cambridge Bibliography of English Literature, ed. Frederick W. Bateson (New York: Macmillan, and Cambridge: The University Press, 1941), 4 vols.

67 Allen R. Benham, *English Literature from Widsith to the Death of Chaucer: A Source Book* (New Haven: Yale University Press, 1916).

68 John Edwin Wells, *A Manual of the Writings in Middle English, 1050–1400* (New Haven: Yale University Press, and London: Oxford University Press, 1916); the Seventh Supplement appeared in 1938.

69 A Transcript of the Register of the Company of Stationers of London, 1554–1640, ed. Edward Arber (London: privately printed, 1875–77), 5 vols.; *A Transcript of the Registers of the Worshipful Company of Stationers from 1640 to 1708*, ed. G. E. B. Eyre (London: privately printed, 1913–14), 3 vols.

70 Term Catalogues 1668–1709 A. D., with a Number for Easter Term 1711 A. D., ed. Edward Arber (London: privately printed, and New York: Dodd, 1903–06), 3 vols.

71 William Carew Hazlitt, *Handbook of the Popular Poetical, and Dramatic Literature of Great Britain, from the Invention of Printing to the Restoration* (London: J. R. Smith, 1857) and *idem, Bibliographical Collections and Notes on Early English Literature, 1475–1700* (London: Quaritch, 1876–1903), 6 vols.; there is an index to these materials: G. J. Gray, *General Index to Hazlitt's Handbook and His Bibliographical Collections* (London: Quaritch, 1893).

72 Alfred William Pollard and Gilbert Richard Redgrave, *A Short-title Catalogue of Books Printed in England, Scotland, and Ireland and of English Books Printed Abroad, 1475–1640* (London: The Bibliographical Society, 1926). The *STC* is not perfect, since there are omissions and since, in some instances, issues or printings are listed as editions; nevertheless, the book is immensely valuable. In using it, one should remember that it does not attempt, except with the rarest books, to make a census of copies. Its purpose is to list the most accessible copies; thus if there is a copy of a work in the British Museum, the presence of another copy in the Lambeth Palace Library may be ignored. If there is also a copy in the Bodleian Library at Oxford, that fact will be mentioned, as will the presence of a copy in Cambridge; but the presence of a second copy in Oxford or in Cambridge will not be indicated. For some corrections to the *STC* see F. B. Williams, Jr., "Corrections to the *STC*", *LTLS*, September 12, 1935, p. 565. There is also Donald Goddard Wing, *Short-Title Catalogue of Books Printed in England, Scotland, Ireland, Wales, and British America and of English Books Printed in Other Countries, 1641–1700* (New York: The Index Society, 1945–); this work is to be complete in three volumes, of which the first appeared in 1945.

73   Thomas Corser, *Collectanea Anglo-Poetica* (Manchester: The Chatham Society, 1860–83), 5 vols.

74   William John Courthope, *A History of English Poetry* (New York and London: Macmillan, 1895–1910), 6 vols.

75   George Saintsbury, *Historical Manual of English Prosody* (London: Macmillan, 1910).

76   Thomas Warton, *The History of English Poetry from the Close of the Eleventh Century to the Commencement of the Eighteenth Century* (London: T. Tegg, 1840), 3 vols.

77   John Colin Dunlop, *History of Prose Fiction,* ed. Henry Wilson (London: G. Bell and Sons, 1906), 2 vols.

78   Ernest Albert Baker, *The History of the English Novel* (London: Witherby, 1924–39), 10 vols.

79   William Frank Bryan and Ronald Salmon Crane, *The English Familiar Essay* (Boston: Ginn, 1916ᶜ)

80   Ronald Salmon Crane and Frederick Benjamin Kaye, *A Census of British Newspapers and Periodicals 1620–1800* (Chapel Hill, N. C.: University of North Carolina Press, and London: Cambridge University Press, 1927).

81   *Tercentenary Handlist of English and Welsh Newspapers, Magazines, and Reviews* (London: The Times, 1920).

82   Wilhelm Creizenach, *Geschichte des neueren Dramas* (Halle: M. Niemeyer, 1911–23), 5 vols.

83   Allardyce Nicoll, *The Development of the Theatre: a Study of Theatrical Art from the Beginnings to the Present Day* (New York: Harcourt Brace, 1937).

84   Roy Caston Flickinger, *The Greek Theatre and Its Drama,* 4th ed. (Chicago: University of Chicago Press, 1936ᶜ).

85   Kathleen Marguerite Lea, *Italian Popular Comedy* (Oxford: Clarendon Press, 1934), 2 vols.

86   Karl Young, *The Drama of the Medieval Church* (Oxford: Clarendon Press, 1933), 2 vols.

87   [Sir] E[dmund] K[erchever] Chambers, *The Mediæval Stage* (London: Oxford University Press, 1903), 2 vols.

88   *Idem, The Elizabethan Stage* (Oxford: Clarendon Press, 1923), 4 vols.

89 Allardyce Nicoll, *A History of Restoration Drama, 1660–1700* (Cambridge: Cambridge University Press, 1923); *idem, A History of Early Eighteenth Century Drama, 1700–1750* (Cambridge: Cambridge University Press, 1925); *idem, A History of Late Eighteenth Century Drama, 1750–1800* (Cambridge: Cambridge University Press, 1927); and *idem, A History of Early Nineteenth Century Drama, 1800–1850* (Cambridge: Cambridge University Press, 1930). See also *idem, British Drama, an Historical Survey from the Beginnings to the Present Time* (London: G. G. Harrap, 1925ᶜ); 3rd ed. rev. (New York: Crowell, 1932ᶜ).

90 Walter Wilson Greg, *A Bibliography of the English Printed Drama to the Restoration* (London: Bibliographical Society, 1939–   ); only Vol. I has thus far appeared.

91 John Payne Collier, *The History of English Dramatic Poetry to the Time of Shakespeare and Annals of the Stage to the Restoration* (London: G. Bell and Sons, 1879), 3 vols.

92 F[rederick] G[ard] Fleay, *A Bigraphical Chronicle of the English Drama 1559–1642* (London: Reeves and Turner, 1891), 2 vols.

93 Gerard Langbaine, *An Account of the English Dramatick Poets* (Oxford: printed for L. L. by G. West and H. Clements, 1691).

94 [Sir] A[dolphus] W[illiam] Ward, *A History of English Dramatic Literature to the Death of Queen Anne* (London and New York: Macmillan, 1899), 3 vols.

95 *Cambridge History of American Literature,* ed. William P. Trent, John Erskine, Stuart P. Sherman, and Carl Van Doren (New York: Macmillan, and Cambridge: Cambridge University Press, 1931), 4 vols. A more recent work is *Literary History of the United States,* ed. R. E. Spiller (New York: Macmillan, 1948), 3 vols.

96 John George Bartholomew, *A Literary and Historical Atlas of America* (New York: Dutton, and London: J. M. Dent and Sons, 1930).

97 Charles Evans, *American Bibliography* (New York: Peter Smith, 1941–42), 12 vols.

98 Willard O. Waters, *American Imprints, 1640–1797, in the Huntington Library* (Cambridge, Mass.: Harvard University Press, 1933). See also Edward H. O'Neill, *A Description and Analysis of the Bibliography of American Literature* (Philadelphia: The Pennsylvania Historical Survey, 1941). The *American Imprints Inventory,* prepared by the Division of Women's and Professional Projects, Works Progress Administration, and published during the years 1937 to 1942, consists of some thirty-five volumes covering such fields as Missouri, 1808–50; Minnesota, 1849–65; Arizona, 1860–90; Chicago, 1851–71; Kentucky, 1787–1810 and 1811–20; Nevada, 1859–90; Alabama, 1807–40; New Jersey, 1784–1800; Kansas, 1854–76; Sag Harbor, Long Island, 1791–1820; and the like.

99 Perry Miller and Thomas Herbert Johnson, *The Puritans* (New York: American Book Co., 1938ᶜ).

100 Moses Coit Tyler, *A History of American Literature During the Colonial Times 1607–1765* (New York and London: Putnam's, 1897), 2 vols.

101   Idem, *The Literary History of the American Revolution 1763–1783* (New York: Putnam's, 1897), 2 vols.

102   Patrick Kevin Foley, *American Authors, 1795–1895* (Boston: privately printed, 1897). See also Merle Devore Johnson, *American First Editions*, revised and enlarged by Jacob Blanck (New York: R. R. Bowker, 1942).

103   Fred Benjamin Millet, *Contemporary American Authors: a Critical Survey of 219 Bio-bibliographies* (New York: Harcourt Brace, 1940).

104   Gay Wilson Allen, *American Prosody* (New York: American Book Co., 1935ᶜ).

105   Oscar Wegelin, *Early American Poetry: A Compilation of the Titles of Volumes of Verse and Broadsides by Writers Born or Residing in North America, North of the Mexican Border*, 2nd ed. (New York: Peter Smith, 1930), 2 vols. in 1. See also Horace Gregory and Marya Zaturenska, *History of American Poetry 1900–1940* (New York: Harcourt Brace, 1946).

106   Lyle Henry Wright, *American Fiction, 1774–1850: A Contribution toward a Bibliography* (San Marino, California: The Huntington Library, 1939).

107   Arthur H[obson] Quinn, *American Fiction: an Historical and Critical Survey* (New York and London: Appleton-Century, 1936ᶜ).

108   Adeline M. Conway, *The Essay in American Literature* (New York: New York University, 1914).

109   Hariette Merrifield Forbes, *New England Diaries 1602–1800* (Topsfield, Mass.: privately printed, 1923).

110   Clarence S[aunders] Brigham, *History and Bibliography of American Newspapers 1690–1820* (Worcester, Mass.: American Antiquarian Society, 1947).

111   Winifred Gregory, *American Newspapers 1821–1936* (New York: H. W. Wilson Company, 1937). See also *Union List of Serials in the United States and Canada,* ed. Winifred Gregory (New York: H. W. Wilson Company, 1943).

112   Arthur H[obson] Quinn, *A History of the American Drama from the Beginning to the Civil War* (New York and London: Harper's, 1923), and *idem, A History of the American Drama from the Civil War to the Present Day* (New York: Crofts, 1936), 2 vols.

113   George C. D. Odell, *Annals of the New York Stage* (New York: Columbia University Press, 1927–   ); Vol. XV, covering the period 1891–94, appeared in 1949.

114   [Robert] Burns Mantle, *The Best Plays of 1919/20* [to 1924–25] *and the Year Book of the Drama in America* (Boston: Small Maynard, 1920–25); *ibid.,* 1925/26– (New York: Dodd Mead, 1926–   ); see also *idem, The Best Plays of 1899 to 1909 . . .* (Philadelphia: Blakiston, 1944) and *The Best Plays of 1909 to 1919 . . .* (New York: Dodd Mead, 1933).

115   Eleanor Prescott Hammond, *Chaucer: A Bibliographical Manual* (New York: Macmillan, 1908); Dudley David Griffin, *Bibliography of Chaucer, 1908 to 1924* (Seattle, Washington: University of Washington,

1926); William Edgar Martin, Jr., *Chaucer Bibliography 1925–1933* (Durham, N. C.: Duke University Press, 1935); and Caroline Frances Eleanor Spurgeon, *Five Hundred Years of Chaucer Criticism and Allusion (1357–1900)* (Cambridge: Cambridge University Press, 1925), 3 vols.

116 Richard Herne Shepherd, *The Bibliography of Coleridge* (London: F. Hollings, 1900); John Louis Haney, *A Bibliography of Samuel Taylor Coleridge* (Philadelphia: privately printed, 1903); Thomas J. Wise, *A Bibliography of the Writings in Prose and Verse of Samuel Taylor Coleridge* (London: Bibliographical Society, 1913); *idem, Coleridgiana: Being a Supplement to the Bibliography of Coleridge* (London: Bibliographical Society, 1919); Virginia Wadlow Kennedy, *Samuel Taylor Coleridge: A Selected Bibliography* . . . (Baltimore: Enoch Pratt Free Library, 1935).

117 John C. Eckel, *First Editions of the Writings of Charles Dickens and Their Values: A Bibliography* (London: Chapman, 1913).

118 Geoffrey Keynes, *A Bibliography of Dr. John Donne, Dean of Saint Paul's*, 2nd ed. (Cambridge: Cambridge University Press, 1932).

119 Hugh Macdonald, *John Dryden: A Bibliography of Early Editions and of Drydeniana* (Oxford: Clarendon Press, 1939).

120 Clark S. Northup, *Bibliography of Thomas Gray* (New Haven: Yale University Press, 1917).

121 A. P. Webb, *Bibliography of the Works of Thomas Hardy, 1865–1916* (London: Hollings, 1916).

122 Robert Wooster Stallman, "Annotated Bibliography of A. E. Housman: A Critical Study", *PMLA*, LX (1945), 463–502.

123 David Harrison Stevens, *Reference Guide to Milton from 1800 to the Present Day* (Chicago: University of Chicago Press, 1930ᶜ); and Harris Francis Fletcher, *Contributions to a Milton Bibliography, 1800–1930: Being a List of Addenda to Stevens'* Reference Guide to Milton (Urbana, Illinois: University of Illinois, 1931).

124 Reginald Harvey Griffith, *Alexander Pope, A Bibliography* (Austin, Texas: University of Texas, 1922).

125 Thomas J. Wise and J. P. Smart, *Complete Bibliography of the Writings in Prose and Verse of John Ruskin, with a List of the More Important Ruskiniana* (London: Clay, 1893), 2 vols.

126 William Ruff, *A Bibliography of the Poetical Works of Sir Walter Scott, 1796–1832* (Edinburgh: Edinburgh Bibliographical Society, 1938).

127 Walter Ebisch and Levin Schucking, *A Shakespeare Bibliography* (Oxford: Clarendon Press, 1931); *idem, Supplement for the Years 1930–35* (Oxford: Clarendon Press, 1937).

128 C. L. and V. M. Broad, *Dictionary to the Plays and Novels of Bernard Shaw, with a Bibliography of His Works and of the Literature Concerning Him, with a Record of the Principal Shavian Productions* (London: Black, 1929).

129 Frederic Ives Carpenter, *A Reference Guide to Edmund Spenser* (Chicago: University of Chicago Press, 1923); Francis R. Johnson, *A Critical Bibliography of the Works of Edmund Spenser Printed Before 1700* (Baltimore: Johns Hopkins Press, 1933); and Dorothy F. Atkinson, *Edmund Spenser: A Bibliographical Supplement* (Baltimore: Johns Hopkins Press, 1937).

130 H. Teerink, *Bibliography of the Writings in Prose and Verse of Jonathan Swift* (The Hague: Nijhoff, 1937).

131 Geoffrey H. Wells, *The Works of H. G. Wells, 1887–1925: A Bibliography, Dictionary, and Subject Index* (London: Rutledge, and New York: H. W. Wilson Company, 1926).

132 Robert E. Spiller and Philip C. Blackburn, *A Descriptive Bibliography of the Writings of James Fenimore Cooper* (New York: R. R. Bowker, 1934).

133 Ames W. Williams and Vincent Starrett, *Stephen Crane: A Bibliography* (Glendale, California: John Valentine, 1948).

134 Thomas Herbert Johnson, *Printed Writings of Jonathan Edwards, 1703–1758: A Bibliography* (Princeton, N. J.: Princeton University Press, 1940).

135 George Willis Cooke, *A Bibliography of Ralph Waldo Emerson* (Boston and New York: Houghton Mifflin, 1908).

136 Nina Eliza Browne, *Bibliography of Nathaniel Hawthorne* (Boston: Houghton Mifflin, 1915).

137 William M. Gibson and George Arms, *A Bibliography of William Dean Howells* (New York: New York Public Library, 1948).

138 William R. Langfield, *Washington Irving: A Bibliography* . . . (New York: New York Public Library, 1933), and Stanley T. Williams and Mary Allen Edge, *A Bibliography of the Writings of Washington Irving* (New York: Oxford University Press, 1936).

139 Eunice C. Hamilton, "Biographical and Critical Studies of Henry James, 1941–1948", *AmLit*, XX (1948–49), [424]–35.

140 George Willis Cooke, *A Bibliography of James Russell Lowell* (Boston and New York: Houghton Mifflin, 1906), and Luther Samuel Livingston, *A Bibliography of the First Editions in Book Form of the Writings of James Russell Lowell* (New York: privately printed, 1914).

141 Edgar M. Branch, "A Chronological Bibliography of the Writings of Samuel Clemens to June 8, 1867", *AmLit*, XVIII (1946–47), [109]–59.

142 Thomas James Holmes, *Cotton Mather: A Bibliography of His Works* (Cambridge, Mass.: Harvard University Press, 1940).

143 *Idem, Increase Mather: A Bibliography* (Cleveland, Ohio: privately printed, 1930).

144 Paul Stephen Clarkson, *A Bibliography of William Sidney Porter* (*O. Henry*), (Caldwell, Idaho: Caxton Press, 1938).

145 Moriz Grolig, *Edgar Allan Poe Bibliographie* (Nimden (Westfalen): J. C. C. Bruns hof-buchhandlung, 1907), and Charles Frederick Heartman, *A Bibliography of First Printings of the Writings of Edgar Allan Poe* (Hattiesburg, Miss.: The Book Farm, 1943).

146 Lucius Beebe and Robert J. Bulkley, Jr., *A Bibliography of the Writings of Edwin Arlington Robinson* (Cambridge, Mass.: Dunston House Book Shop, 1931); Charles Beecher Hogan, *A Bibliography of Edwin Arlington Robinson* (New Haven: Yale University Press, and London: Oxford

University Press, 1936); and Lillian Lippincott, *A Bibliography of the Writings and Criticisms of Edwin Arlington Robinson* (Boston: F. W. Faxon, 1937).

147 Samuel Arthur Jones, *Bibliography of Henry David Thoreau, with an Outline of His Life* (New York: Rowfant Club of Cleveland, 1894), and J. S. Wade, "A Contribution to the Bibliography from 1909 to 1936 of Henry David Thoreau", *Journal of the New York Entomological Society*, XLVII (1939), [163]–203.

148 Gay Wilson Allen, *Twenty-five Years of Walt Whitman Bibliography, 1918–1942* (Boston: H. W. Faxon, 1943ᶜ), and Frank Shay, *The Bibliography of Walt Whitman* (New York: Friedmans', 1920).

149 Thomas Franklin Currier, *A Bibliography of John Greenleaf Whittier* (Cambridge, Mass.: Harvard University Press, 1937).

150 Albert S. Cook, *A Concordance to Beowulf* (Halle: M. Niemeyer, 1911).

151 Alexander Cruden, *A Complete Concordance to the Old and New Testaments* (London and New York: F. Warne, 1936ᶜ).

152 Leslie N. Broughton and Benjamin F. Stelter, *A Concordance to the Poems of Robert Browning* (New York: G. E. Stechert, 1924–25), 2 vols.

153 J. B. Reid, *Complete Word and Phrase Concordance to the Poems and Songs of Robert Burns* (Glasgow: Kerr, 1889).

154 John S. P. Tatlock and Arthur G. Kennedy, *Concordance to the Complete Works of Geoffrey Chaucer and to* The Romaunt of the Rose (Washington, D. C.: Carnegie Institution, 1927).

155 Sister Eugenia Logan, *A Concordance to the Poetry of Samuel Taylor Coleridge* (St. Mary of the Woods, Indiana: privately printed, 1940).

156 Bradford Allen Booth and Claude E. Jones, *Concordance to the Poetical Works of William Collins* (Berkeley, California: University of California Press, 1939).

157 John Nave, *Concordance to the Poetical Works of William Cowper* (London: S. Low, 1887).

158 Homer Carroll Combs and Zay Rusk Sullens, *A Concordance to the English Poems of John Donne* (Chicago: Packard, 1940ᶜ).

159 John Ramsden Tutin, *Concordance to FitzGerald's Translation of* The Rubáiyát *of Omar Khayyám* (London and New York: Macmillan, 1900).

160 William Doremus Paden and Clyde Kenneth Hyder, *Concordance to the Poems of Oliver Goldsmith* (Lawrence, Kansas: privately printed, 1940).

161 Albert S. Cook, *Concordance to the English Poems of Thomas Gray* (Boston: Houghton Mifflin, 1908).

162 Malcolm MacLeod, *Concordance to the Poems of Robert Herrick* (London: Oxford University Press, 1936).

163 Clyde Kenneth Hyder, *A Concordance to the Poems of A. E. Housman* (Lawrence, Kansas: privately printed, 1940).

164 Dane Lewis Baldwin, *Concordance to the Poems of John Keats* (Washington, D. C.: Carnegie Institution, 1917).

165 Charles Crawford, *Concordance to the Works of Thomas Kyd* (Louvain: Uystpruyst, 1906–10).

166 Idem, *The Marlowe Concordance* (Louvain: Uystpruyst, 1911–32), 3 vols.

167 John Bradshaw, *Concordance to the Poetical Works of John Milton* (London: Sonnenschein, 1894), and Lane Cooper, *Concordance to the Latin, Greek, and Italian Poems of John Milton* (Halle: Niemeyer, 1923). See also Laura Emma Lockwood, *Lexicon to the English Poetical Works of John Milton* (London and New York: Macmillan, 1907), and Frank Allen Patterson, *An Index to the Columbia Edition of the Works of John Milton* (New York: Columbia University Press, 1940), 2 vols.

168 Edwin Abbott, *A Concordance to the Works of Alexander Pope* (London: Chapman and Hall, 1875).

169 Mary Victoria Cowden-Clarke, *Complete Concordance to Shakespeare* (London: Vickers, and New York: Scribner's, 1889); John Bartlett, *New and Complete Concordance or Verbal Index to Words, Phrases, and Passages in the Dramatic Works of Shakespeare, with a Supplementary Concordance to the Poems* (London: Macmillan, 1894); and Helen Kate Furness, *Concordance to Shakespeare's Poems*, 4th ed. (Philadelphia: Lippincott, 1916).

170 Frederick S. Ellis, *Lexical Concordance to the Works of Percy Bysshe Shelley* (London: Quaritch, 1892).

171 Charles Grosvenor Osgood, *A Concordance to the Poems of Edmund Spenser* (Washington, D. C.: Carnegie Institution, 1915).

172 Arthur Ernest Baker, *Concordance to the Poetical and Dramatic Works of Alfred Lord Tennyson* (London: K. Paul, and New York: Macmillan, 1914); *idem, Concordance to* The Devil and the Lady (London: Golden Vista Press, 1931).

173 Lane Cooper, *Concordance to the Poems of William Wordsworth* (London: Smith, Elder, and New York: Dutton, 1911).

174 Eva Catherine Hangen, *Concordance to the Complete Works of Sir Thomas Wyatt* (Chicago: University of Chicago Press, 1941).

175 George Shelton Hubbell, *A Concordance to the Poems of Ralph Waldo Emerson* (New York: H. W. Wilson Company, 1932).

176 Evangeline M. O'Connor, *Analytical Index to the Works of Nathaniel Hawthorne* (Boston: Houghton Mifflin, 1882ᶜ).

177 Philip Graham and Joseph Jones, *A Concordance to the Poems of Sidney Lanier* (Austin, Texas: University of Texas Press, 1939).

178 Bradford Allen Booth and Claude Edward Jones, *A Concordance to the Poetical Works of Edgar Allan Poe* (Baltimore: Johns Hopkins Press, 1941).

179 Charles Mills Gayley, *An Introduction to the Methods and Materials of Literary Criticism* (Boston: Ginn, 1889).

180 Charles Mills Gayley and Benjamin Kurtz, *Methods and Materials of Literary Criticism* (Boston: Ginn, 1920).

181 George Saintsbury, *A History of Criticism and Literary Taste in*

Europe from the Earliest Texts to the Present Day (Edinburgh and London: Blackwood, 1900–04).

182 G[eorge] Gregory Smith, *Elizabethan Critical Essays* (Oxford: Clarendon Press, 1904), 2 vols.

183 Joel E. Spingarn, *Critical Essays of the Seventeenth Century* (Oxford: Clarendon Press, 1908–09), 3 vols.

184 A. Bosker, *Literary Criticism in the Age of Johnson* (Groningen: J. B. Wolters, 1930); John W. Draper, *Eighteenth Century English Æsthetics: A Bibliography* (Heidelberg: C. Winter, 1931); Willard H. Durham, *Critical Essays of the Eighteenth Century, 1700–1725* (New Haven: Yale University Press, 1915); and James Edward Tobin, *Eighteenth Century English Literature and Its Background: A Bibliography* (New York: Fordham University Press, 1939).

185 George E. DeMille, *Literary Criticism in America: A Preliminary Survey* (New York: L. MacVeagh, and Toronto: Longmans Green, 1931ᶜ). See also Irving Babbitt *et al.*, *Criticism in America* (New York: Harcourt Brace, 1924); Norman Foerster, *American Criticism: A Study in Literary Theory from Poe to the Present* (Boston: Houghton Mifflin, 1928); Morton D. Zabel, *Literary Opinions in America* (New York: Harper, 1937); Henri Peyre, *Writers and Their Critics* (Ithaca, N. Y.: Cornell University Press, 1944); and Carl H. Grabo, *The Creative Critic* (New York: Doubleday, 1948).

186 Sister Mary Cleophas Costello, *Between Fixity and Flux: A Study of the Concept of Poetry in the Criticism of T. S. Eliot* (Washington, D. C.: Catholic University of America Press, 1947).

187 Leonard Bloomfield, *Language* (New York: Holt, 1933ᶜ).

188 Willem L. Graff, *Language and Languages* (New York and London: Appleton, 1932).

189 Louis H[erbert] Gray, *The Foundations of Language* (New York: Macmillan, 1939).

190 Albert C[roll] Baugh, *A History of the English Language* (New York and London: Appleton-Century, 1935ᶜ).

191 Edward D. Myers, *The Foundations of English* (New York: Macmillan, 1940).

192 *A New English Dictionary on Historical Principles Founded Mainly on the Materials Collected by the Philological Society,* ed. Sir J. A. H. Murray *et al.* (Oxford: Clarendon Press, 1888–1928), 10 vols.

193 *Webster's New International Dictionary of the English Language,* 2nd ed. (Springfield, Mass.: G. and C. Merriam, 1942).

194 Joseph Bosworth and T. Northcote Toller, *An Anglo-Saxon Dictionary* (Oxford: Clarendon Press, 1898), with a Supplement by T. Northcote Toller (Oxford: Clarendon Press, 1908–21).

195 Francis H[einrich] Stratmann, *A Middle English Dictionary,* ed. Henry Bradley (Oxford: Clarendon Press, 1891).

196 Joseph Wright, *The English Dialect Dictionary* (London: H. Froude, and New York: Putnam's, 1898–1905). See also Nathan Bailey, *English*

Dialect Words of the Eighteenth Century as Shown in the "Universal Etymological Dictionary" of Nathaniel Bailey (London: Trübner, 1882).

197 A Dictionary of American English on Historical Principles, ed. Sir William A. Craigie and James R. Hulbert (Chicago: University of Chicago Press, 1938–44), 4 vols.

198 George P[hilip] Krapp, *The English Language in America* (New York: Century, 1925), 2 vols.

199 H[enry] L[ouis] Mencken, *The American Language: An Inquiry into the Development of English in the United States*, 4th ed. (New York: Knopf, 1936), and *idem, Supplement I: The American Language* (New York: Knopf, 1945); see also Harold Wentworth, *American Dialect Dictionary* (New York: Crowell, 1944), and Lester V. Berry and Melvin Van Den Bark, *The American Thesaurus of Slang with Supplement: A Complete Reference Book of Colloquial Speech* (New York: Crowell, 1947).

200 McKerrow, *Introduction to Bibliography*, pp. 145–62.

201 Esdaile, *Student's Manual of Bibliography*, pp. 248–71.

202 W. W. Greg, "A Formulary of Collation", *The Library*, 4th Series, XIV (1933–34), 365–82; see also the introduction to his *A Bibliography of the English Printed Drama to the Restoration*, Vol. I.

203 *The Text of the Canterbury Tales*, ed. John Matthews Manly and Edith Rickert, 8 vols. (Chicago: University of Chicago Press, 1940ᶜ), I, 23.

204 Ibid.

205 Ibid., p. 562.

206 Ibid., p. 94.

207 Ibid., p. 26.

208 Haselden, *Scientific Aids for the Study of Manuscripts*, pp. 64–65.

209 John Livingston Lowes, *The Road to Xanadu*, rev. ed. (Boston and New York: Houghton Mifflin, [1930]).

PART III

THE METHODS OF RESEARCH

Chapter One: Problems of Editing

1 Robert Greene, *Works*, ed. A[lexander] B[alloch] Grosart, 15 vols. (London: privately printed, 1881–83), II, [ix–xi].

2 André Morize, *Problems and Methods*, p. 38.

3 Thomas Nashe, *Works*, ed. R[onald] B[runlees] McKerrow, 5 vols. (London: A. H. Bullen [for Vols. I–IV] and Sidgwick and Jackson [for Vol. V], 1904–[1910]), I, 147–48.

4 Bernard Mandeville, *Fable of the Bees*, ed. F[rederick] B[enjamin] Kaye, 2 vols. (Oxford: Clarendon Press, 1924), I, xxxiii–xxxv.

5 Ibid., p. ix.

6 G. I. Duthie, *The 'Bad' Quarto of* Hamlet (Cambridge: Cambridge University Press, and New York: Macmillan, 1941).

Textual studies devoted to collation and attempts to establish the filiation of texts include: Charlotte D'Evelyn, "An East Midland Recension of *The Pricke of Conscience*", *PMLA*, XLV (1930), 180–200; Marion Crane Carroll and Rosemond Tuve, "Two Manuscripts of the Middle English *Anonymous Riming Chronicle*", *PMLA*, XLVI (1931), 115–54; Margaret Kilgour, "The Manuscript Source of Caxton's Second Edition of the *Canterbury Tales*", *PMLA*, XLIV (1929), 186–201, with a comment by W. W. Greg, "The MS Source of Caxton's Second Edition of the *Canterbury Tales*", *PMLA*, XLIV (1929), 1251–53, and a reply by Margaret Kilgour, *ibid.*, p. 1253; E. E. Neil Dodge, "The Text of the *Gerusalemme Liberata* in the Versions of Carew and Fairfax", *PMLA*, XLIV (1929), 681–95, with a comment by Walter L. Bullock, "Carew's Text of the *Gerusalemme Liberata*," *PMLA*, XLV (1930), 330–35. Studies concerned mainly with the evolution of a text are: J. S. P. Tatlock, "The *Canterbury Tales* in 1400", *PMLA*, L (1935), 100–39; Arthur M. Sampley, "The Text of Peele's *David and Bethsabe*," *PMLA*, XLVI (1931), 659–71; Joseph S. G. Bolton, "The Authentic Text of *Titus Andronicus*", *PMLA*, XLIV (1929), 765–88; Gerda Okerlund, "The Quarto Version of *Henry V* as a Stage Adaptation," *PMLA*, XLIX (1934), 810–34; Allison Gaw, "Is Shakespeare's *Much Ado* a Revised Earlier Play?" *PMLA*, L (1935), 715–38; and Bertrand Harris Bronson, *"The Caledonian Muse"*, *PMLA*, XLVI (1931), 1202–20. Two studies by Kenneth Walter Cameron, *"Othello*, Quarto 1, Reconsidered", *PMLA*, XLVII (1932), 671–83, and "The Text of *Othello*: An Analysis", *PMLA*, XLIX (1934), 762–96, are devoted chiefly to the evaluation of a text. An article by Clara Marburg, "Notes on the Cardigan Chaucer Manuscript", *PMLA*, XLI (1926), 229–51, involves description and collation. Roberta D. Cornelius, "A New Text of an Old Ballad", *PMLA*, XLVI (1931), 1025–33, and George Winchester Stone, Jr., "Garrick's Long Lost Alteration of *Hamlet*", *PMLA*, XLIX (1934), 890–921, give transcriptions of a text. Oliver Farrar Emerson, "More Notes on *Pearl*," *PMLA*, XLII (1927), 807–31, is devoted to suggested emendations. W. W. Greg, "Text of *The Gypsies Metamorphosed*", *PMLA*, XLIX (1934), 963; Samuel A. Tannenbaum, "Corrections to the Text of *Believe As You List*", *PMLA*, XLII (1927), 777–81; and Robert Witbeck Babcock, "The Reverend Montague Summers as Editor of Otway", *PMLA*, XLVIII (1933), 948–52, point out editorial errors.

7 C. F. Tucker Brooke, "The Authorship of the Second and Third Parts of 'King Henry VI' ", *Transactions of the Connecticut Academy of Arts and Sciences*, XVII (1912), 141–211; Madeleine Doran, *Henry VI—Parts II and III, Their Relation to the Contention and the True Tragedy* (Iowa City: State University of Iowa, [1928]), University of Iowa Humanistic Studies, Vol. IV, No. 4; Peter Alexander, *Shakespeare's Henry VI and Richard III* (Cambridge: Cambridge University Press, 1929); Robert A. Law, "Shakespeare's Earliest Plays", *SP*, XXVIII (1931), 631–38; Clayton Alvis Greer, "The Relation of *Richard III* to *The True Tragedy of Richard Duke of York*

and *The Third Part of Henry VI"*, *SP*, XXIX (1932), 543–50; *idem*, "The York and Lancaster Quarto-Folio Sequence", *PMLA*, XLVIII (1933), 655–704; W. W. Greg, *"Henry VI* and the *Contention Plays"*, *PMLA*, L (1935), 919–20; Lucille King, "Text Sources of the Folio and Quarto *Henry VI"*, *PMLA*, LI (1936), 702–18; Clayton Alvis Greer, "The Place of *1 Henry VI* in the York-Lancaster Tetralogy", *PMLA*, LIII (1938), 687–701.

8 James R. Kreuzer, "The Twelve Profits of Anger", *PMLA*, LIII (1938), 78–85.

9 Mendal G. Frampton, *"The Brewbarret Interpolation in the York Play* the *Sacrificium Cayme and Abell"*, *PMLA*, LII (1937), 895–900.

10 Germaine Dempster, "A Chapter of the Manuscript History of the *Canterbury Tales"*, *PMLA*, LXIII (1948), 456–84.

11 Raymond A. Houk, "The Evolution of *The Taming of the Shrew"*, *PMLA*, LVII (1942), 1009–38.

12 Leo Kirschbaum, "An Hypothesis Concerning the Origin of the Bad Quartos", *PMLA*, LX (1945), 697–715.

13 John S. Diekhoff, "The Text of *Comus*, 1634 to 1645", *PMLA*, LII (1937), 705–27.

14 John Edwin Wells, *"Lyrical Ballads, 1800:* Cancel Leaves", *PMLA*, LIII (1938), 207–29.

15 Nashe, *Works*, ed. McKerrow, II, 196–97.

16 Morize, *Problems and Methods*, pp. 53–54.

17 *Ibid.*, p. 51.

18 Edwin Wolf, 2nd, " 'If Shadows Be a Picture's Excellence': An Experiment in Critical Bibliography", *PMLA*, LXIII (1948), 831–57.

19 W. W. Greg, *Principles of Emendation in Shakespeare* (London: Oxford University Press, 1928); this is the Annual Shakespeare Lecture of the British Academy for 1928, with some forty pages of notes added, and was first printed in the *Proceedings of the British Academy*, XIV (1928), 147–216.

20 *Ibid.*, p. [3].

21 *Ibid.*, p. 5.

22 *The Plays and Poems of William Shakespeare*, ed. Malone, 21 vols. (F. C. and J. Rivington and others, 1821), XVII, 318–20.

23 W. W. Greg, *Principles of Emendation in Shakespeare*, p. 4.

24 Nashe, *Works*, ed. McKerrow, I, 33.

25 Shakspere, *Hamlet*, ed. W. G. Clark and W. Aldis Wright, I, ii, 129.

26 W. W. Greg, *op. cit.*, pp. 27–28.

27 Ronald B. McKerrow, *Prolegomena for the Oxford Shakespeare* (Oxford: Clarendon Press, 1939), pp. vi–viii.

28 *Ibid.*, p. vii.

29 John Robert Moore, in a personal letter to me.

30 *The Mirror for Magistrates*, ed. Lily B[ess] Campbell (Cambridge: Cambridge University Press, 1938).

31 Sir Thomas More, *The English Works of Sir Thomas More*, ed. W. E. Campbell and others (London: Eyre and Spottiswoode, 1931–), in 7 vols., of which the first two have appeared.

32 Michael Drayton, *The Works of Michael Drayton,* ed. J. William Hebel (Oxford: Basil Blackwell, 1931–33), 4 vols.

33 Christopher Marlowe, *The Works and Life of Christopher Marlowe,* ed. R. H. Case and others (London: Methuen, [1930–33]), 6 vols.

34 Edmund Spenser, *The Works of Edmund Spenser,* ed. Edwin Greenlaw and others (Baltimore: Johns Hopkins Press, 1932–47), 8 vols. in 9.

35 Roger Boyle, *The Dramatic Works of Roger Boyle, Earl of Orrery,* ed. William Smith Clark, II (Cambridge, Mass.: Harvard University Press, 1937), 2 vols.

36 George Herbert, *The Works of George Herbert,* ed. F. E. Hutchinson (New York: Oxford University Press, 1941).

37 Ben Jonson, *Ben Jonson,* ed. C. H. Herford and Percy and Evelyn Simpson (Oxford: Oxford University Press, 1925–   ), in 10 vols., of which eight have now appeared.

38 John Milton, *The Works of John Milton,* ed. Frank Allen Patterson and others (New York: Columbia University Press, and London: Humphrey Milford, 1931–38), 18 vols. in 21.

39 Joseph Addison, *Letters,* ed. Walter Graham (London: Oxford University Press, 1941).

40 James Boswell, *Life of Johnson,* ed. George Birkbeck Hill, revised by L. F. Powell (Oxford: Clarendon Press, 1934), 6 vols.

41 Lord Chesterfield, *Letters of the 4th Earl of Chesterfield,* ed. Bonamy Dobree (London: Eyre and Spottiswoode, 1932), 6 vols.

42 John Dennis, *The Critical Works of John Dennis,* ed. Edward N. Hooker (Baltimore: Johns Hopkins Press, 1939–43), 2 vols.

43 Alexander Pope, *The Twickenham Edition of the Poems of Alexander Pope,* ed. John Butt and others (New York: Oxford University Press, 1939–   ); to be complete in 10 vols. Vol. II, *The Rape of the Lock and Other Poems,* ed. Geoffrey Tillotson, was published in 1940; Vol. IV, *Imitations of Horace,* ed. John Butt, appeared in 1939; and Vol. V, *Dunciad,* ed. James Sutherland, in 1943.

44 Jonathan Swift, *The Poems of Jonathan Swift,* ed. Harold Williams (Oxford: Clarendon Press, 1937), 3 vols.

45 *Idem, The Prose Works of Jonathan Swift,* ed. Herbert Davis (Oxford: Basil Blackwell for the Shakespeare Head Press, 1939–40), 3 vols.

46 Horace Walpole, *Horace Walpole's Correspondence,* ed. W. S. Lewis and others (New Haven: Yale University Press, and London: Humphrey Milford, 1937–39), 8 vols.

47 John Keats, *The Poetical Works of John Keats,* ed. H. W. Garrod (Oxford: Clarendon Press, 1939).

48 William Wordsworth, *The Poetical Works of William Wordsworth,* ed. E[rnest] DeSélincourt and Helen Derbishire (New York: Oxford University Press, 1940–   ); four vols. have appeared.

49 William Byrd, *The Writings of "Colonel William Byrd, of Westover in Virginia, esqr",* ed. John Spencer Bassett (New York: Doubleday Page, 1901).

50 Benjamin Franklin, *The Writings of Benjamin Franklin,* ed. Albert Henry Smythe (New York and London: Macmillan, 1905–07), 10 vols.

51 Sidney Lanier, *The Centennial Edition of the Writings of Sidney Lanier,* ed. Charles R. Anderson (Baltimore: Johns Hopkins Press, 1945), 10 vols.

52 Nathaniel Hawthorne, *The American Notebooks,* ed. Randall Stewart (New Haven: Yale University Press, and London: Humphrey Milford, 1932).

53 Edgar Allan Poe, *Poems,* ed. Killis Campbell (Boston: Ginn, 1917).

54 Herman Melville, *Collected Poems of Herman Melville,* ed. Howard P. Vincent (Chicago: Packard, 1947–   ); only Vol. I has thus far appeared.

Chapter Two: Problems in Biography

1 Samuel Johnson, *The Rambler,* No. 60.

2 James Boswell, *The Life of Samuel Johnson,* Modern Library ed. (New York: Modern Library, [1931]), p. 10.

3 Hazelton Spencer, *The Art and Life of William Shakespeare* (New York: Harcourt Brace, 1940ᶜ), pp. 47–50, 69–70.

4 See, for example, [Sir] E[dmund] K[erchever] Chambers, *William Shakespeare,* 2 vols. (Oxford: Oxford University Press, 1930), II, 35–52; also Rupert Taylor, "John Shakespeare, Corviser of Stratford-on-Avon and the Balsall Shakespeares", *PMLA,* LV (1940), 721–26.

5 Nashe, *Works,* ed. McKerrow, V, 1–34.

6 John Edwin Bakeless, *Christopher Marlowe* (New York: William Morrow, 1937), pp. 353–58; and Frederick S[amuel] Boas, *Christopher Marlowe* (Oxford: Oxford University Press, 1940), pp. 315–28.

7 J[ohn] Leslie Hotson, *The Death of Christopher Marlowe* (London: Nonsuch Press, and Cambridge, Mass.: Harvard University Press, 1925); a more popular and equally interesting account of this discovery is contained in Professor Hotson's article "Tracking Down a Murderer", *Atlantic Monthly,* CXXV (1925), 733–41. Other contributions to the story are mentioned by Dr. Boas in *Christopher Marlowe,* pp. 304–5.

8 M. S. Giuseppi, *A Guide to the Manuscripts in the Public Record Office* (London: H. M. Stationery Office, 1923), 2 vols.

9 E. K. Chambers, *op. cit.,* II, 41–52.

10 Bakeless, *op. cit.,* p. 240.

11 A. C. Baugh, "Kirk's Life Records of Thomas Chaucer", *PMLA,* XLVII (1932), 461–515.

12 *Idem,* "Thomas Chaucer, One Man or Two?", *PMLA,* XLVIII (1933), 328–39; see also John M. Manly, "Thomas Chaucer, Son of Geoffrey", [London] *Times Literary Supplement,* August 3, 1933, p. 525.

13 Russel Krauss, "William Chaumbre, Kinsman of Thomas Chaucer", *PMLA,* XLIX (1934), 954–55.

14 Nellie Slayton Aurner, "Sir Thomas Malory—Historian?", *PMLA,* XLVIII (1933), 362–91.

15 Pearl Hogrefe, "Sir Thomas More's Connection with the Roper Family", *PMLA*, XLVII (1932), 523–33.

16 Edwin R. Casady, "A Reinterpretation of Surrey's Character and Actions", *PMLA*, LI (1936), 626–35.

17 Raymond Jenkins, "Spenser and the Clerkship in Munster", *PMLA*, XLVII (1932), 109–21.

18 Austin K. Gray, "Some Observations on Christopher Marlowe, Government Agent", *PMLA*, XLIII (1928), 682–700.

19 Hubert H. Hoeltje, "Emerson, Citizen of Concord", *AmLit*, XI (1939–40), [367]–78.

20 G. E. Bentley, "Records of Players in the Parish of St. Giles Cripplegate", *PMLA*, XLIV (1929), 789–826.

21 Emma Marshall Denkinger, "Actors' Names in the Registers of St. Botolph Aldgate", *PMLA*, XLI (1926), 91–109.

22 Fred S. Tupper, "Mary Palmer, Alias Mrs. Andrew Marvell", *PMLA*, LIII (1938), 367–92.

23 Kenneth Forward, "De Quincey's *Cessio Bonorum*", *PMLA*, LIV (1939), 511–25.

24 Alwin Thaler, *"Faire Em* (and Shakspere's Company?) in Lancashire", *PMLA*, XLVI (1931), 647–58.

25 Claude Lloyd, "Edmund Waller as a Member of the Royal Society", *PMLA*, XLIII (1928), 162–65 and *idem*, "John Dryden and the Royal Society", *PMLA*, XLV (1930), 967–76.

26 *Henslowe's Diary*, ed. W. W. Greg (London: A. H. Bullen, 1904–8), 2 vols.

27 E. H. C. Oliphant, "Who Was Henry Porter?", *PMLA*, XLIII (1928), 572–75.

28 Alfred Jackson, "Play Notices from the Burney Newspapers 1700–1703", *PMLA*, XLVIII (1933), 815–49.

29 Reproduced in Thomas Kyd, *Works*, ed. F. S. Boas (Oxford: Clarendon Press, 1901), and in *English Literary Autographs, 1550–1650: Part I. Dramatists*, ed. W. W. Greg, no. XV (b).

30 Bakeless, *Christopher Marlowe*, pp. 169–70.

31 Gabriel Harvey, *Foure Letters and Certeine Sonnets*, ed. G. B. Harrison (London: John Lane, [1922]), pp. 18–24.

32 Nashe, *Works*, ed. McKerrow, I, 287–88.

33 Greene, *Works*, ed. Grosart, I, xlvii.

34 *The Plays and Poems of Robert Greene*, ed. J. Churton Collins (Oxford: Oxford University Press, 1905), I, 49.

35 Greene, *The Blacke Bookes Messenger*, ed. G. B. Harrison (London: John Lane, [1924]), p. viii.

36 Ed. W. W. Greg, Vol. I, *passim*.

37 Harold Jenkins, *The Life and Work of Henry Chettle* (London: Sidgwick and Jackson, 1934), p. 29.

38 *Ibid.*, p. 10.

39 Henry Chettle, *Kind-hartes Dreame,* ed. G. B. Harrison (London: John Lane, [1923]), pp. 6–7.

40 J. S. P. Tatlock, "Muriel: The Earliest English Poetess", *PMLA,* XLVIII (1933), 317–21.

41 Marguerite Hearsey, "New Light on the Evidence for Swift's Marriage", *PMLA,* XLII (1927), 157–61.

42 Helen Sard Hughes, "More Popeana: Items from an Unpublished Correspondence", *PMLA,* XLIV (1929), 1090–98.

43 Randall Stewart, "Recollections of Hawthorne by His Sister Elizabeth", *AmLit,* XVI (1944–45), [316]–31.

44 Jennie A. Morgan, "Early Reminiscences of Walt Whitman", *AmLit,* XIII (1941–42), [9]–17.

45 *Cambridge History of English Literature,* IX, 76.

46 Greene, *Works,* ed. Grosart, I, 157, n. c*

47 *Ibid.,* p. 16.

48 *Ibid.,* p. 19, n. 1.

49 Coolidge Otis Chapman, "The Musical Training of the *Pearl* Poet", *PMLA,* XLVI (1931), 177–81.

50 Rudolf Kirk, "References to the Law in *Piers the Plowman*", *PMLA,* XLVIII (1933), 322–37.

51 William Nelson, "Skelton's Quarrel with Wolsey", *PMLA,* LI (1936), 377–98.

52 Charles A. Rouse, "Was Heywood a Servant of the Earl of Southampton?", *PMLA,* XLV (1930), 787–90.

53 J. Milton French, "A New Letter by John Milton", *PMLA,* XLIX (1934), 1069–70.

54 *Idem,* "Milton as a Historian", *PMLA,* L (1935), 469–79.

55 Fannie E. Ratchford, "Charlotte Brontë's Angrian Cycle of Stories", *PMLA,* XLIII (1928), 494–501.

56 Tremaine McDowell, "A Freshman Poem by Emerson", *PMLA,* XLV (1930), 326–29.

57 Irving T. Richards, "Longfellow in England: Unpublished Extracts from His Journal", *PMLA,* LI (1936), 1123–40.

58 K. L. Knickerbocker, "Browning's Letters to Isabella Blagden", *PMLA,* LIV (1939), 565–78, and William O. Raymond, "Browning's Letters to Isabella Blagden: An Addendum", *PMLA,* LV (1940), 614–15.

59 Donald Ramsay Roberts, "The Death Wish of John Donne", *PMLA,* LXII (1947), 958–76.

60 Gerald Giles Grubb, "The Editorial Policies of Charles Dickens", *PMLA,* LVIII (1943), 1110–24.

61 Herbert E. Greene, "Browning's Knowledge of Music", *PMLA,* LXII (1947), 1095–99.

62 Arthur H. Nethercot, "Oscar Wilde and the Devil's Advocate", *PMLA,* LIX (1944), 833–50.

63 Charlton G. Laird, "Tragedy and Irony in *Knickerbocker's History*", *AmLit,* XII (1940–41), [157]–72.

64 J. W. Thomas, "A Hitherto Unpublished Poem by Margaret Fuller", *AmLit*, XV (1943–44), [411]–15.

65 Merton M. Sealts, "Herman Melville's 'I and My Chimney' ", *AmLit*, XIII (1941–42), [142]–54.

66 Walter Blair, "Mark Twain, New York Correspondent", *AmLit*, XI (1939–40), [247]–59; John B. Hoben, "Mark Twain's *A Connecticut Yankee:* A Genetic Study", *AmLit*, XVIII (1946–47), [197]–218; Bradford A. Booth, "Mark Twain's Friendship with Emeline Beach", *AmLit*, XIX (1947–48), [219]–30; and Arthur L. Vogelback, "Mark Twain: Newspaper Contributor", *AmLit*, XX (1948–49), [111]–28.

67 Bradford A. Booth, "Bret Harte Goes East: Some Unpublished Letters", *AmLit*, XIX (1947–48), [318]–35.

68 G. E. Jensen, "Bunner's Letters to Gilder", *AmLit*, XVII (1945–46), [161]–69.

69 Victor A. Elconin, "Stephen Crane at Asbury Park", *AmLit*, XX (1948–49), [275]–89.

70 Reginald L. Cook, "Robert Frost's Asides on His Poetry", *AmLit*, XIX (1947–48), [351]–59.

71 Theodore Howard Banks, "Sidney's *Astrophel and Stella* Reconsidered", *PMLA*, L (1935), 403–12.

72 W. Nelson Francis, "The Original of the *Ayenbite of Inwit*", *PMLA*, LII (1937), 893–95.

73 Donald Weeks, "Samuel Rogers: Man of Taste", *PMLA*, LXII (1947), 472–86; another article on Samuel Rogers is Joseph J. Firebaugh, "Samuel Rogers and American Men of Letters", *AmLit*, XIII (1941–42), [331]–45.

74 B. B. Gamzue, "Elizabeth and Literary Patronage", *PMLA*, XLIX (1934), 1041–49.

75 Helen Estabrook Sandison, "Arthur Gorges, Spenser's Alcyon and Ralegh's Friend", *PMLA*, XLIII (1928), 645–74.

76 Austin Warren, "To Mr. Pope: Epistles from America", *PMLA*, XLVIII (1933), 61–73.

77 Lewis Mansfield Knapp, "The Naval Scenes in *Roderick Random*", *PMLA*, XLIX (1934), 593–98.

78 James H. Pershing, "Keats: When Was He Born and When Did He Die?", *PMLA*, LV (1940), 802–14.

79 William Charvat, "Melville's Income", *AmLit*, XV (1943–44), [251]–61.

80 Sculley Bradley, "Lowell, Emerson, and the *Pioneer*", *AmLit*, XIX (1947–48), [231]–44.

81 William Charvat, "Thomas Bancroft", *PMLA*, XLVII (1932), 753–58.

82 Townsend Scudder, 3rd, "A Chronological List of Emerson's Lectures on His British Lecture Tour of 1847–1848", *PMLA*, LI (1936), 243–48.

83 T. P. Harrison, Jr., "The Relations of Spenser and Sidney", *PMLA*, XLV (1930), 712–31; but see also J. M. Purcell, "The Relations of Spenser and Sidney", *PMLA*, XLVI (1931), 940.

84 Charles E. Ward, "The Publication and Profits of Dryden's *Virgil*", *PMLA*, LIII (1938), 807–12.

85 Kathleen M. Lynch, "Congreve's Irish Friend, Joseph Keally", *PMLA*, LIII (1938), 1076–87, and *idem*, "Henrietta, Duchess of Marlborough", *PMLA*, LII (1937), 1072–93.

86 Dixon Wecter, "The Missing Years in Edmund Burke's Biography", *PMLA*, LIII (1938), 1102–25.

87 Thomas W. Copeland, "Burke and Dodsley's *Annual Register*", *PMLA*, LIV (1939), 223–45.

88 J. Delancey Ferguson, "New Light on the Burns-Dunlop Estrangement", *PMLA*, XLIV (1929), 1106–15.

89 Robert T. Fitzhugh, "Burns' Highland Mary", *PMLA*, LII (1937), 829–34.

90 Earl Leslie Griggs, "Coleridge and Byron", *PMLA*, XLV (1930), 1085–96.

91 Clarence DeWitt Thorpe, "Keats's Interest in Politics and World Affairs", *PMLA*, XLVI (1931), 1228–45.

92 Franklin Gary, "Charlotte Brontë and George Henry Lewes", *PMLA*, LI (1936), 518–42.

93 Ruth Crosby, "Robert Mannyng of Brunne: A New Biography", *PMLA*, LVII (1942), 15–28.

94 Leah Dennis, "Thomas Percy: Antiquarian vs. Man of Taste", *PMLA*, LVII (1942), 140–54.

95 Kenneth Neill Cameron, "Shelley vs. Southey: New Light on an Old Quarrel", *PMLA*, LVII (1942), 489–512.

96 Edwin H. Zeydel, "Washington Irving and Tieck", *PMLA*, XLVI (1931), 946–47.

97 Oscar Cargill, "Nemesis and Nathaniel Hawthorne", *PMLA*, LII (1937), 848–62, and Austin Warren, "Hawthorne, Margaret Fuller, and 'Nemesis'", *PMLA*, LIV (1939), 615–18.

98 Harry R. Warfel, "Margaret Fuller and Ralph Waldo Emerson", *PMLA*, L (1935), 576–94.

99 Harold Blodgett, "Hawthorne as Poetry Critic: Six Unpublished Letters to Lewis Mansfield", *AmLit*, XII (1940–41), [173]–84.

100 Max L. Griffin, "Whittier and Hayne: A Record of Friendship", *AmLit*, XIX (1947–48), [41]–58.

101 S. V. Gapp, "Notes on John Cleveland", *PMLA*, XLVI (1931), 1075–86.

102 J. Milton French, "George Wither in Prison", *PMLA*, XLV (1930), 959–66.

103 John C. Hodges, "Fresh Manuscript Sources for a Life of William Congreve", *PMLA*, LIV (1939), 432–38.

104 Harrison Gray Platt, Jr., "Astrea and Celadon: An Untouched Portrait of Aphra Behn", *PMLA*, XLIX (1934), 544–59.

105 Lewis M. Knapp, "Ann Smollett, Wife of Tobias Smollett", *PMLA*, XLV (1930), 1035–49.

106 Sidney L. Gulick, Jr., "The Publication of Chesterfield's *Letters to His Son*", *PMLA*, LI (1936), 165–77.

107 Donald Francis Connors, "Thomas Morton of Merry Mount: His First Arrival in New England", *AmLit*, XI (1939–40), [160]–66.

108 David V. Erdman, "Lord Byron as Rinaldo", *PMLA*, LVII (1942), 189–231.

109 Dixon Wecter, "Walt Whitman as Civil Servant", *PMLA*, LVIII (1943), 1094–1109.

110 Lewis P. Curtis, "The First Printer of *Tristram Shandy*", *PMLA*, XLVII (1932), 777–89; see also John M. Yoklavich, "Notes on the Early Editions of *Tristram Shandy*", *PMLA*, LXIII (1948), 508–19.

Among other recent articles dealing with biography may be mentioned Marjorie Anderson, "Alice Chaucer and Her Husbands", *PMLA*, LX (1945), 24–47; William Nelson, "Thomas More, Grammarian and Orator", *PMLA*, LVIII (1943), 337–52; Charles Eaton Burch, "Defoe and His Northern Printers", *PMLA*, LX (1945), 121–28; Rae Blanchard, "Was Sir Richard Steele a Freemason?", *PMLA*, LXIII (1948), 903–17; Cecilia Hennel Hendricks, "Thomas De Quincey, Symptomatologist", *PMLA*, LX (1945), 838–40; Wallace W. Douglas, "Wordsworth as Business Man", *PMLA*, LXIII (1948), 625–41; Harold E. Briggs, "Keats's Conscious and Unconscious Reactions to Criticism of *Endymion*", *PMLA*, LX (1945), 1106–29; John Tyree Fain, "Ruskin and His Father", *PMLA*, LIX (1944), 236–42; Stewart W. Holmes, "Browning: Semantic Stutterer", *PMLA*, LX (1945), 231–55; Gertrude Reese, "Robert Browning and His Son", *PMLA*, LXI (1946), 784–803; Edgar Finley Shannon, Jr., "Tennyson and the Reviewers 1830–1842", *PMLA*, LVIII (1943), 181–94; Cecil Lang, "Swinburne and American Literature: With Six Hitherto Unpublished Letters", *AmLit*, XIX (1947–48), [336]–50; Dixon Wecter, "Thomas Paine and the Franklins", *AmLit*, XII (1940–41), [306]–17; *idem*, "Francis Hopkinson and Benjamin Franklin", *AmLit*, XI (1939–40), [200]–17; W. C. Desmond Pacey, "Washington Irving and Charles Dickens", *AmLit*, XVI (1944–45), [332]–39; John T. Flanagan, "Joseph Kirkland, Pioneer Realist", *AmLit*, XI (1939–40), [273]–84; Richard G. Lillard, "Contemporary Reaction to 'The Empire City Massacre' ", *AmLit*, XVI (1944–45), [198]–203; Fred W. Lorch, "Mark Twain and the 'Campaign that Failed' ", *AmLit*, XII (1940–41), [454]–70; Bradford A. Booth, "Unpublished Letters of Bret Harte", *AmLit*, XVI (1944–45), [131]–42; Robert R. Hubach, "Three Uncollected St. Louis Interviews of Walt Whitman", *Amlit*, XIV (1942–43), [141]–47; Luther W. Courtney, "O. Henry's Case Reconsidered", *AmLit*, XIV (1942–43), [361]–71; and Edwin Harrison Cady, "The Neuroticism of William Dean Howells", *PMLA*, LXI (1946), 229–38.

111 A[lexander] C[orbin] Judson, *Life of Edmund Spenser* (Baltimore: Johns Hopkins Press, 1945); this is Vol. VIII of the Variorum Spenser, edited by Edwin Greenlaw and others (Baltimore: Johns Hopkins Press, 1932–47), 8 vols. in 9.

342 *Methods of Research (III, ii, 112)*

112 J. E. Bakeless, *Christopher Marlowe,* and F. S. Boas, *Christopher Marlowe.*

113 E. K. Chambers, *William Shakespeare*; Hazelton Spencer, *The Art and Life of William Shakespeare*; and Marchette [Gaylord] Chute, *Shakespeare of London* (New York: Dutton, 1949).

114 Arthur Bryant, *Samuel Pepys* (New York: Macmillan, and Cambridge: Cambridge University Press, 1933–35), 2 vols.

115 George Wiley Sherburn, *The Early Career of Alexander Pope* (Oxford: Oxford University Press, 1934).

116 Joseph Wood Krutch, *Samuel Johnson* (New York: Holt, 1944.

117 Alan Dugald McKillop, *Samuel Richardson, Printer and Novelist* (Chapel Hill, N. C.: University of North Carolina Press, 1936).

118 David Morris Low, *Edward Gibbon, 1737–1794* (London: Chatto and Windus, 1937).

119 Lewis Gibbs [Joseph Walter Cove], *Sheridan: His Life and His Theatre* (New York: Morrow, 1948).

120 Newman Ivey White, *Shelley* (New York: Knopf, 1940).

121 Hyder Edward Rollins, *The Keats Circle* (Cambridge, Mass.: Harvard University Press, 1948).

122 Peter Quennel, *John Ruskin; the Portrait of a Prophet* (New York: Viking Press, 1949).

123 Ola Elizabeth Winslow, *Jonathan Edwards, 1703–1758* (New York: Macmillan, 1940).

124 Ralph Leslie Rusk, *Life of Ralph Waldo Emerson* (New York: Scribner's, 1949).

125 Odell Shepard, *Pedlar's Progress: The Life of Bronson Alcott* (Boston: Little, Brown, 1937).

126 Randall Stewart, *Nathaniel Hawthorne; a Biography* (New Haven: Yale University Press, 1948), and Robert Cantwell, *Nathaniel Hawthorne, the American Years* (New York: Rinehart, 1948), to be complete in two volumes.

127 Lawrance [Roger] Thompson, *Young Longfellow* (New York: Macmillan, 1938), and Carl L. Johnson, *Professor Longfellow of Harvard* [University of Oregon Monographs, Studies in Literature and Philology, No. 5], (Eugene, Oregon: University of Oregon Press, 1944).

128 Joy Bayless, *Rufus Wilmot Griswold: Poe's Literary Executor* (Nashville, Tenn.: Vanderbilt University Press, 1943).

129 Henry Seidel Canby, *Thoreau* (Boston: Houghton Mifflin, 1939), and Joseph Wood Krutch, *Henry David Thoreau* (New York: Sloane, 1948).

130 George Frisbie Whicher, *This Was a Poet* (New York and London: Scribner's, 1938).

131 DeLancey Ferguson, *Mark Twain: Man and Legend* (Indianapolis, Ind.: Bobbs-Merrill, 1943).

132 William Peirce Randel, *Edward Eggleston* (New York: King's Crown Press, 1946).

133 Vera McWilliams, *Lafcadio Hearn* (Boston: Houghton Mifflin, 1946).

134 Carl Sandburg, *Abraham Lincoln,* Sangamon ed. (New York: Scribner's, 1940), 6 vols.

135 Robert Greene, *Plays and Poems,* ed. Collins, I, 12.

136 J. Leslie Hotson, "Tracking Down a Murderer," *Atlantic Monthly,* CXXXV (1925), 736–40.

137 Storojenko, for example (Robert Greene, *Works,* ed. Grosart, I, 155), and Collins (*op. cit.,* I, 52).

Chapter Three: Problems of Authenticity and Attribution

1 H. M. Paull, *Literary Ethics* (New York: Dutton, 1929), p. 43.

2 *Dictionary of National Biography,* s. n. "Ritson, Joseph".

3 *Camb. Hist. Eng. Lit.,* II, 203–4.

4 Samuel A. Tannenbaum, " 'More About the Bookie of Sir Thomas Moore' ", *PMLA,* XLIII (1928), 767–78; W. W. Greg, " 'T. Goodal' in *Sir Thomas More*", *PMLA,* XLIV (1929), 633–34; Samuel A. Tannenbaum, "Dr. Greg and the 'Goodal' Notation in *Sir Thomas Moore*", *PMLA,* XLIV (1929), 934–38; W. W. Greg, " 'T. Goodal' in *Sir Thomas More*", *PMLA,* XLVI (1931), 268–71; *idem, PQ,* XI (1932), 410; Samuel A. Tannenbaum, "Dr. Tannenbaum Replies", *PQ,* XII (1933), 88–90.

5 A[lfred] W[illiam] Pollard, *Shakespeare Folios and Quartos* (London: Methuen, 1909), pp. 93–94.

6 John Carter and Graham Pollard, *An Enquiry into the Nature of Certain Nineteenth Century Pamphlets* (London: Constable, and New York: Scribner's, 1934), pp. 44 and 47.

7 *Ibid.,* pp. 56–70.

8 Ronald S[almon] Crane, *New Essays by Oliver Goldsmith* (Chicago: University of Chicago Press, 1927), p. xx.

9 K[atherine] C. Balderston, "Dr. Johnson and Burney's *History of Music*", *PMLA,* XLIX (1934), 966–68.

10 Thomas Wellsted Copeland, "Edmund Burke and the Book Reviews in Dodsley's *Annual Register*", *PMLA,* LVII (1942), 448–68.

11 Carolyn W. and Lawrence H. Houtchens, "Three Early Works Attributed to Dickens", *PMLA,* LIX (1944), 226–35.

12 Rollo G. Silver, "Whitman in 1850: Three Uncollected Articles", *AmLit,* XIX (1947–48), [301]–17.

13 Richard Bentley, *Dissertations upon the Epistles of Phalaris . . . and upon the Fables of Æsop,* ed. Alexander Dyce, 2 vols. (London: Macpherson, 1836), I, 355–430; II, 222–37.

14 Frederick Lafayette Jones, "An Experiment with Massinger's Verse", *PMLA,* XLVII (1932), 727–40.

15 *Ibid.,* p. 740.

16 John Archer Gee, "Tindale and the 1533 English *Enchiridion* of Erasmus", *PMLA,* XLIX (1934), 460–71.

17 Wilbur L. Cross, *The History of Henry Fielding*, 3 vols. (New Haven: Yale University Press, 1918), I, 307.

18 Robert Joseph Kane, "Joseph Hall and *Work for Chimney-Sweepers*", *PMLA*, LI (1936), 407–13.

19 Bernard Freyd, "Spenser or Anthony Munday?—A Note on the *Axiochus*", *PMLA*, L (1935), 903–8; Professor Padelford, in a reply (pp. 908–13) did not find the suggestion convincing, pointing out that the spellings referred to can be found in Spenser.

20 Edward S. Parsons, "The Authorship of the Anonymous Life of Milton", *PMLA*, L (1935), 1057–64.

21 Hope Emily Allen, "On the Author of the *Ancren Riwle*", *PMLA*, XLIV (1929), 635–80.

22 Arthur M. Sampley, "Plot Structure in Peele's Plays as a Test of Authorship", *PMLA*, LI (1936), 689–701.

23 George C. Williams, "Did Thomson Write the Poem *To the Memory of Mr. Congreve?*" *PMLA*, XLV (1930), 1010–13.

24 Agnes Duncan Kuersteiner, "E. K. is Spenser", *PMLA*, L (1935), 140–55.

25 *Encyclopædia Britannica*, 14th ed., *s.v.* "Scottish Literature".

26 Oscar Cargill, "The Langland Myth", *PMLA*, L (1935), 35–56.

27 Raymond A. Houk, "Versions of Lindsay's *Satire of the Three Estates*", *PMLA*, LV (1940), 396–405.

28 Henry David Gray, "Thomas Kyd and the First Quarto of *Hamlet*", *PMLA*, XLII (1927), 721–35.

29 John Robert Moore, "The Songs in Lyly's Plays", *PMLA*, XLII (1927), 623–40.

30 John Carter and Graham Pollard, *An Enquiry . . . 19th Century Pamphlets*, p. 228.

31 *Ibid.*, pp. 302–4.

32 Oscar Cargill, "The Authorship of the *Secunda Pastorum*", *PMLA*, XLI (1926), 810–31.

33 Frances A. Foster, "Was Gilbert Pilkington Author of the *Secunda Pastorum?*", *PMLA*, XLIII (1928), 124–36.

34 Henry B. Hinckley, "The Date, Author, and Sources of the *Owl and the Nightingale*", *PMLA*, XLIV (1929), 329–59; the discussion of authorship covers pages 341–43.

35 Edwin Johnston Howard, "Cynewulf's *Christ* 1665–1693", *PMLA*, XLV (1930), 354–67.

36 Carleton Brown, "Chaucer's *Wreched Engendring*", *PMLA*, L (1935), 997–1011; J. S. P. Tatlock, "Has Chaucer's *Wretched Engendering* Been Found?" *MLN*, LI (1936), 275–84; Germaine Dempster, "Did Chaucer Write *An Holy Medytacion?*" *MLN*, LI (1936), 284–95; Carleton Brown, "An Affirmative Reply", *MLN*, LI (1936), 296–300; Germaine Dempster, "Chaucer's *Wretched Engendering* and *An Holy Meditation*", *MP*, XXXV (1937–38), 27–29; Beatrice D. Brown, "Chaucer's *Wreched Engendrynge*",

MP, XXXV (1937–38), 325–33; Mildred Webster, "The Vocabulary of *An Holy Medytacion*", *PQ*, XVII (1938), 359–64.

37 Coolidge Otis Chapman, "The Authorship of the *Pearl*", *PMLA*, XLVII (1932), 346–53.

38 Fred L. Jones, "*The Trial of Chivalry*, a Chettle Play", *PMLA*, XLI (1926), 304–24.

39 Harold Jenkins, *The Life and Work of Henry Chettle*, pp. 255–60.

40 Wilbur D. Dunkel, "The Authorship of *Anything for a Quiet Life*", *PMLA*, XLIII (1928), 793–99.

41 *Idem*, "The Authorship of *The Puritan*", *PMLA*, XLV (1930), 804–8.

42 *Idem*, "The Authorship of *The Revenger's Tragedy*", *PMLA*, XLVI (1931), 781–85.

43 *Idem*, "Did Not Rowley Merely Revise Middleton?" *PMLA*, XLVIII (1933), 799–805.

44 Cyrus L. Day, "Thomas Randolph's Part in the Authorship of *Hey for Honesty*", *PMLA*, XLI (1926), 325–34.

45 *Idem*, "Thomas Randolph and *The Drinking Academy*", *PMLA*, XLIII (1928), 800–9.

46 G. C. Moore Smith, "*The Drinking Academy* and Its Attribution to Thomas Randolph", *PMLA*, XLIV (1929), 631–33.

47 *The Drinking Academy*, ed. Hyder E. Rollins and Samuel A. Tannenbaum (Cambridge, Mass.: Harvard University Press, 1930).

48 G. C. Moore Smith, review of Thomas Randolph, *The Drinking Academy* in *RES*, VI (1930), 476–83.

49 Hyder E. Rollins, "Thomas Randolph, Robert Baron, and *The Drinking Academy*", *PMLA*, XLVI (1931), 786–801.

50 Roswell G. Ham, "Dryden's Dedication for *The Music of the Prophetesse*, 1691", *PMLA*, L (1935), 1065–75.

51 Archie M. Bangs, "*Mephistophiles in England; Or, The Confessions of a Prime Minister*", *PMLA*, XLVII (1932), 200–19.

52 *Ibid.*, p. 210.

53 Mendal G. Frampton, "Gilbert Pilkington Once More", *PMLA*, XLVII (1932), 622–35.

54 Ernest Brennecke, Jr., "Shakespeare's Musical Collaboration with Morley", *PMLA*, LIV (1939), 139–44.

55 John Cuyus Hodges, "The Ballad in Congreve's *Love for Love*", *PMLA*, XLVIII (1933), 953–54.

56 Rae Blanchard, "A Prologue and Epilogue for Nicholas Rowe's *Tamerlane*", *PMLA*, XLVII (1932), 772–76.

57 Frances Winwar, "Dante Gabriel's or William Michael's?" *PMLA*, XLVIII (1933), 312–15.

58 Robert H. Elias, "The First American Novel", *AmLit*, XII (1940–41), [419]–34.

59 Lewis P. Curtis, "Forged Letters of Laurence Sterne", *PMLA*, L (1935), 1076–1106.

60   Ronald S. Crane, *New Essays by Oliver Goldsmith*, p. 98, n. 1.

61   Helen Pennock South, " 'The Question of Halsam' ", *PMLA*, L (1935), 362–71.

62   *Camb. Hist. Eng. Lit.*, II, 184, 190.

63   Greene, *Works*, ed. Grosart, I, lxix.

64   *Camb. Hist. Eng. Lit.*, V, 151–52.

65   C[harles] M[ills] Gayley, *Representative English Comedies*, 3 vols. (New York and London: Macmillan, 1913–16), I, 401.

66   Maxwell B. Gold, "Swift's Admission to Mrs. Whiteway Confirmed", *PMLA*, XLIX (1934), 964–65.

67   Sidney L. Gulick, Jr., "Jonathan Swift's 'The Day of Judgment' ", *PMLA*, XLVIII (1933), 850–55.

68   Myron F. Brightfield, "Lockhart's *Quarterly* Contributors", *PMLA*, LIX (1944), 491–512.

69   John D. Kern, Elisabeth Schneider, and Irwin Griggs, "Lockhart to Croker on the *Quarterly*", *PMLA*, LX (1945), 175–98.

70   Frederick L. Jones, "Hogg and *The Necessity of Atheism*", *PMLA*, LII (1937), 423–26.

71   Kenneth Forward, " 'Libellous Attack' on De Quincey", *PMLA*, LII, (1937), 244–60.

72   William Reitzel, "Sir Walter Scott's Review of Jane Austen's *Emma*", *PMLA*, XLIII (1928), 487–93.

73   Walter Graham, "Scot and Mr. Reitzel", *PMLA*, XLIV (1929), 309.

74   William Reitzel, *PMLA*, XLIV (1929), 310.

75   Charles Beecher Hogan, "Sir Walter Scott and *Emma*", *PMLA*, XLV, (1930), 1264–66.

76   Kenneth Thorpe Rowe, "The Countess of Pembroke's Editorship of the *Arcadia*", *PMLA*, LIV (1939), 122–38; see also *idem*, "Elizabethan Morality and the Folio Revisions of Sidney's *Arcadia*", *MP*, XXXVII (1939), 151–72.

77   Charles A. Rouse, "Thomas Heywood and *The Life and Death of Hector*", *PMLA*, XLIII (1928), 151–72.

78   Thomas F. Mayo, "The Authorship of *The History of John Bull*", *PMLA*, XLV (1930), 274–82.

79   Richard J. Hooker, "John Dickinson on Church and State", *AmLit*, XVI (1944–45), [82]–93.

80   Erwin G. Gudde, "An American Version of *Munchausen*", *AmLit*, XIII (1941–42), [372]–90.

81   For an application of the method advocated in the text see Chauncey Elwood Sanders, "Robert Greene and his 'Editors' ", *PMLA*, XLVIII (1933), 392–417; Harold Jenkins, "On the Authenticity of *Greene's Groatsworth of Wit* and *The Repentance of Robert Greene*", *RES*, XI (1935), 28–41, points out the weaknesses in the case set forth in that article but does not prove that the two works in question are all that they purport to be.

Among other articles dealing with matters of attribution may be mentioned

Donald J. McGinn, "Nashe's Share in the Marprelate Controversy", *PMLA*, LIX (1944), 952–84; *idem*, "The Real Martin Marprelate", *PMLA*, LVIII (1943), 84–107; Ralph W. Berringer, "Thomas Campion's Share in *A Booke of Ayres*", *PMLA*, LVIII (1943), 938–48; Percy Simpson, "The Problem of Authorship of *Eastward Ho*", *PMLA*, LIX (1944), 715–25; Karl J. Arndt, "The Cooper-Sealsfield Exchange of Criticism", *AmLit*, XV (1943–44), [18]–24; Ralph M. Wardle, "Who Was Morgan Odoherty?", *PMLA*, LVIII (1943), 617–27; and Randolph C. Randall, "Authors of the *Port Folio* Revealed by the Hall Files", *AmLit*, XI (1939–40), [379]–416. Two articles dealing with authenticity are: Austin Wright, "The Veracity of Spence's *Anecdotes*", *PMLA*, LXII (1947), 123–29, and Sidney E. Lind, "Poe and Mesmerism", *PMLA*, LXII (1947), 1077–94.

Chapter Four: Problems of Source-Study

1 Robert W. Kenny, "Ralph's *Case of Authors:* Its Influence on Goldsmith and Isaac D'Israeli", *PMLA*, LII (1937), 104–13.

2 Robert H. Wilson, "Reed and Warton on the *Old Wives Tale*", *PMLA*, LV (1940), 605–8.

3 H. C[hichester] Hart, "Robert Greene's Prose Works", *Notes and Queries*, 10th Series, IV (1905), 1–5, 81–84, 162–64, 224–27, 483–85; Roselle Gould Goree, "Concerning Repetitions in Greene's Romances", *PQ*, III (1924), 69–75; C. J. Vincent, "Further Repetitions in the Works of Robert Greene", *PQ*, XVIII (1939), 73–77.

4 Cooper used, in *The Two Admirals*, material from his own *The History of the Navy of the United States of America*, but added material from Lord Collingwood's *Letters*; see Richard H. Ballinger, "Origins of James Fenimore Cooper's *The Two Admirals*", *AmLit*, XX (1948–49), [20]–30. Whitman turned some of his own early prose into poetry; see Willie T. Weathers, "Whitman's Poetic Translations of His 1855 Preface", *AmLit*, XIX (1947–48), [21]–40.

5 Hyder E. Rollins, "Deloney's Sources for Euphuistic Learning", *PMLA*, L (1935), 413–22.

6 J. M. Purcell, "Sidney's *Astrophel and Stella* and Greville's *Cælica*", *PMLA*, L (1935), 413–22.

7 Maurice Kelley, "Milton's Debt to Wolleb's *Compendium Theologiæ Christianæ*", *PMLA*, L (1935), 156–65.

8 *Ibid.*, p. 165.

9 Miriam Gabriel and Paul Mueschke, "Two Contemporary Sources of Sheridan's *The Rivals*", *PMLA*, XLIII (1928), 249–50.

10 Pierrepont H. Nichols, "William Dunbar as a Scottish Lydgatian", *PMLA*, XLVI (1931), 224. Other studies emphasizing the author's originality include W. K. Wimsatt, Jr., "Poe and the Chess Automaton", *AmLit*, XI (1939–40), [138]–51, and Charles Roberts Anderson, "The Genesis of *Billy Budd*", *AmLit*, XII (1940–41), [329]–46.

11   Roger Sherman Loomis, "The Visit to the Perilous Castle", *PMLA*, XLVIII (1933), 1000–35.

12   Beatrice Daw Brown, "Exemplum Materials Underlying *Macbeth*", *PMLA*, L (1935), 700–14.

13   Lee Monroe Ellison, "Elizabethan Drama and the Works of Smollett", *PMLA*, XLIV (1929), 842–62.

14   The influence of Wilkins and Ross upon Milton is brought out in Grant McColley, "Milton's Dialogue on Astronomy: The Principal Immediate Sources", *PMLA*, LII (1937), 128–62, and that of Servetus in Martin A. Larson, "Milton and Servetus: A Study in the Sources of Milton's Theology", *PMLA*, XLI (1926), 891–934. The influence of John Norris upon James Thomson is discussed in Herbert Drennon, "James Thomson and John Norris", *PMLA*, LIII (1938), 1094–1101; and that of Thomas Taylor on William Blake in Frederick Pierce, "Blake and Thomas Taylor", *PMLA*, XLIII (1928), 1121–41, and on Shelley in James A. Notopoulos, "Shelley and Thomas Taylor", *PMLA*, LI (1936), 502–17. Another study of this sort is Victor M. Hamm, "A Seventeenth-Century French Source for Hurd's *Letters on Chivalry and Romance*", *PMLA*, LII (1937), 820–28.

15   Keith Huntress, "Melville's Use of a Source for *White-Jacket*", *AmLit*, XVII (1945–46), [66]–74.

16   *Problems and Methods of Literary History*, pp. 87–96.

17   John Livingston Lowes, *The Road to Xanadu*.

18   *Ibid.*, p. 4, n. *

19   Lucille King, "Text Sources of the Folio and Quarto *Henry VI*", *PMLA*, LI (1936), 702–18.

20   *Ibid.*, p. 718

21   J. Burke Severs, "The Source of Chaucer's *Melibeus*", *PMLA*, L (1935), 92–99.

22   Douglas Bush, "Notes on Marlowe's *Hero and Leander*", *PMLA*, XLIV (1929), 760–64.

23   Rupert Taylor, "A Tentative Chronology of Marlowe's and Some Other Elizabethan Plays", *PMLA*, LI (1936), 643–88.

24   Mary Matheson Wills, "Marlowe's Role in Borrowed Lines", *PMLA*, LII (1937), 902–5.

25   Fred L. Jones, *"The Trial of Chivalry*, a Chettle Play", *PMLA*, XLI (1926), 304–24.

26   Harold Jenkins, *The Life and Work of Henry Chettle*, pp. 259–60.

27   Douglas Bush, "Notes on Keats's Reading", *PMLA*, L (1935), 785–806.

28   Alice Harmon, "How Great Was Shakespeare's Debt to Montaigne?", *PMLA*, LVII (1942), 988–1008.
Other studies based on parallel passages include Keith Huntress, "Another Source for Poe's *Narrative of Arthur Gordon Pym*", *AmLit*, XVI (1944–45), [19]–25 (see also D. M. McKeithan, "Two Sources of Poe's *Narrative of Arthur Gordon Pym*", *University of Texas Bulletin*, XIII (1933), 127–37, and J. O. Bailey, "Sources for Poe's *Arthur Gordon Pym*, 'Hans Pfaal', and

Other Pieces", *PMLA*, LVII (1942), 513–35); J. O. Bailey, "Poe's 'Palæstine' ", *AmLit*, XIII (1941–42), [44]–58; Gladys Carmen Bellamy, "Mark Twain's Indebtedness to John Phœnix", *AmLit*, XIII (1941–42), [29]–43; Paul G. Brewster, "*Jurgen* and *Figures of Earth* and the Russian Skazki", *AmLit*, XIII (1941–42), [305]–19; and Clara Blackburn, "Continental Influences on Eugene O'Neill's Expressionistic Dramas", *AmLit*, XIII (1941–42), [109]–33.

29 *PMLA*, XLV (1930), 169–79.

30 David H. Greene, "*The Shadow of the Glen* and *The Widow of Ephesus*", *PMLA*, LXII (1947), 233–38.

31 *Proceedings of the British Academy*, XII (1926), 98 ff.

32 Marie Padgett Hamilton, "Notes on Chaucer and the Rhetoricians", *PMLA*, XLVII (1932), 403–9.

33 Don Cameron Allen, "The Classical Scholarship of Francis Meres", *PMLA*, XLVIII (1933), 418–25.

34 J. Burke Severs, "Chaucer's Source MSS for the *Clerkes Tale*", *PMLA*, XLVII (1932), 431–52.

35 Clyde K. Hyder, "Swinburne's *Laus Veneris* and the Tannhäuser Legend", *PMLA*, XLV (1930), 1202–13.

36 John C. Pope, "Prufrock and Raskolnikov", *AmLit*, XVII (1945–46), [213]–30.

37 *Idem*, "Prufrock and Raskolnikov Again: A Letter from Eliot", *AmLit*, XVIII (1946–47), [319]–21.

38 R. B. McKerrow, "A Note on 'Henry VI, Part II' and 'The Contention of York and Lancaster' ", *RES*, IX (1933), 157–69, and Lucille King, "*2 and 3 Henry VI*—Which Holinshed?", *PMLA*, L (1935), 745–51.

39 *Problems and Methods of Literary History*, pp. 96–127.

40 D. T. Starnes, "Barnabe Riche's 'Sappho Duke of Mantua' ", *SP*, XXX (1933), 455–72.

41 Willard Thorp, "Redburn's Prosy Old Guidebook", *PMLA*, LIII (1938), 1146–56.

42 Coolidge Otis Chapman, "Virgil and the *Gawain*-Poet", *PMLA*, LX (1945), 16–23.

43 John E. Hankins, "Spenser and the Revelation of St. John", *PMLA*, LX (1945), 364–81, and Dorothy F. Atkinson, "The Pastorella Episode in *The Færie Queene*", *PMLA*, LIX (1944), 361–72.

44 Vincent Luciani, "Bacon and Guicciardini", *PMLA*, LXII (1947), 96–113.

45 Willie T. Weathers, "Edward Taylor, Hellenistic Puritan", *AmLit*, XVIII (1946–47), [18]–26, and Nathalia Wright, "The Morality Tradition in the Poetry of Edward Taylor", *AmLit*, XVIII (1946–47), [1]–17.

46 George E. Hastings, "How Cooper Became a Novelist", *AmLit*, XII (1940–41), [20]–51, and Harold H. Scudder, "Cooper's *The Crater*", *AmLit*, XIX (1947–48), [109]–26; see also Dorothy Dondore, "The Debt of Two Dyed-in-the-Wool Americans to Mrs. Grant's *Memoirs*: Cooper's *Satanstoe* and Paulding's *The Dutchman's Fireside*", *AmLit*, XIII (1941–42), [52]–58.

47 J. D. Yohannan, "The Influence of Persian Poetry upon Emerson's Work", *AmLit*, XV (1943–44), [25]–41.

48 *Problems and Methods*, pp. 101–2.

49 Pauline Aiken, "Arcite's Illness and Vincent of Beauvais", *PMLA*, LI (1936), 361–69.

50 Raymond Jenkins, "The Sources of Drayton's *Battaile of Agincourt*", *PMLA*, XLI (1926), 280–93.

51 Mildred Gayler Christian, "Middleton's Acquaintance with the *Merrie Conceited Jests of George Peele*", *PMLA*, L (1935), 753–60.

52 Lane Cooper, "Dr. Johnson on Oats and Other Grains", *PMLA*, LII (1937), 785–802.

53 Charles B. Qualia, "French Dramatic Sources of Bulwer-Lytton's *Richelieu*", *PMLA*, XLII (1927), 177–84.

54 Clyde K. Hyder, "Wilkie Collins and *The Woman in White*", *PMLA*, LIV (1939), 297–303.

55 Perry D. Westbrook, "Horace's Influence on Shakespeare's *Antony and Cleopatra*", *PMLA*, LXII (1947), 392–98.

56 Edgar Hill Duncan, "Jonson's *Alchemist* and the Literature of Alchemy", *PMLA*, LXI (1946), 699–710.

57 Harold H. Scudder, "Cooper and the Barbary Coast", *PMLA*, LXII (1947), 784–92.

58 John Robert Moore, "A New Source for *Gulliver's Travels*", *SP*, XXXVIII (1941), 66–80.

59 Ralph L. Collins, "Moore's *The Foundling*—An Intermediary", *PQ*, XVII (1938), 139–43.

60 Carleton Brown, "*Beowulf* and the *Blickling Homilies* and Some Textual Notes", *PMLA*, LIII (1938), 905–16.

61 James A. Work, "Echoes of the Anathema in Chaucer", *PMLA*, XLVII (1932), 419–30.

62 Oliver Farrar Emerson, "Saint Ambrose and Chaucer's *Life of St. Cecilia*", *PMLA*, XLI (1926), 252–61.

63 Roberta D. Cornelius, "Corones Two", *PMLA*, XLII (1927), 1055–57.

64 Donald C. Dorian, "Milton's *Epitaphium Damonis*, Lines 181–97", *PMLA*, LIV (1939), 612–13.

65 Wilbur Gaffney, "The Allegory of the Christ-Knight in *Piers Plowman*", *PMLA*, XLVI (1931), 155–68.

66 G. R. Owst, "The 'Angel' and the 'Goliardeys' of Langland's Prologue", *MLR*, XX (1925), 270–79.

67 Clara W. Crane, "A Source for Spenser's Story of Timias and Belphœbe", *PMLA*, XLIII (1928), 635–44.

68 Merrit Y. Hughes, "Virgillian Allegory and *The Færie Queene*," *PMLA*, XLIV (1929), 696–705.

69 Roland M. Smith, "Una and Duessa", *PMLA*, L (1935), 917–19.

70 Israel James Kapstein, "Shelley and Cabanis", *PMLA*, LII (1937), 238–43.

71 Henry B. Hinckley, "The Date, Author, and Sources of the *Owl and the Nightingale*", *PMLA*, XLIV (1929), 329–59.

72 Albert C. Baugh, "A Source for the Middle English Romance, *Athelston*", *PMLA*, XLIV (1929), 377–82.

73 Sanford Brown Meech, "Chaucer and the *Ovide Moralisé*—A Further Study", *PMLA*, XLVI (1931), 182–204.

74 Coolidge Otis Chapman, "Chaucer on Preachers and Preaching", *PMLA*, XLIV (1929), 178–85.

75 John Livingston Lowes, "Moneta's Temple", *PMLA*, LI (1936), 1098–1113.

76 I. J. Kapstein, "The Symbolism of the Wind and the Leaves in Shelley's 'Ode to the West Wind' ", *PMLA*, LI (1936), 1069–79.

77 Leicester Bradner, "The Growth of *Wuthering Heights*", *PMLA*, XLVIII (1933), 129–46.

78 Clyde K. Hyder, "The Mediæval Background of Swinburne's *The Leper*", *PMLA*, XLVI (1931), 1280–88.

79 Henry A. Pochmann, "Irving's German Tour and Its Influence on His Tales", *PMLA*, XLV (1930), 1150–87.

80 H. Arlin Turner, "Hawthorne's Literary Borrowings", *PMLA*, LI (1936), 543–62.

81 Robert Lee Wolff, "The Genesis of 'The Turn of the Screw' ", *AmLit*, XIII (1941–42), [1]–8, and Francis X. Roellinger, Jr., "Psychical Research and 'The Turn of the Screw' ", *AmLit*, XX (1948–49), [401]–23.

82 Rosemond Tuve, "The Red Cross Knight and Mediæval Demon Stories", *PMLA*, XLIV (1929), 714; the article covers pp. 706–14.

83 Aurélien Digeon, "Autour de Fielding: I. Miss Fielding, son frère, et Richardson", *Revue Germanique*, XI (1920), 209–19.

84 Roland M. Smith, "Spenser's Irish River Stories", *PMLA*, L (1935), 1047–56.

85 Sara Ruth Watson, "Sidney at Bartholomew Fair", *PMLA*, LIII (1938), 125–28.

86 "Equine Quartering in *The Owl and the Nightingale*", *PMLA*, LII (1937), 935–45.

87 *Ibid.*, p. 944.

88 Charles Washburn Nichols, "Fielding's Satire on Pantomime", *PMLA*, XLVI (1931), 1107–12.

89 Lewis Mansfield Knapp, "The Naval Scenes in *Roderick Random*", *PMLA*, XLIX (1934), 593–98.

90 Ruth C. Wallerstein, "Personal Experience in Rossetti's *House of Life*", *PMLA*, XLII (1927), 492–504.

91 Nathalia Wright, "The East Tennessee Background of Sidney Lanier's *Tiger-Lilies*", *AmLit*, XIX (1947–48), [127]–38.

92 George Witter Sherman, "The Influence of London on *The Dynasts*", *PMLA*, LXIII (1948), 1017–28.

93 Theodore Howard Banks, "Sidney's *Astrophel and Stella* Reconsidered", *PMLA*, L (1935), 412; the article begins on p. 403.

94 George Winchester Stone, Jr., *"A Midsummer Night's Dream* in the Hands of Garrick and Coleman", *PMLA,* LIV (1939), 467–82.

95 Leicester Bradner, "The First English Novel: A Study of George Gascoigne's *Adventures of Master F. J.*", *PMLA,* XLV (1930), 543–52.

96 John W. Draper, " 'Honest Iago' ", *PMLA,* XLVI (1931), 724–37.

97 Nadine Page, "The Public Repudiation of Hero", *PMLA,* L (1935), 739–44.

98 John W. Draper, "Olivia's Household", *PMLA,* XLIX (1934), 806; the article begins on p. 797.

99 Roy W. Battenhouse, *"Measure for Measure* and Christian Doctrine of the Atonement", *PMLA,* LXI (1946), 1029–59.

100 See, for example, Fred Manning Smith, "The Relation of Coleridge's *Ode on Dejection* to Wordsworth's *Ode on Intimations of Immortality",* *PMLA,* L (1935), 224–34.

101 Leslie Spence, "Tamburlaine and Marlowe", *PMLA,* XLII (1927), 604–22.

102 Paul Mueschke and Jeannette Fleisher, "Jonsonian Elements in the Comic Underplot of *Twelfth Night",* *PMLA,* XLVIII (1933), 722–40.

103 Arthur H. Nethercot, "The Dramatic Background of Royall Tyler's *The Contrast",* *AmLit,* XII (1940–41), [435]–46.

104 Bertrand Evans, "Manfred's Remorse and Dramatic Tradition", *PMLA,* LXII (1947), 752–73.

105 E. Wayne Marjarum, "Wordsworth's *View of the State of Ireland",* *PMLA,* LV (1940), 608–11.

106 Eleanor Dickinson Blodgett, "Bacon's *New Atlantis* and Campanella's *Civitatis Solis*: A Study in Relationships", *PMLA,* XLVI (1931), 763–80.

107 S. Foster Damon, "Milton and Marston", *PMLA,* XLII (1927), 873–74.

108 Daniel Morley McKeithan, "The Occasion of *MacFlecknoe",* *PMLA,* XLVII (1932), 766–71.

109 John Harrington Smith, "Genesis of *The Borderers",* *PMLA,* XLIX (1934), 922–30.

110 Wayne Burns and Emerson Grant Sutcliffe, *"Uncle Tom* and Charles Reade", *AmLit,* XVII (1945–46), [333]–47.

111 E[ustace] M[andeville] W[etenhall] Tillyard, *Milton* (London: Chatto and Windus, 1946, and New York: Macmillan, 1947), p. 298.

112 Wylie Sypher, "Chatterton's *African Eclogues* and the Deluge", *PMLA,* LIV (1939), 246–60.

113 Wallace Cable Brown, "Prose Fiction and English Interest in the Near East, 1775–1825", *PMLA,* LIII (1938), 827–36.

114 Charles B. Woods, "Notes on Three of Fielding's Plays", *PMLA,* LII (1937), 359–73.

115 Ibid., p. 360.

116 Ibid., pp. 362–68.

117 Ibid., p. 373.

118 Helen Sandison, "An Elizabethan Basis for a Hardy Tale?", *PMLA,* LIV (1939), 610–12.

119 Gertrude Van Arsdale Ingalls, "Some Sources of Goldsmith's *She Stoops to Conquer*", *PMLA*, XLIV (1929), 565–68.

120 Wayne Burns, "The Sheffield Flood: A Critical Study of Charles Reade's Fiction", *PMLA*, LXIII (1948), 686–95.

121 Henry F. Pommer, "Herman Melville and the Wake of the *Essex*", *AmLit*, XX (1948–49), [290]–304.

122 Elisabeth Lee Buckingham, "Campion's *Arte of English Poesie* and Middleton's *Chaste Maid in Cheapside*", *PMLA*, XLIII (1928), 784–92.

123 Francis P. Magoun, Jr., "The Source of Chaucer's *Rime of Sir Thopas*", *PMLA*, XLII (1927), 833–44; the source suggested is the Ile d'Or episode in *Libeaus Desconus*.

124 Thomas H. McNeal, *"The Clerk's Tale* as a Possible Source for *Pandosto*", *PMLA*, XLVII (1932), 453–60.

125 Oscar James Campbell, "The Relation of *Epicœne* to Aretino's *Il Marescalco*", *PMLA*, XLVI (1931), 752–62.

126 T. P. Harrison, Jr., "A Probable Source of Beaumont and Fletcher's *Philaster*", *PMLA*, XLI (1926), 294–303.

127 C. R. Baskervill, "Sidney's *Arcadia* and *The Tryall of Chevalry*", *MP*, X (1912), 197–201, and Frederic L. Jones, "Another Source for *The Trial of Chivalry*", *PMLA*, XLVII (1932), 668–70.

128 Joseph Toy Curtiss, "Butler's *Sidrophel*", *PMLA*, XLIV (1929), 1077–78; the article begins on p. 1066.

129 Charles J. Hill, "Shenstone and Richard Graves's *Columella*", *PMLA,* XLIX (1934), 566–76.

130 M. Ray Adams, "Joseph Fawcett and Wordsworth's Solitary", *PMLA,* XLVIII (1933), 508–28.

131 Paul Mueschke and Earl Leslie Griggs, "Wordsworth as the Prototype of the Poet in Shelley's *Alastor*", *PMLA*, XLIX (1934), 229–45, and Marcell Kessel, "The Poet in Shelley's *Alastor*", *PMLA*, LI (1936), 302–12.

132 A. Lionel Stevenson, *"Vanity Fair* and Lady Morgan", *PMLA,* XLVIII (1933), 547–51.

133 Alfred A. Kern, "Hawthorne's *Feathertop* and R. L. R.", *PMLA*, LII (1937), 503–10.

134 Hallett D. Smith, *"A Woman Killed with Kindness*", *PMLA*, LIII (1938), 138–47.

135 Robert T. Fitzhugh, "Burns' Highland Mary", *PMLA*, LII (1937), 829–34.

136 Olin H. Moore, "Shakespeare's Deviations from *Romeus and Iuliet*", *PMLA*, LII (1937), 68–74.

137 Beatrice Daw Brown, "Marlowe, Faustus, and Simon Magus", *PMLA*, LIV (1939), 82–121.

138 M. F. Ashley Montagu, "Tyson's *Orang-Outang, Sive Homo Sylvestris*", *PMLA*, LIX (1944), 84–89.

139 Carlos Baker, "The Source-Book for Hudson's *Green Mansions*", *PMLA*, LXI (1946), 252–57.

140 Roger Sherman Loomis, "Gawain, Gwri, and Chuchulinn", *PMLA*, XLIII (1928), 384–96.

141 Robert W. Seitz, "The Irish Background of Goldsmith's Social and Political Thought", *PMLA*, LII (1937), 405–11.

142 C. M. Webster, "The Satiric Background of the Attack on the Puritans in Swift's *A Tale of a Tub*", *PMLA*, L (1935), 210–23, and Clarence M. Webster, "Swift and Some Earlier Satirists of Puritan Enthusiasm", *PMLA*, XLVIII (1933), 1141–53.

143 George Arms, "The Literary Background of Howells's Social Criticism", *AmLit*, XIV (1942–43), [260]–76.

144 Among these may be mentioned Edwin Greenlaw, "Spenser and Lucretius", *SP*, XVII (1920), 320–59; *idem*, "Some Old Religious Cults", *SP*, XX (1923), 216 ff.; *idem*, "Spenser's '*Mutabilitie*'", *PMLA*, XLV (1930), 684–703; H. M. Belden, "Alanus de Insulis, Giles Fletcher, and the 'Mutabilitie' Cantos", *SP*, XXVI (1929), 142–44; Ronald B. Levinson, "Spenser and Bruno", *PMLA*, XLIII (1928), 675–81; and Evelyn May Albright, "Spenser's Cosmic Philosophy and His Religion", *PMLA*, XLIV (1929), 715–59.

145 Constance Miriam Syford, "The Direct Source of the Pamela-Cecropia Episode in the *Arcadia*", *PMLA*, XLIX (1934), 472–89.

146 Newton P. Stallknecht, "Wordsworth and Philosophy", *PMLA*, XLIV (1929), 116–43, and *idem*, "Wordsworth's *Ode to Duty* and the Schöne Seele", *PMLA*, LII (1937), 230–37.

147 Dorothy S. Bucks and Arthur H. Nethercot, "Ibsen and Herne's *Margaret Fleming*: A Study of the Early Ibsen Movement in America", *AmLit*, XVII (1945–46), [311]–33. See also Arthur Hobson Quinn, "Ibsen and Herne—Theory and Facts", *AmLit*, XIX (1947–48), [171]–77, and Dorothy S. Bucks and Arthur H. Nethercot, "A Reply to Professor Quinn", *ibid.*, pp. 177–80.

148 Harold Golder, "Bunyan and Spenser", *PMLA*, XLV (1930), 237; the article begins on p. 216.

149 Wilson C. Clough, "Henry Vaughan and the Hermetic Philosophy", *PMLA*, XLVIII (1933), 1108–30.

150 Herbert Drennon, "Henry Needler and Shaftesbury", *PMLA*, XLVI (1931), 1095–1106.

151 Grace Warren Landrum, "More Concerning Chapman's Homer and Keats", *PMLA*, XLII (1927), 986–1009.

152 Hugh H. MacMullan, "The Satire of Walker's *Vagabond* on Rousseau and Godwin", *PMLA*, LII (1937), 215–29; see also above, n. 15.

153 Wilbur Gaffney, "The Allegory of the Christ-Knight in *Piers Plowman*", *PMLA*, XLVI (1931), 155–68.

154 Benjamin S. Harrison, "Medieval Rhetoric in the *Book of the Duchess*", *PMLA*, XLIX (1934), 428–42.

155 Gordon Hall Gerould, "The Gawain Poet and Dante: A Conjecture", *PMLA*, LI (1936), 31–36.

156 William Ringler, "The Immediate Source of Euphuism", *PMLA*, LIII (1938), 678–86.

157 Ruth C. Wallerstein, "The Style of Drummond of Hawthornden in Its Relation to His Translations", *PMLA*, XLVIII (1933), 1090–1107; this article speaks of indebtedness to Petrarch, Tasso, Marino, Sannazarro, and others. Herbert H. Umbach, "The Rhetoric of Donne's Sermons", *PMLA*, LII (1937), 354–58, traces Donne's style to Keckermann's *Rhetoricæ Ecclesiasticæ* and to Tertullian as well as to the King James Bible. A difference of opinion exists as to the reason for a change in Abraham Cowley's prose style; see Richard F. Jones, "Science and English Prose Style in the Third Quarter of the Seventeenth Century", *PMLA*, XLV (1930), 977–1009; *idem*, *PMLA*, XLVI (1931), 965–67; and Arthur H. Nethercot, "Concerning Cowley's Prose Style", *PMLA*, XLVI (1931), 962–65.

158 David H. Greene, "Synge's Unfinished Deirdre", *PMLA*, LXIII (1948), 1314–21.

159 F. DeWolfe Miller, "The Basis for Poe's 'The Island of the Fay'", *AmLit*, XIV (1942–43), [135]–40.

160 Margaret Farrand Thorp, "Shakespeare and the Fine Arts", *PMLA*, XLVI (1931), 672–93.

161 John M. Manly, "Shakespeare Himself", *Memorial Volume to Shakespeare and Harvey* (Austin, Texas: University of Texas, 1916).

162 Walter Dexter and J[ames] W[illiam] T[homas] Ley, *The Origin of Pickwick* (London: Chapman and Hall, [1936]).

163 Robert Louis Stevenson, *Works*, South Seas edition (New York: Scribner's, 1925), VI, xvi–xvii and xxvii–xxviii.

164 J. Milton French, "Othello among the Anthropophagi", *PMLA*, XLIX (1934), 807–9.

165 Claude Lloyd, "Shadwell and the Virtuosi", *PMLA*, XLIV (1929), 472–94.

166 Harold H. Scudder, "Thackeray and Sir Martin Archer Shee", *PMLA*, LXI (1946), 203–10.

Additional examples of source study are: Dudley R. Johnson, "'Homicide' in the *Parson's Tale*", *PMLA*, LVII (1942), 51–56; Marshall W. Stearns, "The Planet Portraits of Robert Henryson", *PMLA*, LIX (1944), 911–27; Robert H. Wilson, "The 'Fair Unknown' in Malory", *PMLA*, LVIII (1943), 1–21; Elizabeth M. Nugent, "Sources of John Rastell's *The Nature of the Four Elements*", *PMLA*, LVII (1942), 74–88; Johnstone Parr, "More Sources of Rastell's *Interlude of the Four Elements*", *PMLA*, LX (1945), 48–58; G. J. Engelhardt, "The Relation of Sherry's *Treatise of Schemes and Tropes* to Wilson's *Arte of Rhetorique*", *PMLA*, LXII (1947), 76–82; D. T. Starnes, "Shakespeare and Apuleius", *PMLA*, LX (1945), 1021–50; Fred Manning Smith, "The Relation of *Macbeth* to *Richard the Third*", *PMLA*, LX (1945), 1003–20; Raymond A. Houk, "*Doctor Faustus* and *A Shrew*", *PMLA*, LXII

(1947), 950–57; Ralph H. Singleton, "Milton's *Comus* and the *Comus* of Erycius Puteanus", *PMLA*, LVIII (1943), 949–57; Gretchen Ludke Finney, "Chorus in *Samson Agonistes*", *PMLA*, LVIII (1943), 649–64; Samuel Kliger, "The 'Urbs Æterna' in *Paradise Regained*", *PMLA*, LXI (1946), 474–91; John F. Moore, "The Originality of Rochester's *Satyr Against Mankind*", *PMLA*, LVIII (1943), 393–401; E. L. McAdam, Jr., "Johnson's Lives of Sarpi, Blake, and Drake", *PMLA*, LVIII (1943), 466–76; Winifred Lynskey, "Pluche and Derham, New Sources of Goldsmith", *PMLA*, LVII (1942), 435–45; William Palmer Hudson, "Archibald Alison and William Cullen Bryant", *AmLit*, XII (1940–41), [59]–68; W. K. Wimsatt, Jr., "What Poe Knew about Cryptography", *PMLA*, LVIII (1943), 754–79; Nathalia Wright, "Biblical Allusion in Melville'sProse", *AmLit*, XII (1940–41), [185]–99; Lyndon Upson Pratt, "A Possible Source of *The Red Badge of Courage*", *AmLit*, XI (1939–40), [1]–10; and Russell K. Alspach, "Some Sources of Yeats's *The Wanderings of Oisin*", *PMLA*, LVIII (1943), 849–66.

Chapter Five: Problems in Chronology

1   *Problems and Methods*, p. 133.

2   See McKerrow, *Introduction to Bibliography*, p. 101, n. 1.

3   C. M. Briquet, *Les Filigranes* is the standard work on watermarks; see above, p. 12.

4   John Carter and Graham Pollard, *An Enquiry . . . Nineteenth Century Pamphlets*, pp. 42–55.

5   See McKerrow, *Printers' and Publishers' Devices . . . 1485–1640*, p. li.

6   Leicester Bradner, "Henry Cheke's *Freewyl*", *PMLA*, XLIX (1934), 1036–40.

7   E[velyn] M[ay] Albright, "Spenser's Reason for Rejecting the Cantos of Mutability", *SP*, XXV (1928), 93–127; *idem*, "On the Dating of Spenser's Mutability Cantos", *SP*, XXVI (1929), 482–98.

8   Douglas Bush, "The Date of Spenser's *Cantos of Mutability*", *PMLA*, XLV (1930), 954–57.

9   Lisle C. John, "The Date of the Marriage of Penelope Devereux", *PMLA*, XLIX (1934), 961–62.

10   Ella T. Riske, "The Date and Occasion of Waller's *Panegyric to My Lord Protector*", *PMLA*, XLIII (1928), 1201–2.

11   John C. Hodges, "The Composition of Congreve's First Play", *PMLA*, LVIII (1943), 971–76.

12   James F. Fullington, "The Dating of Shenstone's Letters", *PMLA*, XLVI (1931), 1128–36.

13   George W. Whiting, "A Pseudonymous Reply to Milton's *Of Prelatical Episcopacy*", *PMLA*, LI (1936), 430–35.

14   Haldeen Braddy, "The Two Petros in the 'Monkes Tale'", *PMLA*, L (1935), 69–80.

15 Leicester Bradner, "Henry Cheke's *Freewyl*", *PMLA*, XLIX (1934), 1036–40.

16 Philip H. Gray, Jr., "Lenten Casts and the Nursery: Evidence for the Dating of Certain Restoration Plays", *PMLA*, LIII (1938), 781–94.

17 Charles Eugene Ward, "The Dates of Two Dryden Plays", *PMLA*, LI (1936), 186–92.

18 See Henry B. Hinckley, "The Date, Author, and Sources of the *Owl and the Nightingale*", *PMLA*, XLIV (1929), 329–59; Frederick Tupper, "The Date and Historical Background of *The Owl and the Nightingale*," *PMLA*, XLIX (1934), 406–27; and Kathryn Huganir, "Further Notes on the Date of *The Owl and the Nightingale*", *Anglia*, LXIII (1939), 113–34.

19 Leicester Bradner, "Henry Cheke's *Freewyl*", *PMLA*, XLIX (1934), 1036–40.

20 Minnie E. Wells, "The *South English Legendary* in Its Relation to the *Legenda Aurea*," *PMLA*, LI (1936), 337–60.

21 Oscar Cargill, "The Date of the A-Text of Piers Ploughman", *PMLA*, XLVII (1932), 354–62; Bernard F. Huppé, "The A-Text of *Piers Plowman* and the Norman Wars", *PMLA*, LIV (1939), 37–64; and Eleanor H. Kellogg, "Bishop Brunton and the Fable of the Rats", *PMLA*, L (1935), 57–68.

22 Sister Mary Aquinas Devlin, "The Chronology of Bishop Brunton's Sermons", *PMLA*, LI (1936), 300–2; a later article by the same author is "Bishop Thomas Brunton and His Sermons", *Speculum*, XIV (1939), 324–44.

23 Mendal G. Frampton, "The Date of the Flourishing of the 'Wakefield Master' ", *PMLA*, L (1935), 631–60.

24 William Nelson, "Skelton's *Speak, Parrot*", *PMLA*, LI (1936), 59–82.

25 H. L. R. Edwards, "The Dating of Skelton's Later Poems", *PMLA*, LIII (1938), 601–11; for a reply, rejoinder, and sur-rejoinder, see *ibid.*, pp. 611–22.

26 See above, n. 19.

27 William Cliff Martin, "The Date and Purpose of Spenser's *Veue*", *PMLA*, XLVII (1932), 137–43.

28 Garrett Mattingly, "The Date of Shakespeare's Sonnet CVII", *PMLA*, XLVIII (1933), 705–21; see also below, p. 363, n. 16.

29 Donald J. McGinn, "A New Date for *Antonio's Revenge*", *PMLA*, LIII (1938), 129–37.

30 Louise Pound, "On the Dating of the English and Scottish Ballads", *PMLA*, XLVII (1932), 10–16.

31 Albert H. Tolman, *"Mary Hamilton:* The Group Authorship of Ballads", *PMLA*, XLII (1927), 422–32.

32 J. Milton French, "That Late Villain Milton", *PMLA*, LV (1940), 102–15; see also Maurice Kelley, "Addendum: The Later Career of Daniel Skinner", *PMLA*, LV (1940), 116–18.

33 Eleanor Grace Clark, "The York Plays and the *Gospel of Nichodemus*", *PMLA*, XLIII (1928), 153–61.

34 Rupert Taylor, "A Tentative Chronology of Marlowe's and Some Other Elizabethan Plays", *PMLA*, LI (1936), 643–88.

35 Mary Matheson Wills, "Marlowe's Role in Borrowed Lines", *PMLA*, LII (1937), 902–5.

36 Raymond A. Houk, "Shakespeare's *Shrew* and Greene's *Orlando*", *PMLA*, LXII (1947), 657–71.

37 John C. Hodges, "The Dating of Congreve's Letters", *PMLA*, LI (1936), 153–64.

38 M. Channing Linthicum, "The Date of *Cambyses*", *PMLA*, XLIX (1934), 959–61.

39 Mendal G. Frampton, "The Date of the 'Wakefield Master': Bibliographical Evidence", *PMLA*, LIII (1938), 86–117.

40 John Harrington Smith, "The Date of Some Wakefield Borrowings from York", *PLMA*, LIII (1938), 595–600.

41 Frederick M. Padelford, "The *Cantos of Mutabilitie*: Further Considerations Bearing on the Date", *PMLA*, XLV (1930), 704–11.

42 J. M. Purcell, "The Date of Spenser's *Mutabilitie Cantos*", *PMLA*, L (1935), 917; the article begins on p. 914.

43 *Ibid.*, p. 917.

44 Roland Bassett Botting, "The Composition of the *Shepheardes Calender*", *PMLA*, L (1935), 423–34.

45 Mody C. Boatright, "Scott's Theory and Practice Concerning the Use of the Supernatural in Prose Fiction in Relation to the Chronology of the Waverley Novels", *PMLA*, L (1935), 235–61, and Robert D. Mayo, "The Chronology of the Waverley Novels: The Evidence of the Manuscripts", *PMLA*, LXIII (1948), 935–49.

Other studies in chronology include Johnstone Parr, "The Date and Revision of Chaucer's *Knight's Tale*", *PMLA*, LX (1945), 307–24; Mendal G. Frampton, "The Processus Talentorum (Towneley XXIV)", *PMLA*, LIX (1944), 646–54; Emmett L. Avery and A. H. Scouten, "A Tentative Calendar of Daily Theatrical Performances in London, 1700–1701 to 1704–05", *PMLA*, LXIII (1948), 114–80; James A. Notopoulos, "The Dating of Shelley's Prose", *PMLA*, LVIII (1943), 477–98; Arthur Stuart Pitt, "The Sources, Significance, and Date of Franklin's 'An Arabian Tale' ", *PMLA*, LVII (1942), 155–68; William B. Hamilton, "The Theater in the Old Southwest: The First Decade at Natchez", *AmLit*, XII (1940–41), [471]–85; Roger P. McCutcheon, "The First English Plays in New Orleans", *AmLit*, XI (1939–40), [183]–99; and Carl F. Strauch, "The Background for Emerson's 'Boston Hymn' ", *AmLit*, XIV (1942–43), [36]–47.

Chapter Six: Problems of Success and Influence

1 Clarence Gohdes, "The 1876 English Subscription for Whitman", *MLN*, L (1935), 252–58.

2 Bernard M. Wagner, "New Allusions to *A Game at Chesse*", *PMLA*, XLIV (1929), 827–34.

3 Kenneth N. Cameron and Horst Frenz, "The Stage History' of Shelley's *The Cenci*", *PMLA*, LX (1945), 1080–1105.

4 Charles C. Bell, "A History of Fairfax Criticism", *PMLA*, LXII (1947), 644–56.

5 Austin Warren, "Crashaw's Reputation in the Nineteenth Century", *PMLA*, LI (1936), 769–85.

6 Frederic T. Blanchard, *Fielding the Novelist: A Study in Literary Reputation* (New Haven: Yale University Press, 1926).

7 Lee Elbert Holt, "Samuel Butler's Rise to Fame", *PMLA*, LVII (1942), 867–78.

8 J. D. Jump, "Ruskin's Reputation in the Eighteen-Fifties: The Evidence of the Three Principal Weeklies", *PMLA*, LXIII (1948), 678–85.

9 Walter Blair, "The Popularity of Nineteenth-Century American Humorists", *AmLit*, III (1931–32), [175]–84.

10 Elmer B. Potter, "The Paradox of Congreve's *Mourning Bride*", *PMLA*, LVIII (1943), 977–1001.

11 Willard Thorp, " 'Grace Greenwood' Parodies *Typee*", *AmLit*, IX (1937–38), [455]–57.

12 Erwin G. Gudde, "E. Th. A. Hoffmann's Reception in England", *PMLA*, XLI (1926), 1005–10.

13 Austin Warren, "To Mr. Pope: Epistles from America", *PMLA*, XLVIII (1933), 61–73.

14 Thomas P. Haviland, *The* Roman de Longue Haleine *on English Soil* (Philadelphia: privately printed, 1931); see also *idem*, "The Serpent in Milady's Library", *University of Pennsylvania Library Chronicle*, IV (1936), 57–61.

15 E. Preston Dargan, "Byron's Fame in France", *Virginia Quarterly Review*, II (1926), 530–41.

16 Clarence Gohdes, "Longfellow and His Authorized British Publishers", *PMLA*, LV (1940), 1165–79.

17 Harold Blodgett, "Walt Whitman in England", *American Mercury*, XVII (1929), 490–96.

18 Charles Anderson, "Melville's English Debut", *AmLit*, XI (1939–40), [23]–38.

19 George Sanderlin, "The Repute of Shakespeare's Sonnets in the Early Nineteenth Century", *MLN*, LIV (1939), 462–66.

20 Charles E. Burch, "Notes on the Contemporary Popularity of Defoe's *Review*", *PQ*, XVI (1937), 210–13.

21 Charles R. Anderson, "Contemporary American Opinions of *Typee* and *Omoo*", *AmLit*, IX (1937–38), [1]–25.

22 Hyder Edward Rollins, *Keats' Reputation in America to 1848* (Cambridge, Mass.: Harvard University Press, 1946).

23 Richard Clarence Harrison, "Walt Whitman and Shakespeare", *PMLA*, XLIV (1929), 1201–38.

24 David Lee Clark, "Shelley and Shakespeare", *PMLA*, LIV (1939), 287; the article extends from p. 261 to p. 287. See also Sara Ruth Watson, "Shelley and Shakespeare: An Addendum", *PMLA*, LV (1940), 612–13.

25 Edith Peairs, "The Hound, the Bay Horse, and the Turtle-Dove: A Study of Thoreau and Voltaire", *PMLA*, LII (1937), 863–69.

26 Earle Vonard Weller, "Keats and Mary Tighe", *PMLA*, XLII (1927), 963–85.

27 Merrit Y. Hughes, "Virgil and Spenser", *University of California Publications in English*, II (1929), 263–418.

28 A[shley] H[orace] Thorndike, *The Influence of Beaumont and Fletcher on Shakespeare* (Worcester, Mass.: C. B. Wood, 1901).

29 Floyd Dell, "Keats' Debt to Robert Burton", *Bookman*, LXVII (1928), 13–17.

30 H. E. Briggs, "Swift and Keats", *PMLA*, LXI (1946), 1101–8.

31 John F. Ross, "The Character of Poor Richard: Its Sources and Alteration", *PMLA*, LV (1940), 785–94.

32 Thomas P. Haviland, "A Measure for the Early Freneau's Debt to Milton", *PMLA*, LV (1940), 1033–40.

33 John Livingston Lowes, "*The Witch of Atlas* and *Endymion*", *PMLA*, LV (1940), 203–6.

34 Hill Shine, "The Influence of Keats upon Rossetti", *Englische Studien*, LXI (1926–27), 183–210.

35 Clarice Short, "William Morris and Keats", *PMLA*, LIX (1944), 513–23.

36 Wilmon Brewer, *Shakespeare's Influence on Walter Scott* (Boston: Cornhill, 1925).

37 P. L. Carver, "The Influence of Maurice Morgann", *RES*, VI (1930), 320–22.

38 John Hawley Roberts, "'Vision and Design' in Virginia Woolf", *PMLA*, LXI (1946), 835–47.

39 Vivienne Koch Macleod, "The Influence of Ibsen on Joyce", *PMLA*, LX (1945), 879–98.

40 Joseph M. Beatty, Jr., "Churchill's Influence on Minor Eighteenth Century Satirists", *PMLA*, XLII (1927), 162–76.

41 Jesse Sidney Goldstein, "Two Literary Radicals: Garland and Markham in Chicago, 1893", *AmLit*, XVII (1945–46), [152]–60.

42 Rufus A. Coleman, "Trowbridge and Whitman", *PMLA*, LXIII (1948), 262–73.

43 Norman L. Torrey, "Bolingbroke and Voltaire—A Fictitious Influence", *PMLA*, XLII (1927), 788–97.

44 Edmund L. Freeman, "Bacon's Influence on John Hall", *PMLA*, XLII (1927), 385–99.

45 Elizabeth Atkins, "Points of Contact between Byron and Socrates", *PMLA*, XLI (1926), 402–23.

46 John Brooks Moore, "Emerson on Wordsworth", *PMLA*, XLI (1926), 179–92.

47 David Lee Clark, "Shelley and Bacon", *PMLA*, XLVIII (1933), p. 546; the article begins on p. 529.

48 Eleanor Sickels, "Shelley and Charles Brockden Brown", *PMLA*, XLV (1930), 1116–28.

49 Albert Morton Turner, "A Study of Clough's *Mari Magno*", *PMLA*, XLIV (1929), 569–89.

50 Reuben Arthur Brower, "Dryden's Epic Manner and Virgil", *PMLA*, LV (1940), 119–38.

51 John H. Wilson, "The Influence of Beaumont and Fletcher on Restoration Drama", *Ohio State University Contributions in Language and Literature*, No. 4 (1928). See also Donald J. Rulfs, "Beaumont and Fletcher on the London Stage 1776–1833", *PMLA*, LXIII (1948), 1245–64.

52 Ralph M. Wardle, "Thomas Vaughan's Influence upon the Poetry of Henry Vaughan", *PMLA*, LI (1936), 936–52.

53 A[lexander] C[orbin] Judson, "The Source of Henry Vaughan's Ideas Concerning God in Nature", *SP*, XXIV (1937), 529–606.

54 Wayne Burns, "Pre-Raphaelitism in Charles Reade's Early Fiction", *PMLA*, LX (1945), 1149–64, and A. Dwight Culler, "Edward Bysshe and the Poet's Handbook", *PMLA*, LXIII (1948), 858–85.

55 Pierrepont Herrick Nichols, "Lydgate's Influence on the Aureate Terms of the Scottish Chaucerians", *PMLA*, XLVII (1932), 516–22.

56 Henry R. Fairclough, "The Influence of Virgil upon the Forms of English Verse", *Classical Journal*, XXVI (1930–31), 74–94.

57 James R. Foster, "The Abbé Prévost and the English Novel", *PMLA*, XLII (1927), 443–64.

58 R. W. Babcock, "The Mediaeval Setting of Chaucer's *Monk's Tale*", *PMLA*, XLVI (1931), 205–13.

59 Grace Jameson, "Irish Poets of Today and Blake", *PMLA*, LIII (1938), 575–92.

60 Ralph Hinsdale Goodale, "Schopenhauer and Pessimism in Nineteenth Century English Literature", *PMLA*, XLVII (1932), 260; the article covers pp. 241–61.

61 James H. Warner, "The Reaction in Eighteenth-Century England to Rousseau's Two *Discours*", *PMLA*, XLVIII (1933), 471–87.

62 Ruth O. Rose, "Poetic Hero-Worship in the Late Eighteenth Century", *PMLA*, XLVIII (1933), 1182–1202.

63 William P. Cummings, "The Influence of Ovid's *Metamorphoses* on Spenser's 'Mutabilitie' Cantos", *SP*, XXVIII (1931), 241–56.

64 Richmond P. Bond, "–IAD: A Progeny of the *Dunciad*", *PMLA*, XLIV (1929), 1099–1105.

65 William S. Clark, "The Sources of the Restoration Heroic Play", *RES*, IV (1928), 49–63; Kathleen M. Lynch, "Conventions of Platonic Drama in the Heroic Plays of Orrery and Dryden", *PMLA*, XLIV (1929), 456–71; William S. Clark, "The Platonic Element in the Restoration Heroic Play", *PMLA*, XLV (1930), 623–24; reply by Professor Lynch, *ibid.*, pp. 625–26.

66 C. H. Maynadier, *"Ivanhoe* and Its Literary Consequences", *MLN,* XLI (1926), 45–47.

67 Charles Sears Baldwin, "Cicero on Parnassus", *PMLA,* XLII (1927), 106–12.

68 Robert Withington, " 'Vice' and 'Parasite'. A Note on the Evolution of the Elizabethan Villain", *PMLA,* XLIX (1934), 743–51.

69 Theodore Hornberger, "Painters and Paintings in the Writings of F. Hopkinson Smith", *AmLit,* XVI (1944–45), [1]–10.

70 Lieut. Cyrille Arnsvon, "Theodore Dreiser and Painting", *AmLit,* XVII (1945–46), [113]–26.

71 Eleanor K. Hemingham, "Old English Precursors of *The Worcester Fragments", PMLA,* LV (1940), 291–307.

72 Clark H. Slover, "Early Literary Channels between Britain and Ireland", [University of Texas] *Studies in English,* No. 6 (1926), pp. 5–52; *idem,* "Early Literary Channels between Ireland and Britain", [University of Texas] *Studies in English,* No. 7 (1927), pp. 5–111; Arthur C. L. Brown, "The Irish Element in King Arthur and the Grail", *Mediæval Studies in Memory of Gertrude Schoepperle Loomis* (Paris: H. Champion, and New York: Columbia University Press, 1927), pp. 95–111.

73 James H. Warner, *"Émile* in Eighteenth-Century England", *PMLA,* LIX (1944), 773–91.

74 Stephen Leacock, "Homer and Humbug", in *Behind the Beyond* (New York: Dodd Mead, 1919), p. 189.

Other treatments of success include Thomas P. Haviland, "Préciosité Crosses the Atlantic", *PMLA,* LIX (1944), 131–41; Dudley R. Hutcherson, "Poe's Reputation in England and America, 1850–1909", *AmLit,* XIV (1942–43), [211]–33; Joseph Remenyi, "Walt Whitman in Hungarian Literature", *AmLit,* XVI (1944–45), [181]–85; Arthur Lawrence Vogelback, "The Publication and Reception of *Huckleberry Finn* in America", *AmLit,* XI (1939–40),[260]–72; *idem, "The Prince and the Pauper:* A Study in Critical Standards", *AmLit,* XIV (1942–43), [48]–54; David H. Dickason, "Stephen Crane and the *Philistine", AmLit,* XV (1943–44), [279]–87; Clarence Gohdes, "British Interest in American Literature During the Latter Part of the Nineteenth Century as Reflected by Mudie's Select Library", *AmLit,* XIII (1941–42), [356]–62; and Martin Staples Schockley, "The Reception of *The Grapes of Wrath* in Oklahoma", *AmLit,* XV (1943–44), [351]–61.

Examples of studies in influence include Joshua H. Neumann, "Milton's Prose Vocabulary", *PMLA,* LX (1945), 102–20; Lyon N. Richardson, "What Rutherford B. Hayes Liked in Emerson", *AmLit,* XVII (1945–46), [22]–32; Dagmar Renshaw LeBreton, "Orestes Brownson's Visit to New Orleans in 1855", *AmLit,* XVI (1944–45), [110]–14; Maurice Browning Cramer, "Browning's Literary Reputation at Oxford 1855–1859", *PMLA,* LVII (1942), 232–40; and Lee Elbert Holt, "E. M. Forster and Samuel Butler", *PMLA,* LXI (1946), 804–19.

Chapter Seven: Problems of Interpretation

1 Tyrus Hillway, "Taji's Quest for Certainty", *AmLit*, XVIII (1946–47), [27]–34.

2 Gordon Hall Gerould, "The Social Status of Chaucer's Franklin", *PMLA*, XLI (1926), 262–79.

3 Emma P. M. Dieckmann, "The Meaning of *burdoun* in Chaucer", *MP*, XXVI (1928–29), 279–82.

4 Harbert Hartman, "Prince Hal's 'Shew of Zeale' ", *PMLA*, XLVI (1931), 720–23.

5 Waldo H. Dunn, "Hamlet's 'Fatness' ", *LTLS*, May 26, 1927, p. 375.

6 Hubert H. Hoeltje, *"L'Allegro,* Lines 53–55", *PMLA*, XLV (1930), 201–3.

7 Mallie J. Murphy, *"The Rambler,* No. 191", *PMLA*, L (1935), 926–28.

8 Kerby Neill, "Spenser's Acrasia and Mary Queen of Scots", *PMLA*, LX (1945), 682–88; Allan H. Gilbert, "Belphœbe's Misdeeming of Timias", *PMLA*, LXII (1947), 622–43.

9 Paul E. McLane, "Spenser's Morrell and Thomalin", *PMLA*, LXII (1947), 936–49.

10 Donald J. McGinn, "The Allegory of the 'Beare' and the 'Foxe' in Nashe's *Pierce Penilesse*", *PMLA*, LXI (1946), 431–53.

11 Lloyd Douglas, " 'A Severe Animadversion on Bossu' ", *PMLA*, LXII (1947), 690–706.

12 Marion Clyde Wier, "Shelley's 'Alastor' Again", *PMLA*, XLVI (1931), 947–50, and Evan K. Gibson, *"Alastor:* A Reinterpretation", *PMLA*, LXII (1947), 1022–45.

13 J. M. Ariail, " 'The Grammarian's Funeral'—A Note", *PMLA*, XLVIII (1933), 954–56.

14 Theodore H. Banks, "Spenser's Rosalind: A Conjecture", *PMLA*, LII (1937), 335–39.

15 Genevieve Crotty, "The Exeter *Harrowing of Hell:* A Re-Interpretation", *PMLA*, LIV (1939), 349–58.

16 Garrett Mattingly, "The Date of Shakespeare's Sonnet CVII", *PMLA*, XLVIII (1933), 705–21; a number of contributions on the same subject were published in the "Correspondence" columns of the [London] *Times Literary Supplement* during the year 1933.

17 E. P. Kuhl, "Malvolio's 'Please One, and Please All' ", *PMLA*, XLVII (1932), 903–4.

18 B. Sprague Allen, "Tom Coryat and Juliet's 'Balcony' ", *PMLA*, XLVIII (1933), 945–48.

19 Florence Teager, "Chaucer's Eagle and the Rhetorical Colors", *PMLA*, XLVII (1932), 410–18.

20 Kemp Malone, "A Note on *Beowulf* 1231", *MLN*, XLI (1926), 466–67.

21 Franz Montgomery, "A Note on the Reeve's Prologue", *PQ*, X (1931), 404–5.

22 Alwin Thaler, "Queen Elizabeth and Benedick's 'Partridge Wing' ", *MLN*, XLI (1926), 527–29.

23 W. Roy Mackenzie, "Standing Water", *MLN*, XLI (1926), 283–93.

24 John W. Draper, "Shakespeare's 'Star-Crossed Lovers' ", *RES*, XV (1939), 16–34.

25 Donald R. Roberts, "Miching Mallico", *LTLS*, April 18, 1936, p. 336.

26 George M. Harper, "Milton's 'Two-Handed Engine' ", *LTLS*, June 16, 1927, p. 424; Donald C. Dorian, "Milton's 'Two-Handed Engine' ", *PMLA*, XLV (1930), 204–15; Donald A. Stauffer, "Milton's 'Two-Handed Engine' ", *MLR*, XXXI (1936), 57–60; and Marian H. Studly, "That Two-Handed Engine", *English Journal*, College Edition, XXVI (1937), 148–51.

27 George W. Whiting, "The Golden Compasses in 'Paradise Lost' ", *N & Q*, CLXXII (1937), 294–95, and Grant McCollay, "Milton's Golden Compasses", *N & Q*, CLXXVI (1939), 97–98.

28 Newell F. Ford, "The Meaning of 'Fellowship with Essence' in *Endymion*", *PMLA*, LXII (1947), 1061–76.

29 Tyrus Hillway, "Taji's Abdication in Herman Melville's *Mardi*", *AmLit*, XVI (1944–45), [204]–7.

30 Ichiyé Hayawaka, "A Note on the Madmen's Scene in Webster's *The Duchess of Malfi*", *PMLA*, XLVII (1932), 907–9.

31 Theodore H. Banks, "The Banquet Scene in *Paradise Regained*", *PMLA*, LV (1940), 773–76.

32 Kenneth Neill Cameron, "The Planet-Tempest Passage in *Epipsychidion*", *PMLA*, LXIII (1948), 950–72.

33 Elisabeth Schneider, "The 'Dream' of *Kubla Khan*", *PMLA*, LX (1945), 784–801, and Charles S. Bouslog, "The Symbol of the Sod-Seat in Coleridge", *PMLA*, LX (1945), 802–10.

34 A. H. Krappe, "Who Was the Green Knight?", *Speculum*, XIII (1938), 206–15.

35 Paul L. Wiley, "The Phaeton Symbol in *John Brown's Body*", *AmLit*, XVII (1945–46), [231]–42.

36 R. E. Watters, "Melville's 'Isolatoes' ", *PMLA*, LX (1945), 1138–48.

37 Louise Dauner, "The Pernicious Rib: E. A. Robinson's Concept of Feminine Character", *AmLit*, XV (1943–44), [139]–58; see also *idem*, "Avon and Cavender: Two Children of the Night", *AmLit*, XIV (1942–43), [55]–65.

38 William Savage Johnson, "The 'Savior' in the Poetry of Robinson Jeffers", *AmLit*, XV (1943–44), [159]–68.

39 Arthur E. Du Bois, "The Unity of *Beowulf*", *PMLA*, XLIX (1934), 374–405.

40 Arthur Mizener, "Character and Action in the Case of Criseyde", *PMLA*, LIV (1939), 65–81.

41 George Winchester Stone, Jr., "An Interpretation of the A-Text of *Piers Plowman*", *PMLA*, LIII (1938), 656–77, and Howard William Troyer, "Who Is Piers Plowman?", *PMLA*, XLVII (1932), 368–84.

42 S. A. Small, "The Political Import of the Norton Half of *Gorboduc*", *PMLA*, XLVI (1931), 641–46.

43 Irving T. Richards, "The Meaning of Hamlet's Soliloquy", *PMLA*, XLVIII (1933), 741–66, and Harold L. Walley, "Shakespeare's Conception of *Hamlet*", *PMLA*, XLVIII (1933), 777–98.

44 Dorothy Waples, "Suggestions for Interpreting *The Marble Faun*", *AmLit*, XIII (1941–42), [224]–39.

45 Walter H. French, "The Meaning of Chaucer's *Envoy to Scogan*", *PMLA*, XLVIII (1933), 289–92.

46 Walter Clyde Curry, "Destiny in Chaucer's *Troilus*", *PMLA*, XLV (1930), 129–68.

47 Elizabeth Nitchie, "The Moral of the *Ancient Mariner* Reconsidered", *PMLA*, XLVIII (1933), 867–76; for the article to which this is a reply, see below, n. 65.

48 George G. Williams, "Who Was 'Cenus' in the Poem *To the Memory of Mr. Congreve?*", *PMLA*, XLIV (1929), 495–500.

49 Raymond Jenkins, "Drayton's Relation to the School of Donne, as Revealed in the *Shepherd's Sirena*", *PMLA*, XXXVIII (1923), 557–87; J. William Hebel, "Drayton's *Sirena*", *PMLA*, XXXIX (1924), 814–36; and Raymond Jenkins, "Drayton's *Sirena* Again", *PMLA*, XLII (1927), 129–39.

50 Nelson Sherwin Bushnell, "Natural Supernaturalism in *The Tempest*", *PMLA*, XLVII (1932), 684–98, and Elmer Edgar Stoll, "*The Tempest*", *PMLA*, XLVII (1932), 699–726.

51 Rosalie Feltenstein, "Melville's 'Benito Cereno' ", *AmLit*, XIX (1947–48), [244]–55.

52 Charlotte Lefever, "Richardson's Paradoxical Success", *PMLA*, XLVIII (1933), 856–60.

53 John Arthos, "The Poetry of E. E. Cummings", *AmLit*, XIV (1942–43), [372]–90.

54 William Nelson, "Skelton's Quarrel with Wolsey", *PMLA*, LI (1936), 377–98.

55 Claude L. Finney, "Keats's Philosophy", *PQ*, V (1926), 1–19; Royall Snow, "Heresy Concerning Keats", *PMLA*, XLIII (1928), 1142–49; Mary Evelyn Shipman, "Orthodoxy Concerning Keats", *PMLA*, XLIV (1929), 929–34; John Hawley Roberts, "Poetry of Sensation or of Thought?", *PMLA*, XLV (1930), 1129–39; *idem*, "The Significance of *Lamia*", *PMLA*, L (1935), 550–61; and James Ralston Caldwell, "The Meaning of *Hyperion*", *PMLA*, LI (1936), 1080–97. On Shelley, Raymond D. Havens, "Shelley's *Alastor*", *PMLA*, XLV (1930), 1098–1115; Paul Mueschke and Earl L. Griggs, "Wordsworth as the Prototype of the Poet in Shelley's *Alastor*", *PMLA*, XLIX (1934), 229–45; Marcel Kessel, "The Poet in Shelley's *Alastor*: A Criticism and a Reply", *PMLA*, LI (1936), 302–12 (a rejoinder by Paul Mueschke and Earl L. Griggs is on pp. 310–12); and E. Wayne Marjarum, "The Symbolism of Shelley's 'To a Skylark' ", *PMLA*, LII (1937), 911–13.

56 F. Barron Freeman, "The Enigma of Melville's 'Daniel Orme' ", *AmLit*, XVI (1944–45), [208]–11.

57   Frederic I. Carpenter, "The Values of Robinson Jeffers", *AmLit*, XI (1939–40), [353]–66.

58   H. Willard Reninger, "Norris Explains *The Octopus:* A Correlation of His Theory and Practice", *AmLit*, XII (1940–41), [218]–27.

59   Kemp Malone, "Hrethric", *PMLA*, XLII (1927), 268–313.

60   S. J. Herben, "Beowulf, Hrothgar, and Grendel", *Archiv*, CLXXIII (1938), 24–30.

61   L. J. Mills, "The Meaning of *Edward II*", *MP*, XXXII (1934), 11–31.

62   Alexander Corbin Judson, "Spenser's Theory of Courtesy", *PMLA*, XLVII (1932), 122–36.

63   Viola B. Hulbert, "A New Interpretation of Spenser's *Muipotmos*", *SP*, XXV (1931), 128–48; Josephine Waters Bennett, "Spenser's Garden of Adonis", *PMLA*, XLVII (1932), 46–80; Brents Stirling, "The Philosophy of Spenser's 'Garden of Adonis'", *PMLA*, XLIX (1934), 501–38; Isabel E. Rathborne, "Another Interpretation of *Muipotmos*", *PMLA*, XLIX (1934), 1050–68; and Rudolf B. Gottfried, "Spenser's *View* and Essex", *PMLA*, LII (1937), 645–51.

64   Albert W. Upton, "Allusions to James I and His Court in Marston's *Fawn* and Beaumont's *Woman Hater*", *PMLA*, XLIV (1929), 1048–65.

65   Newton P. Stallknecht, "The Moral of the *Ancient Mariner*", *PMLA*, XLVII (1932), 559–69; for a reply to this article, see above, n. 47.

66   Samuel Kliger, "Hebraic Lore in Maxwell Anderson's *Winterset*", *AmLit*, XVIII (1946–47), [219]–32.

67   Frederick Tupper, "The Date and Historical Background of *The Owl and the Nightingale*", *PMLA*, XLIX (1934), 406–27.

68   Irene Pettit McKeehan, "*Guillaume de Palerme*", *PMLA*, XLI (1926), 785–809.

69   John M. Manly, "Sir Thopas: A Satire", *Essays and Studies by Members of the English Association*, XIII (1928), 52–73.

70   Theodore W. Douglas, "What Is the *Parlement of Foules?*", *MLN*, XLIII (1929), 378–84; Haldeen Braddy, "*The Parlement of Foules:* A New Proposal", *PMLA*, XLVI (1931), 1007–19; *idem, "The* Parlement of Foules *in Its Relation to Contemporary Events*", in *Three Chaucer Studies* (New York: Oxford University Press, 1932). Professor Manly's review of the last-named work (*RES*, X (1934), 257–73) evoked a reply by the author (*RES*, XI (1935), 204–9) and a rejoinder by Professor Manly (*RES*, XI (1935), 209–13).

71   Oscar Cargill and Margaret Schlauch, "*The Pearl* and Its Jeweler", *PMLA*, XLIII (1928), 105–23.

72   Oscar Cargill, "The Date of the A-Text of *Piers Ploughman*", *PMLA*, XLVII (1932), 354–62.

73   Bernard F. Huppé, "The A-Text of *Piers Plowman* and the Norman Wars", *PMLA*, LIV (1939), 37–64.

74   Nellie Slayton Aurner, "Sir Thomas Malory—Historian?", *PMLA*, XLVIII (1933), 362–91.

75   William Nelson, "Skelton's *Speak, Parrot*", *PMLA*, LI (1936), 59–82.

76   C. W. Lemmi, "The Allegorical Meaning of Spenser's *Muipotmos*", *PMLA*, XLV (1930), 732–48.

77   Emma Marshall Denkinger, "Spenser's *Muipotmos* Again", *PMLA*, XLVI (1931), 272–76; one of the points in this argument is based upon the assumption that the marriage of Penelope Devereux to Lord Riche took place in the spring of 1581. On this matter, see above, p. 200. Another reply to Mr. Lemmi's article is Ernest A. Strathmann, "The Allegorical Meaning of Spenser's *Muipotmos*", PMLA, XLVI (1931), 940–45.

78   J. M. Purcell, *PMLA*, XLVI (1931), 945–46.

79   Raymond Jenkins, "Spenser: The Uncertain Years 1584–89", *PMLA*, LIII (1938), 350–62.

80   William Cliff Martin, "The Date and Purpose of Spenser's *Veue*," *PMLA*, XLVII (1932), 137–43.

81   John W. Draper, "Classical Coinage in the *Færie Queene*", *PMLA*, XLVII (1932), 97–108.

82   Ruth Hudson, "Greene's *James IV* and Contemporary Allusions to Scotland", *PMLA*, XLVII (1932), 652–67.

83   Dixon Wecter, "Shakespeare's Purpose in *Timon of Athens*", *PMLA*, XLIII (1928), 701–21.

84   Michele De Filippis, "Milton and Manso: Cups or Books?", *PMLA*, LI (1936), 745–56.

85   John Robert Moore, "Contemporary Satire in Otway's *Venice Preserved*", *PMLA*, XLIII (1928), 166–81.

86   John Stafford, "Patterns of Meaning in *Nights with Uncle Remus*", *AmLit*, XVIII (1946–47), [89]–108.

87   Evelyn May Albright, "The Folio Version of *Henry V* in Relation to Shakespeare's Times", *PMLA*, XLIII (1928), 722–56.

88   Greene, *Works*, ed. Grosart, III, 128–39; the source material is found on pp. 439–45 of the 1614 edition of Bowes' translation of Primaudaye.

89   C. W. Lemmi, "The Allegorical Meaning of Spenser's *Muipotmos*", *PMLA*, XLV (1930), 732–48; the significance of this evidence was challenged by Ernest A. Strathmann (see above, n. 77), and Mr. Lemmi replied in "Astery's Transformation in *Muipotmos*", *PMLA*, L (1935), 913–14.

90   A. Philip McMahon, "Francis Bacon's Essay *Of Beauty*", *PMLA*, LX (1945), 716–59.

91   Winfield H. Rogers, "The Significance of Fielding's *Temple Beau*", *PMLA*, LV (1940), 440–44.

92   Harold E. Briggs, "Keats, Robertson, and *That Most Hateful Land*", *PMLA*, LIX (1944), 184–99.

93   Donald Weeks, "Image and Idea in Yeats' *The Second Coming*", *PMLA*, LXIII (1948), 281–92.

94   James R. Caldwell, "Dating a Spenser-Harvey Letter", *PMLA*, XLI (1926), 568–74.

95   James H. Hewlett, "Interpreting a Spenser-Harvey Letter", *PMLA*, XLII (1927), 1060–65.

96 See above, n. 69, and Chaucer, *Canterbury Tales,* ed. J. M. Manly (New York: Holt, 1928ᶜ), pp. 629 ff.

97 William Witherle Lawrence, "Satire in *Sir Thopas*", *PMLA,* L (1935), 81–91.

98 *Specimens of the Pre-Shaksperean Drama,* ed. John Matthews Manly, 2 vols. (Boston: Ginn, 1897ᶜ), II, 53–54, 59–60.

99 O. F. Emerson, "The Punctuation of *Beowulf* and Literary Interpretation", *MP,* XXIII (1926), 393–405.

100 Joseph S. Graydon, "Defense of Criseyde", *PMLA,* XLIV (1929), 141–77; there is a reply to this article by J. Milton French, "A Defense of Troilus", *PMLA,* XLIV (1929), 1246–51, and another by Joseph M. Beatty, "Mr. Graydon's Defense of Criseyde", *SP,* XXVI (1929), 470–81.

101 Graydon, *op. cit.,* pp. 156–57.

102 Bertrand H. Bronson, "A Note on Gadshill, *Our Setter*", *PMLA,* XLV (1930), 749–53.

103 Laura Hibbard Loomis, "Arthur's Round Table", *PMLA,* XLI (1926), 771–84.

104 M. Channing Linthicum, " 'My Jewish Gaberdine' ", *PMLA,* XLIII (1928), 757–66.

105 Pauline K. Angell, "Light on the Dark Lady: A Study of Some Elizabethan Libels", *PMLA,* LII (1937), 652–74; a reply to this article—T. W. Baldwin, "Light on the Dark Lady", *PMLA,* LV (1940), 598–99—evoked further contributions (*PMLA,* LV (1940), 599–602).

106 John Robert Moore, "The Contemporary Significance of Middleton's *Game at Chesse*", *PMLA,* L (1935), 761–68.

107 Fredson T. Bowers, "Middleton's *Fair Quarrel* and the Duelling Code", *JEGP,* XXXVI (1937), 40–65.

108 Brother Augustine Philip, "The Exeter Scribe and the Unity of the *Crist*", *PMLA,* LV (1940), 903–9.

109 Haldeen Braddy, "Chaucer and Graunson: The Valentine Tradition", *PMLA,* LIV (1939), 359–68.

110 Henry Willis Wells, "The Philosophy of Piers Plowman", *PMLA,* LIII (1938), 339–49.

111 Maurice Kelley, "The Theological Dogma of *Paradise Lost,* III, 173–202", *PMLA,* LII (1937), 75–79.

112 G. R. Elliott, "Spectral Etching in the Poetry of Thomas Hardy", *PMLA,* XLIII (1928), 1185–95.

113 Evelyn May Albright, "Shakespeare's *Richard II* and the Essex Conspiracy", *PMLA,* XLII (1927), 686–720; Ray Heffner, "Shakespeare, Hayward, and Essex", *PMLA,* XLV (1930), 754–80; Evelyn May Albright, "Shakespeare's *Richard II,* Hayward's History of Henry IV, and the Essex Conspiracy", *PMLA,* XLVI (1931), 694–719; Ray Heffner, "Shakespeare, Hayward, and Essex Again", *PMLA,* XLVII (1932), 898–99; reply by Miss Albright, pp. 899–901.

Among other studies in interpretation may be mentioned: Marie Padgett Hamilton, "The Religious Principle in *Beowulf*", *PMLA,* LXI (1946), 309–30;

Margaret Schlauch, "The Marital Dilemma in the *Wife of Bath's Tale*", *PMLA*, LXI (1946), 416–30; Allan H. Gilbert, "Spenserian Armor", *PMLA*, LVII (1942), 981–87; Jefferson B. Fletcher, "The Puritan Argument in Spenser", *PMLA*, LVIII (1943), 634–48; Mary K. Woodworth, "The Mutability Cantos and the Succession", *PMLA*, LIX (1944), 985–1002; W. W. Lawrence, "Hamlet and Fortinbras", *PMLA*, LXI (1946), 673–98; Ernest William Talbert, "The Interpretation of Jonson's Courtly Spectacles", *PMLA*, LXI (1946), 454–73; Howard J. Bell, Jr., "*The Deserted Village* and Goldsmith's Social Doctrines", *PMLA*, LIX (1944), 747–72; Kenneth Neill Cameron, "The Political Symbolism of *Prometheus Unbound*", *PMLA*, LVIII (1943), 728–53; Elmer Edgar Stoll, "Symbolism in Coleridge", *PMLA*, LXIII (1948), 214–33; J. O. Bailey, "An Early American Utopian Fiction", *AmLit*, XIV (1942–43), [285]–93; Edgar Hill Duncan, "Lowell's 'Battle of the Kettle and the Pot'", *AmLit*, XV (1943–44), [127]–38; Louise Dauner, "Myth and Humor in the Uncle Remus Fables", *AmLit*, XX (1948–49), [129]–43; and Genevieve W. Foster, "The Archetypal Imagery of T. S. Eliot", *PMLA*, LX (1945), 567–85.

Chapter Eight: Problems in Technique

1 Helene B. Bullock, "Thomas Middleton and the Fashion in Playmaking", *PMLA*, XLII (1927), 766–76.

2 Robert Ralston Cawley, "Sir Thomas Browne and His Reading", *PMLA*, XLVIII (1933), 426–70.

3 John S. Diekhoff, "Critical Activity of the Poetical Mind: John Milton", *PMLA*, LV (1940), 748–72.

4 Frank T. Thompson, "Emerson's Theory and Practice of Poetry", *PMLA*, XLIII (1928), 1170–84. Among other studies of the origin of a technique might be mentioned Weldon M. Williams, "The Genesis of John Oldham's *Satyrs upon the Jesuits*", *PMLA*, LVIII (1943), 958–70, and Bard McNulty, "Milton's Influence on Wordsworth's Early Sonnets", *PMLA*, LXII (1947), 745–51.

5 Agnes K. Getty, "The Mediæval-Modern Conflict in Chaucer's Poetry", *PMLA*, XLVII (1932), 385–402.

6 Erma M. Gill, "The Plot-Structure of *The Comedy of Errors* in Relation to Its Sources", [University of Texas] *Studies in English*, X (1930), 13–65.

7 Paul Mueschke and Jeannette Fleisher, "A Re-Evaluation of Vanbrugh", *PMLA*, XLIX (1934), 848–89.

8 Rudolf Kirk, "References to the Law in *Piers the Plowman*", *PMLA*, XLVIII (1933), 322–27.

9 Roland Bassett Botting, "The Composition of the *Shepheardes Calender*", *PMLA*, L (1935), 423–34.

10 Allison Gaw, "Is Shakespeare's *Much Ado* a Revised Earlier Play?", *PMLA*, L (1935), 715–38.

370 Methods of Research (III, viii, 11)

11 Mody C. Boatright, "Scott's Theory and Practice Concerning the Use of the Supernatural in Prose Fiction in Relation to the Chronology of the Waverley Novels", *PMLA,* L (1935), 235–61; but see also Chapter V, n. 45.

12 Karl Young, "Chaucer's 'Troilus and Criseyde' as Romance", *PMLA,* LIII (1938), 38–63.

13 Robert A. Pratt, "Chaucer's Use of the *Teseide*", *PMLA,* LXII (1947), 598–621.

14 Freda L. Townsend, "Sidney and Ariosto", *PMLA,* LXI (1946), 97–108.

15 Daniel C. Boughner, "The Psychology of Memory in Spenser's *Færie Queene*", *PMLA,* XLVII (1932), 89–96.

16 Helen Phipps Houck, "Mabbe's Paganization of the *Celestina*", *PMLA,* LIV (1939), 422–31.

17 John William Ashton, "Conventional Material in Munday's *John a Kent and John a Cumber*", *PMLA,* XLIX (1934), 752–61.

18 Janette Harrington, "Wordsworth's *Descriptive Sketches* and *The Prelude,* Book VI", *PMLA,* XLIV (1929), 1144–58, and Edward Niles Hooker, "*Descriptive Sketches* and *The Prelude,* Book VI", *PMLA,* XLV (1930), 619–23.

19 Willard Thorp, "Redburn's Prosy Old Guidebook", *PMLA,* LIII (1938), 1146–56.

20 Jared Wenger, "Character-Types of Scott, Balzac, Dickens, Zola", *PMLA,* LXII (1947), 213–32.

21 Arthur E. Du Bois, "The Unity of *Beowulf*", *PMLA,* XLIX (1934), 374–405.

22 Henry W. Wells, "The Construction of *Piers Plowman*", *PMLA,* XLIV (1929), 123–40.

23 Clark H. Slover, "*Sire Degarre:* A Study of a Mediæval Hack Writer's Methods", [University of Texas] *Studies in English,* XI (1931), 6–23.

24 Arthur M. Sampley, "Plot Structure in Peele's Plays as a Test of Authorship", *PMLA,* LI (1936), 689–701.

25 Alwin Thaler, "The 'Lost Scenes' of *Macbeth*", *PMLA,* XLIX (1934), 835–47.

26 Edgar C. Knowlton, "The Plots of Ben Jonson", *MLN,* XLIV (1929), 77–86.

27 Wilbur D. Dunkel, *The Dramatic Technique of Thomas Middleton in His Comedies of London Life* (Chicago: privately printed, 1925).

28 Theodore Baird, "The Time-Scheme of *Tristram Shandy* and a Source", *PMLA,* LI (1936), 803–20.

29 Rufus Putney, "The Plan of *Peregrine Pickle*", *PMLA,* LX (1945), 1051–65.

30 Katherine F. Gleason, *The Dramatic Art of Robert Browning* (Boston: privately printed [1927]).

31 Emerson Grant Sutcliffe, "Plotting in Reade's Novels", *PMLA,* XLVII (1932), 834–63; *idem*, "Unique and Repeated Situations and Themes in Reade's Fiction", *PMLA,* LX (1945), 221–30.

32 R. F. Blackmur, "The Craft of Herman Melville", *Virginia Quarterly Review*, XLV (1938), 266–82.

33 Carl J. Weber, "Chronology in Hardy's Novels", *PMLA*, LIII (1938), 314–20; John P. Emery, "Chronology in Hardy's *Return of the Native*", *PMLA*, LIV (1939), 618–19; reply by Mr. Weber, *PMLA*, LIV (1939), 620. See also Albert A. Murphree and Carl F. Strauch, "The Chronology of *The Return of the Native*", *MLN*, LIV (1939), 491–97.

34 Carleton Brown, "The Evolution of the Canterbury 'Marriage Group'", *PMLA*, XLVIII (1933), 1041–59; *idem*, "Author's Revision in the *Canterbury Tales*", *PMLA*, LVII (1942), 29–50.

35 George Wesley Whiting, "Conrad's Revision of Six of His Short Stories", *PMLA*, XLVIII (1933), 552–57; *idem*, "Conrad's Revision of 'The Lighthouse' in *Nostromo*", *PMLA*, LII (1937), 1183–90.

36 Phyllis Bartlett, "Chapman's Revisions in His *Iliads*", *ELH*, II (1935), 92–119.

37 Willa McClung Evans, "An Early Lovelace Text", *PMLA*, LX (1945), 382–85.

38 Kerby Neill, "Structure and Symbol in Crashaw's *Hymn in the Nativity*", *PMLA*, LXIII (1948), 101–13.

39 Tremaine McDowell, "Bryant's Practice in Composition and Revision", *PMLA*, LII (1937), 474–502.

40 Leon T. Dickinson, "Mark Twain's Revisions in Writing *The Innocents Abroad*", *AmLit*, XIX (1947–48), [139]–57.

41 Royal A. Gettmann, "Henry James's Revision of *The American*", *AmLit*, XVI (1944–45), [279]–95.

42 *Idem*, "George Moore's Revisions of *The Lake, The Wild Goose,* and *Esther Waters*", *PMLA*, LIX (1944), 540–55.

43 Theodore H. Banks, Jr., "Miltonic Rhythm; A Study of the Relation of the Full Stops to the Rhythm of *Paradise Lost*", *PMLA*, XLII (1927), 140–45.

44 John S. Diekhoff, "Rhyme in *Paradise Lost*", *PMLA*, XLIX (1934), 539–43.

45 R. W. Short, "The Metrical Theory and Practice of Thomas Campion", *PMLA*, LIX (1944), 1003–18.

46 Arnold Stein, "Donne's Prosody", *PMLA*, LIX (1944), 373–97.

47 Louise Propst, *An Analytical Study of Shelley's Versification* (Iowa City: The University, [1932]), University of Iowa Humanistic Studies, Vol. V, No. 3.

48 Elizabeth Jackson, "Notes on the Stanza of Rossetti's 'The Blessed Damozel'", *PMLA*, LVIII (1943), 1050–56.

49 Kathryn Anderson McEuen, "Emerson's Rhymes", *AmLit*, XX (1948–49), [31]–42.

50 W. L. Werner, "Poe's Theories and Practice in Poetic Technique", *AmLit*, II (1930–31), [156]–65.

51 Bruce Robert McElderry, Jr., "Archaism and Innovation in Spenser's Poetic Diction", *PMLA*, XLVII (1932), 144–70.

52 Wilson C. Clough, "The Use of Color Words by Edgar Allen [*sic*] Poe", *PMLA,* XLV (1930), 598–613. A more extensive study of color in literature is Sigmund Skard, *The Use of Color in Literature: A Survey of Research* (Philadelphia: American Philosophical Society, 1946), first published in *Proceedings of the American Philosophical Society,* XC (1946), 163–249.

53 Clough, *op. cit.,* p. 613.

54 Karl Litzenburg, "The Diction of William Morris: A Discussion of His Translations from the Old Norse with Particular Reference to His Pseudo-English Vocabulary, with Some Remarks on the Theory of Translating from the Old Norse", *Arkiv för Nördisk Filologi,* LIII (1938), 327–63.

55 Helen Casey, "Synge's Use of the Anglo-Irish Idiom", *English Journal,* College Edition, XXVII (1938), 773–76.

56 Joseph Prescott, "James Joyce: A Study in Words", *PMLA,* LIV (1939), 304–15.

57 John Boal Douds, "Donne's Technique of Dissonance", *PMLA,* LII (1937), 1051–61. Another study of metaphysical poetry is Alice Stayert Brandenburg, "The Dynamic Image in Metaphysical Poetry", *PMLA,* LVII (1942), 1039–45.

58 Douds, *op. cit.,* p. 1061.

59 James Whaler, "The Miltonic Simile", *PMLA,* XLVI (1931), 1034–74.

60 *Idem,* "Animal Simile in *Paradise Lost"*, *PMLA,* XLVII (1932), 534–53.

61 Lorena M. Gary, "Rich Colors and Ominous Shadows", *South Atlantic Quarterly,* XXXVII (1938), 41–45.

62 Lois Ware, "Poetic Conventions in *Leaves of Grass"*, *SP,* XXVI (1929), 47–57.

63 Autrey Nell Wiley, "Reiterative Devices in *Leaves of Grass"*, *AmLit,* I (1929–30), [161]–70.

64 C. C. Batchelor, "The Style of the Beowulf: A Study of the Composition of the Poem", *Speculum,* XII (1937), 330–42.

65 Germaine Dempster, *Dramatic Irony in Chaucer,* in *Stanford University Publications, University Series, Language and Literature,* IV (1932), No. 3.

66 Paull F. Baum, "Characterization in the 'Knight's Tale' ", *MLN,* XLVI (1931), 302–4.

67 A. C. Howell, "A Note on Ben Jonson's Literary Methods", *SP,* XXVIII (1931), 710–19.

68 Daniel C. Boughner, "Notes on Hooker's Prose", *RES,* XV (1939), 194–200.

69 John S. Diekhoff, "The Punctuation of *Comus"*, *PMLA,* LI (1936), 757–68.

70 Tom B. Haber, "The Chapter-Tags in the Waverley Novels", *PMLA,* XLV (1930), 1140–49.

71 Richard Gordon Lillard, "Irony in Hardy and Conrad", *PMLA*, L (1935), 316–22.

72 Phillip Shaw, "The Position of Thomas Dekker in Jacobean Prison Literature", *PMLA*, LXII (1947), 366–91.

73 Herbert H. Umbach, "The Rhetoric of Donne's Sermons", *PMLA*, LII (1937), 354–58.

74 Arnold Stein, "Donne and the Couplet", *PMLA*, LVII (1942), 676–96.

75 Wallace Cable Brown, "Gay's Mastery of the Heroic Couplet", *PMLA*, LXI (1946), 114–25.

76 J. Milton French, "Milton as Satirist", *PMLA*, LI (1936), 414–29.

77 Harold H. Watts, "Lytton's Theories of Prose Fiction", *PMLA*, L (1935), 274–89.

78 Robert Price, "Mrs. Catherwood's Early Experiments with Critical Realism", *AmLit*, XVII (1945–46), [140]–51.

79 Robert M. Estrich, "Chaucer's Maturing Art in the Prologues to the *Legend of Good Women*", *JEGP*, XXXVI (1937), 326–37.

80 David H. Greene, *"The Tinker's Wedding*, A Revaluation", *PMLA*, LXII (1947), 824–27.

81 Frederick Brache, "Understatement in Old English Poetry", *PMLA*, LII (1937), 915–34.

82 Roger Sherman Loomis, "The Visit to the Perilous Castle: A Study of the Arthurian Modification of an Irish Theme", *PMLA*, XLVIII (1933), 1000–35.

83 Mary A. Hill, "Rhetorical Balance in Chaucer's Poetry", *PMLA*, XLII (1927), 845–61.

84 Ola E. Winslow, *Low Comedy as a Structural Element in English Drama from the Beginnings to 1642* (Chicago: University of Chicago Libraries, 1926).

85 Robert Withington, " 'Vice' and 'Parasite'. A Note on the Evolution of the Elizabethan Villain", *PMLA*, XLIX (1934), 743–51.

86 Alwin Thaler, "Shakspere and the Unhappy Happy Ending", *PMLA*, XLII (1927), 736–61, and Samuel Asa Small, "The Ending of *The Two Gentlemen of Verona*", *PMLA*, XLVIII (1933), 767–76.

87 Kathleen M. Lynch, "Conventions of Platonic Drama in the Heroic Plays of Orrery and Dryden", *PMLA*, XLIV (1939), 456–71.

88 Fletcher Collins, Jr., "Music in the Craft Cycles", *PMLA*, XLVII (1932), 613–21.

89 Harvey Eagleson, "Costume in the Middle English Metrical Romances", *PMLA*, XLVII (1932), 339–45.

90 Earle R Davis, "Dickens and the Evolution of Caricature", *PMLA*, LV (1940), 231–40.

91 Alexander Brede, "Theories of Poetic Diction in Wordsworth and Others and in Contemporary Poetry", *Papers of the Michigan Academy*, XIV (1931), 537–65.

92   Houghton W. Taylor, " 'Particular Character': An Early Phase of a Literary Evolution", *PMLA*, LX (1945), 161–74.

93   Carl J. Weber, "The Restoration of Hardy's Starved Goldfinch", *PMLA*, LV (1940), 617–19.

94   Alan S. Downer, "Nature to Advantage Dressed: Eighteenth Century Acting", *PMLA*, LVIII (1943), 1002–37.

95   A. E. Zucker, "The Genealogical Novel, A New Genre", *PMLA*, XLIII (1928), 551–60; other contributions to this discussilon are: Arthur Burkhard, "The Genealogical Novel in Scandinavia," *PMLA*, XLIV (1929), 310–13; A. E. Zucker, *"The Genealogical Novel Again"*, *PMLA*, XLIV (1929), 925–27; and Arthur Burkhard, "Thomas Mann's Indebtedness to Scandinavia", *PMLA*, XLV (1930), 615.

96   Alan Reynolds Thompson, "Melodrama and Tragedy", *PMLA*, XLIII (1928), 810–35; there is a reply to this article by Clara F. McIntyre, "The Word 'Universality' as Applied to Drama", *PMLA*, XLIV (1929), 927–29.

97   Harold C. Binkley, "Essays and Letter-Writing", *PMLA*, XLI (1926), 342–61.

98   Louise Pound, "A Recent Theory of Ballad-Making", *PMLA*, XLIV (1929), 622–30; this article was prompted by Gordon Hall Gerould's "The Making of Ballads", *MP*, XXI (1923–24), 15–28.

99   R. W. Babcock, "The Mediæval Setting of Chaucer's *Monk's Tale"*, *PMLA*, XLVI (1931), 205–13.

100   Philip Schuyler Allen, *The Romanesque Lyric. Studies in Its Background and Development from Petronius to the Cambridge Songs (50–1050), with Renderings into English Verse by Howard Mumford Jones* (Chapel Hill, N. C.: University of North Carolina Press, 1928).

101   Henry B. Hinckley, "The Framing Tale", *MLN*, XLIX (1934), 69–80.

102   T. H. Vail Motter, *The School Drama in England* (London: Oxford University Press, and New York: Longmans, 1929).

103   Charles Read Baskervill, *The Elizabethan Jig and Related Song Drama* (Chicago: University of Chicago Press, [1929]).

104   Francis White Weitzmann, "Notes on the Elizabethan *Elegie"*, *PMLA*, L (1935), 435–43.

105   John Erskine, *The Elizabethan Lyric* (New York: Columbia University Press, 1905).

106   DeWitt Talmage Starnes, "Bilingual Dictionaries of Shakespeare's Day", *PMLA*, LII (1937), 1005–18.

107   E. N. S. Thompson, *The Seventeenth-Century English Essay*, in *University of Iowa Humanistic Studies*, III (1926), No. 3.

108   Robert Gale Noyes, "Conventions of Song in Restoration Tragedy", *PMLA*, LIII (1938), 162–88.

109   Autrey Nell Wiley, "Female Prologues and Epilogues in English Plays", *PMLA*, XLVIII (1933), 1060–79.

110   Bertha Monica Stearns, "Early English Periodicals for Ladies (1700–1760)", *PMLA*, XLVIII (1933), 38–60.

111   Marion K. Bragg, *The Formal Eclogue in Eighteenth Century Eng-*

land, in *University of Maine Studies,* Second Series, No. 6 (1926); see also R. F. Jones, "Eclogue Types in English Poetry of the Eighteenth Century", *JEGP,* XXIV (1925), 33–60.

112 Newell W. Sawyer, *The Comedy of Manners from Sheridan to Maugham* (Philadelphia: University of Pennsylvania Press, and London: Milford and Oxford University Press, 1931).

113 Ina Beth Sessions, "The Dramatic Monologue", *PMLA,* LXII (1947), 503–16.

114 Howard Mumford Jones, "Methods in Contemporary Biography", *English Journal,* College Edition, XXI (1932), 43–51, 113–22.

115 Edmund Lester Pearson, *Dime Novels; or, Following an Old Trail in Popular Literature* (Boston: Little, Brown, and Toronto: McClelland and Stewart, 1929).

116 Louis B. Wright, "Animal Actors on the English Stage before 1642", *PMLA,* XLII (1927), 656–69

117 Richmond P. Bond, *English Burlesque Poetry 1700–1750,* in *Harvard Studies in English,* VI (1932).

118 C. A. Moore, "Whig Panegyric Verse, 1700–1760", *PMLA,* XLI (1926), 362–401.

119 Robert M. Myers, "Neo-Classical Criticism of the Ode for Music", *PMLA,* LXII (1947), 399–421.

120 John W. Draper, "The Metrical Tales in XVIII-Century England", *PMLA,* LII (1937), 390–97.

121 Richard C. Boys, "The Beginnings of the American Poetical Miscellany, 1714–1800", *AmLit,* XVII (1945–46), [127]–39.

122 Virginia Shull, "Clerical Drama in Lincoln Cathedral, 1318 to 1561", *PMLA,* LII (1937), 946–66.

123 Irene Pettit McKeehan, "The Book of the Nativity of St. Cuthbert", *PMLA,* XLVIII (1933), 981–99.

124 C. O. Chapman, *"The Parson's Tale:* A Medieval Sermon", *MLN,* XLIII (1928), 229–34.

125 F. G. Black, "The Technique of Letter Fiction in English from 1740 to 1800", *Harvard Studies and Notes in Philology and Literature,* XV (1933), 291–312.

126 Wilmon Brewer, *Sonnets and Sestinas* (Boston: Cornhill Publishing Co., 1937).

127 Among the many studies of the novel, or of fiction in general, may be mentioned Bliss Perry, *A Study of Prose Fiction* (Boston and New York: Houghton Mifflin, 1902); Clayton [Meeker] Hamilton, *Materials and Methods of Fiction* (New York: Baker and Taylor, 1908); Ernest Bernbaum, "The Views of the Great Critics on the Historical Novel", *PMLA,* XLI (1926), 424–41; Walter L. Myers, *The Later Realism: A Study of Characterization in the English Novel* (Chicago: University of Chicago Press, 1927); Annie Russell Marble, *A Study of the Modern Novel, British and American* (New York and London: Appleton, 1928); Carl H. Grabo, *The Technique of the Novel* (New York: Scribner's, 1928ᶜ); Walter L. Myers, "The Novel

Dedicate", *Virginia Quarterly Review,* VIII (1932), 410–18; Joseph W. Beach, *The Twentieth Century Novel: Studies in Technique* (New York and London: Century, 1932ᶜ); Pelham Edgar, *The Art of the Novel from 1700 to the Present Time* (New York: Macmillan, 1933); G[odfrey] F[rank] Singer, *The Epistolary Novel: Its Origin, Decline, and Residuary Influence* (Philadelphia: University of Pennsylvania Press, 1933); John T. Frederick, "New Techniques in the Novel", *English Journal,* XXIV (1935), 355–63; Harlan H. Hatcher, *Creating the Modern American Novel* (New York: Farrar and Rinehart, 1935ᶜ); Albert M. Turner, *The Making of "The Cloister and the Hearth"* (Chicago: University of Chicago Press, 1938); Percy Lubbock, *The Craft of Fiction* (New York: Peter Smith, 1947), originally published in 1929; George Snell, *The Shapers of American Fiction, 1798–1947* (New York: E. P. Dutton, 1947); Alexander Cowie, *The Rise of the American Novel* (New York: American Book Co., 1948), and Willa Cather, *Willa Cather on Writing* (New York: Knopf, 1949).

128 E. J. MacEwan, *Freytag's Technique of the Drama* (Chicago: Scott Foresman, 1894ᶜ)—English translation of the 5th ed. of Gustav Freytag, *Die Technik des Dramas* (Leipzig, 1863); C[harles] E[dwyn] Vaughan, *Types of Tragic Drama* (London: Macmillan, 1908); Clayton Hamilton, *The Theory of the Theatre* (New York: Henry Holt, 1910); George Pierce Baker, *Dramatic Technique* (Boston: Small, Maynard, 1912ᶜ); Ferdinand Brunetière, *The Law of the Drama* (New York: Columbia University Press, 1914); Dorothy Kaucher, "Modern Dramatic Technique", *University of Missouri Studies,* III (1928), 1–183; M[uriel] C[lara] Bradbrook, *Themes and Conventions of Elizabethan Tragedy* (Cambridge: Cambridge University Press, 1936); and Moody E. Prior, *The Language of Tragedy* (New York: Columbia University Press, 1947).

129 Lu Emily Pearson, "Isolable Lyrics of the Mystery Plays", *ELH,* III (1936), 228–52, and William D[arby] Templeman, "The Place of the Lyric in Elizabethan Drama before 1600", *Western Reserve Studies,* II, No. 2 (1916), 28–36.

Among other studies in technique may be mentioned Leonard F. Dean, "Literary Problems in More's *Richard III*", *PMLA,* LVIII (1943), 22–41; Richard D. Altick, "Symphonic Imagery in *Richard II*", *PMLA,* LXII (1947), 339–65; Robert Adger Law, *"Richard the Third:* A Study in Shakespeare's Composition", *PMLA,* LX (1945), 689–96; Phyllis Brooks Bartlett, "Stylistic Devices in Chapman's *Iliads*", *PMLA,* LVII (1942), 661–75; Johnstone Parr, "The Horoscope in Webster's *The Duchess of Malfi*", *PMLA,* LX (1945), 760–65; John S. Diekhoff, "The Function of the Prologues in *Paradise Lost*", *PMLA,* LVII (1942), 697–704; Richard H. Fogle, "Empathic Imagery in Keats and Shelley", *PMLA,* LXI (1946), 163–91; Carlisle Moore, "Carlyle's 'Diamond Necklace' and Poetic History", *PMLA,* LVIII (1943), 537–57; Paul A. Cundiff, "The Clarity of Browning's Ring Metaphor", *PMLA,* LXIII (1948), 1276–82; J. C. Bailey, "Hardy's 'Mephistophelian Visitants'", *PMLA,* LXI (1946), 1146–84; Roy P. Basler, "Abraham Lincoln's Rhetoric", *AmLit,* XI (1939–40), [167]–82; R. W. Short, "The Sentence Structure of

Henry James", *AmLit*, XVIII (1946–47), [71]–88; and William M. Gibson, "Materials and Form in Howells's First Novels", *AmLit*, XIX (1947–48), [158]–66.

Chapter Nine: Problems in the History of Ideas

1 Matthew Arnold, *Essays in Criticism* (London: Macmillan, 1869), "The Function of Criticism at the Present Time", pp. 5 and 36.

2 Arthur O. Lovejoy, "Reflections on the History of Ideas", *Journal of the History of Ideas*, I (1940), 3–23, and *idem*, *The Great Chain of Being* (Cambridge, Mass.: Harvard University Press, 1936), Introduction.

3 James Phillips, Jr., *The State in Shakespeare's Greek and Roman Plays* (New York: Columbia University Press, 1942).

4 L. C. Knights, *Drama and Society in the Age of Jonson* (London: Chatto and Windus, 1942).

5 Malcolm Mackenzie Ross, "Elizabethan Society and Letters", *University of Toronto Quarterly*, XII (1943), [244]–54.

6 Arthur O. Lovejoy, "Reflection on the History of Ideas", *Journal of the History of Ideas*, I (1940), 6.

7 Emile Durkheim, *The Rules of Sociological Method*, 8th ed., tr. Sarah A. Solovay and John H. Mueller, ed. George E. G. Catlin (Chicago: University of Chicago Press, 1938).

8 Charles A. Beard, "Written History as an Act of Faith", *American Historical Review*, XXXIX (1933–34), 219–31; *The Idea of National Interest* (New York: Macmillan, 1934); "That Noble Dream", *American Historical Review*, XLI (1935–36), 74–87; *The Discussion of Human Affairs* (New York: Macmillan, 1936); *Economic Bases of Politics* (New York: Knopf, 1945), rev. ed., first published in 1922; and, in collaboration with Alfred Vagts, "Currents in Historiography", *American Historical Review*, XLII (1936–37), 460–83.

9 Carl Lotus Becker, *Every Man His Own Historian* (New York: Crofts, 1935); "What Is Historiography?", *American Historical Review*, XLIV (1938–39), 20–28; *Modern Democracy* (New Haven: Yale University Press, 1941); *New Liberties for Old* (New Haven: Yale University Press, and London: Oxford University Press, 1941); *The Declaration of Independence: A Study in the History of Political Ideas* (New York: Harcourt Brace, 1922, and Knopf, 1942); *Freedom and Responsibility in the American Way of Life* (New York: Knopf, 1945); and *Progress and Power* (New York: Knopf, 1949), first published in 1936.

10 Jacques Barzun, *Race; a Study in Modern Superstition* (New York: Harcourt Brace, 1937ᶜ); *Of Human Freedom* (Boston: Little, Brown, 1939); *Romanticism and the Modern Ego* (Boston: Little, Brown, 1943); and, in collaboration with Hajo Holborn, Herbert Heaton, Dumas Malone, and George La Piana, *The Interpretation of History*, ed. Joseph R. Strayer (Princeton: Princeton University Press, 1943).

11　Merle Eugene Curti, *The Growth of American Thought* (New York and London: Harper, [1943]); and *The Roots of American Loyalty* (New York: Columbia University Press, 1946).

12　Bernard Smith, *Forces in American Criticism* (New York: Harcourt Brace, 1939ᶜ).

13　Karl Mannheim, *Rational and Irrational Elements in Contemporary Society* (London: Oxford University Press, 1934); *Ideology and Utopia* (New York: Harcourt Brace, 1936); *Man and Society in an Age of Reconstruction* (New York: Harcourt Brace, [1940]); and *Diagnosis of Our Time* (New York: Oxford University Press, 1944).

Mention should also be made of Howard Mumford Jones, *Ideas in America* (Cambridge, Mass.: Harvard University Press, 1944) and Arthur O. Lovejoy, *Essays in the History of Ideas* (Baltimore: Johns Hopkins Press, 1948).

14　Arthur O. Lovejoy, "Reflections on the History of Ideas", *JHL*, I (1940), 7.

15　*Idem*, "On the Discrimination of Romanticisms", *PMLA*, XXIX (1924), 229–53, and "The Meaning of Romanticism for the Historian of Ideas", *Journal of the History of Ideas*, II (1941), 257–78. Other discussions of romanticism include Frederick E. Pierce, "Romanticism and Other Isms", *JEGP*, XXVI (1927), 451–66, and John C. Blankengel, George R. Havens, Hoxie N. Fairchild, Kenneth McKenzie, F. Courtney Tarr, and Elizabeth Nitchie, "Romanticism: A Symposium", *PMLA*, LV (1940), 1–60; see also below, n. 17.

16　Francis White Weitzmann, "Notes on the Elizabethan *Elegie*", *PMLA*, L (1935), 435–43.

17　Arthur O. Lovejoy, "Optimism and Romanticism", *PMLA*, XLII (1927), 921–45.

18　Murray W. Bundy, *Theory of Imagination* (Urbana, Illinois: University of Illinois, 1927); see also the next work following.

19　*Idem*, " 'Invention' and 'Imagination' in the Renaissance", *JEGP*, XXIX (1930), 535–45.

20　Solomon F. Gingerich, "The Conception of Beauty in the Works of Shelley, Keats, and Poe", *Essays and Studies in English and Comparative Literature by Members of the English Department of the University of Michigan* (1932), pp. 169–94.

21　Joseph W. Beach, *The Concept of Nature in Nineteenth-Century Poetry* (New York: Macmillan, 1936).

22　John W. Draper, "The Theory of the Comic in Eighteenth-Century England", *JEGP*, XXXVII (1938), 207–23.

23　Alfred Owen Aldridge, "Shaftesbury and the Test of Truth", *PMLA*, LX (1945), 129–56.

24　Norman Foerster, "Emerson on the Organic Principle in Art", *PMLA*, XLI (1926), 193–208.

25　Arthur E. Du Bois, "The Cult of Beauty: A Study of John Masefield", *PMLA*, XLV (1930), 1218–57.

26 Alfred Owen Aldridge, "Jonathan Edwards and William Godwin on Virtue", *AmLit*, XVIII (1946–47), [308]–18.

27 B. Sprague Allen, "The Dates of *Sentimental* and Its Derivatives", *PMLA*, XLVIII (1933), 303–7; another study of sentimentalism is Mildred Davis Doyle, *Sentimentalism in American Periodicals 1741–1800* (New York: New York University, 1944).

28 William E. Alderman, "Shaftesbury and the Doctrine of Moral Sense in the Eighteenth Century", *PMLA*, XLVI (1931), 1087–94.

29 C. R. Sanders, "Coleridge, F. D. Maurice, and the Distinction between the Reason and the Understanding", *PMLA*, LI (1936), 459–75.

30 Clarence DeWitt Thorpe, "Addison and Some of His Predecessors on 'Novelty' ", *PMLA*, LII (1937), 1114–29.

31 Charles G. Smith, "Spenser's Theory of Friendship", *PMLA*, XLIX (1934), 490–500; see also *idem, Spenser's Theory of Friendship* (Baltimore: Johns Hopkins Press, 1936).

32 George C. Taylor, "Shakespeare's Attitude toward Love and Honor in *Troilus and Cressida*", *PMLA*, XLV (1930), 781–86.

33 Elizabeth Geen, "The Concept of Grace in Wordsworth's Poetry", *PMLA*, LVIII (1943), 689–715.

34 Floyd Stovall, "Shelley's Doctrine of Love", *PMLA*, XLV (1930), 283–303.

35 Elsa Chapin, "The Literary Interests of Sir Francis Bryan: A Study in Early Tudor Ideas", [University of Chicago] *Abstracts of Theses*, Humanistic Series, VIII (1932), 429–33.

36 Alwin Thaler, "Shakespeare on Style, Imagination, and Poetry", *PMLA*, LIII (1938), 1019–36.

37 Richard F. Jones, "Richard Mulcaster's View of the English Language", *Washington University Studies,* Humanistic Series, XIII (1926), 267–303.

38 Ernest A. Strathmann, "Sir Walter Ralegh on Natural Philosophy", *MLQ*, I (1940), 49–61.

39 John Robert Moore, *Daniel Defoe and Modern Economic Theory*, in *Indiana University Studies*, No. 104 (1935 for 1934).

40 F. M. Darnall, "Swift's Belief in Immortality", *MLN*, XLVII (1932), 448–51.

41 Rae Blanchard, "Richard Steele and the Status of Women", *SP*, XXVI (1929), 325–55.

42 George R. Potter, "Mark Akenside, Prophet of Evolution", *MP*, XXIV (1927), 55–64.

43 Lionel Stevenson, "Brooke's *Universal Beauty* and Modern Thought", *PMLA*, XLIII (1928), 198–209.

44 Alan D. McKillop, "Mrs. Radcliffe on the Supernatural in Poetry", *JEGP*, XXI (1932), 352–59.

45 Clarence DeWitt Thorpe, "Keats's Interest in Politics and World Affairs", *PMLA*, XLVI (1931), 1228–45.

46 Francis W. Palmer, "The Bearing of Science on the Thought of Arthur Hugh Clough", *PMLA*, LIX (1944), 212–25.

47 Fred A. Dudley, "Matthew Arnold and Science", *PMLA*, LVII (1942), 275–94.

48 Ruth C. Child, *The Æsthetic of Walter Pater* (New York: Macmillan, 1940).

49 William O. Raymond, "Browning and Higher Criticism", *PMLA*, XLIV (1929), 590–621.

50 David Williams, "More Light on Franklin's Religious Ideas", *American Historical Review*, XLIII (1938), 803–13.

51 Arthur I. Ladu, "Channing and Transcendentalism", *AmLit*, XI (1939–40), [129]–37.

52 *Idem*, "The Political Ideas of Orestes A. Brownson", *PQ*, XII (1933), 280–89.

53 Clifton Joseph Furness, "Walt Whitman's Politics", *American Mercury*, XVI (1929), 459–66.

54 Edwin Mims, "The Social Philosophy of Ellen Glasgow", *Journal of Social Forces*, IV (1926), 495–503.

55 T[homas] S[tearns] Eliot, "The Humanism of Irving Babbitt", *Forum*, LXXX (1928), 37–44.

56 Philip A. Smith, "Bishop Hall, 'Our English Seneca' ", *PMLA*, LXIII (1948), 1191–1204.

57 Elbert N. S. Thompson, "The Philosophy of Thomas Traherne", *PQ*, VIII (1929), 97–112.

58 Newton P. Stallknecht, "Wordsworth and Philosophy", *PMLA*, XLIV (1929), 1116–43; and *idem*, "Nature and Imagination in Wordsworth's Meditation upon Mt. Snowden", *PMLA*, LII (1937), 835–47. See also Melvin Rader, "The Transcendentalism of William Wordsworth", *MP*, XXVI (1928–29), 169–90.

59 Robert P. Falk, "Thomas Paine: Deist or Quaker?", *Pennsylvania Magazine of History and Biography*, LXII (1938), 52–63.

60 William Charvat, "Prescott's Political and Social Attitudes", *AmLit*, XIII (1941–42), [320]–30.

61 Frederic I. Carpenter, "William James and Emerson", *AmLit*, XI (1939–40), [39]–57.

62 George J. Becker, "Albion W. Tourgée: Pioneer in Social Criticism", *AmLit*, XIX (1947–48), [59]–72.

63 Hyatt Howe Waggoner, "Hart Crane's Bridge to Cathay", *AmLit*, XVI (1944–45), [115]–30.

64 Woodburn O. Ross, "Concerning Dreiser's Mind", *AmLit*, XVIII (1946–47), [233]–43.

65 Martin A. Larson, *The Modernity of Milton* (Chicago: University of Chicago Press, 1927ᶜ).

66 William P. Dunn, *Sir Thomas Browne: A Study in Religious Philosophy* (Menasha, Wisconsin: privately printed, 1926).

67 Clarence D. Thorpe, *The Mind of John Keats* (New York: Oxford University Press, 1926).

68 Newton Arvin, *Hawthorne* (Boston: Little, Brown, 1926).

69 Lewis Mumford, *Herman Melville* (New York: Literary Guild, 1929).

70 Genevieve Taggard [Mrs. Robert L. Wolf], *The Life and Mind of Emily Dickinson* (New York and London: Knopf, 1930).

71 Putnam Fennell Jones, "Milton and the Epic Subject from British History", *PMLA*, XLII (1927), 901–9.

72 Richard Croom Beatty, "Criticism in Fielding's Narratives and His Estimate of Critics", *PMLA*, XLIX (1934), 1087–1100.

73 Arthur L. Cooke, "Henry Fielding and the Writers of Heroic Romance", *PMLA*, LXII (1947), 984–94.

74 W. F. Gallaway, Jr., "The Sentimentalism of Goldsmith," *PMLA*, XLVIII (1933), 1167–81.

75 Harold H. Watts, "Lytton's Theories of Prose Fiction", *PMLA*, L (1935), 274–89.

76 Emerson Grant Sutcliffe, "*Fœmina Vera* in Charles Reade's Novels", *PMLA*, XLVI (1931), 126–79.

77 Donald Smalley, "A Parleying with Aristophanes", *PMLA*, LV (1940), 823–38.

78 Ruth C. Child, "Swinburne's Mature Standards of Criticism", *PMLA*, LII (1937), 870–79.

79 Allan G. Halline, "Maxwell Anderson's Dramatic Theory", *AmLit*, XVI (1944–45), [63]–81.

80 Lane Cooper, "Coleridge, Wordsworth, and Mr. Lowes", *PMLA*, XLIII (1928), 582–92.

81 Dixon Wecter, "Burke's Theory Concerning Words, Images, and Emotions", *PMLA*, LV (1940), 167–81.

82 Ernest Marchand, "The Literary Opinions of Charles Brockden Brown", *SP*, XXXI (1934), 541–66.

83 Charles Howell Foster, "Hawthorne's Literary Theory", *PMLA*, LVII (1942), 241–54.

84 Robert P. Falk, "Critical Tendencies in Richard Grant White's Shakespeare Commentary", *AmLit*, XX (1948–49), [144]–54.

85 Laurence Barrett, "Young Henry James, Critic", *AmLit*, XX (1948–49), [385]–400.

86 Thomas M. Raysor, "Coleridge's Criticism of Wordsworth", *PMLA*, LIV (1939), 496–510.

87 Harry Hayden Clark, "Lowell's Criticism of Romantic Literature", *PMLA*, XLI (1926), 209–28.

88 Harry T. Baker, "Hazlitt as a Shakesperean Critic", *PMLA*, XLVII (1932), 191–99.

89 William D. Templeman, "Thoreau, Moralist of the Picturesque", *PMLA*, XLVII (1932), 864–89; James G. Southworth, *"Thoreau, Moralist of* the Picturesque", *PMLA*, XLIX (1934), 971–74: and Fred W. Lorch, "Thoreau and the Organic Principle in Poetry", *PMLA*, LIII (1938), 286–302.

90 Morris U. Schappes, "William Ernest Henley's Principles of Criticism", *PMLA*, XLVI (1931), 1289–1301.

91 Ruth C. Child, "Is Walter Pater an Impressionistic Critic?", *PMLA*, LIII (1938), 1172–85.

92 Arthur Robinson, "Meredith's Literary Theory and Science: Realism Versus the Comic Spirit", *PMLA*, LIII (1938), 857–68.

93 William D. Briggs, "Political Ideas in Sidney's *Arcadia*", *SP*, XXVIII (1931), 137–61; see also *idem*, "Sidney's Political Ideas", *SP*, XXIX (1932), 534–42.

94 T. C. Wedel, "On the Philosophical Background of *Gulliver's Travels*", *SP*, XXIII (1926), 434–50.

95 Olive B. White, "Richard Taverner's Interpretation of Erasmus in *Proverbes or Adagies*", *PMLA*, LIX (1944), 928–43.

96 Hoxie N. Fairchild, "Hartley, Pistorius, and Coleridge", *PMLA*, LXII (1947), 1010–21.

97 Hyatt Howe Waggoner, "T. S. Eliot and *The Hollow Men*", *AmLit*, XV (1943–44), [101]–26.

98 Agnes K. Getty, "Chaucer's Changing Conceptions of the Humble Lover", *PMLA*, XLIV (1929), 202–16.

99 Sister Eugenia, "Coleridge's Scheme of Pantisocracy and American Travel Accounts", *PMLA*, XLV (1930), 1069–84.

100 J. V. Nash, "The Religious Evolution of Darwin", *Open Court*, XLII (1928), 449–63.

101 Charles Child Walcutt, "The Three Stages of Theodore Dreiser's Naturalism", *PMLA*, LV (1940), 266–89.

102 Ralph M. Wardle, "Mary Wollstonecraft, *Analytical Reviewer,*" *PMLA*, LXII (1947), 1000–9.

103 Mildred Silver, "Emerson and the Idea of Progress", *AmLit*, XII (1940–41), [1]–19, and Marjory M. Moody, "The Evolution of Emerson as an Abolitionist", *AmLit*, XVII (1945–46), [1]–21.

104 Adeline R. Tintner, "The Spoils of Henry James", *PMLA*, LXI (1946), 239–51.

105 Daniel C. Boughner, "The Psychology of Memory in Spenser's *Fœrie Queene*", *PMLA*, XLVII (1932); see also Louise C. Turner Forest, "A Caveat for Critics against Invoking Elizabethan Psychology", *PMLA*, LXI (1946), 651–72.

106 Laurens Joseph Mills, "The Friendship Theme in Orrery's Plays", *PMLA*, LIII (1938), 795–806.

107 Dorothy Richardson, "Saintsbury and Art for Art's Sake in England", *PMLA*, LIX (1944), 243–60.

108 Marjorie Nicolson, "Kepler, the *Somnium*, and John Donne", *Journal of the History of Ideas*, I (1940), 259–80.

109 Otto F. Kranshaar, "Lotze's Influence on the Pragmatism and Prac-

tical Philosophy of William James", *Journal of the History of Ideas,* I (1940),
439–58; see also *idem,* "Lotze's Influence on the Psychology of William
James", *Psychological Review,* XLIII (1936), 235–57; *idem,* "What James's
Philosophical Orientation Owed to Lotze", *Philosophical Review,* XLVII
(1938), 517–26; and *idem,* "Lotze as a Factor in the Development of James's
Radical Empiricism and Pluralism", *Philosophical Review,* XLVIII (1939),
455–71.

110 Estelle Kaplan, *Philosophy in the Poetry of Edwin Arlington Robinson* (New York: Columbia University Press, 1940).

111 John S[mith] Harrison, *Platonism in English Poetry of the Sixteenth
and Seventeenth Centuries* (New York: Columbia University Press and Macmillan, and London: Macmillan, 1903).

112 M. Ellwood Smith, "Æsop, a Decayed Celebrity", *PMLA,* XLVI
(1931), 225–36.

113 Charles Sears Baldwin, *Medieval Rhetoric and Poetic (to 1400)
Interpreted from Representative Works* (New York: Macmillan, 1928).

114 John Livingston Lowes, *Convention and Revolt in Poetry* (Boston and
New York: Houghton Mifflin, 1919).

115 Laurens J[oseph] Mills, *One Soul in Bodies Twain* (Bloomington,
Indiana: Principia Press, 1937).

116 Ruth L. Anderson, *Elizabethan Psychology and Shakespeare's Plays,*
in *University of Iowa Studies,* Humanistic Series, III, No. 4 (1927).

117 Carroll Collier Moreland, "Ritson's Life of Robin Hood", *PMLA,* L
(1935), 522–36.

118 Paul Spencer Wood, "Native Elements in English Neo-Classicism",
MP, XXIV (1926–27), 201–8.

119 Raymond D. Havens, "Changing Taste in the Eighteenth Century:
A Study of Dryden's and Dodsley's Miscellanies", *PMLA,* XLIV (1929),
501–63.

120 Hoxie N[eale] Fairchild, *The Noble Savage: A Study in Romantic
Naturalism* (New York: Columbia University Press, 1928).

121 J. N. Vedder, "The Nature of Romanticism", *Faculty Papers of
Union College,* I (1930), 95–114.

122 Eleanor M. Sickels, *The Gloomy Egotist: Moods and Themes of
Melancholy from Gray to Keats* (New York: Columbia University Press,
1929).

123 Ernest S. Bates, "Mad Shelley: A Study in the Origins of English
Romanticism", *Fred Newton Scott Papers* (Chicago: University of Chicago
Press, and London: Cambridge University Press, 1929), pp. 117–40.

124 Edward E. Cassady, "Muckraking in the Gilded Age", *AmLit,* XIII
(1941–42), [134]–41.

125 Notley S. Maddox, "Literary Nationalism in *Putnam's Magazine,*
1853–1857", *AmLit,* XIV (1942–43), [117]–25.

126 Robert E. Streeter, "Association Psychology and Literary Nationalism
in the *North American Review,* 1815–1825", *AmLit,* XVII (1945–46), [243]–
54.

127 Robert D. Williams, "Antiquarian Interest in Elizabethan Drama before Lamb", *PMLA*, LIII (1938), 434–44.

128 Wallace Cable Brown, "Prose Fiction and English Interest in the Near East, 1775–1825", *PMLA*, LIII (1938), 827–36.

129 Joseph Bunn Heidler, *The History, from 1700 to 1800, of English Criticism of Prose Fiction,* in *University of Illinois Studies in Language and Literature,* XIII (1928).

130 George G. Williams, "The Beginnings of Nature Poetry in the Eighteenth Century", *SP*, XXVII (1930), 583–608.

131 Elizabeth Cox Wright, "Continuity in XV Century English Humanism", *PMLA*, LI (1936), 370–76, and W. Gordon Zeeveld, "Richard Morison, Official Apologist for Henry VIII", *PMLA*, LV (1940), 406–25.

132 Ralph Hinsdale Goodale, "Schopenhauer and Pessimism in Nineteenth Century English Literature", *PMLA*, XLVII (1932), 241–61.

133 Arthur O. Lovejoy and George Boas, *Primitivism and Related Ideas in Antiquity,* Vol. I of *A Documentary History of Primitivism and Related Ideas,* eds. Arthur O. Lovejoy, Gilbert Chinard, George Boas, and Ronald S. Crane (Baltimore: Johns Hopkins Press, 1935–   ).

134 George Williamson, "The Restoration Revolt against Enthusiasm", *SP*, XXX (1933), 571–630; see also below, n. 143.

135 William E. Alderman, "Shaftesbury and the Doctrine of Optimism in the Eighteenth Century", *Transactions of the Wisconsin Academy,* XXVIII (1933), 297–305.

136 William Haller, *The Rise of Puritanism* (New York: Columbia University Press, 1938).

137 C[hauncey] B[rewster] Tinker, *Nature's Simple Plan* (Princeton: Princeton University Press, 1922).

138 Lynn Thorndike, "The Survival of Medieval Intellectual Interest into Early Modern Times", *Speculum*, II (1927), 147–59.

139 Lester Kruger Born, "The Perfect Prince: A Study in Thirteenth and Fourteenth Century Ideals", *Speculum*, III (1928), 470–504.

140 C. H. Haskins, "The Spread of Ideas in the Middle Ages", *Speculum,* I (1926), 19–30.

141 Louis B. Wright, "The Renaissance Middle-Class Concern over Learning", *PQ*, IX (1931), 273–96.

142 Idem, *Middle-Class Culture in Elizabethan England* (Chapel Hill, N. C.: University of North Carolina Press, 1925).

143 Clarence M. Webster, "Swift and Some Earlier Satirists of Puritan Enthusiasm", *PMLA*, XLVIII (1933), 1141–53.

144 W. F. Gallaway, Jr., "The Conservative Attitude toward Fiction, 1770–1830", *PMLA*, LV (1940), 1041–59.

145 C[hauncey] B[rewster] Tinker, *The Salon and English Letters* (New York: Macmillan, 1915).

146 G. Harrison Orians, "Censure of Fiction in American Romances and Magazines 1789–1810", *PMLA*, LII (1937), 195–214.

147 William C. Frierson, "The English Controversy over Realism in Fiction, 1885–1895", *PMLA*, XLIII (1928), 533–50.

148 Clarence Decker, "Victorian Comment on Russian Realism", *PMLA*, LII (1937), 542–49.

149 William C. Frierson and Herbert Edwards, "Impact of French Naturalism on American Critical Opinion 1877–1892", *PMLA*, LXIII (1948), 1007–16.

150 Clyde K. Hyder, "The Medieval Background of Swinburne's *The Leper*", *PMLA*, XLVI (1931), 1280–88.

151 Erika von Erhardt-Siebold, "Harmony of the Senses in English, German, and French Romanticism", *PMLA*, XLVII (1932), 577–92.

152 Louis I. Bredvold, "The Tendency toward Platonism in Neo-Classical Æsthetics", *ELH*, I (1934), 91–119.

153 Raymond D. Havens, "Changing Taste in the Eighteenth Century", *PMLA*, XLIV (1929), 501–36; Edward Niles Hooker, "The Discussion of Taste, from 1750 to 1770, and the New Trends in Literary Criticism", *PMLA*, XLIX (1934), 577–92; and R. W. Babcock, "The Idea of Taste in the Eighteenth Century", *PMLA*, L (1935), 922–26.

154 Clarence R. Decker, "The Æsthetic Revolt against Naturalism in Victorian Criticism", *PMLA*, LIII (1938), 844–56.

155 Frederic E. Faverty, "Legends of Joseph in Old and Middle English", *PMLA*, XLIII (1928), 79–104.

156 Roscoe E. Parker, "The Reputation of Herod in Early English Literature", *Speculum*, VIII (1933), 59–67.

157 M. Channing Linthicum, " 'Something Browner than Judas's' ", *PMLA*, XLVII (1932), 905–7.

158 William G. Bowling, "The Wild Prince Hal in Legend and Literature", *Washington University Studies*, Humanistic Series, XIII (1926), 205–34, and D. T. Starnes, "More about the Prince Hal Legend", *PQ*, XV (1936), 358–66.

159 Beatrice Daw Brown, "Medieval Prototypes of Lorenzo and Jessica", *MLN*, XLIV (1929), 227–32.

160 Archibald A. Hill, "Diomede: The Traditional Development of a Character", *Essays and Studies in English and Comparative Literature by Members of the English Department of the University of Michigan* (1932), pp. 1–25.

161 Allen H. Godbey, "The Devil in Legend and Literature", *Open Court*, XLVII (1933), 385–97.

162 Robert Withington, "The Development of the Vice", *Essays in Memory of Barrett Wendell* (Cambridge, Mass.: Harvard University Press, 1926), pp. 153–67; *idem*, "The Ancestry of the 'Vice' ", *Speculum*, VII (1932), 525–29; see also the note following.

163 *Idem*, " 'Vice' and 'Parasite'. A Note on the Evolution of the Elizabethan Villain", *PMLA*, XLIX (1934), 743–51.

164 Louis B[ernard] Salomon, *The Rebellious Lover in English Poetry* (Philadelphia: University of Pennsylvania Press, 1931); also published without notes as *Devil Take Her* (Philadelphia: University of Pennsylvania Press, 1932).

165 Ruth Kelso, *The Institution of the Gentleman in English Literature of the Sixteenth Century: A Study in Renaissance Ideals* (Urbana, Illinois: University of Illinois Press, 1929).

166 Ezra Kempton Maxfield, "The Quakers in English Stage Plays before 1800", *PMLA*, XLV (1930), 256–73, and John Wilson Bowyer, "Quakers on the English Stage", *PMLA*, XLV (1930), 957–58.

167 John Harrington Smith, "Tony Lumpkin and the Country Booby Type in Antecedent English Comedy", *PMLA*, LVIII (1943), 1038–49.

168 Helaine Newstead, "The Besieged Ladies in Arthurian Romance", *PMLA*, LXIII (1948), 803–30.

169 Harold F. Watson, *The Sailor in English Fiction and Drama 1550–1800* (New York: Columbia University Press, 1931).

170 John E. Hankins, "Caliban the Bestial Man", *PMLA*, LXII (1947), 793–801.

171 Kenneth C. Slagle, *The English Country Squire as Depicted in English Prose Fiction from 1740 to 1800* (Philadelphia: privately printed, 1938).

172 Robert L. Shurter, "The Utopian Novel in America", *South Atlantic Quarterly*, XXXIV (1935), 137–44; a more recent study of Utopian fiction is J. O. Bailey, *Pilgrims through Time and Space* (New York: Argus Books, 1947).

173 Phillips D. Carleton, "The Indian Captivity", *AmLit*, XV (1943–44), [169]–80, and Roy Harvey Pearce, "The Significances of the Captivity Narrative", *AmLit*, XIX (1947–48), [1]–20.

174 Arnold M. Rose, *The Negro's Morale: Group Identification and Protest* (Minneapolis: University of Minnesota Press, 1949).

175 Ina Corinne Brown, *The Story of the American Negro* (New York: Friendship Press, 1950), rev. ed.; first published in 1936.

176 Idem, *Race Relations in a Democracy* (New York: Harper, 1949).

177 Bliss Perry, *The American Mind* (Boston and New York: Houghton Mifflin, 1912).

178 Henry Steele Commager, *The American Mind* (New Haven: Yale University Press, 1950).

179 Vernon Louis Parrington, *Main Currents in American Thought* (New York: Harcourt Brace, 1927–30), 3 vols.

180 Oscar Cargill, *Intellectual America: Ideas on the March* (New York: Macmillan, 1941).

181 Van Wyck Brooks, *Literature in New England: The Flowering of New England 1815–1865; New England: Indian Summer 1865–1915* (Garden City, N. Y.: Garden City Publishing Co., [1944]); the first of these two works was published in 1936, the second in 1940.

182 Wesley Frank Craven, *The Southern Colonies in the Seventeenth Century, 1607–1689* (Baton Rouge, La.: Louisiana State University Press and the Littlefield Fund for Southern History of the University of Texas, 1949); this is Vol. I of *A History of the South*, eds. Wendell Holmes Stephenson and E. Merton Coulter, to be complete in ten volumes, of which four volumes have thus far been published.

183 Hardin Craig, *The Enchanted Glass: The Elizabethan Mind in Literature* (New York: Oxford University Press, 1936).

184 Perry Miller, *The New England Mind: The Seventeenth Century* (New York: Macmillan, 1939).

185 Roy Franklin Nichols, *The Disruption of American Democracy* (New York: Macmillan, 1948).

186 Evarts Boutell Greene, *The Revolutionary Generation, 1763–1790* (New York: Macmillan, 1943); this is Vol. IV of *A History of American Life,* eds. Arthur M. Schlesinger and Dixon Ryan Fox (New York: Macmillan, 1927–   ), of which thirteen volumes have been published.

187 William Charvat, *The Origins of American Critical Thought, 1810– 1835* (Philadelphia: University of Pennsylvania Press, and London: Milford and Oxford University Press, 1936).

188 Norman Foerster, *American Criticism: A Study in Literary Theory from Poe to the Present* (Boston and New York: Houghton Mifflin, 1928).

189 Raymond G[arfield] Gettell, *History of American Political Thought* (New York and London: Century, 1928).

190 Henry Alonzo Myers, *Are Men Equal? An Inquiry into the Meaning of American Democracy* (New York: Putnam's, 1945).

191 Thomas G. Manning, David M. Potter, and Wallace E. Davies, *Government and the American Economy, 1870–Present* (New York: Henry Holt, 1950).

192 Albert Post, *Popular Freethought in America 1825–1850* (New York: Columbia University Press, 1943).

193 Sidney Warren, *American Freethought, 1860–1914* (New York: Columbia University Press, 1943).

194 Leonard J. Trinterud, *The Forming of an American Tradition: A Reexamination of Colonial Presbyterianism* (Philadelphia: Westminster Press, 1949).

195 Kenneth P. Williams, *Lincoln Finds a General: A Military Study of the Civil War,* Vols. I and II of four (New York: Macmillan, 1949).

196 Francis Shoemaker, *Æsthetic Experience and the Humanities* (New York: Columbia University Press, 1943).

197 Homer C. Hockett and Arthur M. Schlesinger, *The Political and Social Growth of the American People,* 3rd ed. (New York: Macmillan, 1940–41), 2 vols.

198 Dixon Wecter and others, *Changing Patterns in American Civilization* (Philadelphia: University of Pennsylvania Press, 1949).

199 *Years of the Modern,* ed. John W. Chase (New York: Longmans, 1949).

200 Michael Kraus, *The Atlantic Civilization: Eighteenth Century Origins* (Ithaca, N. Y.: Cornell University Press, 1949).

201 Halvdan Koht, *The American Spirit in Europe* (Philadelphia: University of Pennsylvania Press, 1949).

202   Sir John Marriott, *English History in English Fiction* (New York: Dutton, 1941), and Homer E. Woodbridge, *Sir William Temple* (New York: Modern Language Association, and London: Oxford University Press, 1940).

203   Joseph B. Collins, *Christian Mysticism in the Elizabethan Age* (Baltimore: Johns Hopkins Press, 1940), and Howard W. Hintz, *The Quaker Influence in American Literature* (New York: Revell, 1940).

204   G. C. Coulton, *Studies in Mediæval Thought* (London and New York: Thomas Nelson and Sons, 1940).

205   *The Letters of Saint Boniface,* tr. Ephraim Emerton (New York: Columbia University Press, 1940), and Frank J. Klingberg, *Anglican Humanitarianism in Colonial New York* (Philadelphia: The Church Historical Society, 1940).

Articles in the field of the history of ideas include Eugene F. Bradford, "Anglo-Saxon Melancholy", *Harvard University Summaries of Theses . . . 1927* (Cambridge, Mass.: Harvard University Press, 1931), pp. 148–50; Marjorie Nicolson, "The Early Stages of Cartesianism in England", *SP*, XXVI (1929), 356–74; Esther E. Burch, "The Sources of New England Democracy: A Controversial Statement in Parringston's *Main Currents in American Thought*", *AmLit*, I 1929–30), [115]–40; George L. Marsh, "The Early Reviews of Shelley", *MP*, XXVII (1929–30), 73–95; R. W. Babcock, "The Attack of the Late Eighteenth Century upon Alterations of Shakespeare's Plays", *MLN*, XLV (1930), 446–51; *idem*, "The Attitude toward Shakespeare's Learning in the Late Eighteenth Century", *PQ*, IX (1930), 116–22; Lily B[ess] Campbell, "Theorie of Revenge in Renaissance England", *MP*, XXVIII (1930–31), 281–96; W. Lee Ustick, "Changing Ideals of Aristocratic Character and Conduct in Seventeenth-Century England", *MP*, XXX (1932–33), 147–66; C. H. Faust, "The Background of the Unitarian Opposition to Transcendentalism", *MP*, XXXV (1937–38), 297–324; Neal Frank Doubleday, "Hawthorne and Literary Nationalism", *AmLit*, XII (1940–41), [447]–53; Hyatt Howe Waggoner, "The Humanistic Idealism of Robert Frost", *AmLit*, XIII (1941–42), [207]–23; Z. S. Fink, "The Theory of the Mixed State and the Development of Milton's Political Thought", *PMLA*, LVII (1942), 705–36; David H. Dickason, "Benjamin Orange Flower, Patron of the Realists", *AmLit*, XIV (1942–43), [148]–56; Baxter Hathaway, "John Dryden and the Function of Tragedy", *PMLA*, LVIII (1943), 665–73; Olive Wrenchel Parsons, "Whitman the Non-Hegelian", *PMLA*, LVIII (1943), 1073–93; Hannah Graham Belcher, "Howells's Opinions on the Religious Conflicts of His Age as Exhibited in Magazine Articles", *AmLit*, XV (1943–44), [262]–78; Margaret Denny, "Cheever's Anthology and American Romanticism", *AmLit*, XV (1943–44), [1]–9; Eleanor M. Sickels, "Archibald MacLeish and American Democracy", *AmLit*, XV (1943–44), [223]–37; Ruth Mohl, "Theories of Monarchy in *Mum and the Sothsegger*", *PMLA*, LIX (1944), 26–44; R. E. Watters, "Melville's 'Sociality'", *AmLit*, XVII (1945–46), [33]–49; Edward S. Le Comte, "Milton's Attitude Towards Women in the *History of Britain*", *PMLA*, LXII (1947), 977–83; Arthur H. Nethercot, "The Quintessence of Idealism; Or, The Slaves of Duty", *PMLA*, LXII

(1947), 844–59; Warrington Winters, "Dickens and the Psychology of Dreams", *PMLA*, LXIII (1948), 984–1006; and Daniel Stempel, "Lafcadio Hearn: Interpreter of Japan", *AmLit*, XX (1948–49), [1]–19.

Among more extensive works in the field may be mentioned George T. Buckley, *Atheism in the English Renaissance* (Chicago: University of Chicago Press, 1932); H. M. Knappen, *Tudor Puritanism* (Chicago: University of Chicago Press, 1939); John Paul Pritchard, *Return to the Fountains: Some Classical Sources of American Criticism* (Durham, N. C.: Duke University Press, 1942); Arthur Alphonse Ekirch, *The Idea of Progress in America, 1815– 1860* (New York: Columbia University Press, 1944); Kenneth Walter Cameron, *Emerson the Essayist* (Raleigh, N. C.: Thistle Press, 1945), 2 vols.; Arthur M. Schlesinger, Jr., *The Age of Jackson* (Boston: Little, Brown, 1945); Bernard Smith, *The Democratic Spirit* (New York: Knopf, 1945); Harvey Wish, *Contemporary America: The National Scene since 1900* (New York and London: Harper, [1945]); Howard Mumford Jones, *Education and World Tragedy* (Cambridge, Mass.: Harvard University Press, 1946); Herbert W. Schneider, *A History of American Philosophy* (New York: Columbia University Press, 1946); Van Wyck Brooks, *The Times of Melville and Whitman* (New York: Dutton, 1947); Louis M. Hacker, *The Shaping of the American Tradition* (New York: Columbia University Press, 1947), 2 vols.; Lloyd R. Morris, *Postscript to Yesterday: the Last Fifty Years* (New York: Random House, 1947)—see also *idem, Not So Long Ago* (New York: Random House, 1949); Henry Bamford Parkes, *The American Experience: An Interpretation of the History and Civilization of the American People* (New York: Knopf, 1947); Eric Fischer, *Passing of the European Age* (Cambridge, Mass.: Harvard University Press, 1948), first published in 1943; Dixon Wecter, *The Age of the Great Depression, 1929–1941* (New York: Macmillan, 1948); Max Ascoli, *The Power of Freedom* (New York: Farrar, Straus, 1949); *The Heritage of America*, eds. Henry Steele Commager and Allan Nevins (Boston: Little, Brown, 1949); Gilbert Highet, *The Classical Tradition: Greek and Roman Influences on Western Literature* (Oxford: Oxford University Press, 1949); Arthur M. Schlesinger, *Paths to the Present* (New York: Macmillan, 1949); Arthur M. Schlesinger, Jr., *The Vital Center* (New York: Houghton Mifflin, 1949); Peter Viereck, *Conservatism Revisited* (New York: Scribner's, 1949); and Henry Steele Commager, *Majority Rule and Minority Rights* (New York: Peter Smith, 1950), rev. ed., first published in 1943.

Chapter Ten: Problems in Folklore

1 Translated by A. W. Ryder (Chicago: 1925ᶜ); for a good account of the whole Panchatantra tradition, and indeed of the whole field of Indic fiction, see Bolte and Polívka, *Anmerkungen zu den Kinder- und Hausmärchen der Brüder Grimm*, IV, 286 ff.

2 Edited by N. M. Penzer (London: 1924–28).

3 Translated and edited by E. Lancereau (Paris: 1882).

4 Translated and edited by R. Schmidt (Stuttgart: 1899).

5 Included in the *Ocean of Story* (see above, n. 2), and available almost completely in A. W. Ryder, *Twenty-Two Goblins* (London: 1917).

6 Translated and edited by F. Edgerton (Cambridge, Mass.: 1926).

7 Ed. E. B. Cowell (Cambridge, England: 1893–1907), 6 vols.

8 Translated by George Rosen (Leipzig: n.d.).

9 Ed. Killis Campbell (Boston: 1907); this edition contains a good discussion of the whole tradition.

10 For full bibliographical and comparative treatment and summaries of all the tales see V. Chauvin, *Bibliographie des Ouvrages Arabes* (Liége: 1892–1923), 12 vols. The best English translations are those of Lane (London: 1839–41), 3 vols., and Burton (Benares: 1885), 10 vols.

11 Cf. M. Gaster, *The Exempla of the Rabbis* (London: 1924); M. J. bin Gorion, *Der Born Judas* (Leipzig: 1918–   ), 6 vols.

12 J. G. Frazer, *Apollodorus: the Library* (London: 1921), 2 vols.

13 Lucius Apuleius, *The Golden Ass* . . . , tr. W. Adlington (London: Heinemann, and New York: Macmillan, 1915).

14 Ed. H. Oesterley (Berlin: 1872); English translation by C. Swan (London: 1888). Good discussions are found in S. J. Herrtage, *The Early English Versions of the Gesta Romanorum,* in EETS, No. 33 (1879) and in Herbert, *Catalogue of Romances in the British Museum,* III, 183 ff.

15 Ed. T. F. Crane (London: 1890).

16 Neither the *Scala Celi* (Lübeck: 1476) nor the *Summa Predicantium* (Basel: 1479; the latest edition Antwerp: 1614) have appeared in modern editions.

17 For a definitive treatment of the exemplum, see J. Wetter, *L'Exemplum dans la littérature . . . du Moyen Age* (Paris: 1927).

18 A good summary of the Æsop material is given in J. Jacobs, *The Fables of Æsop* (London: 1894); many of the texts are in Hervieux, *Les Fabulistes Latins* (Paris: 1883–99), 5 vols. See also Ward, *Catalogue of Romances in the British Museum* (London: 1893), II, 272 ff.

19 For a bibliography see Bolte's edition of Pauli's *Schimpf und Ernst* (Berlin: 1924), II, 243 ff.

20 A considerable series of these have been published by Hyder Rollins, the most important being *The Pepys Ballads A Handfull of Pleasant Delights* (1924), *The Pack of Autolycus* (1927), *A Pepysian Garland* (1922), *Cavalier and Puritan* (1923), and *Old English Ballads* (1920). The Ballad Society has issued, among others, *The Roxburghe Ballads* and the *Bagford Ballads* in their publications beginning in 1869 (London).

21 See also, for folk music, Herzog, *Research in Primitive and Folk Music in the United States* (Washington: American Council of Learned Societies, 1936), Bulletin 24.

22 A good summary appears in A. Taylor, *The Black Ox,* in *FF Communications* No. 70 (Helsinki: 1927), pp. 3–15, and K. Krohn, *Die Folkloristische Arbeitsmethode* (Oslo: 1926).

23 See Archer Taylor, *Edward and Sven i Rosengard* (Chicago: 1931).

24 See Aarne, *Vergleichende Rätselforschungen,* in *FF Communications* Nos. 26–28 (Helsinki: 1918).

25 See Elsa Enäjärvi-Haavio, *The Game of Rich and Poor,* in *FF Communications* No. 100 (Helsinki: 1923).

26 See M. Haavio, *Kettenmärchenstudien,* in *FF Communications* Nos. 88, 99 (Helsinki: 1929–31), 2 vols.; A. Wesselski, "Das Märchen vom Tode des Huhnchens und andere Kettenmärlein", *Hessische Blätter für Volkskunde,* XXXII (1933), 1–51; A. Taylor, "A Classification of Formula Tales", *Journal of American Folklore,* XLVI (1934), 77 ff.

27 For a suggestive treatment of this subject, see H. Naumann, *Primitive Gemeinschaftskultur* (Jena: 1921).

28 See, for example, Bolte and Polívka, *Anmerkungen zu den Kinder- und Hausmärchen der Brüder Grimm,* IV, 1 ff.; A. Wesselski, *Versuch einer Theorie des Märchens* (Reichenberg: 1931); K. Wehrhan, *Die Sage* (Leipzig: 1908); H. Honti, *Volksmärchen und Heldensage,* in *FF Communications* No. 95 (Helsinki: 1931); also *Handwörterbuch des deutschen Märchens, passim;* A. Taylor, *The Proverb* (Cambridge, Mass.: 1931); Richard Jente, "A Review of Proverb Literature since 1920", *Corona* [Studies in Celebration of the 80th Birthday of Samuel Singer] (Durham, N. C.: 1941), pp. 23–44.

29 In Harvard *Studies and Notes,* XI (1907).

30 See K. Krohn, *Kalavalastudien,* in *FF Communications* Nos. 53, 69, 71, 72, 75, and 76 (Helsinki: 1924–28).

31 See, for example, F. W. Panzer, *Studien zur Germanischen Sagengeschichte* (München: 1910), 2 vols. (Beowulf, Sigfrid); F. von der Leyen, *Die Märchen in der Göttersagen der Edda* (Berlin: 1899).

32 See Herzog, "Musical Typology in Folksong", *Southern Folklore Quarterly,* I (June, 1937), 49–55.

Appendix A

SPECIMEN BIBLIOGRAPHIES

I Works on Bibliography and Methods of Research

AINSLIE, DOUGLAS, see CROCE, BENEDETTO

AVEY, ALBERT E., *The Functions and Forms of Thought* (New York: Henry Holt, 1912)

BERRY, G. G., see LANGLOIS, C. V.

BLACK, JOHN BENNETT, *The Art of History* (London: Methuen, 1926)

BOAS, F[rederick] S[amuel], "Some Aspects of Research", *School and Society,* XVIII (July 28, 1923), 98–102

BYRNE, M[uriel] ST. C[lare], "Anthony Munday's Spelling as a Literary Clue", *The Library,* 4th series, IV (1923–24), 9–23

CLARK, A[lbert] C[urtis], *The Descent of Manuscripts* (Oxford: Clarendon Press, 1918)

COFFEY, PETER, *The Science of Logic* (New York: Longmans, Green, 1912), 2 vols.

COLE, GEORGE WATSON, *Compiling a Bibliography* (New York: *Library Journal,* 1902)

COOLEY, W[illiam] F[orbes], and others, *An Introduction to Reflective Thinking* (Boston: Houghton, Mifflin, 1923)

CROCE, BENEDETTO, *History, Its Theory and Practice,* tr. Douglas Ainslie (New York: Harcourt, Brace, 1921)

CRUMP, C[harles] G[eorge,], *History and Historical Research* (London: Routledge, 1928)

CURL, MERVIN JAMES, *Expository Writing* (Boston: Houghton, Mifflin, 1919)

DEWEY, JOHN, *How We Think* (Boston: D. C. Heath, 1910)

DOW, EARLE W., *Principles of a Note-System for Historical Studies* (New York: Century, 1924)

DUFF, E[dward] G[ordon], see MADAN, F[alconer]

ESDAILE, ARUNDELL, *The Sources of English Literature: A Guide for Students* (Cambridge: Cambridge University Press, 1928)

―――, *A Student's Manual of Bibliography* (London: Allen and Unwin, and New York: Scribner's, 1931)

FLING, FRED M[orrow], *The Writing of History* (New Haven: Yale University Press, 1920)

FREEMAN, EDWARD A[ugustus], *Methods of Historical Study* (London: Macmillan, 1886)

GEORGE, H[ereford] B[rooke], *Historical Evidence* (Oxford: Clarendon Press, 1919)

GIBSON, S[trickland], see MADAN, F[alconer]

GREG, W[alter] W[ilson], "A Formulary of Collation", *The Library,* 4th series, XIV (1933–34), 365–82

―――, "What Is Bibliography?", *Transactions of the Bibliographical Society* [London], XII (1911–13), 40–53

―――, see POLLARD, A[lfred] W[illiam]

HUTCHINS, MARGARET; JOHNSON, ALICE S.; and WILLIAMS, MARGARET S., *Guide to the Use of Libraries. A Manual for College and University Students* (New York: H. W. Wilson, 1923), 2nd ed.

JEVONS, W[illiam] S[tanley], *Elementary Lessons in Logic* (New York: Macmillan, 1901)

―――, *The Principles of Science* (New York: Macmillan, 1887)

JOHNSON, ALICE S., see HUTCHINS, MARGARET

JOHNSON, ALLEN, *The Historian and Historical Evidence* (New York: Scribner's, 1926)

JUSSERAND, JEAN JULES, and others, *The Writing of History* (New York: Scribner's, 1926)

LANGLOIS, Ch[arles] V[ictor], and SEIGNOBOS, Ch[arles], *Introduction to the Study of History,* tr. G. G. Berry (London: Duckworth, and New York: Henry Holt, [1898].

McKERROW, RONALD B[runlees], *An Inroduction to Bibliography for Literary Students* (Oxford: Clarendon Press, 1928), 2nd impression, with corrections

MADAN, F[alconer]; DUFF E[dward] G[ordon]; and GIBSON, S[trickland], "Standard Descriptions of Printed Books", *Proceedings and Papers of the Oxford Bibliographical Society,* Vol. I, Pt. 1 (1923), 56–64

A Manual of Style (Chicago: University of Chicago Press, 1949), 11th ed.

MARSHALL, RICHARD L., *The Historical Criticism of Documents* (New York: Macmillan, 1920)

MOORE, MARGARET F., *Two Select Bibliographies of Medieval Historical Study* (London: Constable, 1912)

MUDGE, ISADORE GILBERT, *Bibliography* (Chicago: American Library Association, 1915)

MURRAY, DAVID, *Bibliography, Its Scope and Methods* (Glasgow: Maclehose, 1916)

PAETOW, L[ouis] J[ohn], *A Guide to the Study of Medieval History* (New York: Crofts, 1931)

PIGOTT, [Sir] F[rancis] T[aylor], "Practical Notes on Historical Research",

Transactions of the Royal Historical Society, 4th series, V (1922), 132–49

POLLARD, A[lfred] W[illiam], "Elizabethan Spelling as a Literary and Bibliographical Clue", *The Library,* 4th series, IV (1923–24), 1–8

————, and GREG, W[alter] W[ilson], "Some Points in Bibliographical Description", *Transactions of the Bibliographical Society* [London], IX (1906–8), 31–52

REEDER, WARD G., *How to Write a Thesis* (Bloomington, Illinois: Public School Publishing Co., 1925)

ROBINSON, DANIEL S[ommer], *The Principles of Reasoning* (New York: Appleton, 1928)

ROGERS, WALTER T., *A Manual of Bibliography* (London: H. Gravel, 1891)

SCHLUTER, W[illiam] C[harles], *How to Do Research Work* (New York: Prentice-Hall, 1926)

SEIGNOBOS, Ch[arles], see LANGLOIS, Ch[arles] V[ictor]

SEVERANCE, H[enry] O[rmal], "How Periodicals Aid Research", *Library Journal,* LIII (1928), 590–92

SHOTWELL, JAMES T., *Introduction to the Study of History* (New York: Columbia University Press, 1923)

TEGGART, F[rederick] J[ohn], *Theory of History* (New Haven: Yale University Press, 1925)

VAN HOESEN, H[enry] B[artlett] and WALTER, FRANK K[eller], *Bibliography, Practical, Enumerative, and Historical* (New York: Scribner's, 1928)

VINCENT, JOHN M[artin], *Historical Research* (New York: Peter Smith, 1929)

WALTER, FRANK K[eller], see VAN HOESEN, H[enry] B[artlett]

WESTWAY, F[rederic] W[illiam], *Scientific Method—Its Philosophy and Practice* (London: Blackie and Son, 1931)

WILLIAMS, IOLO A[neurin], *Elements of Book-Collecting* (London: Mathews and Marrot, and New York: F. A. Stokes, 1927)

WILLIAMS, MARGARET S., see HUTCHINS, MARGARET

II Heuristic (The Science of Finding Things)

BAKER, ERNEST A. The Uses of Libraries. London, 1927

BECKER, G[USTAV]. *Catalogi Bibliothecarum Antiqui.* Berlin, 1885

DE RICCI, SEYMOUR, with the assistance of J. W. WILSON. *Census of Medieval and Renaissance Manuscripts in the United States and Canada.* Washington, 1934

DOWLING, MARGARET. "Public Record Office Research: The Equity Side of Chancery, 1558–1714", *Review of English Studies,* VIII (1932), 185–200

GARDTHAUSEN, V[IKTOR EMIL]. *Sammlungen und Kataloge griechischer Handschriften.* 1903. (Offprint from *Byzantinische Archiv*)

GIUSEPPI, M[ONTAGUE] S[PENCER]. *A Guide to the Manuscripts Preserved in the Public Record Office.* London, 1923–24. 2 vols.

GOTTLIEB, TH[EODORE]. *Über mittelalterliche Bibliotheken.* Leipzig, 1890

HAENEL, G[USTAV]. *Catalogi librorum manuscriptorumque qui in bibliothecis Galliæ, Helvetiæ, Belgii, Britanniæ, Hispaniæ, Lusitaniæ asservantur.* Leipzig, 1830

JAMES, MONTAGUE RHODES. *The Wanderings and Homes of Manuscripts.* London and New York, 1919

MEADS, DOROTHY M. "Searching Local Records", *Review of English Studies,* IV (1928), 173–90, 301–22

DE MONTFAUCON, BERNARD. *Bibliotheca Bibliothecarum.* Paris, 1739. 2 vols.

RYE, REGINALD ARTHUR. *The Students' Guide to the Libraries of London.* London, 1927

WEINBERGER, W[ILHELM]. *Catalogus Catalogorum.* Vienna and Leipzig, 1902

WILSON, J. W., see DE RICCI, SEYMOUR

III   Paper

1   Aitken, P. Henderson, "Some notes on the history of paper-making", *Transactions of the Bibliographical Society* [London], XIII (1913–15), 201–17

2   Alibaux, Henri, "Le controle des dates par le filigrane du papier", *Le vieux papier, Bulletin de la Société Archéologique, Historique, et Artistique,* XVII (October, 1928), *fascicule* 118, pp. 271–80

3   Bevan, E[dward] J[ohn], see Cross, Charles Frederick

4   Briquet, C[harles] M[oise], *Les filigranes* (Paris, A. Picard & fils, 1907), 4 vols.

5   Butler, Frank C., *The story of paper-making* (Chicago, J. W. Butler Paper Company, 1901)

6   Cross, Charles Frederick, and Bevan, E[dward] J[ohn], *A text-book of paper-making* (London, E. and F. N. Spon, 1920), 5th ed.

7   Heawood, Edward, "Papers used in England after 1600", *The library,* 4th series, XI (1930–31), 263–99, 466–98

8   ——, "The position on the sheet of early watermarks", *The library,* 4th series, IX (1928–29), 38–47

9   ——, "Sources of early English paper-supply", *The library,* 4th series, X (1929–30), 282–307, 427–54

10   ——, "The use of watermarks in dating old maps and documents", *The geographical journal,* LXIII (1924), 391–412

11   Jahans, Gordon A., "A brief history of paper", *The book-collector's quarterly,* XV (July–September, 1934), 42–58

12   Jenkins, Rhys, "Early attempts at paper-making in England, 1495–1586", *Library association record,* II (1900), 479–88. See also pp. 577–88 and *ibid.,* III (1901), 239 ff.

IV   Ink

Caneparius, Petrus Maria. *De Atramentis cujuscunque Genesis Opus.* Rotterdam, 1718.
Carvalho, David N. *Forty Centuries of Ink.* New York, 1904.
Hepworth, T. C., see Mitchell, C. Ainsworth.
Mitchell, C[harles] Ainsworth. *Ink.* London, 1923.
——, and Hepworth, T. C. *Inks: Their Composition and Manufacture . . .* 3rd ed. London, 1924.

V   Printing

H. G. Aldis, *The Printed Book* (New York: Macmillan, 1940), revised by John Carter and E. A. Crutchley.
Pierce Butler, *The Origin of Printing in Europe* (Chicago: University of Chicago Press, 1940).
John Carter, see H. G. Aldis.
R[obert] W[illiam] Chapman, *Cancels* (London: Constable, and New York: R. R. Smith, 1930).
——, "Cancels and Stubs", *The Library,* 4th series, VIII (1927–28), 264–68.
E. Crous, G. Fumagalli, Charles Mortet, Maurits Sabbe, James P. R. Lyell, H. R. Plomer, Lauritz Nielsen, L. C. Wharton, G. P. Winship, and Lawrence C. Wroth, *Printing: a Short History of the Art* (London: Grafton, 1927), ed. R. A. Peddie.
E. A. Crutchley, see H. G. Aldis.
Hugh William Davies, *Devices of the Early Printers 1457–1560: Their History and Development* (London: Grafton, 1935).
F[rederic] S[utherland] Ferguson, "Additions to *Title-Page Borders 1485–1640*", *The Library,* 4th series, XVII (1936–37), 264–311.
——, see R[onald] B[runlees] McKerrow.
G. Fumagalli, see E. Crous.
Harry R. Hoppe, "John Wolfe, Printer and Publisher", *The Library,* 4th Series, XIV (1933–34), 241–88.
Alfred Forbes Johnson, *A Catalogue of Engraved and Etched English Title-Pages* (Oxford: Bibliographical Society [London], 1934).
——, *One Hundred Title-Pages, 1500–1800* (London: John Lane, 1928).
A. E. M. Kirkwood, "Richard Field, Printer", *The Library,* 4th series, XII (1931–32), 1–39.
James P. R. Lyell, see E. Crous.
Douglas C. McMurtrie, *The Golden Book* (Chicago: Covici, 1928).
R[onald] B[runlees] McKerrow, "Edward Allde as a Typical Trade Printer", *The Library,* 4th series, X (1929–30), 121–62.

──────, *Printers' and Publishers' Devices Used in England and Scotland 1485–1640* (London: Bibliographical Society [London], 1913).

──────, "The Use of the Galley in Elizabethan Printing", *The Library*, 4th series, II (1921–22), 97–108.

──────, and F[rederic] S[utherland] Ferguson, *Title-Page Borders Used in England and Scotland 1485–1640* (London: the Bibliographical Society [London], 1932).

Stanley Morrison, *A Review of Recent Typography in England, the United States, France, and Germany* (Cambridge [England]: Fleuron, 1927).

Charles Mortet, see E. Crous.

Lauritz Nielsen, see E. Crous.

R. A. Peddie, see E. Crous.

Henry R. Plomer, "Eliots Court Press", *The Library*, 4th series, III (1922–23), 194–209.

──────, see E. Crous.

Maurits Sabbe, see E. Crous.

Charles Sayle, "Initial Letters in Early English Printed Books", *Transactions of the Bibliographical Society* [London], VII (1902–4), 15–47.

──────, "Reynold Wolfe", *Transactions of the Bibliographical Society* [London], XIII (1913–15), 171–92.

Percy Simpson, *Proof-Reading in the Sixteenth, Seventeenth, and Eighteenth Century* (London: Oxford University Press, 1935).

A. H. Smith, *A Description of the Hand-Press in the Department of English, at University College, London* (London: privately printed, 1934).

Daniel B. Updike, *Printing Types, Their History, Forms, and Use, a Study in Survivals* (Cambridge [Mass.]: Harvard University Press, 1922), 2 vols.

Beatrice Warde, "Type Faces, Old and New", *The Library*, 4th series, XVI (1935–36), 121–43.

L. C. Wharton, see E. Crous.

J[ohn] Dover Wilson, "Richard Schilders and the English Puritans", *Transactions of the Bibliographical Society* [London], XI (1909–11), 65–134.

G. P. Winship, see E. Crous.

Lawrence C. Wroth, see E. Crous.

VI   Bindings

Cyril Davenport, "Forgeries in Bookbinding", *The Library*, 2nd series, II (1901), 389–95.

Strickland, Gibson, "The Localization of Books by their Bindings", *Transactions of the Bibliographical Society* [London], VIII (1904–6), 25–28.

Ernst Philip Goldschmidt, *Gothic and Renaissance Bookbindings* (London: Benn, 1928).

Wolfgang Meyer, *Bibliographie de Buchbinderei-Literatur* (Leipzig: Hiersemann, 1925).

LAWRENCE TAYLOR, see WEALE.

W. H. JAMES WEALE, *Bookbindings and Rubbings of Bindings in the National Art Library* (London: H. M. Stationery Office, 1898), 2 vols.

————, and LAWRENCE TAYLOR, *Early Stamped Bookbindings in the British Museum* (London: Longmans, Green, 1922).

VII   The Care and Preservation of Books and Manuscripts

CLARK, John Willis. *The Care of Books*. Cambridge, 1901.

The Cleaning and Restoring of Museum Exhibits. London, 1921.

FITZPATRICK, John Clement. *Notes on the Care, Cataloguing, Calendaring, and Arranging of Manuscripts*. Washington, 1921.

FOWLER, G. Herbert, *Care of County Muniments*. 2nd ed. Westminster, 1928.

IIAMS, Thomas M. "Preservation of Rare Books and Manuscripts in the Huntington Library", *The Library Quarterly*, II (1932), 375–86.

JENKINSON, Hilary. *A Manual of Archive Administration*. Oxford, 1922.

JOHNSON, Charles. *The Care of Documents and Management of Archives*. London, 1919.

MINIER, Dee W. "Mildew and Books", *The Library Journal*, LVII (1932), 931–36.

SANDERS, Jephtha P. "The Preservation of Manuscripts and Bindings", *The Library Journal*, LVII (1932), 936–38.

Spons' Workshop Receipts for Manufacturers, Mechanics, and Scientific Amateurs. London, 1924. 4 vols.

VIII   Palæography and Abbreviations

1   BERNHEIMER, CARLO, *Palæographia Ebraica* (Firenze, 1924).

2   BYRNE, MURIEL ST. CLARE, "Elizabethan Handwriting for Beginners", *Review of English Studies*, I (1925), 198–209.

3   CAPPELLI, ADRIANO, *Lexicon Abbreviatorum* . . . , 3rd ed. (Milano, 1929).

4   CHAMPOLLION-FIGEAC, A. L., *Paléographie des Classiques Latins* (Paris, 1884–1900).

5   CHASSANT, ALPHONSE ANTOINE LOUIS, *Dictionnaire des Abrévations Latines et Françaises*, 5th ed. (Paris, 1884).

6   CHATELAIN, EMIL LOUISE MARIE, *Introduction à la Lecture des Notes Tironiennes* (Paris, 1900).

7   CRUMP, CHARLES GEORGE, and JACOB, ERNEST FRASER, *The Legacy of the Middle Ages* (Oxford, 1926); see chapter on "Handwriting" by Elias Avery Lowe (pp. 197–226).

8   *Facsimiles of Ancient Manuscripts*, 1st series (London, 1903–12), 2 vols.

9   *Facsimiles of Ancient Manuscripts*, 2nd series (London, 1913–26).

10 *Facsimiles of Manuscripts and Inscriptions,* 1st series (London, 1873–83), 3 vols.

11 *Facsimiles of Manuscripts and Inscriptions,* 2d series (London, 1884–94), 2 vols.

12 GARDTHAUSEN, VIKTOR EMIL, *Griechische Paläographie* (Leipzig, 1911).

13 GREG, WALTER WILSON, *English Literary Autographs, 1550–1650* (London, 1925–28), 3 vols.

14 JENKINSON, HILARY, "Elizabethan Handwritings", *The Library,* 4th series, III (1922–23), 1–34.

15 ———, "English Current Writing and Early Printing", *Transactions of the Bibliographical Society* [London], XIII (1915), 273–95.

16 ———, *The Later Court Hand in England from the Fifteenth to the Seventeenth Century* (Cambridge [England], 1927), 2 vols.

17 ———, see JOHNSON, CHARLES.

18 JOHNSON, CHARLES, and JENKINSON, HILARY, *English Court Hand* (Oxford, 1915).

19 KELLER, WOLFGANG, *Angelsächsische Paläographie* (Berlin, 1906), 2 vols.

20 KENYON, SIR FREDERIC GEORGE, *The Palæography of Greek Papyri* (Oxford, 1899).

21 LACEY, ARTHUR DOUGLAS, see WILKS, JOHN.

22 LOWE, ELIAS AVERY, *Codices Latini Antiquores* (Oxford, 1934).

23 ———, see CRUMP, CHARLES GEORGE, and JACOB, E. F.

24 McKERROW, RONALD BRUNLEES, "The Capital Letters in Elizabethan Handwriting", *Review of English Studies,* III (1927), 28–36.

25 MADAN, FALCONER, *Books in Manuscript,* 2nd ed., revised (New York, 1927).

26 MARTIN, CHARLES TRICE, *The Record Interpreter,* 2nd ed. (London, 1892).

27 ———, see WRIGHT, ANDREW.

28 MILLARES, CARLO AGUSTIN, *Paleografía Española* (Barcelona and Buenos Aires, 1929), 2 vols.

29 NELIS, HUBERT, *L'Écriture et les Scribes* (Bruxelles, 1918).

30 PAUES, ANNA C., "Runes and Manuscripts", *Cambridge History of English Literature,* I, 7–20.

31 PROU, JEAN MAURICE, *Manuel de Paléographie* (Paris, 1892).

32 REUSENS, EDMOND HENRI JOSEPH, *Éléments de Paléographie* (Louvain, 1899).

33 SANDYS, SIR JOHN EDWIN, *A Companion to Latin Studies* (London, 1910); see chapter on "Palaeography" by Sir Edward Maunde Thompson (pp. 765–91).

34 SKEAT, WALTER WILLIAM, *Twelve Facsimiles of Old English Manuscripts* (Oxford, 1892).

35 STEFFENS, FRANZ, *Lateinische Paläographie* (Berlin and Leipzig, 1909).

36 TANNENBAUM, SAMUEL AARON, *The Handwriting of the Renaissance* (New York, 1930).

37 ——, *Problems in Shakespere's Penmanship* (New York, 1927).

38 THOMPSON, SIR EDWARD MAUNDE, *Handbook of Greek and Latin Palæography* (New York, 1893).

39 ——, *An Introduction to Greek and Latin Palæography* (Oxford, 1912).

40 ——, see SANDYS, SIR JOHN EDWIN.

41 VAN HOESEN, HENRY BARTLETT, *Roman Cursive Writing* (Princeton, 1915).

42 WALTHER, JOHANN LUDOLF, *Lexicon Diplomaticum* . . . (Göttingen, 1747).

43 WATTENBACH, WILHELM, *Das Schriftwesen im Mittelalter* (Leipzig, 1896).

44 WILKS, JOHN, and LACEY, ARTHUR DOUGLAS, *Catalogue of Works Dealing with the Study of Western Palæography* (London, 1921).

45 WRIGHT, ANDREW, *Court-Hand Restored,* ed. Charles Trice Martin, 10th ed. (London, 1912).

IX   Chronology

1 BOND, JOHN JAMES, *Handy-book of rules and tables for verifying dates* (London, 1869).

2 CAPPELLI, ADRIANO, *Cronologia, cronografia e calendario perpetuo* . . . (Milan, 1930).

3 FIELDEN, F. J., see NILSSON, MARTIN.

4 FRY, EDWARD ALEXANDER, *Almanacks for students of English history* (London, 1915).

5 GINZEL, FRIEDRICH KARL, *Handbuch der mathematischen und technischen Chronologie* (Leipzig, 1906–14), 3 vols.

6 GRANT, JULIUS, *Books and documents, dating, permanence, and preservation* (London, 1937).

7 GROTEFEND, HERMANN, *Zeitrechnung des deutschen Mittelalters und Neuzeit* (Hanover, 1891–98).

8 MAS-LATRIE, LOUIS, *Trésor de chronologie d'histoire et de géographie pour l'étude et l'emploi des documents du moyen âge* (Paris, 1889).

9 NICOLAS, SIR NICHOLAS HARRIS, *The chronology of history* (London, 1838).

10 NILSSON, MARTIN, *Primitive time-reckoning,* tr. F. J. Fielden (Lund, 1920).

11 POOLE, REGINALD LANE, *Medieval reckoning of time* (London, 1921).

X *Epigraphy* (The Science of Inscriptions)

CAGNAT, René, Cours d'épigraphie latine (Paris, 1890).
EGBERT, James Chidester, Introduction to the study of Latin inscriptions (New York, 1923), revised ed.
SANDYS, Sir John Edwin, Latin epigraphy (Cambridge [England], 1927).

XI *Heraldry*

BURKE, Sir John Bernard. The General Armory of England, Scotland, Ireland, and Wales. London, 1884. 2 vols.
COLANERI, Giustino. Bibliografia araldica e genealogica d'Italia. Roma, 1904.
COPINGER, W[alter] A[rthur]. Heraldry Simplified. Manchester, 1910.
FAIRBAIRN, James. Fairbairn's Crests of the Leading Families in Great Britain and Ireland. Edinburgh and London, 1860. 2 vols.
FOX-DAVIES, Arthur Charles. A Complete Guide to Heraldry. London, 1925.
GATFIELD, George. Guide to Printed Books and Manuscripts Relating to English and Foreign Heraldry and Genealogy. London, 1892.
GRANT, Francie James. The Manual of Heraldry. Edinburgh, 1929.
PAPWORTH, John Woody. An Alphabetical Dictionary of Coats of Arms. London, 1858–74.
RENESSE, de, Théodore, Comte. Dictionnaire des figures héraldique. Bruxelles, 1894–1903. 7 vols.
RIETSTAP, Johannes Baptist. Armorial general. Gouda, 1884. 12th ed. 2 vols.

XII *Diplomatics*

ALAIN DEBOURD, Manuel de diplomatique française et pontificale (Paris, 1929), 2 vols.
HARRY BRESSLAU, Handbuch der Urkundenlehre für Deutschland und Italien (Leipzig, 1889).
EUGENE DEPREZ, Études de diplomatique anglaises (Paris, 1908).
ARTHUR GIRY, Manuel de diplomatique (Paris, 1925), new ed.
HUBERT HALL, A formula book of English official historical documents (Cambridge [England]. 1908–9), 2 vols.
———, Studies in English official historical documents (Cambridge [England], 1908).
ARMANDO LODOLINI, Elementi di diplomatica (Milano, 1926).
THOMAS MADOX, Formulare Anglicanum (London, 1702).
JOHANN LUDOLF WALTHER, Lexicon diplomaticum . . . (Göttingen, 1747).

XIII   *Sphragistics* (The Science of Seals)

1   Edmund Clarence Richard Armstrong, *Irish Seal-Matrices and Seals* (Dublin, 1913).
2   Walter de Gray Birch, *Catalogue of Seals in the Department of Manuscripts in the British Museum* (London, 1887–1900), 6 vols.
3   ———, *History of Scottish Seals* (Stirling, 1905), 2 vols.
4   ———, *Seals* (London, 1907).
5   L. Douet d'Arcq, *Collection des Sceaux* (Paris, 1863–68), 3 vols.
6   Germain Demay, *Inventaire des Sceaux de l'Artois et de la Picardie* (Paris, 1877).
7   ———, *Inventaire des Sceaux de la Bourgogne* (Paris, 1912).
8   ———, *Inventaire des Sceaux de la Flandre* (Paris, 1873), 2 vols.
9   ———, *Inventaire des Sceaux de la Normandie* (Paris, 1881).
10   Fernando De Sagarra, *Sigillografia Catalana* (Barcelona, 1916).
11   *Durham, Catalogue of the Seals in the Treasury and Chapter of* (Kendal, 1911–21), 2 vols.
12   Hugh Sadler Kingsford, "Seals", in *Helps for Students of History* (London, 1920).
13   Henry Laing, *Descriptive Catalogue of . . . Ancient Scottish Seals from 1094 to the Commonwealth* (Edinburgh, 1850–86), 2 vols.
14   ———, *Supplemental Descriptive Catalogue of Ancient Scottish Seals, Royal, Baronial, Ecclesiastical, and Municipal . . . from 1150 to the Eighteenth Century* (Edinburgh, 1866).
15   Sir Henry Churchill Maxwell Lyte, *Historical Notes on the Use of the Great Seal of England* (London, 1926).
16   William Rae MacDonald, *Scottish Armorial Seals* (Edinburgh, 1904).
17   Nicodème Mariette, "Bibliographie Générale de la Sigillographie", *Bibliographie Moderne*, XXII (1924–5), 130–61.
18   Gale Pedrick, *Borough Seals of the Gothic Period* (London, 1904).
19   ———, *Monastic Seals of the XIIIth Century* (London, 1902).
20   Reginald Lane Poole, "Seals and Documents", *Proceedings of the British Academy*, IX (1919).
21   Otto Posse, *Die Siegel des Adels der Wettiner Lande bis zum Jahre 1500* (Dresden, 1903–11), 4 vols.
22   ———, *Die Siegel der deutschen Kaiser und Könige von 751 bis 1806* (Dresden, 1909–13), 5 vols.
23   Joseph Hippolyte Roman, *Manuel de Sigillographie française* (Paris, 1912).
24   Mario Tosi, *Bullaria e Bullatores della Cancelleria pontificia*, in *Gli Archivi Italiani* (Siena, 1917).

XIV   *The Application of Science to Research*

1   ANDERSSON, HUGO, *Codex Argenteus Upsaliensis* (Upsala: Almquist &
    Wiksell, 1927).
2   ———, see SVEDBERG, T.
3   BENDIKSON, L[ODEWYK], "Charred Documents", *Library Journal*, LVIII
    (1933), 243–44.
4   ———, "A New Type of an Ultra-Violet Light Source for Documentary
    Photography", *Library Journal*, LIX (1934), 690–92.
5   ———, "Phototechnical Problems: Some Results Obtained at the Hunt-
    ington Library", *Library Journal*, LVII (1932), 789–94.
6   ———, and HASELDEN, R[EGINALD] B[ERTI], "The Detection of Manu-
    script Forgeries", *Library Journal*, LIX (1934), 442.
7   COLES, ALFRED C., *Critical Microscopy* (London: J. & A. Churchill,
    1921).
8   DOLD, P. ALBAN, "Untersuchungsergebnisse einer doppelt reskribierten
    Wolfenbütteler Handschrift mittels Fluoreszenz-Photographie," *Zen-
    tralblatt für Bibliothekswesen*, XXXIV (1917), 231–44.
9   FASSBINDER, JOSEPH, "Das Photographieren von Handschriften", *Photo-
    graphische Mitteilungen*, XLVI (1909), 195–99.
10 FRAZER, PERSIFOR, "The Application of Composite Photography to Hand-
    writing and Especially to Signatures", *Proceedings of the American
    Philosophical Society*, XXIII (1886), 433–41.
11 ———, *Bibliotics, or Study of Documents*, 3rd ed. (New York: Lippin-
    cott, 1901).
12 GAGE, SIMON HENRY, *The Microscope* (Ithaca, N. Y.: Comstock, 1925).
13 GIBSON, KASSON STANFORD, and HARRIS, FOREST K., *The Lovibond Color
    System: I, A Spectrophotometric Analysis of the Lovibond Glasses*
    (Washington: U. S. Government Printing Office, 1927), Scientific
    Papers of the Bureau of Standards, No. 547.
14 GROSS, HANS, "Leserlicher machen verblasster Schriften", *Archiv für
    Kriminal-Anthropologie und Kriminalistik*, LXI (1915), 273–75.
15 ———, see KALLEN, H. M.
16 HARRIS, FOREST K., see GIBSON, KASSON STANFORD.
17 HASELDEN, R[EGINALD] B[ERTI], *Scientific Aids for the Study of Manu-
    scripts* (Oxford: Bibliographical Society [London], 1935).
18 ———, see BENDIKSON, L[ODEWYK].
19 KALLEN, H. M., *Criminal Psychology* (Boston: Little, Brown, 1911);
    English translation of HANS GROSS, *Handbuch der Untersuchungs-
    richter als System der Kriminalistik* (Munich, 1908).
20 KÖGEL, RAPHAEL, "Die Neue Palimpsestphotographie", *Photographische
    Korrespondenz*, No. 658 (1915), pp. 1–11.
21 ———, "Die Photographie unleserlicher und unsichtbarer Schriften der

Palimpsests", *Studien und Mitteilungen zur Geschichte des Benedik-terordens,* XXXIII (1912), 309–15.

22 ———, "Die Palimpsestphotographie in einfacher und billiger Ausfüh-rung", *Zeitschrift für Reproduktionstechnik,* XIX (1917), 90–94.

23 KÜGEL, GUSTAV, "Die äquimensurale Ultraviolett- und Fluoreszenz-Photo-graphie", *Abderhaldens Handbuch der biologischen Arbeitsmethoden* (Berlin and Vienna, 1928), section 2, part 2, no. 7.

24 ———, "Ein neuer Typ der Ultraviolett-Fluoreszenz-photographie," *Zentralblatt für Bibliothekswesen,* XLVII (1930), 656.

25 KRUMBACHER, KARL, *Die Photographie im Dienste der Geisteswissen-schaften* (Leipzig: Teubner, 1906).

26 *Lifa-Licht-Filter Handbuch* (Augsburg: Kellner, 1928).

27 LOVIBOND, JOSEPH WILLIAMS, *Measurement of Light and Color Sensa-tions* (London: George Gill & Sons, 1893).

28 MEIER, GABRIEL, "Die Fortschritte der Paläographie mit Hilfe der Photographie", *Zentralblatt für Bibliothekswesen,* XVII (1900), 1–32, 113–30.

29 MITCHELL, C[HARLES] AINSWORTH, *Documents and Their Scientific Examination* (London: Charles Griffin & Co., 1922).

30 OSBORN, ALBERT SHERMAN, *Questioned Documents,* 2nd ed. (Albany, N. Y.: Boyd Printing Co., 1929).

31 *Photomicrography,* 9th ed. (Rochester, N. Y.: Eastman Kodak Co., 1927).

32 QUIRKE, ARTHUR J., *Forged, Anonymous, and Suspect Documents* (Lon-don: Routledge, 1930).

33 REISS, RUDOLPH ARCHIBALD, *Manuel de police scientifique* (Lausanne: Payot, 1911).

34 ———, *La Photographie judiciaire* (Paris: J. De Francia, 1903).

35 RIEDER, KARL, "Praktisches zur Handschriftenphotographie", *Zentralblatt für Bibliothekswesen,* XXVII (1910), 215–17.

36 RORIMER, JAMES J., *Ultra-Violet Rays and Their Use in the Examination of Works of Art* (New York: Metropolitan Museum of Art, 1931).

37 ROSTAGNO, ENRICO, "Della riproduzione de palinsesti e d'un nuovo sistema italiano ad esso applicato", *Rivista delle Biblioteche e degli Archivi,* XXVI (1915), 58–67.

38 SPITTA, EDMUND J., *Microscopy* (London: Murray, 1920).

39 STAINIER, LOUIS, "Études de Procédés techniques, les meilleurs et les plus économiques à recommander pour la reproduction des manuscrits, des monnaies et des sceaux", *Actes du Congrès international . . . tenu à Liége . . . août 1905* (Bruxelles, 1905), pp. 75–98.

40 SVEDBERG, T., and ANDERSSON, HUGO, "Fluorescence Photography by Means of the New Wratten Ultra-violet Filter", *The Photographic Journal,* LXIII (January, 1923), 30–32.

41 TANNENBAUM, SAMUEL AARON, "Bibliotics", *The Critical Crown,* I (1928), 6–10.

42 TOUT, THOMAS FREDERICK, "Medieval Forgers and Forgeries", *Bulletin of the John Rylands Library,* V (1919).

43 WIEDEMANN, EILHARD, "Über Photographie von Handschriften und Drucksachen", *Zentralblatt für Bibliothekswesen,* XXIII (1906), 22–25.

44 *Wratten Light Filters,* 11th ed. (Rochester, N. Y.: Eastman Kodak Co., 1932).

Appendix B

SPECIMENS OF BIBLIOGRAPHICAL,
CRITICO-BIBLIOGRAPHICAL,
AND SUBJECT NOTES

BIBLIOGRAPHICAL NOTE—FOR A BOOK

Greene, Robert
The Plays and Poems of Robert Greene,
ed. J[ohn] Churton Collins
(Oxford: Oxford University Press, 1905), 2 vols.

CRITICO-BIBLIOGRAPHICAL NOTE—FOR THE SAME BOOK

Greene, Robert, *The Plays and Poems of Robert Greene,*
ed. J[ohn] Churton Collins (Oxford: Oxford University Press,
1905), 2 vols.

Review by W. W. Greg, *MLR,* I (1905–6), 238–51:

"The common sense displayed in the general introduction is rendered nugatory by the results there attained
being contradicted in other parts of the work. The labour
expended on the notes is largely misapplied owing to a
failure to distinguish between what is relevant and what
is not." (p. 251)

BIBLIOGRAPHICAL NOTE—FOR A PERIODICAL ARTICLE

Cole, George Watson,
"Bibliography—A Forecast",
Papers of the Bibliog. Soc. of Am.,
XIV (1920), 1–19

CRITICO-BIBLIOGRAPHICAL NOTE—FOR THE SAME ARTICLE

Cole, George Watson
"Bibliography—A Forecast"
Papers of the Bibliog. Soc. of Am.
XIV (1920), 1–19

> Contains the unexpurgated version of Greene's attack on the Harveys as contained in the apparently unique copy of the first issue of the *Quippe* now in the Huntington Library.

SUBJECT NOTE REPRESENTING A PRIMARY SOURCE

Relations with other writers:
   failure of friends to visit

Bodleian
Malone 575*

Robert Greene, *Repentance* (1592)

[C3ᵛ]

"But heere note, that though I knew how to get a friend, yet I had not the gift nor reaſon how to keepe a friend: for hee that was my deareſt friend, I would bee ſure ſo to behaue my ſelfe towards him, that he ſhoulde euer after profeſſe to bee my vtter enemie, or elſe vowe neuer after to come in my company."

See also C1ᵛ

". . . I left the Vniuerſitie and away to London, where (after I had continued ſome ſhort time, & driuen my ſelf out of credit with ſundry of my frends) I became an Author . . ."

SUBJECT NOTE REPRESENTING A SECONDARY SOURCE

Relations with other writers:

   failure of friends to visit

Collins, *Plays and Poems,* I, 23

"But unhappily though he knew how to get a friend, he had not, he tells us, the gift or reason how to keep one, and he was very soon [after 1589 or 1590] to estrange almost all who had been intimate with him."

SUBJECT NOTE REPRESENTING A SECONDARY SOURCE

Relations with other writers:
    failure of friends to visit

Lodge was on voyage with Cavendish from 1591 to 1593
See *DNB, s. n.* Cavendish, Thomas.
Also *Encyclopædia Britannica, s. n.* Lodge, Thomas.

SUBJECT NOTE REPRESENTING ORIGINAL OPINION

Relations with other writers:
    failure of friends to visit

May not friends have been afraid G. had the plague?

Appendix C

SPECIMEN THESIS PAGES

SPECIMEN THESIS PAGES IN ROUGH DRAFT FORM

Before we leave the question of Greene's friendships, it may be well to consider briefly the tradition that he was not on good terms with his old companions at the time of his death. Collins expressed the belief in these words: "But unhappily though he knew how to get a friend, he had not, he tells us, the gift or reason how to keep one, and he was very soon [after 1589 or 1590] to estrange almost all who had been intimate with him." [41] This tradition rests

[41] Greene, *Plays and Poems,* ed. Collins, I, 23.

in part upon two statements of Greene, both in the *Repentance,*[42] and in part

[42] Ed. 1592, pp. [C1ᵛ] and [C3ᵛ]; in the Bodley Head Quarto edition these statements will be found on pp. 20 and 24–25.

upon the circumstances of his death. The very doubtful value of statements such as those in the *Repentance* I have pointed out elsewhere; [43] and the

[43] Chauncey Sanders, "Robert Greene and His 'Editors'", *PMLA,* XLVIII (1933), 404–17.

conditions under which Greene is supposed to have died are not as clear as tradition would imply.

It has been assumed that Greene's friends had all drifted away from him before his death because, it was said, none of his friends visited him during his last illness.[44] We have nothing but Gabriel Harvey's word to support such

[44] Cf. Greene, *Plays and Poems,* ed. Collins, I, 45.

a belief; [45] but even if it be true that none of Greene's friends visited him just

[45] Gabriel Harvey, *Works,* ed. Grosart, I, 176.

before his death,[46] it does not follow that they were no longer his friends or

[46] In the *Repentance* there is reference to a friend who brought Greene word from his wife just before his death; see Bodley Head Quarto ed., p. 32.

that there was anything strange in his relations with them. It must be remembered that the plague was abroad in London in the summer of 1592; Nashe had fled from the city to escape it, probably before August 8.[47] It is perfectly

[47] *Pierce Penilesse* was entered in the *Stationers' Register* (ed. Arber, II, 619) on that date; and Nashe complains (*Works,* ed. McKerrow, I [153]) that he, being in the country when the book was published, was given no opportunity to correct it.

possible that Greene died of the plague, for Gabriel Harvey's unsubstantiated story of the "fatall banquet of pickle herring" [48] or the "surfett of pickle

[48] *Foure Letters,* ed. Bodley Head Quarto, p. 21.

herringe and rennish wine" [49] does not prove that the cause of Greene's death

[49] *Ibid.,* p. [13].

was either indigestion or alcoholism. There is reason to doubt the truth of any statement concerning Greene made by Harvey, an avowed enemy; moreover, there are some indications that Harvey's statements were not meant to be taken seriously. If Harvey's remarks were jesting ones, we can understand what is otherwise a rather strange phraseology in Nashe's reference in *Strange Newes.*[50]

[50] *Works,* ed. McKerrow, I, 287: ". . . that fatall banquet of Rhenish wine and pickled hearing (if thou wilt needs haue it so), . . ."

Since there is apparently either attempted humor or abuse in two of the details of Gabriel's first remark, there may well be a jest or an insult in the reference to a surfeit. Harvey's words are:

> My next business was to enquire after the famous Author: who was reported to lye dangerously sicke in a shoemakers house near Dow-gate; not of the plague, or the pockes, as a Gentleman saide, but of a surfett of pickle herringe and rennish wine, or as some suppose, of an exceeding feare.[51]

[51] *Foure Letters,* ed. Bodley Head Quarto, p. [13].

This may seem neither humorous nor abusive; but it must be remembered that Gabriel was never noted for his wit, and that this was written before practice and an excellent teacher had given him a certain proficiency in the art of abuse. The indications that this remark was not meant to be a serious statement of fact lie in the connotation of two of the four suggested causes of Greene's illness, and in the nature of the last element.

The "exceeding feare" we may understand from what follows, was a fear of retaliation from the Harveys for Greene's attack on them in his *Quippe for*

an Upstart Courtier; and not even Gabriel could have seriously maintained
that that was the real cause of Greene's mortal illness. That Harvey's allusion
to the pox may be merely abusive is suggested by his use of the word in his
New Letter of Notable Contents (1593).[52] The same possibility lies in the

[52] Harvey, *Works,* ed. Grosart, I, 272–73: "When the sweet Youth haunted
Aretine, and *Rabelays,* the two monstrous wittes of their languages, who so shaken
with the furious feauers of the One; or so attainted with the French Pockes of the
other?"

reference to "pickle herringe and rennish wine"; for pickled herring seems to
have been associated with drunkenness,[53] with poverty,[54] and with lechery.[55]

[53] For evidence of the association in England of fish with drinking see Gabriel
Harvey, *Works,* ed. Grosart, II, 113–14; Nashe, *Works,* ed. McKerrow, III, 268;
Westward for Smelts, ed. Halliwell, p. 6. For the association of pickled herring,
specifically, with drinking see Nashe, *op. cit.,* p. 223; and Samuel Rowlands, *Letting
of Humours Blood,* pp. 77–78. In Nashe, *op. cit.,* p. 149, red herring are spoken of
as requiring an accompanying beverage. In the introduction to *Festive Songs,* ed.
Sandys, p. liv, a number of "shoeing horns" or "pullers" are mentioned, among them
red herring and pickled herring; unfortunately, the only evidence Sandys cites is
the passage now in question.

[54] See Nashe, *op. cit.,* I, 171; III, 287; IV, 100; and V, 152.

[55] Lodge, in *Wits Miserie,* p. 52, says of Fornication, one of the offspring of
Asmodeus, "If he take vp commodities, it is Cocksparrows, Potatos, and Herringes,
and the hottest wines are his ordinary drink to increase his courage."

Harvey's reference to a surfeit of pickled herring and Rhenish wine may be,
then, merely a gibe at Greene's personal habits and at the nature of the "fatall
banquet".[56]

[56] It may be worth noting that there is a somewhat similar use of the word
"surfet" in Lyly's *Pappe with an Hatchet* (*Works,* ed. Bond, III, 389): "Bastard
Senior was with them at supper, and I thinke tooke a surfet of colde and raw
quipps."

Whatever may have been the cause of Greene's death, it would have been
natural for his friends to suspect, in the summer of 1592, when they heard of
his illness, that he had the plague. To remain away from him, under those
circumstances, was not unfriendly, but prudent.[57] Moreover, Nashe [58] and

[57] Lodge, in his *Treatise of the Plague* (*Works,* ed. Hunterian Club, IV, 22),
wrote: "First of all, therefore, it behooueth euery man to haue speciall care that he
frequent not any places or persons infected, neither that he suffer such to breath
vpon him: . . ." It will be remembered that Lodge was a physician as well as a
writer.

[58] Nashe seems to have been with Archbishop Whitgift at the palace at Croydon;
see Nashe, *op. cit.,* V, 21.

Lodge,[59] the only persons whose friendship with Greene can be very satisfac-

[59] See *DNB, s. n.* Cavendish, Thomas; or *Encyclopædia Britannica,* 14th ed., *s. n.*
Lodge, Thomas.

torily established, were not in London. The pathetic picture of the graceless author, bereft, by his own wilfulness, of all his old friends, may actually represent the conditions under which Greene died; but there is nothing to justify the common acceptance of that situation as a fact. Without better evidence than has yet been presented, it must remain, like many another detail in the traditional biography of Greene, a possibility—at most, a probability.

Before we leave the question of Greene's friendships, it may be well to consider briefly the tradition that he was not on good terms with his old companions at the time of his death. Collins expressed the belief in these words: "But unhappily though he knew how to get a friend, he had not, he tells us, the gift or reason how to keep one, and he was very soon [after 1589 or 1590] to estrange almost all who had been intimate with him." [41] This tradition rests in part upon two statements of Greene, both in the *Repentance*,[42] and in part upon the circumstances of his death. The very doubtful value of statements such as those in the *Repentance* I have pointed out elsewhere; [43] and the conditions under which Greene died are not as clearly known as tradition would imply.

It has been assumed that Greene's friends had all drifted away from him before his death because, it was said, none of them visited him during his last illness.[44] We have nothing but Gabriel Harvey's word to support such a belief; [45] but even if it be true that none of Greene's friends visited him just before his death,[46] it does not follow that they were no longer his friends or that there was anything strange in his relations with them. It must be remembered that the plague was abroad in London in the summer of 1592; Nashe had fled from the city to escape it, probably before August 8.[47] It is perfectly possible that Greene died of the plague, for Gabriel Harvey's unsubstantiated story of the "surfett of pickle herringe and rennish wine" [48] or the "fatall banquet of pickle herring" [49] does not prove that the cause of Greene's death was either indigestion or alcoholism. There is reason to doubt the truth of any statement concerning Greene, made by Harvey, an avowed enemy; moreover, there are some indications that Harvey's statements were not meant to be taken seriously. If Harvey's remarks were jesting ones, we can understand

---

[41] Greene, *Plays and Poems*, ed. Collins, I, 23.

[42] Ed. 1592, pp. [C1ᵛ] and [C3ᵛ]; in the Bodley Head Quarto ed. these statements will be found on pp. 20 and 24–25.

[43] Chauncey Sanders, "Robert Greene and His 'Editors'", *PMLA*, XLVIII (1933), 404–17.

[44] Cf. Greene, *op. cit.*, p. 45.

[45] Gabriel Harvey, *Works*, ed. Grosart, I, 176.

[46] In the *Repentance* there is reference to a friend who brought Greene word from his wife just before his death; see Bodley Head Quarto ed., p. 32. See also Nashe, *Works*, ed. McKerrow, I, 287–88.

[47] *Pierce Penilesse* was entered in the *Stationers' Register* (ed. Arber, II, 619) on that date; and Nashe later complained (*Works*, ed. McKerrow, I [153], that he, being in the country when the book was published, was given no opportunity to correct it.

[48] *Foure Letters*, ed. Bodley Head Quarto, p. [13].

[49] *Ibid.*, p. 21.

what is otherwise a rather strange phraseology in Nashe's reference in *Strange Newes*.[50]

Since there is apparently either attempted humor or abuse in two of the details accompanying one of Gabriel's remarks, there may well be a jest or an insult in the reference to a surfeit. Harvey's words are:

> My next businesse was to enquire after the famous Author; who was reported to lye dangerously sicke in a shoemakers house near Dow-gate: not of the plague, or the pockes, as a Gentleman saide, but of a surfett of pickle herringe and rennish wine, or as some suppose, of an exceeding feare.[51]

This may seem neither humorous nor very abusive; but it must be remembered that Gabriel was never noted for his wit, and that this was written before practice and an excellent teacher had given him a certain proficiency in the art of abuse. The indications that this remark was not meant to be a serious statement of fact lie in the connotations of two of the four suggested causes of Greene's illness, and in the nature of the last element.

The "exceeding feare", we may understand from what follows, was a fear of retaliation from the Harveys for Greene's attack on them in his *Quippe for an Upstart Courtier*; and not even Gabriel could have seriously maintained that that was the real cause of Greene's mortal illness. That Harvey's allusion to the pox may be merely abusive is suggested by his use of the word in his *New Letter of Notable Contents* (1593).[52] The same possibility lies in the reference to "pickle herringe and rennish wine"; for pickled herring seems to have been associated with drunkenness,[53] with poverty,[54] and with lechery.[55] Harvey's reference to a surfeit of pickled herring and Rhenish wines

---

[50] Nashe, *op. cit.*, p. 287: ". . . that fatall banquet of Rhenish wine and pickled herring (if thou wilt needes haue it so), . . ."

[51] Harvey, *op. cit.*, ed. Bodley Head Quarto, p. [13].

[52] Harvey, *Works*, ed. Grosart, I, 272–73: "When the sweet Youth haunted *Aretine,* and *Rabelays,* the two monstrous wittes of their languages, who so shaken with the furious feauers of the One; or so attainted with the French pockes of the other?"

[53] For evidence of the association in England of fish with drinking see Gabriel Harvey, *op. cit.*, II, 113–14; Nashe, *Works,* ed. McKerrow, III, 268; *Westward for Smelts,* ed. Halliwell, p. 6. For the association of pickled herring specifically, with drinking, see Nashe, *op. cit.*, p. 223; and Samuel Rowlands, *Letting of Humours Blood,* pp. 77–78. In Nashe, *op. cit.*, p. 149, red herring are spoken of as requiring an accompanying beverage. In the introduction to *Festive Songs,* ed. Sandys, p. liv, a number of "shoeing horns" or "pullers"—i.e., thirst-provokers—are mentioned, among them, red herring and pickled herring; unfortunately, the only evidence Sandys cites is the passage now in question.

[54] See Nashe, *Works,* ed. McKerrow, I, 171; III, 287; IV, 100; and V, 152.

[55] Lodge, in *Wits Miserie,* p. 52, says of Fornication, one of the offspring of Asmodeus, "If he take vp commodities, it is Cocksparrows, Potatos, and Herringes, and the hottest wines are his ordinary drink to increase his courage."

may be, then, merely a gibe at Greene's personal habits and at the nature of the "fatall banquet".[56]

Whatever may have been the cause of Greene's death, it would have been natural for his friends to suspect, in the summer of 1592, when they heard of his illness, that he had the plague. To remain away from him, under those circumstances, was not unfriendly but prudent.[57] Moreover, Nashe [58] and Lodge,[59] the only persons whose friendship with Greene can be very satisfactorily established, were not in London. The pathetic picture of the graceless author, bereft, by his own wilfulness, of all his old friends, and dying in abject poverty, may represent the conditions under which Greene died; but there is nothing to justify the common acceptance of that situation as a fact. Without better evidence than has yet been presented, it must remain, like many another detail in the traditional biography of Greene, a possibility—at most, a probability.

---

[56] It may be worth noting that there is a somewhat similar use of the word "surfet" in Lyly's *Pappe with an Hatchet* (*Works,* ed. Bond, III, 389): "Bastard *Senior* was with them at supper, and I thinke tooke a surfet of colde and raw quipps."

[57] Lodge, in his *Treatise of the Plague* (*Works,* ed. Hunterian Club, IV, 22), wrote: "First of all, therefore, it behooueth euery man to haue speciall care that he frequent not any places or persons infected, neither that he suffer such to breath vpon him: . . ." It will be remembered that Lodge was a physician as well as a writer.

[58] Nashe, *op. cit.,* V, 21.

[59] See *DNB, s. n.* Cavendish, Thomas.

Index

(NOTE: The multiplicity of names and titles cited in this book makes a complete index impracticable. What follows is a list of subjects, with page numbers indicating the place or places in which each term is defined, explained, or otherwise treated at some length. Incidental occurrences of the term elsewhere in the book are ignored.)